Building the Black Metropolis

THE NEW BLACK STUDIES SERIES

Edited by Darlene Clark Hine and Dwight A. McBride

A list of books in the series appears at the end of this book.

Building the Black Metropolis

African American Entrepreneurship in Chicago

EDITED BY
ROBERT E. WEEMS JR.
AND JASON P. CHAMBERS

UNIVERSITY OF
ILLINOIS PRESS
Urbana, Chicago, and Springfield

Library of Congress Cataloging-in-Publication Data
Names: Weems, Robert E., 1951– editor. | Chambers, Jason, editor.
Title: Building the black metropolis : African American
    entrepreneurship in Chicago / edited by Robert E. Weems Jr. and
    Jason P. Chambers.
Description: Urbana : University of Illinois Press, [2017] | Series: The
    new black studies series | Includes bibliographical references and
    index. |
Identifiers: LCCN 2017005983 (print) | LCCN 2017022585 (ebook) |
    ISBN 9780252050022 (ebook) | ISBN 9780252041426 (cloth : alk.
    paper) | ISBN 9780252082948 (pbk. : alk. paper)
Subjects: LCSH: African American businesspeople—
    Illinois—Chicago—History. | African American business
    enterprises—Illinois—Chicago—History. | Entrepreneurship—
    Illinois—Chicago—History. | African Americans—Illinois—
    Chicago—Economic conditions. | African Americans—Illinois—
    Chicago—Social conditions.
Classification: LCC F548.9.N4 (ebook) | LCC F548.9.N4 B85 2017 (print)
    | DDC 305.896/073077311—dc23
LC record available at https://lccn.loc.gov/2017005983

Contents

Acknowledgments

The publication of a co-edited book cannot be completed without the cooperation of contributors. Therefore, first and foremost, we want to thank the colleagues that contributed essays to this book. Their important research, along with the Introduction and individual chapters produced by the co-editors, promises to make a substantive contribution to the historiography of Black Chicago and black business history.

We also want to thank Dawn Durante of the University of Illinois Press. She has been an unflagging supporter of this project and did a superb job of shepherding it through the review and publication process. On a related note, we want to thank the colleagues who reviewed earlier drafts of this manuscript. Their incisive comments and suggestions were invaluable.

Another note of thanks is due to our employers, Wichita State University and the University of Illinois at Urbana-Champaign. Both institutions have provided valuable assistance to this and our other research and publication efforts. We also want to acknowledge our friends and colleagues across the country that have also provided encouragement and support for this and our other research and publication efforts.

Last, but not least, we want to thank our families—wife Nisha and daughters Morgan, Madison, and Mya, and wife Dr. Lisa Liggins-Chambers and children Jordyn, Jada, and Jason II—for their love, inspiration, and encouragement.

Building the Black Metropolis

Introduction

One story regarding the founding of Chicago states that the city's name is derived from the Potawatomi term for "let's make a deal." Although the *Encyclopedia of Chicago* disputes this assertion, it states that "economic and business concerns have not merely shaped but [have] determined Chicago's destiny."[1] Significantly, in the context of the present volume, Jean Baptiste Point DuSable, a person of African descent, is regarded as simultaneously being Chicago's first permanent non–Native American inhabitant and its first entrepreneur. Although much of DuSable's life remains unknown, his entrepreneurial prowess is well documented. As Thomas A. Meehan commented, "it is remarkable that every contemporary report about DuSable describes him as a man of substance. Undoubtedly he owned one of the most complete [trading] establishments in the Middle West outside of Detroit and St. Louis."[2]

Perhaps fittingly, DuSable established a historical precedent for the commercial skills exhibited by the individuals featured in this volume. Even today, no one knows how DuSable, "some two hundred miles from the nearest center of civilization," established a trading post that "could supply flour, pork, and bread to a party of at least four, evidently had hogs, fields under cultivation, his own flour mill, and also someone to bake bread." Nevertheless, "DuSable had all of these things and many other accommodations—which makes one wonder at the ingenuity of a man who could have such a fine establishment in the midst of a wilderness."[3]

Standing on the shores of Lake Michigan, Chicago today is home to over 6 million residents. This bustling metropolis, variously referred to as "the City of Big

Shoulders," "the Windy City" and sometimes "the Capital of the Midwest," has a history that could fill a library of books. Politicians and gangsters, inventors and movie stars, and just regular citizens have helped the city evolve (sometimes forcefully and sometimes violently) into one of the world's great urban centers.

Yet Black Chicago is somewhat different than the larger city. At various points in history, the vision of Black Chicago as both a metaphorical and real city-within-the-city nurtured and supported generations of its African American residents. As the city grew, residents of African descent built upon DuSable's foundation in myriad ways. Geographically segregated in Chicago for much of its history and victimized by repeated outbreaks of violence, extralegal reprisals, and social and economic restrictions, blacks built a viable commercial enclave within Chicago. Still, notwithstanding the centrality of business enterprise in the evolution of the Black Metropolis, the economic history of Black Chicago remains relatively understudied. This gap is especially glaring as compared to studies of black political and cultural history. The present volume seeks to fill this gap through its examination of African American business experiences across a range of industries in the city.

As Juliet E. K. Walker noted in *The History of Black Business in America*, it is important to understand and analyze blacks' efforts to endure within a system of slavery, violence, and racism that has long been part of their experience in America.[4] Thus it is important not to merely state that blacks were unable to build the independent Black Metropolis in Chicago that they originally envisioned, but to understand the strategies they utilized to try to do so. Moreover, in this volume the authors strive to understand black business enterprises as they were, rather than for what they failed to become. Black business owners in Chicago ran the gamut from the small street-level entrepreneur who earned just enough to keep his or her business open, to the titans of black enterprise (men and women such as Robert Abbott, Jesse Binga, Annie Malone, and Anthony Overton). Also, moving beyond the "respectable elements" of the black entrepreneurial class, this volume includes a discussion of its less respectable elements—the policy operators.[5]

Robert Abbott, publisher of the *Chicago Defender*, was a staunch advocate of African Americans' migration out of the South and into the industrial North. He set the date of May 15, 1917, for what he called "the Great Northern Drive." This target date, he hoped, would spur blacks to continue their movement northward and away from the violence and restrictions of the South. In hindsight, it is clear that the Great Migration of African Americans into Chicago (and other northern cities) provided an important stimulus for black business formation in the North. Accordingly, the essays in this volume seek to analyze the impact of the migration North through the lens of black entrepreneurship and business development. As more African Americans streamed into Chicago, their presence created a growing consumer market that fired the imaginations and aspirations of local black entrepreneurs and their supporters. Consequently, succeeding decades witnessed the promotion of racial economic solidarity that could move the dream of a self-sustaining Black Metropolis from the realm of fantasy into an observable reality.[6]

In this volume we seek to place African American entrepreneurial development in its proper framework. In the process we argue that, in their reactions to Chicago's racial hostility, African Americans responded by creating business enterprises that helped form a solid economic foundation for the Black Metropolis. Furthermore, the conception of the Black Metropolis needs to be properly contextualized to not only include its structural or geographical elements, but also as a source of racial agency. Specifically, the Black Metropolis was a place where blacks turned the disadvantages of their segregation into opportunities. As Chicagoan Claude Barnett, founder of the Associated Negro Press, said to an associate: "If we are to have segregated institutions, we ought to get whatever economic values go with such forced solidarity." Barnett, a graduate of Tuskegee, shared Booker T. Washington's belief that black equality could come only with the support of a solid economic foundation. Without such a foundation, blacks would always be subject to the whims of luck, providence, or white benevolence.[7] Moreover, this mindset contributed to the development of what we are calling "the Chicago Network" of community and entrepreneurial support.

The "Myth" of Black Business

It is important to establish at the outset our position on black business and entrepreneurship. First, it has to be pointed out that businesses fail. This is a simple fact, but it is often overlooked in the analysis of African American business. Discussions of African American business failure tend not to acknowledge that these enterprises, like others, can fail for reasons completely outside the control of the owner. Yet with black business failures (or limited growth), the implication is that failure resulted because the owner inherently lacked the capacity for business. In other words, analyses of black businesspersons have implied that their failure came not for reasons connected to business and economics, but instead because their owners lacked the requisite qualities of successful entrepreneurs. This notion has often been repeated in analyses of black business, perhaps none more scathing than that of one of its initial architects: E. Franklin Frazier in his 1957 book *Black Bourgeoisie*.

Frazier, largely refusing to acknowledge the impact of slavery, Jim Crow racism, and violence, mocked black business as a "myth." Further, he lambasted black business owners for trying to build an independent black economy that could fuel their business growth. In so doing, he implicitly linked black business owners' failure with their lack of skill, expertise, and vision. Ironically, historic black entrepreneurs could clearly see the value of owning enterprises in mining, timber, industrial manufacturing, mineral extraction, steel, meat-packing, railroads, or other pursuits that were fueling American fortunes to dizzying heights. But those areas were often closed to those same entrepreneurs for reasons ranging from the costs of development and operation to racial proscriptions on their participation.

Beyond Frazier, there exists in American scholarship an entire genre that denigrates historic African American business development as compared to that exhibited by European and Asian immigrants. For example, in her work on "middleman minorities," Edna Bonacich lauds the manner in which members of foreign-born populations have used their insularity to spur their own economic development. In the process she asks how they, in implicit contrast to African Americans, had found economic success while blacks did not. This specious comparison between the foreign-born and African Americans, in terms of economic development, appears in much of the historical and sociological literature on African American entrepreneurs. Moreover, as John Sibley Butler noted, the literature on entrepreneurship has traditionally been laudatory of the businesses developed by minority entrepreneurs except when that examination has included African American ones.[8]

Economist Abram Harris, in his 1936 classic *The Negro as Capitalist*, put forth another denigration of historic African American entrepreneurship. He wrote:

> The organization and failure of banking among Negroes is part and parcel of the historical effort of the members of the Negro upper class to emulate within their circumscribed existence, economic habits, social values, and the business ideals that dominate the surrounding white world. It is, in brief, a phase of an attempt to lay the economic foundation for a Black Bourgeoisie class. But the development of such a class and the institutions on which its existence depends necessitates a larger amount of trade, industry, and commerce than Negro life will ever afford.[9]

The failure of Harris's analysis is that he based his critique on a perception of blacks' failure in attempts to act or be white. Rather, as Adam Green noted in *Selling the Race*, their actions were based less on attempts to be "white" than they were efforts to be prosperous within the market system of the United States.[10]

A topic usually absent in discourse on historic black business development is how actual (and threatened) racial violence and hostility against blacks negatively affected their wealth accumulation and business formation. Moreover, even such "nonviolent" acts of racial discrimination such as mainstream banks' refusal to loan money to black entrepreneurs, merchants forcing black entrepreneurs to pay higher wholesale prices, or municipal "social customs" that kept black businesses from expanding beyond the confines of black neighborhoods are rarely acknowledged. Certainly all entrepreneurs deal with a competitive landscape: for customers, retail locations, raw materials, distribution options, logistical challenges, and countless other things. But only African Americans have, in addition to those challenges, also dealt with ones related to being black in a historically hostile white-controlled society. In the end, we must balance the criticism of black entrepreneurs for what they did not do, with a careful analysis that acknowledges what they were able to accomplish within the marketplace. As Butler argued, "while Japanese, Italians, Jews, and other ethnics developed business activities and were free to place their enterprises in the major growth areas of their cities of residence (and, of course, in their own neighborhoods) and take full advantage of the free enterprise system, Afro-Americans found themselves limited by law and unable to pursue this simple tenet of free enterprise."[11]

Thus the position of this work is that a proper evaluation of black business ownership must include an acknowledgment of the forces arrayed against African American entrepreneurship. Despite American rhetoric, the realm of business was not a level playing field, but was one skewed against substantive African American business formation. It was a situation that often did not allow blacks to participate, or to sell their products or services to a wider (i.e., white) market, or to get the capital they needed to fuel their entrepreneurial visions. Furthermore, whites repeatedly placed other obstacles in the path of black entrepreneurs. For instance, white property owners regularly refused to sell commercial property to black firms that sought to expand their operations. Of the commercial real estate on Chicago's South Side, a *Time* writer observed in the late 1930s, "Virtually all of this property belongs to whites, most of them Jews, and they make it tough for Negroes to go into business in these prize areas. Leases generally have clauses forbidding Negro tenants; and if a Negro manages to wangle a lease anyway, he is apt to find his rent tripled when the lease comes up for renewal."[12] Was race the only inhibiting factor? Of course not; it would be ahistorical to suggest otherwise. Nevertheless, we should not pretend that it was a nonexistent or meaningless one. Certainly blacks have failed in business for reasons disconnected from larger social reasons, but it is also true that "racism, prejudice, and discrimination have locked blacks out of both capital and consumer markets, which consequently limited their access to financial resources, credit, and venture capital."[13]

Before the Black Metropolis

As Christopher R. Reed discusses in the present volume, for much of the nineteenth century the African American population of Chicago remained small. Blacks lived throughout the city, including in racially mixed neighborhoods, and established various kinds of businesses. In fact, several of the most prominent early black entrepreneurs provided services primarily to white clients. Black tailors and barbers had a history of servicing white clientele, particularly among the white elite. Men like tailor John Jones serviced white clients and beyond their business pursuits were often linked to the abolition movement.[14]

The economic and social connections of Chicago's black "old settlers" made them much more supportive of integrationist efforts than those blacks who later embraced the vision of the Black Metropolis. In *Aristocrats of Color*, Willard Gatewood described blacks in Chicago prior to the turn of the century as "committed to the ultimate integration of blacks into the mainstream of American life."[15] However, during the first decades of the twentieth century, Chicago's growing black migrant population largely eschewed the "old settlers" integrationist vision. Instead, African American newcomers to the city advocated the racial solidarity and self-help mindset commonly identified with Booker T. Washington.

The developing vision of the Black Metropolis was also fueled by the hardening of racial lines in the city. After the turn of the century, as more black migrants arrived from the South, the treatment of blacks grew ever more hostile. Concurrently there was the rise of a black business and professional class whose livelihoods were based not on relationships with whites—as had been the case of black elites and successful business owners of the past—but instead were linked to the growing black community. Thus the growing emphasis on self-help and racial solidarity was fueled by both increasing white hostility and blacks' emphasis on community growth through their own efforts.

A City within the City

The train station at Twelfth and Michigan Avenue no longer stands. This terminal of the Illinois Central Railroad eventually became a casualty of urban renewal. Yet for African American migrants to Chicago during the years of the Great Migration, the building was, as *Ebony* publisher John H. Johnson observed, for black migrants as Ellis Island was for European immigrants. These travelers, who left states throughout the old Confederacy, came with their lunches or dinners in brown paper sacks and with as many belongings as they could carry. Most had never seen a building over five stories tall, so when they stepped out from the train platform and looked north toward downtown, they were likely amazed to see a plethora of buildings that seemed to touch the sky. They had stepped into another world, far different from the dusty rural enclaves they had left behind.[16]

Despite clear differences in the physical infrastructure of their old communities and what they observed in their new home, black migrants to Chicago quickly realized that they had not left racial segregation behind. Because of racial bias in Chicago, new black residents were steered toward preexisting black enclaves on the South Side and West Side. This experience was not immediately upsetting to these individuals because, like other new arrivals to the city (such as European immigrants), black migrants sought the comfort of the familiar: to be among people like themselves who could help them navigate this strange new place. Yet unlike their fellow white newcomers, blacks did not possess the option to not live among people like themselves. Eventually, their forced proximity led to Chicago's black community becoming the "second largest Negro city in the world, only New York's Harlem exceeding it in size."[17]

With that size came a new spirit, or ideal of the New Negro, as described by Davarian Baldwin in *Chicago's New Negroes*. In contrast to the old Negro, as Frederick H. H. Robb emphasized, "The New Negro . . . does not seek philanthropy but an opportunity."[18] Blacks in the metropolis viewed themselves as agents of their own desired change, not as chattel awaiting the beneficent white hand that might give them help. Further, the consciousness Baldwin described was encapsulated by Howard Phelps, a writer in the city who argued that "the stability of the Negro rests upon his financial independence. Independence means the employment of race men and women by race business men and women."[19] And in Phelps's understanding, "race" was more than a socio-biological construct, it was also a mindset. A "race" man or woman was not simply someone who was black, but who also recognized his or her duty to work for the benefit of other African Americans. Hence for race entrepreneurs, their responsibility included constructing the Black Metropolis's economic infrastructure. In a world of possibilities, the Black Metropolis represented a place where, in the face of the virulent racism and discrimination present in the larger city, black economic nationalism could create a place where African Americans would not only survive, but thrive.

Admittedly, the racial solidarity envisioned for the Black Metropolis had limits for both consumers and business owners. For example, noted black banker and real estate magnate Jesse Binga was a celebrated race man. Yet, like white landlords, he often charged his black renters more than whites paid for the same kinds of apartments. In contrast to white landlords, however, the additional profits that he made from those renters became part of the investment capital that he used to aid the collective African American community in other ways. For their part, especially in times of personal economic crisis, black shoppers chose to patronize stores with the lowest prices or that extended credit to them even if those stores were not black-owned. Clearly there were struggles between what was good or optimal for the individual versus what benefited the collective race. Thus a tension existed, as Jeffrey Helgeson asserted, between individual and collective interests. While one could strive to meld the two, it was not always possible to do so. How black businesspeople in Chicago balanced these often complementary but sometimes oppositional factors is part of our story, but exploring it in full is beyond the scope of this volume.[20]

Building the Black Metropolis was more than merely an ideal. From today's vantage point, it is easy to overlook how early twentieth-century blacks saw it as both a possibility and a practical necessity. Because blacks were prevented by the rule of force, violence, and tradition from movement beyond their prescribed geographic area, they recognized the necessity of exercising as much independence from whites as possible. As Butler noted, "historical data show that oppressed groups create solidarity in order to turn hostility into a positive force."[21] Hence we must, as Adam Green so eloquently encouraged, see the black business community within the city "as a site of creativity, rather than constraint."[22] In other words, rather than lamenting that blacks did not build more or larger business institutions in Chicago, let us analyze those that they did create within the kinds of structural limitations arrayed against them. What residents hoped might emerge from an independent Black Chicago was as important as what actually did emerge. Additionally, as Green demonstrates, carried to its full fruition, the Black Metropolis could be a base for the greater development of black people as a race, both within the United States and the broader world.[23]

Although new to the city, migrating blacks were not empty vessels waiting to be filled with the dreams and goals of others. Instead, as James Grossman argued, southern blacks brought with them dreams of independence. They were "the dreams of independence through land ownership that had been central to southern black culture since emancipation."[24] Combined with the "entrepreneurial spirit" within the city, that preexisting desire for independence catalyzed the creation of a host of business enterprises. As Black Chicago businessman Jacoby Dickens asserted, "I always wanted to do something for myself, and I always wanted to do it with other black folks because I knew that if I had a business and my customers were black, white people couldn't just come and take those folks away from me."[25]

The geographic proximity of blacks in Chicago represented an unprecedented financial opportunity. Never before had so many blacks been present in so distinctive a locale within easy reach of the aggressive or strategic entrepreneur. The high wages of black employees from the stockyards, steel mills, and slaughterhouses meant that black business owners in Chicago had a huge pool of potential customers with money to spend. That those customers were also neighbors, friends, relatives, and fellow parishioners only added to their viability as potential economic support for the enterprise in question. As a writer in the *New York Daily Mirror* put it: "It is in this sense that their 'black belt' along Wentworth Ave. was an achievement rather than an imposition, which has given Chicago's darktown in the country where Negro dollars are spent in Negro shops, the only Black City with an economic structure of its own."[26] As a result, Black Chicagoans, during the 1920s, widely believed they could demonstrate substantive self-determination in their economic and political lives.[27] Unfortunately, those opportunities and beliefs were doomed by the economic downturn of the late 1920s. Therefore, as Christopher Robert Reed discussed in *The Depression Comes to the South Side*, the "Black Metropolis" all but disappeared during the 1930s as several previously successful black enterprises became casualties of the decade's serious economic crisis.[28]

One of the many changes wrought by the challenges of the Great Depression was the alteration in emphasis on how black consumer power should be utilized. Previously, African American leaders had urged black consumers to use their dollars to support black business development and growth. Yet the decimation of many black enterprises during the 1930s, along with the concurrent decimation of many of the jobs African Americans held before the Great Depression, prompted a reassessment of how to best use blacks' remaining buying power. This led to the "Don't Buy Where You Can't Work" campaigns of the 1930s, which advocated for equal treatment and job opportunities in white-owned commercial establishments.[29]

Although the Depression stifled the dream of the Black Metropolis, the legacy of early twentieth-century black business success served as an important precedent for Black Chicago business formation in the post–World War II era. Some of these enterprises, such as George Johnson's Johnson Products Company, followed the long-standing business model of selling black-produced goods and services to the black consumer market. Other businesses, particularly in the media and communications industry, sold the products and services of white-owned corporations to black consumers. Significantly, John H. Johnson nimbly shifted between the old and newer approaches. After initially starting his publishing empire with the *Negro Digest*, a magazine with no advertising that catered to the literary interests of blacks, he shifted to the creation of *Ebony*. This new magazine, similar to *Negro Digest*, was still sold to black consumers, but it featured mainstream product advertisements. Accordingly, it allowed Johnson to act as a "broker" or "consultant" to white corporations eager to sell their products in the black consumer market. His print efforts were supported by other black media figures, like popular Chicago radio deejay Daddy-O Daylie. Daylie used his show and signature radio style to encourage black women to buy the products of corporations like Proctor & Gamble. Thus this second phase was a kind of partial independence, a melding of the Black Metropolis ideal with the realities of the post-Depression and postwar landscape.[30]

Just as the decades following World War II witnessed a rejuvenation of the broader economy, the notion of a viable Black Metropolis in the Windy City reappeared during those same years. The enthusiasm for a rejuvenation of the ideal seemed justified. For example, black unemployment in the city was relatively low in the late 1940s and early 1950s. Furthermore, during the 1950s the median income of blacks in Chicago was second only to that of blacks in Detroit.[31] Ultimately, the belief in the efficacy of "community control" reached a zenith during the era of Black Power and "Black Capitalism." Yet, similar to the 1930s, when an unstable national economy contributed to rising black unemployment rates and the related decline and disappearance of black commercial enterprises, the economic woes of the 1970s and 1980s also resulted in inordinately high black unemployment and the decline and disappearance of iconic, historic African American businesses.

For black entrepreneurs, the victories of the civil-rights movement came with a complicated impact. On the one hand, they presented blacks with freedoms nearly unimaginable just a generation before. Freedom to move out of the traditional black communities, freedom to indulge in leisure pursuits in formerly restricted downtown areas, and a black consumer population increasingly receiving invitations for their patronage and support from white-owned companies that once refused to acknowledge their existence. Additionally, black professionals now had the opportunity for employment and promotion in major corporations. Yet these understandably welcome opportunities also generated losses. Now competing against larger and often better-funded enterprises, black businesses found themselves in a losing battle for customers. Inherent in this observation is not a lament for the segregated Chicago and America of the past, but a recognition that the legacy of civil rights is multifaceted and complicated in ways we continue to try to understand.

The entrepreneurs of the Black McDonald's Operators Association (BMOA) represent a bridge between the primarily black visions of the Black Metropolis—black entrepreneurs making money developing products and services delivered to black people and the post–civil-rights vision of black entrepreneurs whose very entrepreneurship came via an association with a white-owned company. Their entrepreneurship was developed within the framework of a white corporate structure. It remains to be seen if this model of business formation will proliferate, or if a third manifestation of "Black Metropolis" sentiment will appear as the twenty-first century unfolds.

The Chicago Business Network

In 1885, Isaac Counsellor Harris asserted in *The Colored Men's Professional and Business Directory* that "there seems to be a great degree of race pride, inspiring the better class with an inordinate desire to see each other succeed in whatever pursuit they may perchance engage in. This fact is demonstrated in many instances by the large patronage and co-operation which they received from one another, it being occasionally sufficient enough to support different branches of business where the trade is entirely closed."[32]

During the early to mid-twentieth century, the various manifestations of African American enterprise that existed in Chicago were linked to the underlying sense of community that existed among its black residents. In the United States we often speak of our "six degrees of separation," the concept that we are all only six people away from knowing everyone else in the country. In the concentrated environment of Chicago's black community, the linkages were even closer. Grouped together by both force and choice, tens of thousands of Black Chicagoans lived within blocks of one another. Meaning that publishing magnate John Johnson grew up just a few blocks away from future advertising leader Tom Burrell. Comedian Redd Foxx lived in close proximity to future crooner Nat King Cole, as well as model and actor Richard Roundtree. That is not to say that each of these people automatically knew one another individually. Rather that when one takes an expansive view of their tree of communication, one finds individuals that crossed one another's orbit akin to the crossing points of a Venn diagram. Thus blacks in Chicago, like their fellow citizens, often practiced the maxim "Don't send me nobody that nobody sent." Embedded in that statement is a mindset, related to notions of familiarity and support, that has long been at the root of Chicago's networks, both black and white.[33]

On the degrees of separation between black residents of Chicago, particularly those on the South Side, Timuel Black recalled, "If you were to go from Forty-third to Sixty-third and from the Rock Island tracks over to Cottage Grove, there was just one big neighborhood where everybody knew each other."[34] Even if colored with a little historical hyperbole, Black's description nonetheless clarifies the belief held by other longtime black residents of Chicago that, even within the hundreds of thousands of blacks living in the city, individuals were only one or two people away from knowing every other. It meant not just being a member of the actual community, but also in feeling a sense of community. And from that community came the Chicago network.

The network was built on a foundation of church memberships, professional associations, fraternal orders, high school connections, and social organizations like the Appomattox Club. The Appomattox Club was "a favorite of business and professional men as well and a center of Negro social life in general." A contemporary went further, saying, "every man in Chicago who holds any kind of responsible position or occupies a big place politically, belongs to the Appomattox Club."[35] John Rogers, founder of Ariel Capital Management, said, "There is something in the way that Chicago business leadership, white and black work to make the city stronger and it is part of the history of the town to have interaction between non-profits, government, and business. . . . There is a spirit here of working close together, and knowing fellow entrepreneurs and business leaders really well, as well as the political leadership in the community leadership."[36]

Early in the twentieth century, the Associated Business Clubs (ABC) exemplified the cooperative spirit of black business owners. The ABC, led by three of the top black business leaders of the period—Robert Abbott, Anthony Overton, and Jesse Binga—focused on developing programs to enhance black entrepreneurship throughout the city. These were "titans who had competing interests [but] still managed to coalesce for the sake of economic unity and their group's advancement."[37] Groups like the ABC set the foundation of cooperation for the black business community in Chicago.

Publisher John H. Johnson recalled that the black business community of the 1930s was "small, cohesive and cooperative."[38] It therefore inculcated a spirit of support within the cadre of black entrepreneurs, and it led the men and women business owners of the Black Metropolis to seek out other black entrepreneurs first, before branching into agreements or work with companies owned by nonblacks. For example, Alvin Boutte, founder of a chain of black-owned drugstores and co-founder of Independence Bank, said on selling the bank, "this company is worth a lot more than thirty-eight million dollars, but we wanted to sell it to blacks. We bought it black. We sold it black."[39]

Regardless of organization, the Chicago network emphasized the importance of investment in the community. For example, local black entrepreneurs were urged, when possible, to hire black workers and to cooperate with fellow black businesspeople. Similarly, black consumers were urged to employ black service providers. As a longtime Black Chicago resident recalled, "One of the reasons this city had such a strong black professional class when I was growing up is that segregation pushed us into just a few areas and we all ended up supporting each other's businesses—whether we were lawyers, doctors, or entrepreneurs."[40] This idea was exemplified by the Chicago Negro Chamber of Commerce's slogan: "For economic emancipation, trade with your own."[41] In the post–World War II era, the activities of the Negro Chamber of Commerce and ABC were extended by groups like the 40 Club. These clubs met regularly and enabled black entrepreneurs and business leaders to network with one another, partner with one another, and sit on one another's boards of directors or advisors.[42]

Beyond slogans, evidence indicates black business leaders in Chicago actively implemented these ideals. S. B. Fuller not only advertised in *Ebony* magazine, but also encouraged his salesmen to distribute it. Certainly its success offered Fuller an opportunity to advertise in a magazine directed to his consumer base, but it also enabled him to support the efforts of another black entrepreneur in the city. Fuller's expansive thinking in this area is further demonstrated by his support of the Johnson Products company. After a fire devastated the Johnson Products plant and office building, Fuller called George Johnson, a former employee and now fellow business owner, and told him he could use Fuller's own production facilities to continue to produce his products. The products Johnson sold were not in direct competition with the Fuller Products line, but nonetheless, Fuller's generosity is emblematic of the spirit of support among black business owners in Chicago.[43]

Media and Personal Care Products

The interconnected nature of Chicago's black business community is perhaps best illustrated by those in the media industries. At various times in the city's history, black entrepreneurs actively supported and were supported by local black-owned periodicals, advertising agencies, and musical and television programs. Additionally, companies in those industries also supported the work of black artists, writers, designers, photographers, and those with other skills connected to the production and distribution of media.

Beginning in 1827 with the first black newspaper, *Freedom's Journal*, African Americans have used the media to not just deliver their own news and opinions, but to present themselves as a people with a past, present, and future worthy of study and understanding. Traditionally, if someone examined mainstream media (newspapers, magazines, radio, television, and advertising) to understand the history of the United States, he or she would conclude that blacks played little part other than as slaves and criminals. In this imagined realm, African Americans did not have families, contribute to charities, build businesses, or do virtually anything of value. Consequently, blacks took it upon themselves to establish their own media outlets to tell their own stories.

Black media in Chicago began in 1878 with the founding of the *Chicago Conservator* by Ferdinand L. Barnett. Later, from the *Chicago Defender* newspaper to *The Oprah Winfrey Show*, black-created media in Chicago had an important impact well beyond the city limits. These institutions served as a key part of the economic foundation of the Black Metropolis. Yet as Baldwin, Green, and others have demonstrated, these media enterprises also conveyed important ideas about the black community. More than just businesses, they were creators and distributors of culture that generated discourse on what it meant to be black within the changing U.S. society of the twentieth century.[44]

Robert Abbott was an indefatigable advocate of the protection and advancement of black people. Through the development of a unique editorial style, content, and distribution system using railroad porters to deliver the *Defender* to southern blacks, Abbott circumvented the ways in which southern whites attempted to prevent them from reading the paper. Myiti Sengstacke Rice's essay in the present volume elaborates upon Robert Abbott's business activities in early twentieth-century Chicago.

Later in the century, in 1945, Abbott's fellow Chicagoan John H. Johnson, a migrant from the South who settled in the city in the 1930s, started one of the largest and most successful publishing companies in history, Johnson Publications (JPC). First with *Negro Digest*, then with his flagship publication, *Ebony*, Johnson provided blacks with the kinds of news and imagery that were absent from mainstream media. While some criticized Johnson, and in particular *Ebony*, for providing too much emphasis on blacks' conspicuous consumption or entertainment topics rather than "serious" news, the decades-long popularity of the magazine among black readers is evidence of the success of Johnson's formula. Jason P. Chambers provides an in-depth examination of John H. Johnson's publishing empire in the present volume.[45]

Periodicals like the *Chicago Defender* or *Whip*, *Ebony*, and *Jet* magazines, radio programs popularized by black deejays, and eventually television shows such as *Soul Train* or *The Oprah Winfrey Show* had their home in the city. Black Chicago had a host of advantages that led to it becoming the center of black media in the country. First, led by black newspaper publishers, Chicago was home to media entrepreneurs who recognized the importance of advertising and the distribution of their periodicals. Men like Abbott, and Claude Barnett, founder of the Associated Negro Press, pushed for the kind of advertising support (and revenue) received by mainstream periodicals and news services. Here, they knew, was the real potential value to a newspaper, advertising support by companies eager to reach the paper's readers. And while neither man achieved the kind of advertising support they sought from mainstream companies, both were ably supported (Abbott and the *Defender* especially) by black-owned businesses in the city. Hence the second important factor in Chicago's centrality for black-owned media was the presence of black business owners in the city who used the papers for advertising. From advertisements for Claude Barnett's Nile Queen cosmetic products in the pages of the *Defender* to Anthony Overton's support of the *Half-Century Magazine* and S. B. Fuller's advertising within and distribution of *Ebony* magazine, black entrepreneurs proved key sources of revenue for black media in the city and for catalyzing the development of media vehicles to promote their products. Third, periodicals like the *Defender* also had national distribution, aided in part by Pullman porters, who carried the paper throughout the country. Finally, black media in the city supported and were supported by black-owned companies in partner industries. Black printers, graphic artists, writers, photographers, musicians, and advertising agencies were all present in the city. This reality, combined with the emphasis on working with black-owned businesses in the city when possible, enhanced the presence and success of national black media based in the city, as well as benefited the associated black industries they partnered with.[46]

The development of the television program *Soul Train*, one of the first nationally syndicated programs featuring an African American host (the legendary Don Cornelius), exemplified the power associated with cooperation within Chicago's black business community. The program was sponsored by a black business, Johnson Products, who used that program to advertise their products. Never before had a black-owned company had time on a national television program to sell their products. In later years, that company's advertisements would be created by Burrell Advertising, a Chicago-based black-owned advertising agency.[47]

An examination of black-owned advertising agencies in Chicago, among other things, shows how some Black Chicago female entrepreneurs gained acclaim in non-gender-specific business realms. A prominent example of this phenomenon was Barbara Proctor, who, along with such male counterparts as Tom Burrell and

Vince Cullers, established Chicago as the epicenter of black-owned firms in America's advertising industry. These individuals, along with the pioneering Claude A. Barnett, created enterprises that not only sold their clients' products successfully, but also used their influence to improve the image of African Americans presented in advertisements. As Adam Green has observed, these businesses occupied a "pivotal place in redefining black life and thought nationwide."[48] Jason P. Chambers's essay on Tom Burrell provides an important illumination of this aspect of Chicago's African American business history.

Notwithstanding the importance of *Soul Train*, the appearance of *The Oprah Winfrey Show* in 1985 represents a mega-event in the realm of Black Chicago media history. Winfrey, who moved to Chicago in 1984, developed a programmatic format that made it one of the longest-running and most popular talk shows in history. Moreover, Winfrey, leveraging the fame generated from her wildly popular television program, subsequently branched into other forms of media ownership. Juliet E. K. Walker's reprinted essay on Oprah Winfrey as a business tycoon (originally published in 2002) provides a detailed account of this phenomenon. Although Oprah, since 2002, has gone on to accomplish a variety of other business-related feats (including becoming the first African American female billionaire), Walker's seminal essay provides the most thorough scholarly examination of Oprah's foundational entrepreneurial activities. Winfrey is also heir of a Chicago tradition not only in her media presence, but also as a powerful female entrepreneur.

Oprah Winfrey's meteoric rise as an entrepreneur is all the more significant because of her gender. Traditionally, characteristics (essential to business success) such as self-confidence, aggressiveness, and being a risk-taker have been viewed as masculine. Yet an examination of the history of African American entrepreneurship in Chicago reveals a long-standing presence of successful black women in business. One industry where Chicago African American female entrepreneurs were especially prominent was the provision of personal care products to black women. During the late nineteenth century, black beauty establishments, such as Grace Garnett-Abbey's popular South Side beauty shop, catered to both elite black and white clients.[49] However, with the dawning of the twentieth century, Annie Malone and Madame C. J. Walker created business models that provided black women of all classes the opportunity to have healthy and beautiful hair. Moreover, while Malone and Walker started their enterprises in other cities, Chicago soon became the hub of their respective operations.

Malone, whose "Wonderful Hair Grower" revolutionized the care of African American women's hair, also established St. Louis's Poro College in 1917. This institution—the cornerstone of a building complex that included an auditorium, dining facilities, a theater, a gymnasium, a chapel, and a roof garden—is recognized as the first educational facility that taught black cosmetology.[50] In 1930, Malone moved her business operations to Chicago. In retrospect, this corporate relocation came at an inopportune time. The subsequent Great Depression, along with Malone's bitter second divorce, took a toll on the Poro College founder.[51] Still, her example as a self-made business tycoon continues to serve as a positive example of African American female entrepreneurship.

Madam C. J. Walker, a protégée of Annie Malone, was another historic black female entrepreneur whose drive and determination equaled that of her male counterparts, and in terms of financial success she eclipsed many of them. When Walker died in 1919, another dynamic woman, Chicago's Marjorie Stewart Joyner, became national supervisor of Walker's beauty college system. Besides being a capable administrator in this regard, Joyner, in 1928, invented a breakthrough hair-care product known as the "Permanent Waving Machine." This device, which dramatically extended the amount of time curls would stay in place, became an instant success. Yet, because Joyner secured the patent for the "Permanent Waving Machine" in the context of her position with the Walker Company, she did not personally benefit from her groundbreaking innovation.[52]

The Underground Economy

Beyond its interconnected business community, Black Chicago's gambling-based underground economy contributed mightily to its economic development during the early to mid-twentieth century. Because of overt racial discrimination in America during this period, black entrepreneurs across the country had limited access to traditional sources of capital. In this unfavorable commercial environment, Chicago blacks, seemingly more than their counterparts in other locales, circumvented these obstacles by creating a viable alternative source of business funding.

Regardless of one's view of policy (a forerunner of today's government-sponsored lotteries), policy stations and the capital they generated were a key part of Black Chicago's economy. Policy station owners reinvested portions of their profits back into the community, employed its members, and served as the source of loans to entrepreneurs when traditional banks proved unwilling to do so. As a result, the world of the respectable businesses and that of the policy operators were intertwined in Chicago. Also, to protect themselves from police harassment, black policy station owners paid off unscrupulous white politicians. In addition, it's worth noting that during the first decades of the twentieth century, before policy's ascendance as a major economic influence in Black Chicago, such local African American gambling kingpins as John "Mushmouth" Johnson, Robert T. Motts, and Daniel Jackson employed a similar business model.[53]

By the early 1930s, policy, also referred to as "the numbers game," surpassed games of chance associated with cards and dice as the primary source of gambling revenue in Black Chicago. Nathan Thompson's 2002 book *Kings: The True Story of Chicago's Policy Kings and Numbers Racketeers, and their Battles with the Mafia and United States Government* provides a thorough examination of this phenomenon. According to Thompson, policy was an enterprise controlled by African Americans.

The World War I–era Great Migration dramatically enhanced the potential profits associated with policy. As more and more blacks streamed into the Windy City, many of these newcomers became regular players of the numbers game. By the 1920s, because of policy's growing revenues, a rumor spread that the Chicago-based mobster Al Capone wanted to take control of this lucrative Bronzeville business. In a 1926 meeting with several black policy operators, Capone assured the group that he had no interest in taking over this underground enterprise. Among other things, he reportedly asserted, "I have enough on my hands now managing my own business . . . That's your game . . . you fellows ought to have control of that and get all out of it you can . . . it's a game among your race."[54]

In April 1931, Democrat Anton J. Cermak replaced William Hale "Big Bill" Thompson as mayor of Chicago. Because African Americans had been closely aligned with the deposed Thompson administration, Cermak made a point of punishing local black Republicans. Targets of his political pogrom included Bronzeville policy operators, the vast majority of whom had ties to Thompson.[55] Yet while most South Side policy operators suffered during the Cermak administration, Edward Perry Jones Jr., a Democrat, continued to profit from the numbers game. Moreover, he and his brothers (George and Mack) subsequently became the richest "policy kings" in America and dramatically continued the tradition of melding underground-economy profits with "legitimate" enterprises and community improvement projects.

Similar to his Black Chicago gambling kingpin predecessors, Edward Jones used political leverage to help grow his business. For instance, in 1932 Mayor Cermak reportedly asked for Jones's help in mobilizing Bronzeville voters for the year's upcoming presidential election. Jones and Cermak subsequently agreed that if Jones used his influence to increase the number of registered black Democratic voters in Bronzeville, he (Jones) would be given the right to control all black gambling operations in the Chicago area, free of police interference.[56]

After Cermak's assassination in early 1933, Edward Kelly became Chicago's interim mayor. Among other things, Kelly agreed to honor the honor the agreement that Cermak had made with Ed Jones during the previous year. Consequently, Ed Jones and his brothers controlled black gambling activity in the Chicago area with impunity.[57] This type of political arrangement, not enjoyed by African Americans in other locales, had two important consequences. First, the availability of gambling-funded venture capital helped encourage additional business formation in Bronzeville. Second, the enhanced stature of Black Chicago's business community, stimulated by this dramatic infusion of alternative investment funding, attracted national attention. For instance, in its April 18, 1938, issue, *Time* magazine published an article titled "Business in Bronzeville," which told readers that "although Chicago has 100,000 fewer Negroes than New York, it is the centre of U.S. Negro business; last census figures showed Chicago's Negro establishments had annual net sales of $4,826,897, New York's were only $3,322,274."[58]

This *Time* magazine article also cited the economic power of Ed Jones and his brothers. At the time, white landlords controlled most of the commercial real estate in the increasingly important Forty-Third, Forty-Seventh, and Fifty-First Street shopping districts. For their part, the Jones brothers, to graphically demonstrate their financial independence, purchased outright the Forty-Seventh Street property, where they started "the world's only Negro-owned department store."[59] The Jones brothers' historic Ben Franklin Store, located at 436 East Forty-Seventh Street, opened for business on July 7, 1937. This two-story department store featured 300,000 square feet of "housewares, sporting goods, hardware, cosmetics, clothes, restaurants, a liquor section, and later a currency exchange." The master of ceremonies for the Ben Franklin Store's ribbon-cutting was *Defender* publisher Robert Abbott. In his comments he noted that "the business acumen of the Jones brothers compares favorably with that of any other American businessmen" and that "the Ben Franklin store expresses a new era in race progress." Perhaps even more impressive about the opening of the Ben Franklin Store was its subsequent provision of more than 125 full-time jobs to Bronzeville residents in a variety of capacities.[60]

Based upon the overwhelming success of the Ben Franklin Store, in 1938 the Jones brothers established the Jones Brothers Finer Food Mart, located at 303 East Forty-Third Street. This enterprise, hailed as the most modern grocery store in Bronzeville, featured a "state of the art meat department and free delivery."[61] Later in 1938, as a further demonstration of how the dichotomy between legitimate and illegitimate black business in Chicago had blurred, the Jones brothers helped organize an "Exposition of Negro Business," spotlighting local African American enterprises, held at Bronzeville's Eighth Regiment Armory. The proceedings of this event were mentioned in the April 18, 1938, *Time* article on "Business in Bronzeville."[62] Besides the Jones brothers' use of policy profits to establish personally-owned legitimate business enterprises, they also dispersed funds to enhance the business and professional stature of the larger Bronzeville community. Black Chicago doctors and dentists seeking to start or expand their practices, as well as other prospective community entrepreneurs, relied on the Jones Brothers and other policy kings for needed business loans. As one longtime Black Chicago resident asserted, "Back in those days, if ya [*sic*] didn't have no money and you wanted to open a business, you couldn't go to a bank, so you went to your local policy king."[63]

Black Chicago's policy kings' venture-capital portfolio also included investments in various professional sporting activities. Their infusion of money to help launch Joe Louis's career was especially noteworthy. Besides the Jones brothers, Julian Black was another prominent local policy station operator. Black's passion was boxing, and during the early 1930s he brought Joe Louis, then a virtually unknown fighter from Detroit, to Chicago for a workout. After the young Louis's impressive showing, Black contacted the Jones brothers and other local policy operators requesting additional seed capital to help launch the young Louis's career.[64]

Joe Louis's subsequent rise to national and international prominence generated positive financial and public relations benefits for the Jones brothers and Louis's other Black Chicago policy investors. For instance, two weeks after Louis became an iconic figure in Black America after winning the heavyweight championship on June 22, 1937, he was one of the ribbon cutters at the July 7, 1937, opening of the Jones brothers' Ben Franklin Store. Similarly, one of the featured attractions of the Jones brothers–supported 1938 "Exposition of Negro Business" was an appearance by "the Champ."[65]

Through their wide-ranging spheres of influence, the Jones brothers and other policy kings helped create a community that seemingly was the envy of other African American urban enclaves across the country. No less an observer than the immortal Duke Ellington, who regularly played in Bronzeville venues, retrospectively described Black Chicago in almost surreal terms: "The Southside was together. It was a real us-for-we, we-for-us community. It was a community with 12 Negro Millionaires. No hungry Negroes, no complaining Negroes, no crying Negroes, and no Uncle Toms. It was a community of men and women who were respected, people of great dignity—doctors, lawyers, Policy operators, boot blacks, barbers, beauticians, bartenders, saloon-keepers, night clerks, club owners, cab drivers, stock yard workers, owners of after-hours joints, bootleggers—everything and everybody, but no junkies."[66] The September 1951 issue of *Our World*, one of *Ebony* magazine's early competitors, reinforced Ellington's perceptions and shared them with a national audience through an article titled "Chicago: Money Capital of Negro America." *Our World* described Chicago as a place "which has become famous for the biggest policy wheels, the largest funerals, the flashiest cars, and the prettiest women." Moreover, the Windy City had "built that reputation on only one thing—money."[67]

Most of this article featured such "legitimate" Black Chicago entrepreneurs and executives as Judge H. Parker, owner of the Parker Sausage Company, and Truman K. Gibson, president of the Supreme Liberty Life Insurance Company. Nevertheless, it also mentioned Ted Roe, who had succeeded the Jones brothers as the chief policy king in Chicago, as well as Roe's wife, Carrie, who was described as owning "the best equipped beauty parlor on S. Michigan Avenue." *Our World* also revealed that monies generated by the Jones brothers during their heyday in the 1930s were still generating profits in the early 1950s.[68]

Within a couple years, the gambling profits and economic nationalism that were important underpinnings of Bronzeville's successful commercial activity had dissipated. On August 4, 1952, Ted Roe, after refusing to voluntarily sell his policy business to La Cosa Nostra, was assassinated by a Mafia hit squad.[69] Thus, similar to what had occurred in Harlem a couple of decades earlier, white mobsters subsequently controlled the policy business in Bronzeville. Needless to say, La Cosa Nostra, unlike the previous African American controllers of this enterprise, did not divert a portion of policy's profits into various black community enhancement activities. Will Cooley's essay on Black Chicago's underground economy during the twentieth century provides additional details on how race-based alternative capitalism operated during this period.

Policy's importance as an alternative source of venture capital appears to have been stimulated by the Great Depression's destruction of legitimate Black Chicago banks. In fact, before the economic downturn of the 1930s, Chicago was the undisputed center of black banking activity in the country. As Abram Harris declared in *The Negro as Capitalist*, in 1929 the Binga State Bank and the Douglass National Bank "possessed 36 percent of the combined resources of all Negro banks in the United States."[70] In the present volume, Robert Howard and Robert E. Weems Jr. provide detailed discussions of Jesse Binga and the Binga State Bank and Anthony Overton and the Douglass National Bank.

The Social Impact of Black Business Development

The comedian and social critic Dick Gregory once famously said, "In the North they don't care how big you get as long as you don't get too close."[71] That is not totally accurate. History is replete with numerous examples of how much some whites did care about how "big" black enterprises got. Whites seemingly accepted black business activity as long as it remained of limited profitability and serviced only black consumers. This was a factor recognized by African American entrepreneurs, and in many cases it limited the scope of their business operations and aspirations. For example, in 1947 S. B. Fuller purchased the previously white-owned Boyer Laboratories, which produced the popular Jean Nadal cosmetic line. Since white consumers were the primary market for Jean Nadal products, Fuller's ownership of Boyer Laboratories was kept secret for fear of a potential white backlash. Ultimately, the infamous White Citizens Council did discover Fuller's ownership of Boyer and coordinated a boycott of Jean Nadal products that helped spur the brand's demise.[72] Clovis Semmes's essay in the present volume elaborates upon Fuller's purchase of Boyer Laboratories and the subsequent negative impact it had on his business stature.

While Fuller's experience might appear isolated, it served as an example of the perils of expansion beyond racially acceptable categories. Another example of this phenomenon involved publisher John H. Johnson. In 1950 Johnson, wary about a possible negative response in the white business community, declined an opportunity to invest in *Quick* magazine, a periodical that catered to white readers. This self-imposed business limitation appears to have been linked to fears that his white advertiser clients in *Ebony* might take offense at him expanding beyond his accepted space. Thus, in contrast to earlier black businesses based solely on connections to black consumers, new models like Johnson's, with its linkages to white-owned corporations, could sometimes limit entrepreneurial opportunities.[73]

From a legalistic standpoint, the long-standing racial bias experienced by black entrepreneurs in Chicago (and elsewhere) gradually declined after the May 17, 1954, U.S. Supreme Court decision in the *Brown v. Board of Education* case. In fact, the dismantling of American apartheid did, indeed, open up new opportunities for African American entrepreneurship. For instance, Marcia Chatelain's essay in the present volume discusses the growth of black-owned McDonald's franchises in Chicago commencing in the 1960s.

Also, the post-1954 birth and development of government-sponsored programs to promote black business development contributed mightily to the increased movement of African American entrepreneurs into franchise and other business-related opportunities. For example, in 1964, at the behest of Eugene P. Foley, the administrator of the Small Business Administration (SBA), a business loan provision was added to Title IV of the Economic Opportunity Act. Later manifestations of government support for black business development included Richard Nixon's establishment of the Office of Minority Business Enterprise (OMBE) through Executive Order 11458 on March 5, 1969, and the establishment of the Minority Business Development Agency (MBDA) in 1979, which sought to increase the number of medium- to large-size black firms in such growth industries as energy, communications, and electronics.[74]

As a result of the slaying of Jim Crow and increased government support for African American business aspirations, substantive opportunities were created for some entrepreneurially minded blacks. For instance, David L. Steward, the president and CEO of World Wide Technologies, Inc. (WWT), currently presides over the largest black-owned business in America. Steward, with the early help of the SBA's Section 8(a) program, grew the suburban St. Louis-based WWT from a shoestring operation into an economic juggernaut that had annual revenue of over $6 billion in 2013.[75] Nevertheless, the historic "economic detour" that confined many black enterprises to only serving other blacks remained alive and well in late twentieth-century America. In this volume's concluding chapter, on the impact of racial desegregation on Chicago's African American business community, Robert

E. Weems Jr. discusses how white-owned businesses, and not black ones, were the primary beneficiaries of economic desegregation.

The Black Metropolis in the Twenty-First Century

In recent decades, as many of Black Chicago's historic enterprises have disappeared from the landscape of American business, other locales have emerged as leading centers of African American entrepreneurship. According to a 2015 study titled "Best Places for Black-Owned Businesses," the ten best locales for African American entrepreneurship are Atlanta (GA), Montgomery (AL), Memphis (TN), Washington, D.C., Durham (NC), Savannah (GA), Baton Rouge (LA), Baltimore (MD), Richmond (VA), and Miami (FL). Chicago ranked 39th among the 107 U.S. cities that have a population of at least 100,000 residents. The indices used to determine these rankings were average revenue of black-owned businesses; percentage of black-owned businesses (out of total businesses); percentage of black-owned businesses with paid employees; number of black businesses per 100 black residents; median income of black residents; and the cost-of-living index.[76]

While the future of African American entrepreneurship in Chicago cannot be predicted with precision, one reality remains crystal clear. During the twentieth century, based upon a variety of historical circumstances, the Windy City created a black executive and entrepreneurial class unmatched anywhere else in the country. Moreover, black-owned business enterprises in Chicago had an importance far beyond that of the businesses themselves. As Allan Spear noted, "whatever the real achievements of Negro businessmen, politicians, and civic leaders, the sight of Negroes participating independently in fields that had previously been monopolized by whites became a source of race pride."[77] Thus the men and women of the black business class became more than race leaders; they became race heroes. Whether barber, banker, hair care magnate, or policy king, black entrepreneurs' success became demonstrable proof of blacks' ability to compete with whites regardless of the unfair playing field on which they operated.

Finally, the success of local black entrepreneurs helped fuel the dream of a Black Metropolis. As Timuel Black once asserted, "You could buy anything you needed in our community. You didn't have to shop downtown."[78] The question of whether this statement was true is of course important. But equally important is the fact that many residents of Chicago's South and West Sides believed that they could build a community that was strong enough politically, economically, socially, and culturally to not be dependent on others or to at least be able to protect themselves and their families from the depredations of racism and discrimination. In a nation that continues to experience the negative reverberations of slavery and American apartheid, this mindset, which remains a factor in stimulating black business development and entrepreneurship, has not been totally extinguished.

Notes

1. Peter A. Coclanis, "Business of Chicago," *Encyclopedia of Chicago*, accessed December 19, 2016, at http://www.encyclopedia.chicagohistory.org/pages/198.html.

2. Thomas A. Meehan, "Jean Baptiste Point DuSable, the First Chicagoan," *Journal of the Illinois State Historical Society* 56 (Autumn 1963): 451.

3. Ibid., 449.

4. Juliet E. K. Walker, *The History of Black Business in America: Capitalism, Race, Entrepreneurship* (New York: Macmillan, 1998), xx–xxi. For an example of recent research regarding the local experiences of black entrepreneurs, see Bessie House-Soremekun, *Confronting the Odds: African American Entrepreneurship in Cleveland, Ohio* (Kent, OH: Kent State University Press, 2009).

5. On black patronage of the arts, see Christopher Robert Reed, "African American Cultural Expression in Chicago before the Renaissance: The Performing, Visual, and Literary Arts, 1893–1933," in *The Black Chicago Renaissance*, ed. Darlene Clark Hine and John McCluskey Jr. (Urbana: University of Illinois Press, 2012), 14–15.

6. On Robert Abbott's "Great Northern Drive," see Myiti Sengstacke Rice, *Images of America: Chicago Defender* (Charleston: Arcadia, 2012), 7; Ethan Michaeli, *The Defender: How a Legendary Black Newspaper Changed America, from the Age of the Pullman Porters to the Age of Obama* (Boston: Houghton Mifflin Harcourt, 2016), 61–79.

7. Claude A. Barnett to Robert R. Moton, September 22, 1930, Claude A. Barnett Papers, Box 131, Folder 6. On Barnett's advocacy of the Washington/Tuskegee approach, see Linda J. Evans, "Claude Barnett and the Associated Negro Press," *Chicago History* (1983), 46.

8. Edna Bonacich, "A Theory of Middleman Minorities," *American Sociological Review* 38 (October 1973): 583–94; John Sibley Butler, *Entrepreneurship and Self-Help among Black Americans: A Reconsideration of Race and Economics* (Albany: State University of New York Press, 2005), 239. On the scholarly denigration of African American business beyond that of E. Franklin Frazier, see Earl Ofari Hutchinson, *The Myth of Black Capitalism* (New York: Monthly Review Press, 1970), and Michelle Boyd, *Jim Crow Nostalgia: Reconstructing Race in Bronzeville* (Minneapolis: University of Minnesota Press, 2008), 17–24.

9. Quoted in Abram L. Harris, *The Negro as Capitalist* (Chicago: Urban Research Press, 1992; originally published 1936), 223.

10. Adam Green, *Selling the Race: Culture, Community, and Black Chicago, 1940–1955* (Chicago: University of Chicago Press, 2007), 175.

11. John Sibley Butler, *Entrepreneurship and Self-Help among Black Americans* (Albany: State University of New York Press, 1991), 75. On restrictions of blacks' home and property buying, see St. Clair Drake and Horace R. Cayton, *The Black Metropolis: A Study of Negro Life in a Northern City* (Chicago: The University of Chicago Press, 1993), 79–80.

12. "Business in Bronzeville," *Time* 31 (April 18, 1938): 70.

13. Walker, *The History of Black Business in America*, xix.

14. On services to white elites, see Davarian L. Baldwin, *Chicago's New Negroes: Modernity, the Great Migration, and Black Urban Life* (Chapel Hill: University of North Carolina Press, 2007), 64; Christopher Reed, *Black Chicago's First Century* (Columbia: University of Missouri Press, 2005), 1:200–203. On John Jones, see Charles A. Gliozzo, "John Jones: A Study of a Black Chicagoan," *Illinois Historical Journal* 80 (Autumn 1987): 177–88.

15. Willard Gatewood, *Aristocrats of Color: The Black Elite, 1880–1920* (Bloomington: Indiana University Press, 1990), 119.

16. Evelyn Burrell (longtime resident of the South Side of Chicago and migrant from Alabama), interview by author, August 29, 2012.

17. Drake and Cayton, *Black Metropolis*, 12.

18. Baldwin, *Chicago's New Negroes*, 7.

19. Quoted in ibid.

20. Jeffrey Helgeson, *Crucibles of Black Empowerment: Chicago's Neighborhood Politics from the New Deal to Harold Washington* (Chicago: University of Chicago Press, 2014), 12, 31.

21. Butler, *Entrepreneurship and Self-Help among Black Americans*, 259.

22. Green, *Selling the Race*, 3.

23. Ibid., 9.

24. James R. Grossman, *Land of Hope: Chicago, Black Southerners, and the Great Migration* (Chicago: University of Chicago Press, 1989), 6.

25. Timuel Black, *Bridges of Memory: Chicago's First Wave of Black Migration* (Evanston, IL: Northwestern University Press, 2003), 327; Baldwin, *Chicago's New Negroes*, 6; Helgeson, *Crucibles of Black Empowerment*, 117.

26. Quoted in Harris, *The Negro as Capitalist*, 217.

27. Reed, *The Rise of Chicago's Black Metropolis*; see introduction, Baldwin, *Chicago's New Negroes*, 7–8.

28. Christopher R. Reed, *The Depression Comes to the South Side: Protest and Politics in the Black Metropolis, 1930–1933* (Bloomington: Indiana University Press, 2011), 1.

29. On the transition in emphasis of black consumer power, see Robert E. Weems Jr., *Desegregating the Dollar: African American Consumerism in the Twentieth Century* (New York: New York University Press, 1998), 28–30, and Laura Warren Hill and Julia Rabig, *The Business of Black Power: Community Development, Capitalism, and Corporate Responsibility in Postwar America* (Rochester, NY: University of Rochester Press, 2012), 22–25.

30. On John H. Johnson's role as a "broker," see Dwight E. Brooks, "In Their Own Words: Advertisers' Construction of an African American Consumer Market, the World War II Era." *Howard Journal of Communications* 6 (1995): 49. On Daddy-O Dailey, see Robert E. Weems, "The Revolution Will Be Marketed: American Corporations and Black Consumers during the 1960s," *Radical History Review* 59 (1994): 99.

31. On the rejuvenation of the Black Metropolis ideal, see Drake and Cayton, *Black Metropolis*, 726. On black income and employment see Green, *Selling the Race*, 10–11.

32. Quoted in Reed, *Black Chicago's First Century*, 260.

33. Edward McClelland, *Young Mr. Obama: Chicago and the Making of a Black President* (New York: Bloomsbury Press, 2010), 118.

34. Black, *Bridges of Memory*, 1:389.

35. Quoted in Allan H. Spear, *Black Chicago: The Making of a Negro Ghetto, 1890–1920* (Chicago: University of Chicago Press, 1967), 109.

36. John Rogers (founder of Ariel Capital Management), interview by Jason P. Chambers, July 30, 2012.

37. Reed, *The Rise of Chicago's Black Metropolis*, 110.

38. Mary Fuller Casey, *S. B. Fuller: Pioneer in Black Economic Development* (Jamestown, NC: BridgeMaster Press, 2003), 57.

39. Black, *Bridges of Memory*, 1:273.

40. Graham, *Our Kind of People*, 202.

41. "S. B. Fuller: A Man and His Products," *Black Enterprise* (1975): 48.

42. "Chicago Hailed as Business Capital for Blacks," *Chicago Tribune*, July 30, 1979.

43. On the Johnson-Fuller relationship, see *Bridges of Memory*, 1:359–60; Casey, *S. B. Fuller*, 130–31.

44. Metz T. P. Lochard, "The Negro Press in Illinois," *Journal of the Illinois Historical Society* 56 (Autumn 1963): 572.

45. Hill and Rabig, *The Business of Black Power*, 22–23.

46. Gregory, *The Southern Diaspora*, 126; Baldwin, *Chicago's New Negroes*, 13, 64–65, 80–82.

47. On Johnson products and *Soul Train*, see Black, *Bridges of Memory*, 1:365–66; Christopher P. Lehman, *A Critical History of Soul Train on Television* (Jefferson, NC: McFarland, 2008).

48. Jason Chambers, *Madison Avenue and the Color Line: African Americans in the Advertising Industry* (Philadelphia: University of Pennsylvania Press, 2008), 22–30; Lawrence D. Hogan, *A Black National News Service: The Associated Negro Press and Claude Barnett, 1919–1945* (Rutherford, NJ: Farleigh Dickinson University Press, 1984), 164–65.

49. Baldwin, *Chicago's New Negroes*, 64.

50. "Annie Turnbo Malone: A Generous Entrepreneur," Annie Malone Children and Family Services, accessed December 19, 2016, at http://www.anniemalone.com/annie-turnbo-malone.html; "*Poro Hair & Beauty Culture* (St. Louis: PORO College, 1922), 5–6; Annie Malone," *Gale Encyclopedia of Biography*, accessed December 19, 2016, at http://www.encyclopedia.com/people/history/historians-miscellaneous-biographies/annie-turnbo-malone.

51. "Annie Turnbo Malone: A Generous Entrepreneur."

52. "Marjorie Joyner," Gaius Chamberlin, accessed December 19, 2016, at http://www.blackinventor.com/marjorie-joyner/.

53. Green, *Selling the Race*, 15.

54. Thompson, *Kings*, 21. Although Al Capone apparently appeared willing to permit African Americans to maintain control of Bronzeville's policy game during the 1920s (when his bootlegging operations were booming), one can only wonder what Capone's attitude would have been during the next decade, when the end of Prohibition signaled the end of the illicit alcohol industry. The example of "Dutch" Schultz in New York suggests that Capone, had he been on the scene, would have reconsidered his disinterest in policy. The mobster Schultz, seeking a new income stream, used intimidation and force to take control of the policy business in Harlem. This resulted in Schultz's gaining control of an enterprise that generated upward of $20 million annually.

55. Ibid., 465; Harold F. Gosnell, *Negro Politicians: The Rise of Negro Politics in Chicago* (Chicago: University of Chicago Press, 1935), 126; Walker, *The History of Black Business in America*, 191.

56. Thompson, *Kings*, 20.

57. Ibid., 21.

58. "Business in Bronzeville," 70.

59. Ibid., 72.

60. Thompson, *Kings*, 156, 160, 161.

61. Ibid., 162.

62. "Business in Bronzeville," 72.

63. Thompson, *Kings*, 163.

64. Ibid., 126.

65. Ibid., 160; "Business in Bronzeville," 71.

66. Thompson, *Kings*, 141.

67. "Chicago: Money Capital of Negro America," *Our World* 6 (September 1951): 15.

68. Ibid., 15, 16, 19.

69. Thompson, *Kings*, 331–34.

70. Harris, *The Negro as Capitalist*, 195.

71. Elijah Wald, *Riding with Strangers: A Hitchhiker's Journey* (Chicago: Chicago Review Press, 2006), 206.

72. On the boycott of Fuller's company, see John H. Johnson, *Succeeding against the Odds: The Autobiography of a Great American Businessman* (New York: Amistad Press, 1992), 129.

73. Ben Burns, *Nitty Gritty: A White Editor in Black Journalism* (Jackson: University Press of Mississippi, 1996), 166–68.

74. Robert E. Weems Jr., *Business in Black and White: American Presidents and Black Entrepreneurs in the Twentieth Century* (New York: New York University Press, 2009), 74, 127, 217.

75. "Billion Dollar Businessman Dave Steward Shares Success Secrets," Carolyn M. Brown, accessed December 19, 2016, at http://www.blackenterprise.com/small-business/billion-dollar-businessman-dave-steward-shares-success-secrets/; "BE 100s 2014," accessed December 19, 2016, at http://www.blackenterprise.com/lists/be-100s-2014/.

76. "Best Places for Black-Owned Businesses," Jonathan Todd, accessed December 19, 2016, at http://www.nerdwallet.com/blog/small-business/best-places-for-black-owned-businesses/.

77. Spear, *Black Chicago*, 226.

78. Black, *Bridges of Memory*, vol. 2, unnumbered photograph captioned "Woodson's Shoe Store."

CHAPTER 1

Early Black Chicago Entrepreneurial and Business Activities from the Frontier Era to the Great Migration

The Nexus of Circumstance and Initiative

CHRISTOPHER ROBERT REED

> I have frequently consulted with many of our leading citizens and well-thinking people upon the great need of a work of this kind, and they have earnestly admitted with one accord that a directory of the business, professions and prominent occupations of the enterprising colored people in the city of Chicago would be a work of vast importance, and a reliable medium of authoritative information, while its many advantages would be highly appreciated by all lovers of our race progress . . .
>
> —Isaac C. Harris, *Colored Men's Business Directory*, 1885

To the credit of black initiative and indomitability of spirit, early black Chicago's entrepreneurial and business evolution proceeded along a parallel, yet somewhat submerged, track with the city's overall economic growth and development. This was the case even though black business operations in a frontier setting scarcely forecast the twentieth century's partially realized "Dream of the Black Metropolis," where African Americans exerted some control over their residential and commercial district. Nevertheless, black Chicagoans' nineteenth-century entrepreneurial pursuits served as a bridge and precursor to more accelerated commercial activity during the next millennium.

Chicago's pre–Civil War Era featured incipient African American entrepreneurial pursuits along with established business operations. Black initiative produced and thrived at a time when Chicago accelerated its transformation from a "home market" to a metropolitan economy. As historian Bessie Louise Pierce described this process, Chicago's *town economy*, based upon the coming of the railroads at midcentury, became an *economy of the city*.[1] Existing businesses rested on a base of entrepreneurship and acquisition that reflected the quickening activities of the market revolution. With early black Chicagoans embracing the entrepreneurial and business spirit pervading the nation, white hostility seemed surmountable in this sphere as compared to the area of wage employment where racial constraints restricted black pursuit of material stability.

Despite the odds facing a group held in low esteem and legally recognized bondage nationally, African Americans in Chicago entered fields most readily accessible, such as barbering and personal upkeep. In fact, they operated (and possibly owned) two of the three bathhouses in the city by 1842, while Nelson P. Perry provided spirited entertainment on his violin for "assemblies, balls, and parties."[2] Importantly, an accompanying pattern of business involvement emerged beyond such scattered examples as Abram T. Hall, who owned the first black-owned barbershop by 1844, or the grocer O. G. Hanson, who amicably extended the entrepreneurial John Jones family credit of $2 to ensure their survival when they arrived in the city in 1845. J. W. Norris's *General Directory*, an early combined business list and census, listed four other African American barbers in antebellum Chicago: Oliver C. Henson, John Dixon, Henry Knight, and John Johnson.[3]

Horse-drawn wagons, carts, carriages, or stagecoaches kept mid-nineteenth-century Chicago moving, both inside and outside its borders. While primitively conquering space and time, these conveyances prevented the complete social isolation of Chicago's African American residents. The livery stable business afforded the entrepreneurial Harry Knight the distinction of operating the largest in the city in 1852.[4] Entrepreneur Isaac Atkinson began operating his own stagecoach business by 1858, carrying passengers over fewer and fewer muddy streets and ground-level debris as plank roads miraculously made their appearance. In fact, one late nineteenth-century recollection claimed that "in the early 50's Isaac Atkinson ran a bus which was a rival of Parmalee (the leading transporter of people)."[5] Constituting an essential cog in the fledgling town's transportation network, Atkinson clearly demonstrated that blacks with daring were not to be totally restrained in their quest for economic advancement.

Hauling and distributing Lake Michigan water to the city's residents afforded Isom Artis a comfortable livelihood.[6] Lake water provided Chicagoans a healthier supply than the polluted water from the Chicago River, filled as it was with debris of all types. Artis and other water haulers became known as water men, taking their two-wheeled carts to the foot of the lake at Randolph Street and filling barrels from pails with nature's thirst-quenching nectar. By 1842, the water men faced their first major competition as the Chicago Hydraulic Company began its operations.[7]

Early cattle keeping appeared on the city's periphery, at Thirty-First Street on the south, and Fifth Avenue and Crawford on the far west, a precedent to Chicago's later lucrative livestock industry. An unnamed, yet documented, African American demonstrated his business astuteness in this realm during the early 1850s. Boldly settling with his family away from the crowded city in the vicinity of Racine (then Ann Street) and Lake Street on the city's somewhat isolated West Side, this ambitious African American herded perhaps as many as several dozen cattle.[8] The patriarch of the family had lived an unusual life under bondage in Kentucky. He had been trusted to drive his master's cattle alone into free territory, negotiate the sale, and return to his wife and children with the master's portion of the sale. He eventually bought his own and his family's freedom and settled in 1854 on the western boundary of Chicago.

The most successful and highly publicized African American entrepreneur during this period was "John Jones[, who] conducted his business so well that he was able to purchase important property, including the location at 119 Dearborn Street—now occupied by a prominent Chicago department store—where he set up a merchant tailoring establishment."[9] His worth was listed as being at least $10,000 by 1860, and by the time of the Great Fire of 1871 it had possibly reached an estimated $85,000 to $100,000.[10] As the city's leading black businessman, Jones assumed the mantle of civic and political leadership, as well. He guided the legal fight to end the Illinois Black Codes in March 1865 and became the first African American to be elected to a municipal office in Illinois history in 1872. As a Cook County commissioner, he served two terms in office as Chicago recovered from the conflagration of the previous year.

As post–Civil War Chicago moved into the Gilded Age of the 1880s and 1890s, both white and black enterprises experienced business growth and development. To be sure, the growth and financial successes of black businesses was diminutive when contrasted with the city's economic "Big Three" of merchandiser Marshall Field, meat-packer Philip Armour, and hotelier Potter Palmer. The fact emerged that while white Chicago was developing within its leadership structure a highly discernible upper class based on wealth accruing from impressive gains in both commercial and industrial production, Black Chicago was prevented from building a comparable wellspring for economic advancement. Nonetheless, the proportional growth of Black Chicago commercial enterprises following the Civil War clearly attested to African American entrepreneurial and business vigor, perseverance, and acumen. This awareness prompted Marsha Freeman Edmond, whose correspondence from the period of 1885–89 was later published in a 1930s *Chicago Tribune* series, to write contemporaneously that "dawn has come for the Negro here. When I hear people complain because their progress economically is slow, I feel rather impatient, for it seems to me that, on the contrary, they have accomplished a great deal in the twenty-five years since emancipation. In spite of the heavy handicap of poverty and lack of education, there are many of the race who are property owners. Some of the Negroes of the city are quite prosperous."[11]

In a city basking in the reflected glory of its growing industrial might, the exclusion of African Americans from the manufacturing sector by the 1890s relegated blacks to an economic position of both circumscribed opportunity and limited expectations. This condition persisted despite a perceived prosperity in the eyes of some observers like Marsha Freeman Edmond. Moreover, the potential for Chicago African Americans to amass a fortune through meat-packing, steel production, transportation, or merchandising existed only in the realm of the impossible.

In this restricted economic environment, African Americans, in pursuit of wealth, labored either as employees of others or as small-scale entrepreneurs or businessmen. Of the 14,271 Black Chicago residents enumerated in the 1890 census, 8,080 held employment in the following areas, along with their percentage as part of the city's total working population: domestic and personal service, 4,972 (34%); manufacturing and mechanical, 1,376 (1.9%); trade, 474 (1.3%); transportation and communication, 395 (2.2%); clerical services, 133 (0.4%); professional services, 115 (1.3%); public services, 48 (1.6%); and, agriculture, 7 (2.2%). Five hundred and sixty workers were listed as unclassified workers. Of the total black workforce, 61.5 percent earned their living in the area of domestic and personal services.

Strategically, the city's black entrepreneurs began to focus on the notion of promoting a group economy, in a similar manner to how other groups in America had accomplished their goals. Once again, conditions for success in the North exceeded those in the South with its legal and customary constraints.[12] Moreover, as Chicago's black population grew in both size and consciousness, it was accompanied by an increasing commitment to an ideology of intraracial support for community businesses. In fact, contrary to the popular notion that blacks did not support their own businesses during this period, a major piece of contemporary evidence in Chicago shows otherwise. The following observation, which appeared in Isaac C. Harris's 1885 *Colored Men's Business Directory*, attested to this growing tradition: "There seems to be a great degree of race pride, inspiring the better class with an inordinate desire to see each other succeed in whatever pursuit they may perchance engage in. This fact is demonstrated in many instances by the large patronage and co-operation which they received from one another, it being occasionally sufficient enough to support different branches of business where the trade is entirely colored."[13]

Proponents of racial solidarity and self-help were found not only among businesspersons themselves and a portion of the masses, but also among the ranks of the clergy, as well as community and elite civic leaders. As reported in the December 18, 1886, edition of the *Conservator*, "Is there race pride? Then patronize those that patronize the race. Go buy where they invite you through your *own* newspapers [emphasis added]."[14]

An additional set of circumstances, which affected African American work and wage earning, increased entrepreneurship's allure among blacks. Because of blatant racism, black workers earned their living outside the industrial sphere, so a sense of labor consciousness and workers' solidarity was less likely to be nurtured. Moreover, in the spheres of work, family, and friends, self-employment carried a heightened status and mobility unachievable by the worker whose work was tightly regimented. Entrepreneurship made one truly a master over individual exertions and creativity, and this type of freedom appealed to a group of people whose collective history featured their forced labor for others. Thus, by 1885, Black Chicago counted 110 businesses, with 46 located in the retail sector and 64 in service-related areas.[15]

One early sector of Black Chicago business activity, the print industry, provided uneven financial benefits to its pioneering entrepreneurs. Yet local African American newspapers and directories ultimately provided a major catalyst for business formation.

When Ferdinand L. Barnett launched Chicago's first African American newspaper, the *Conservator*, in 1878, he believed this initiative provided a modicum of financial opportunity. With a growing base of subscribers and readers, he believed this venture could be potentially profitable. Yet the *Conservator* became a financial challenge that prompted Barnett to return full-time to his law practice and pension cases, where greater financial success existed.[16]

In 1885, entrepreneur and businessman Isaac Counsellor Harris, seeking to capitalize from growing black pride and growing black entrepreneurship compiled and published Black Chicago's first business directory, *The Colored Men's Professional and Business Directory*. As the most significant publication since the establishment of the *Conservator*, it represented a newer, more energized promotion of entrepreneurial and business success. Harris, in compiling his directory, observed that Chicago's most assertive, enterprising, and successful African Americans achieved through their own efforts and deserved attention because "none were to the manor born."[17]

By the late nineteenth century, as chronicled in *The Colored Men's Professional and Business Directory*, the diverse ways that Chicago blacks were accumulating wealth had expanded greatly from the pre–Civil War era. African Americans had now moved into such areas as real estate, retail furniture, undertaking, catering, saloon ownership, and the professions. Lewis Bates, who arrived unheralded in the city as a fugitive slave during the Civil War, went on to amass a small fortune in real estate. Uneducated after an early life of uncompensated toil, but determined to achieve the utmost in life, Bates moved steadily upward in his quest for wealth production.

He first toiled in a foundry under the direction of others; then he worked independently as an express man, delivering essential items in a society hungering for the goods necessary to meet its rising consumer needs.[18] He became known for "his excellent judgment, and nearly all his investments are gilt-edged." As chronicled by historian Rayford W. Logan, Lewis Bates, "a former slave in North Carolina lived alone in a dingy room at 400 Dearborn Street . . . [while he] amassed a fortune of some $500,000 through shrewd real-estate dealings. One of his holdings was 'an elegant, new seven-story pressed-brick and terra cotta apartment house worth $80,000 on State Street which he rented to white tenants.'"[19]

The firm of Platt & Goode was a partnership run by the son of J. F. Platt, a man who had prospered in the lumber business and who, on his own, combined his talents with those of a carpenter to prosper in the furniture and lumber business.[20] Later, Platt Place, a street on Chicago's West Side, was named for this successful businessman.[21]

During the late nineteenth century, undertaking became an important business endeavor among Chicago blacks. George T. Kersey, a native of Chatham, Ontario, Canada, reached the city in 1888 and soon went into business with Daniel Jackson, the son of prosperous saloonkeeper Emmanuel Jackson. Later, David McGowan joined them for a brief time before Kersey and McGowan withdrew to form a partnership with another young enterprising risk-taker named Morsell.[22]

The catering trade offered opportunities for African Americans, especially among the growing wealthy North Side white elite. Charles H. Smiley and his wife arrived from Virginia in 1880 and quickly established themselves as ambassadors of service par excellence. Smiley distinguished himself among black caterers during this period and into the new century, earning the sobriquet "Chicago's *colored* caterer" as well as "a sort of Vanderbilt with a darker hue." "No affair on the Gold Coast was considered properly cared for unless handled by the Smiley establishment."[23]

The liquor business offered another avenue to obtain wealth for enterprising late nineteenth-century Chicago blacks. For instance, an August 6, 1885, *Chicago Daily News* article included the following: "you may be surprised to hear that in the liquor business alone upward of $200,000 worth of stock and saloon fixtures are owned by Colored men. In fact, this business seems to be the best adapted of any to the abilities of the Colored man who has saved enough out of his earnings to invest in any kind of business."[24] One such person was Daniel "Uncle Dan" Scott, who arrived in the city in 1872 and immediately joined his brothers in the saloon business. He shrewdly converted his profits into a cartage business solely under his control. When Daniel Scott died in 1895, his worth had reportedly reached $100,000.[25] Later, men such as John "Mushmouth" Johnson, Henry "Teeenan" Jones, and Robert T. "Bob" Motts enhanced their successful saloons with the addition of profitable gambling activities.[26]

Not to be overlooked was Black Chicago's professional community, which contained physicians, dentists, and lawyers. Their prominence in the operating rooms and arguing before the bench extended beyond any limitations imposed by race. Notable names included Dr. Daniel Hale Williams, the first American surgeon to successfully operate on the human heart; Dr. Charles E. Bentley, who developed such skills in dentistry as to become the "father of the dental hygiene movement" to the nation's schoolchildren; and attorney Edward H. Morris, whose legal acumen won him acceptance with some of the city's leading business firms. Attorneys Ferdinand L. Barnett and S. Laing Williams began an acquaintance at the University of Michigan that blossomed into a law partnership of some length. Breaking the glass ceiling to join the professional ranks was the nation's first black female dentist, Ida Gray Nelson, who began her practice in Chicago in 1894. The following year, Ida M. Platt became the first African American woman lawyer in Illinois.[27]

According to 1890 census data, 61.5 percent of Black Chicagoans worked in the relatively noncompetitive areas of domestic service. Nevertheless, friction between African American workers and the city's organized labor movement remained high. Conditions were exacerbated beyond repair in 1892 when members of the supposedly color-blind Knights of Labor in Chicago endorsed the deportation of African Americans to Central Africa in an effort to reduce labor competition. The city's African American workers responded by staging a protest meeting followed by circulating a letter of indignation that attracted sizable coverage in the white press. Psychologically American to the core, Chicago's African Americans reacted with words of indignation, suggesting that "if this country is too small for the Knights of Labor and the Negro, then let the Knights leave."[28]

In the midst of a devastating economic depression, the World's Columbian Exposition, popularly known as the 1893 Chicago World's Fair, became an economic stimulant for established businessmen as well as entrepreneurs. Interestingly, it also served as a magnet for prospective laborers who would expand the city's growing African American consumer market. Importantly, the event attracted the economically zealous who sought to become entrepreneurs. It afforded rising entrepreneurs an opportunity to make their fortunes in the next century, men such as future real-estate magnate and banker Jesse Binga.[29]

On the cusp of a new century, black Chicago's expanding business community fulfilled the necessary functions essential to building viable community life along economic lines. Active business growth was evident up and down the lengthy South State Street Corridor. Still, an analysis of this thoroughfare during 1905 and 1906 revealed a plethora of small businesses engaged in various economic activities, but with limited capital.[30]

Subsequent expansion along the emerging State Street Corridor reflected African Americans' continuous interest in their economic destiny. Black business acumen carved out State Street (adjacent to the Dearborn Street residential corridor), south of Twenty-Second and extending to Thirty-Ninth Street, as the major commercial, retail, and service thoroughfare of Black Chicago. Early on, its recognized epicenter was "the corner of Thirty-first and State where business and professional men had their offices."[31]

The new century's African American business leadership was composed of assertive and imaginative men who possessed a style that contrasted dramatically with the nineteenth-century pioneers, such as the merchant-tailor John Jones. While Jones worked congenially with whites, this newer set of entrepreneurs and businesspersons acted as competitors to white merchants and service producers for the constantly growing African American market. Black dependency on white paternalism gave way to assertiveness and a push for independence. Matching the rapidity with which whites were expanding their businesses operations in all fields at the turn of the century, the more capitalist-minded and risk-taking African Americans did likewise. The names of Jesse Binga, Robert Abbott, and Anthony Overton were destined to become household names mainly due to their actualization of black initiative and the implementation of effective business operations. Moreover, Chicago black businesspersons reflected the national mood of aiming for commercial and retail success. Consequently, a very active branch of Booker T. Washington's National Negro Business League (NNBL) operated throughout this period in Chicago and with widespread appeal and support. For instance, Chicago hosted the NNBL's national convention in 1912. Within a decade, the Associated Business Clubs (ABC) evolved as another manifestation of Black Chicago's interest in maximizing its business and economic potential.[32]

During the late nineteenth century, the news field and publishing offered somewhat limited opportunities for financial success. Still, the excitement of supporting the workings of the fourth estate with its control over popular thought intrigued a new cadre of Black Chicago journalists during the early twentieth century. If nothing else, the self-image of blacks could be presented in a positive fashion, reinforcing group pride and cohesion. In publishing, when the enterprising D. A. Bethea saw fit to tell the story of black business in early twentieth-century Chicago, he compiled the first business directory since Isaac C. Harris's in 1885. Bethea's Celerity Print Shop, located farther south along the State Street Corridor at 4926 State Street, was the publishing home of his *Colored People's Blue Book and Business Directory of Chicago* (1905 and 1906). Concurrently, the prescient Robert S. Abbott started his soon-to-be famous *Chicago Defender* in 1905.

At this time, African Americans depended on news from the major Chicago white dailies as well as from their own black weeklies. The daily *Tribune, Herald, Times, Daily News,* and *Inter Ocean* provided general information on happenings in the city. The latter was extremely popular among blacks because it featured extensive coverage of black activities, liberal editorials and commentaries, and generally a pro-black stance on interracial matters. But with the 1900 census showing twelve African American journalists residing in Chicago, subsequent efforts to expand black publications seemed natural.[33] Frederick G. Detweiler best explained the role of the black press: "It is not surprising if the Negro turns with more than ordinary devotion to the printed page. To him it is an institution peculiarly embodying his group life, something like his church or his lodge, but even more like some public work of art symbolizing his aspiration."[34]

As a rule, Black Chicago's newspapers, before the *Defender*, were small and not especially profitable. Thus they became dependent on partisan reporting. For instance, Julius F. Taylor moved his *Broad Ax* from Salt Lake City in 1899, and once in Chicago it served primarily as an unprofitable shill for the Democratic Party and sounding board of anti-Tuskegee sentiment until 1910. The *Illinois Idea* was run by Sheadrick B. Turner and had a weekly circulation of at least one hundred issues. It countered Taylor's influence by promoting the G.O.P.[35]

Considering its later prominence, Robert Abbott's *Chicago Defender* had a rather inauspicious debut. During the paper's early days, Abbott literally peddled his four-sheet product door-to-door during the daytime hours. In the evening, "he visited every south side barbershop, poolroom, night club, saloon, drugstore and church, indeed anywhere Negroes assembled, selling papers and gathering news and advertisements. He often was made the butt of coarse jokes, but he merely turned his head aside."[36] Importantly, he set out to excel in journalism but made money along the way, eventually becoming a millionaire and a national voice of black advancement in all spheres of endeavor.

During the *Defender*'s early years, Abbott closely observed the success of the *Chicago Tribune* and copied its layout, use of features, and placement of headlines as he set out to revolutionize African American publications both culturally and financially.[37] He also recognized the value of printing sensationalistic, lurid headlines and news of little-known persons from throughout the country, not just reporting on topics of interest locally to Black Chicagoans. Under bylines from Dayton, Ohio, to Mobile, Alabama, to Los Angeles, California, the *Defender* circulated personal, society, and institutional news from across America.

As he transformed himself from an obscure Georgia farm boy into a dominant figure in Black America, Robert Abbott's persona was partially built around his character traits of stubbornness and tenacity to pursue his business aims. His chief biographer, Roi Ottley, commented:

> Though sensitive and sometimes standoffish, he had a magnetic personality and could be suspiciously urbane. He was basically a friendly person with a touch of the common man. He talked with every and anybody . . . His appearance of humility, bordering on the apologetic, was disarming to whites as well as Negroes. But few people ever touched him sufficiently to develop any intimacy . . . He was no

rabble-rouser or backslapper, but he deeply loved the rank and file of his race, and conceded, though he did not wish to have intimate associations with them, "It's the little man who digs ditches in the streets, who is paying me my salary."[38]

An important manifestation of Abbott's business acumen was his use of Chicago Pullman porters, who accounted for 20 percent of the black male laboring force, to bolster the *Defender*'s circulation. This group had the potential to bring quick distribution and recognition for the *Defender*. Abbott was keenly aware that these railroad workers played an influential role in the economic and social currents of Chicago's Black Belt and throughout the nation. Their influence rested in their numbers within the labor force and access to money (limited as it would have been relative to white middle-class and skilled working-class earning power). Since Pullman porters considered themselves a privileged group with expansive fraternal ties within their ranks, Abbott allowed an active porter to write a weekly column about railroad concerns beginning in 1910. The rail columns contained information regarding their ideas about life and racial advancement, details on their labor activities, and advice on social concerns, such as purchasing homes to improve their status. Reciprocating for recognition of their organizational status, the porters distributed copies of the *Defender* free of charge and solicited annual subscriptions.[39]

By 1913, the *Defender*'s growth attracted Booker T. Washington's favorable attention. Subsequent communication between Abbott and Washington centered on developing a journalistic arrangement aimed at telling the Tuskegee story that would be profitable for both parties. For instance, in a December 19, 1913, letter to Abbott, Washington declared, "I am glad that your paper is taking this sensible view." Evidently Abbott, like Washington, a graduate of Hampton (where industrial education was promoted), had commented favorably on that educational focus. Washington mentioned "another thing we must learn sooner or later, and that is, that no matter how much a certain type of white people may promise to do for us in the way of securing 'rights' in the last analysis, we have got to help ourselves."[40] Washington's insistence on pushing for economic self-reliance always found receptive ears in Chicago's black business community. It would be left to Abbott, who was adept at pleasing his readership as well as at splitting ideological hairs (between activist integrationists and gradualists), to show black publishers and journalists the way to financial success.

In the financial arena, successful realtor Jesse Binga served as the archetype for the modern plunge into moneymaking. He was one of six other enterprising African Americans who identified their activities in the 1900 U.S. census as banking and brokerage.[41] Shortly thereafter, in 1908, Binga established the first of his (and the race's) two banks in Chicago (and he proposed to open a third in

1930 as a nationally chartered venture). The first of Binga's three institutions was located on the southeast corner of State and Thirty-Sixth at city lot 3637. Initially, Binga's operation was small. Nevertheless, it reflected his entrepreneurial spirit and business acumen to satisfy Black Chicago's need for reliable financial services. At the time, similar bank openings were occurring throughout the city's immigrant neighborhoods.[42]

An examination of the origins of Chicago's black banking system reveals the first institutions started as private ventures that possessed positive communal implications as neighborhood stabilizers. The establishment of the Binga Bank was followed by the R. W. Hunter & Company Bank, which had both South Side (at Forty-Eighth and State) and West Side (along the main commercial corridor on Lake Street) facilities. Soon, the A. W. Woodfolk Bank began its operations at 3201 South State Street. Black Chicago now had three banks and had laid the foundation for economic penetration into the competitive, lucrative, and tumultuous world of high finance.[43]

That Binga possessed adequate capital to begin his venture made him a rarity among many enterprising African Americans in Chicago and indeed the nation. According to a popular myth, the most obvious source would have been his real estate holdings and his wife Eudora's inheritance of somewhere between $200,000 and $250,000. Moreover, rumor linked his wife's inheritance to the Johnson family fortune in gambling, Mrs. Binga being one of several siblings of the wealthy gambler and political boss John V. "Mushmouth" Johnson.[44] A popular researcher on Chicago observed, "He was the [local black] kingfish of the policy and numbers [racket], gambling, dice games, poker, and faro as played in the Bad Lands and Little Cheyenne Districts [of the white, crime-ridden Levee District]."[45]

Contradicting this belief as to the source of Binga's access to capital is the fact that he had opened his bank in 1908, four years before his 1912 marriage to "Mushmouth" Johnson's sister. Historically, Binga had proven himself a shrewd businessman by his acquisition and sale of western lands in the 1890s and profitable huckstering on Chicago's streets at the time of the world's fair. Just as real estate holdings and sales had created frontier-era Chicago's economy, they continued to play a major role as an economic resource and in wealth creation. Once established in Chicago, Binga acquired real estate along State Street and rented exploitatively to fellow African Americans at a rate advantageous to his accumulation of personal wealth. Jesse Binga's holdings were so extensive that an entire block on State Street from Forty-Seventh to Forty-Eighth carried his imprint as "the Binga Block." Operating from his first major office at 3331 South State Street, he acquired and sold property throughout the South Side, extending his reach even into all-white neighborhoods. In 1905 and 1906 he advertised boldly in the *Chicago Tribune*.[46]

A businessman through and through, Binga had experienced the exuberance of success in the marketplace as a youngster while accompanying his thriving parents in Detroit. Unfettered by the southern tendency to pay deference to whites, Binga envisioned the entire Chicago landscape as having potential from which he could make money. For instance, during the Binga Bank's first days, 80 percent of his customers were white and only 20 percent were African American.[47]

Binga's entrepreneurial exuberance combined public spectacle with economic advancement aimed at sustaining self-reliance. In 1912 he proposed the formation of a permanent local black business association with a capitalization of $150,000 to support an annual carnival resembling a gigantic fair or exposition along State Street. As Binga commented at the first of such community business expositions held that summer, "I want to see *my* people in every line of business there is. I want to see them in neat, clean stores. I want to see them dealing in fruit stores, fish markets. Just think of small Chicago, with 100,000 of *us*, [and] there is not a fish market, and we eat fish, too. Who is getting the bulk of this money? And still you wonder why we can't get work. You are not making it for yourself. They place their money in banks where their children are not given a chance to learn banking" (emphasis added).[48]

Binga was not alone in sensing the possibilities of amassing profits in the real estate arena. T. W. Champion in 1912 formed a business bearing his name, T. W. Champion Realty Agency and Loan Company, and later the Pyramid Building Company. He thus followed a path in pursuing wealth trod by Chicagoans since the city was first platted. The immediate model of these activities might just have been Jesse Binga as he embarked on his three-decade climb to financial success.[49]

In 1911 a very ambitious Anthony Overton left Kansas City to start a business in Chicago exploiting a growing women's market in grooming aids. Imbibing Chicago's infectious nectar of racial pride and economic possibility, Overton contributed to the newest economic surge within the Black Belt. Thinking as Jesse Binga did about African American advancement, Overton committed himself to business excellence and financial success. A recent researcher uncovered another truth about Overton: he "held firmly to a vow that his firm would be composed 'entirely of Negroes.' He made it a point that he would not employ a single white person 'in any capacity' and insisted that 'not a dollar of white capital would be used either directly or indirectly.'"[50]

Overton was born to slave parents in Louisiana in 1864, so he spent only one year and fourteen days in bondage. Overton's attitudes and dreams were shaped by his family's example: "His father was a merchant and it was from him that he inherited the ambition to make good in business."[51] From producing his first product, baking powder, he expanded his business operations to include fifty-two products related to female grooming. The company employed a small salaried work staff and claimed contractual relationships with four hundred commissioned door-to-door salesmen.[52] By 1915, the Overton Hygienic Company expanded its operations and opened a branch office at 3519 South State Street. He listed the company's capitalization at $268,000 (or possibly $286,000) and claimed to be manufacturing sixty-two different items, including baking powder, extracts, and toilet articles. Overton now commanded a workforce that had risen to thirty-two employees.[53] As to his attitude toward his chosen path, he was committed to business as an end in itself. As one observer assessed his approach to business, "It's a game and he likes to play it: it's a test of his skill and his ability; it gives him a chance to match wits with his competitors, to overcome complicated and perplexing problems and mould living institutions to his will."[54]

The field of beauty care and personal upkeep presented opportunities to become successful and prosperous, as evidenced by Overton's chief competitors, Annie Turnbo Malone and her Poro College in St. Louis, and Madame C. J. Walker and her thriving operations in Indianapolis. Consequently, beauty shops and barbershops operated throughout the Black Belt and appeared fearless in competition with whites, whose interest would not fully develop in the field for another seventy-five years.

Directly linked to personal grooming, dressmakers and seamstresses listed in the 1900 census numbered 404 (4 being men) and 147, respectively, indicating that a solid market existed in this area also.[55] Grooming for men provided a profitable business path, as Bethea's *Colored People's Blue Book* listed forty-five barbershops located on State or within a block of State and a dozen or so to be found half a mile away.[56] Bathing facilities were included in several of the establishments, with cigars and tobacco provided, as well.[57]

Paralleling Binga's move into finance, former Pullman porter Sandy J. Trice introduced the black presence into enhanced retail trade when he opened a department store in a partnership at 2918 State Street.[58] The business enjoyed a short life span, from 1905 through 1909, but a meaningful one in that it demonstrated what possibilities of success could lay ahead for others.[59]

Speaking of success, Charles Smiley's catering company, by the early twentieth century, had expanded its commercial influence in the Windy City. Smiley reportedly began his career in late nineteenth-century Chicago with a mere fifty cents in his pocket. But as Booker T. Washington later commented, Smiley "possessed . . . several assets more valuable than mere money. He had a resolute character, good powers of observation, ambition, and brains."[60] At 2111 South Indiana Avenue, three short city blocks east of the State Street Corridor, Smiley's Catering prospered by meeting the needs of a selective white Gold Coast clientele. Smiley's innovations and level of service allowed him to prosper at a time when other African American entrepreneurs were experiencing a decline in white clientele throughout the North. Full service from Smiley's Catering meant that the proprietor assumed total responsibility for an affair, a rarity in that business. This included the most essential goods and services for any wedding—the cake, floral arrangements, canopies, ushers, "security guards who were placed discreetly to watch the gifts," and even delivery of invitations. Smiley ensured safe and timely deliveries by owning the sixteen horses that pulled his wagons.[61] With the death of husband and son, Mrs. Smiley continued the business operations as a sole proprietor until her death.[62]

In the scramble for commercial success in Chicago's growing Black Belt, entrepreneur and gambling czar Robert T. Motts made history in 1905 when he opened his Pekin Theater. Remodeling the site of his original smaller gaming establishment at Twenty-Seventh and State Street, Motts constructed "a little bijou theater, complete in all its details, with a balcony, boxes, fire exits, red axes and all the other attributes of a regulation playhouse." At the same time, an orchestra was formed to accompany an assembled stock company. As a venue for topflight black entertainment that soon appealed to both races, one white newspaper billed it as "the only theater in the country—probably the only regular playhouse in the world—owned, managed and conducted by colored people, presenting with a stock company of colored artists original musical comedies, farces and plays written and composed by colored men . . . in this city."[63]

Controversial among members of the black pulpit, white newspapers, and the white elite, the Pekin Theater represented another African American "first."[64] Motts "demonstrated the ability of the Negro in the trades as well as in the theatrical profession" to operate a business successfully.[65] Still, despite Motts's historic accomplishment in the realm of entertainment ownership, the bulk of theater and club life within the Black Belt remained in white hands throughout the 1920s jazz and blues era.

On the eve of the Great Migration (1916–18), which transformed the economic potential of the Black Belt into the prosperous reality of the Black Metropolis of the 1920s, Black Chicago had visibly demonstrated its ability to fit into the mold of modern America.[66] The nexus of circumstance, found abundantly in the milieu of frontier freedom and later in the laissez-faire spirit of the post-Reconstruction era, continued into the early twentieth century. Moreover, the underlying principle of personal initiative, drawn derivatively from the spirit of Jean Baptiste Pointe DuSable's historic example, produced an impressive entrepreneurial and business history heretofore overlooked, but now recorded and documented.

Notes

1. Bessie Louise Pierce, *A History of Chicago, Vol. II.: From Town to City, 1848–1871* (New York: Knopf, 1940), 4.

2. Bessie Louise Pierce, *A History of Chicago, Vol. I: The Beginning of a City, 1673–1848* (Chicago: University of Chicago Press, 1937), 201, 210.

3. Christopher R. Reed, *Black Chicago's First Century, Vol. I, 1833–1900* (Columbia: University of Missouri Press, 2005), 74.

4. Abram L. Harris, *The Negro as Capitalist* (1936; repr., Gloucester, MA; Peter Smith, 1968), 11.

5. Letters, Marsha Freeman Edmond to Julia Boyd, June 20, 1887, in Herma Clark, "When Chicago Was Young: The Elegant Eighties," *Chicago Sunday Tribune*, June 28, 1936, n.p., in the Atkinson Family Collection, Chicago Historical Society.

6. Frederick H. H. Robb, ed. and comp., *The Negro in Chicago, Vol. I: 1779–1927* (Chicago: Washington Intercollegiate Club, 1927), 227.

7. A. T. Andreas, *History of Chicago, Vol. I* (Chicago: A. T. Andreas, 1885), 185, 186.

8. E. Franklin Frazier, *The Negro Family in the United States* (Chicago: University of Chicago Press, 1939), 140.

9. Arna Bontemps and Jack Conroy, *They Seek a City* (Garden City, NY: Doubleday, Doran, 1945), 47.

10. The 1860 figure comes from Juliet E. K. Walker, *The History of Black Business in America: Capitalism, Race, Entrepreneurship* (New York: Twayne, 1998), 110; the 1871 figures are from Charles R. Branham, "John Jones," in *Encyclopedia of African American Business History* (Westport, CT: Greenwood Press, 1999), 344.

11. Letters from Marsha Freeman Edmond to Julia Boyd of New York, June 20, 1887.

12. Walker, *The History of Black Business in America*, 150.

13. Isaac C. Harris, *The Colored Men's Professional and Business Directory* (Chicago: 1885), n.p.

14. "Note," *Conservator*, December 18, 1886, 3 (photocopied version in author's possession).

15. St. Clair Drake and Horace R. Cayton, *Black Metropolis: A Study of Negro Life in a Northern City* (New York: Harcourt, Brace and World, 1945), 434.

16. Reed, *Black Chicago's First Century*, 205–8, 263–64.

17. Harris, *Colored Men's Directory*, n.p.

18. H. F. Kletzing and W. H. Crogman, *Progress of a Race, or the Remarkable Advancement of the Afro-American* (Atlanta, 1897; repr., New York: Negro Universities Press, 1969), 276.

19. Rayford W. Logan, *The Betrayal of the Negro: From Rutherford B. Hayes to Woodrow Wilson* (New York, 1965; orig. publ. as *The Negro in American Life and Thought: The Nadir, 1877–1901*: New York, 1954), 233, 234.

20. "Colored Lights in Chicago: Citizens of Dark Hue Who Are Prominent in Business and the Professions," *Chicago Daily News*, August 6, 1885, 1; and letters, Martha Freeman Edmond to Julia Boyd. See also Drake and Cayton, *Black Metropolis*, 433.

21. Robb, *The Negro in Chicago*, 2: 227.

22. "Story of Old Settler Reads Like Fiction," *Chicago Defender*, May 3, 1930, 23. Also see Walker, *The History of Black Business in America*, 178.

23. "Chicago Colored People: The Race Problem Is Solving Itself in This City," *Chicago Tribune*, May 4, 1890 (Pro Quest version), 33. Also, "Old Citizens Are Culinary Experts," *Chicago Defender*, May 13, 1933, 16.

24. "Colored Lights in Chicago."

25. Perry R. Duis, *Challenging Chicago: Coping with Everyday Life, 1837–1920* (Urbana: University of Illinois Press, 1998), 262.

26. Christopher Robert Reed, *Knock at the Door of Opportunity: Black Migration to Chicago, 1900–1919* (Carbondale: Southern Illinois University Press, 2014), 90–91.

27. Reed, *Black Chicago's First Century*, 383.

28. "Opinion of the Chicago Colored Women's Club," *Chicago Inter Ocean*, March 13, 1894 [unlocatable], cited in Philip S. Foner and Ronald L. Lewis, eds., *The Black Worker: A Documentary History from Colonial Times to the Present, volume III, The Black Worker During the Era of the Knights of Labor* (Philadelphia: Temple University Press, 1978), 282.

29. See Christopher Robert Reed, *The Rise of Chicago's Black Metropolis, 1920–1929* (Urbana: University of Illinois Press, 2011).

30. D. A. Bethea, comp., *Colored People's Blue Book and Business Directory of Chicago* (Chicago: Celebrity Publishing, 1905); *The Colored People's Blue Book of Chicago* (Chicago: Celebrity Publishing, 1906). Data accumulated from both publications are the source of this analysis. Significantly, conditions had not changed by 2007 in terms of the small size of black businesses where an owner usually had no more than a single employee. See "'A Seat at the Table' for Black Firms," *Chicago Sunday Tribune*, Business Section, September 16, 2007, 1, 6.

31. Harold M. Mayer and Richard C. Wade, *Chicago: Growth of a Metropolis* (Chicago: University of Chicago Press, 1969), 252.

32. Reed, *The Rise of Chicago's Black Metropolis*, 110–12.

33. Richard R. Wright Jr., "The Negro in Chicago," *Southern Workman* 35 (October 1906): 560.

34. Frederick G. Detweiler, *The Negro Press in the United States* (Chicago: University of Chicago Press, 1922), n.p., quoted in Roi Ottley, *The Lonely Warrior: The Life and Times of Robert S. Abbott* (Chicago: Henry Regnery, 1955).

35. Reed, *Black Chicago's First Century*, 232, 339.

36. Ottley, *Lonely Warrior*, 93.

37. Harold F. Gosnell, *Negro Politicians: The Rise of Negro Politics in Chicago* (Chicago: University of Chicago Press, 1935), 102.

38. Ottley, *Lonely Warrior*, 3–5.

39. Reed, *Knock at the Door of Opportunity*, 147, 171.

40. Booker T. Washington to Robert Sengstacke Abbott, December 19, 1913, in Harlan and Smock, Booker T. Washington Papers, vol. 12.

41. Wright, "Negro in Chicago," 562. Interestingly enough, no mention is made of such a grouping in Bethea, *Colored People's Blue Book* (1905/1906).

42. Perry R. Duis, *Challenging Chicago: Coping with Everyday Life, 1837–1920* (Urbana: University of Illinois Press, 2007), 299.

43. Reed, *Knock at the Door of Opportunity*, 172.

44. Henry Brown, "Binga Downfall Ends Spectacular Career," *Chicago Defender*, June 10, 1933, 10.

45. Stephen Longstreet, *Chicago: 1860–1919* (New York: David McKay, 1973), 214, 215; Madrue Chavers-Wright, *The Guarantee: P. W. Chavers—Banker, Entrepreneur, Philanthropist in Chicago's Black Belt of the Twenties* (New York: Wright-Amstead Associates, 1985), 365.

46. *Chicago Tribune*, September 3, 1905, G14; *Chicago Tribune*, November 11, 1906, G11.

47. Louise de Koven Bowen, *The Colored People of Chicago*, n.p. (unpaginated 8, 9). Also see "Mr. Jesse Binga," *The Broad Ax*, December 25, 1909, 2.

48. "The State Street Fair and Carnival Association," *Chicago Defender*, September 7, 1912, 4; Major [and Saunders], *Black Society*, 304.

49. Reed, *Knock at the Door of Opportunity*, 176.

50. Adam Langer, "Black Metropolis," *Reader* (Chicago's free weekly), April 9, 1993, 12.

51. Deton J. Brooks Jr., "Empire Builder: From Slave to Wealth Is Story of Overton," *Chicago Defender*, December 26, 1942, 13.

52. "Anthony Overton, Born Entrepreneur," *Issues & Views* (Spring 1997), http://www.issues-views.com/index.php/sect/1000/article/1006.

53. [W. E. B. Du Bois], "Colored Chicago," *The Crisis* (September 1915): 242.

54. "Daughters," *Chicago Defender*, March 13, 1915, 4; Brooks, "Empire Builder."

55. Wright, "Negro in Chicago," 561.

56. Bethea, *Colored People's Blue Book*, 27, 29–39.

57. Reed, *Knock at the Door of Opportunity*, 181.

58. *Chicago Defender*, September 24, 1932, 7.

59. Allan H. Spear, *Black Chicago: The Making of a Negro Ghetto, 1890–1920* (Chicago: University of Chicago Press, 1967), 113.

60. Juliet E. K. Walker, ed., *Encyclopedia of African American Business History* (Westport, CT: Greenwood Press, 1999), 132. See also "Charles Smiley—Going against the Grain," *Issues & Views* (Fall 1994), http://www.issues-views.com/index.php/sect/1000/article/1004.

61. "Charles Smiley—Going against the Grain," *Issues & Views* (Fall 1994), http://www.issues-views.com/index.php/sect/1000/article/1004.

62. "Old Citizens Are Culinary Experts," *Chicago Defender*, May 12, 1933, 16.

63. Clipping, "Colored Peoples Theater . . . Proves a Success," unknown Chicago newspaper, n.d. (c. 1906) [author's personal possession].

64. See Alfreda M. Duster, ed., *Crusade for Justice: The Autobiography of Ida B. Wells* (Chicago: University of Chicago Press, 1967), chapter 34, "A Negro Theater."

65. "The Event of the Century[, But] Not [the]Year," *The Broad Ax*, July 7, 1906, 1.

66. See Reed, *Knock at the Door of Opportunity*.

CHAPTER 2

Robert Sengstacke Abbott, 1868–1940

MYITI SENGSTACKE RICE

> In this business if you are going to keep ahead of the other fellow,
> you must have initiative and [the] guts to push forward.
> —Robert Sengstacke Abbott to John H. H. Sengstacke

During the first half of the twentieth century, Chicago newspaperman Robert Sengstacke Abbott became a publishing and journalistic giant. Beginning in 1905 the Georgia migrant transformed a four-page, "hand-bill size" publication with an initial investment of 25 cents into a prosperous modern newspaper. The first run of the *Chicago Defender* was 300 copies with a newsstand cost of two cents. To Abbott's credit, "the *Defender* was published continuously without missing an issue for the next fifty years."[1]

Yet success was never guaranteed for either Abbott or the *Defender*, especially during this first of three phases of the paper's evolution. From 1905 to the advent of the Great Migration in 1916, financial collapse always appeared imminent. Then, for a full generation of business operations, roughly 1916 up until the Great Depression, prosperity reigned. In the last period of Abbott's life, which ended in 1940, he successfully relied on his iron will and kept the newspaper viable for his successor, his nephew John H. H. Sengstacke. In the twenty-first century the *Chicago Defender* is no longer controlled by the Abbott-Sengstacke family but has been taken over by another African American–owned corporation. Regardless of that transition in ownership, both Abbott and the *Defender* were an integral part of building Chicago into an entrepreneurial hub for African American business owners. Abbott took careful advantage of his location in Chicago (at the end of the Illinois Central line, which brought tens of thousands of southern blacks to the city) as well as the relative economic and social opportunities that encouraged black business owners to support (via advertising) and be supported by the *Defender*. Hence his presence in the city, links to the black entrepreneurial community, and connections among Pullman porters gave him a significant advantage over black publishers in other cities.

Abbott's eventual success came via a combination of a determination to succeed driven by his father and a careful business vision that combined his ideas for racial uplift with modern publishing and distribution techniques. As the *Defender*'s foreign editor, Dr. Metz T. P. Lochard, observed, "The story of the *Chicago Defender* symbolized the aspirations and enterprise of the Negro people." He then posthumously assessed Abbott's contribution: "Abbott set the tone for the Negro press not only in Illinois, but throughout the United States. The *Chicago Defender* led the groundswell for the national Negro press."[2] In 1944 in his monumental study *An American Dilemma*, Gunnar Myrdal "pronounced Abbott as the greatest single force in Negro journalism, and indeed the founder of the modern Negro press."[3] As both an uncompromising civil-rights advocate and successful businessman, Robert S. Abbott was a standard setter. He was unquestionably a "race man," but he was also one with a careful eye on the profitability of his enterprises. Thus racial support and uplift were key drivers, but so, too, were careful considerations of financial success.

Abbott's mother, Flora, and his stepfather, John Sengstacke, a German immigrant, educator, and part-time minister, raised Abbott on the outskirts of Savannah, Georgia. By the time Robert turned eight, he was receiving individualized religious and educational training from his stepfather, who believed that "intelligence was necessary for Christian salvation." Reverend Sengstacke, however, taught his stepson more than just how to write and read. He told Robert of his social obligation to his race—"the Sengstacke mission." This "mission" for the young man was to become a missionary to educate and uplift his race. Abbott later wrote, "For twenty-five years I have hearkened to the sacred advice of my father, and have endeavored to give expression to my love for him, my Race and humanity through the columns of the *Chicago Defender*."[4]

By the time Abbott was fourteen, he became his stepfather's close companion and often accompanied him on his missionary errands. During this period, Robert also prepared for college. He enrolled at Beach Institute in Savannah, a preparatory school. By 1887, at the age of seventeen, Robert was ready to start college. In October of that year, he entered Claflin University in Orangeburg, South Carolina. In November 1889, at the age of nineteen, Abbott decided to expand on his education and moved to Virginia to begin printing classes at Hampton Institute. Hampton's goal, like that of its alumnus Booker T. Washington, was to produce black men and women productive in the agricultural and industrial fields. Abbott finished his training as a printer in 1893 and remained to complete his academic work in 1896. Looking back on his days at Hampton, he later said that the time spent there was the most pleasurable of his life.[5]

After graduation, Abbott, now twenty-six, headed for Chicago, a city that he had been exposed to while singing with the Hampton Quartet at the World's Columbian Exposition in 1893. Upon arriving, he sought employment as a printer but faced racial obstacles that prohibited him from finding steady work. Employment difficulties and his drive to earn money and status persuaded him to enroll at Kent College of Law in the fall of 1897. Abbott's dream of the comfortable life as a lawyer, however, quickly faded after graduation. When Abbott interviewed with Edward H. Morris, a prominent black attorney in Chicago, Morris told Abbott that he was "a little too dark to make any impression on the courts of Chicago."[6]

After this second encounter with racial discrimination in the workforce, Abbott made the decision to start his own paper in Chicago and become self-sufficient. Abbott knew that starting a paper in Chicago would be no easy task, even with the city's well-established black community. Chicago already had three existing black papers: Julius C. Taylor's *Broad Ax*, S. B. Turner's *Illinois Idea*, and Ferdinand L. Barnett's *Conservator*. If this was not enough competition for the young newspaperman, there were also at least two respected out-of-state black newspapers read in Chicago—the *Indianapolis Freeman*, edited by George L. Knox, and T. Thomas Fortune's *New York Age*. Undaunted, Abbott forged ahead.

So, by the 1900s, Abbott was planning his future as he perfected his typesetting skills at Barnett's *Conservator* offices during the latter's second stint at ownership of that paper. As to locale, Chicago excelled in the early twentieth century as a publishing and printing center in its midwestern location, so it was no wonder that ambitious African Americans quickly and constantly entered the field. It was being reported that by 1927, Black Chicago supported a field of twenty printers, four magazines, and six newspapers.[7]

To build the *Defender*, Abbott relied on creative, unrelenting, popular-based methods of circulation. He coupled these with an ever-expanding distribution network that expanded beyond Chicago's boundaries. Abbott envisioned the *Defender* as a national paper for African Americans, and he continually pressed for an expansion in its distribution. Part of the reason for this emphasis rested on his unique vision for racial uplift among blacks. Although he was from the South, his time and experiences in Chicago led him to the conclusion that the best opportunities for blacks were outside of the South. The distribution of the *Defender* among southern blacks allowed him to communicate that ideal to blacks still residing there. Additionally, his national distribution strategy enabled greater sales for the paper, and in turn the increased circulation benefited advertising sales (the key to sustained profitability for most periodicals). Abbott justly earned the sobriquet etched on his tombstone: "He did for his race in the field of journalism what other great characters

[Washington, Hope, Du Bois, Bethune] accomplished in the field of education. He was an inspiration and builder in the turbulent era in which he lived."[8]

The Publishing Styles of the *Defender*

Abbott's career as a newspaper owner spanned thirty-five years, with the period between 1910 and 1920 viewed as the most important and influential. In this brief span, he helped define a new era in American journalism. During those years he also waged a migration campaign that enticed hundreds of thousands of southern blacks to move North in search of a better life. During this period, more than two-thirds of the *Chicago Defender*'s published copies were sold outside of Chicago, with a tenth of the total going to New York City. The newspaper influenced both blacks and whites in the North and the South, but in various ways. Author Lee Finke wrote, "When a White man reads a Negro paper for the first time it hits him like a bucket of cold water in the face."[9] The racist lore argued that blacks were incapable of sustaining business enterprises or calculated intellectual arguments. The existence and quality of the *Defender* visibly and forcibly contradicted those notions. Further, the economic, social, and cultural success of northern blacks (particularly those in Chicago) highlighted in the *Defender* made that city seem especially promising for blacks in search of opportunities.

Since so many blacks were migrating North, many southern whites were afraid of losing their labor force. Some whites even forbade blacks from going north; some increased recruitment of blacks by providing better pay and more livable conditions. Many southern whites generally condemned the *Defender*. The opposite effect took place among blacks, with the journey to the North representing a sojourn to the Promised Land. Relative to the dismal conditions in the South, the North offered unlimited opportunities in employment, education, and personal security and freedom. Hence for thousands of black migrants, Chicago was their destination and the *Defender* was their guide.[10]

Despite its eventual success, in the earliest days of publication one would have been hard-pressed to see it as an example of anything other than a struggling business. Because he made little if any profit, Abbott paid no salaries. When manager J. Hockley Smiley was hired sometime before 1910, he was promised a salary of $10 weekly but usually received half that amount.[11] The first sports writer, Frank "Fay" Young, used his income as a postal employee to make ends meet. Once again, according to biographer and fellow journalist Roi Ottley, regardless of financial hardships, the *Defender* staff worked as a harmonious team. The spirit of uplift inculcated by Abbott to his staff, as well as his selection of employees who supported that vision, gave those working for the paper an almost missionary zeal for the endeavor.[12]

Abbott had a knack for knowing what his audience wanted, and he gave it to them. In the process, he initially spent a great deal of time strolling along the main social and commercial corridor of black activity, State Street, also referred to as "the Stroll."[13] Here he observed, talked with, and listened to everyone about everything of possible interest to his readers. And beyond just listening, Abbott was careful to highlight the juiciest and most popular local stories in the *Defender*. The *Defender* consequently became the favorite of blacks in the city, as it reported on their lives and any events directly or remotely affecting them. Ottley wrote, "When he announced his new venture many people laughed, even ridiculed the idea. As yet, no one recognized his imagination as talent, nor his aptness for gathering rumor and hearsay and weaving them into stories, which he often did to the delight of his friends."[14] Suddenly for blacks, the goings-on among all elements of black society were deemed important, as were the woes and successes of Pullman porters, his most reliable distribution conduit for spreading the *Defender*'s message across the South. The activities of the porters were often featured in the paper, and Abbott paid them a commission on their sale of the papers and of subscriptions.[15]

According to Carter G. Woodson, the *Defender*'s mainstay in the early years was, of course, its sensationalistic and deliberately lurid articles that appealed to the masses. As a business practice it opened up a new market while meeting the cultural need of increasing the flow of information about African American affairs to an interested black public. No longer was newspaper reading a middle- and upper-class preserve. Instead the paper became required reading for anyone who wanted to be up-to-date on the current news for both Black Chicago and Black America. Overall, Woodson assessed that Abbott had succeeded in making good on his pledge to make the *Defender* "the World's Greatest Weekly," at least for African Americans. "Abbott deserves credit especially for what he did for the Negro press," analyzed Woodson. He continued: "Prior to the success of *The Chicago Defender* Negro newspapers were ordinary sheets that had little influence upon the locality in which they printed. Not a single one had a circulation exceeding 25,000 and most of them considered themselves doing well if the circulation ran as high as 5,000. When Abbott demonstrated, however, the possibility of the newspaper that would cater to the wants of the Negro people in publishing news concerning them and in a way that they could understand and appreciate it, the publications changed their methods and imitated Abbott."[16]

As the business moved toward greater stability, the structure of the *Defender* was Abbott's primary concern. He wanted a first-class operation in both content and location. Consistent with the latter goal, by 1921 Abbott relocated the paper's offices to 3435 South Indiana Avenue, two blocks east of the State Street Corridor.[17] Abbott remodeled these offices with a modern decor uniform with his dream. His personal appeal and the paper's popularity induced five thousand visitors to visit to see firsthand the attractiveness of the new *Defender* offices and plant.

To establish the paper's dominance in a crowded field, and in variance to how a traditional black newspaper presented the news, the *Chicago Defender* shifted from a reliance on rhetorical politics to unsupported sensationalism. Selling papers was the goal. To do so Abbott used an eye-grabbing print size. Huge font sizes blared to potential newsstand readers the lead stories. Lurid and detailed articles about sex crimes, murders, and lynchings, although sometimes stretching the boundaries of good taste and truth, were also undeniably popular. With his focus on popular local and national information, Abbott had more content than he did pages. So by the end of World War I, the *Defender* expanded to thirty-two pages at a price of 10 cents. And while the steamy and violent events described in the *Defender* undeniably aided its popularity, of greater importance was its role as the leading voice of the Great Migration.[18]

Between 1915 and 1925, the *Defender* consistently encouraged African Americans to move to the North, with such headlines as "Millions Prepare to Leave the South Following Brutal Burning of Human." The *Defender* used editorials, cartoons, and articles with blazing headlines to attract attention to the geographic movement. This was no haphazard reporting of events, but instead was a calculated and organized drive fueled by the *Defender* and in particular Abbott's hopes for African Americans. To Abbott, economic success for blacks in the South was impossible. Wages were suppressed by the agricultural system and racial tradition, and blacks were locked into a system designed to limit them. In contrast, while admittedly rife with its own racial challenges, the North gave blacks access to wages and opportunities unimaginable in the South. As a result, through the pages of the *Defender* Abbott urged blacks to get on the trains, get into their cars, or even to walk out of the South. For example, May 15, 1917, was declared the date of the "Great Northern Drive." This was the first major call for blacks to head north. Abbott even went so far as to describe the South as "the land where every foot of land marks a tragedy . . . Every black man for the sake of his wife and daughter should leave, even at a financial sacrifice, every spot in the South where his worth is not appreciated enough to give him the standing of a man."[19]

Meanwhile, befitting his rank as that of a major Chicago publisher with growing wealth and a civic mantle, Abbott's social invitation could appeal to the likes of Jane Addams and the University of Chicago's academic luminaries. A man of diverse images in regard to how he spent his money, Abbott proved himself an astute businessman as he expanded his operations during this period of prosperity by reinvesting what he earned back into the operations of the *Defender*.

The most important visitor in Abbott's life arrived in town, and on May 6, 1921, Flora Abbott Sengstacke, the publisher's mother, proudly unveiled the *Chicago*

Defender's first printing press. Abbott bubbled with excitement. It was to be sure a magnificent moment that day:

> In a sentimental gesture, he brought his mother from Woodville, Georgia to press the button and start the machinery in its initial revolutions . . . There she stood before the presses in an old fashioned long flowing dress and a big wide brimmed hat, her happiness shining through her unsmiling face . . . The Negro employees were seemingly as excited as Abbott himself. *Defender* writer Fay Young whipped off a note to Hampton's *Southern Workman* exulting that the *Defender* had moved into a "three-story modern building with four linotype machines, a four deck Goss straight-line press, and a print shop the likes of which no colored man ever saw before or dreamed of owning." And he added triumphantly, "All this is owned and paid for by a Hampton Graduate."[20]

Acquisition of this plant cut operating costs more than $1,000 weekly, with overhead being modest. He employed sixty-eight workers, all paid below standard wages (except the white unionized printers). Abbott moved to open distribution outlets beyond Chicago in New York, Philadelphia, Los Angeles, Detroit, Toledo, New Orleans, and Louisville. He was now comfortable enough with his business returns to award himself a salary of $200 weekly, and he drew from an outside account of $1,000–2,000 monthly.

Once Richard Jones became business manager, Ottley reported that out of every 10 cents, 1 cent represented profit. Five cents went to expenses such as printing, salaries, mailings, print paper, and so on; the agents' shares amounted to 4 cents; that left 1 cent clear profit.[21] When sociologist Charles S. Johnson wrote of Abbott's accomplishments he observed, "Here [in Chicago] also is the home of the world's greatest weekly—with a circulation of more than a hundred thousand and a plant valued at as many dollars." As a matter of fact, the number of newsstands and agents in the *Defender* network totaled 2,359 coast to coast. The entire physical plant was valued at $1 million. Abbott printed two editions a week on new presses he owned that were worth $100,000 and old ones that were valued at $48,825.[22] Independent black Chicago publishers *Simms's*, along with *Black's Blue Book*, reported the newspaper's circulation was 225,000 copies per week, with an estimated total of 1,200,000 readers for each edition, leading *Simms's* to assess: "The *Chicago Defender* is the greatest achievement in the history of the Race in journalism."[23] Over time as an employer, Abbott's staff reached 100, performing in employment areas of "the kind that had been forbidden to them." Being a racially integrated staff, it was unique. Having to conform to union rules relating to the actual printing of newspapers, Abbott was forced to hire white typesetters and other skilled workers in his plant.[24]

Making money from mass circulation as opposed to advertising made the *Defender* unique, but such was its appeal and its power to expand the spectrum of its reading audience into the thousands that it paved new territory indeed.[25] Accordingly, Frederick H. H. Robb wrote that "porters and cooks and stockyard workers came to look for their *Defender* regularly because they realized that it sought to cater to their needs as no other organ had ever done. They came to look upon the *Defender* as their champion in real deed as well as in name."[26]

Circulation and Distribution Network

Abbott demonstrated the extent of his personal magnetism and business acuity when he enlisted Chicago's labor pool of thousands of Pullman porters, along with scores of peripatetic vaudevillians, to willingly distribute *Defenders* throughout the nation. As they traveled constantly from city to city and region to region, these converts to Abbott's *Defender* program of race advancement spread the news of twentieth-century emancipation. And, sensing the importance of the moment to business success, Roi Ottley wrote that following the death of Booker T. Washington in November 1915, the paper's front-page announcement of the event caused circulation to explode. Blacks were interested in what Washington had accomplished in Tuskegee as well as throughout the nation as a militant exhorter (in the North) of black pride and economic accomplishment. In 1916, 50,000 issues were printed and by 1918, 125,000 issues. These numbers continued increasing in the early 1920s to 200,000 copies, and by 1925, 200,000 copies were printed. Astronomically high numbers for 1929 reached 250,000 copies. Only a national disaster such as the Great Depression could force that number down in 1933, to 100,000 copies.[27]

Local distribution was in the hands of scores upon scores of youngsters, who eventually became Buddies as a part of the Bud Billiken movement. After organizing black youth nationally as members of the Bud Billiken movement to align youth activities along positive lines, Abbott inaugurated an annual parade and picnic in 1929. Dr. Lochard regarded the parade as "a measure of the *Defender's* extraordinary drawing power and prestige."[28] Drawing hundreds, then thousands, it now has reached one million spectators and participants to become the largest ethnic parade in America. Among adults, black vendors throughout the Black Belt and on the West Side were soon convinced to join this crusade to inform a unified community in the process of becoming a formidable Black Metropolis.

Advertising played a dominant role in producing profits for the white media, so Abbott soon took the appropriate steps to increase the *Defender's* revenue stream, as well. He realized that he would be unable to secure advertising without the help of a white businessman as an intermediary to the white business community. The William B. Ziff Company, founded in 1920, was a fledgling Chicago agency that claimed to be able to secure advertising for black newspapers from national firms such as Procter & Gamble. As a consequence of what one reporter remembered as almost daily badgering, Ziff was hired to sell advertising in the 1920s. This mutuality of benefits did not extend to complete fairness in dealing with African Americans, however. Just as Abbott had been forced to compromise on the issue of hiring an all-white corps of printers due to exclusionary union rules, the same situation occurred in regard to employment and Ziff's views on the racial disparities between blacks and whites. Consequently, Abbott required a white man to be his ambassador among the white executives of corporate America, and Ziff, at least, fulfilled that role very well. Through Ziff, Abbott secured advertising contracts he might not have otherwise received. And because of his relationship with Abbott, Ziff was able to acquire a fortune in advertising working with others in the black press at the time.[29]

Management of the *Defender*

When it came to management, Abbott exerted sound control over his *Defender* empire. This was accomplished through successful management choices, with the exception of his brother-in-law, Floridian and attorney Nathan K. Magill, who joined the newspaper in 1924. Presenting Abbott with salutary recommendations, Magill assumed the position of general manager. His salary was commensurate with his abilities and responsibilities, at $27,000 for one year's work. Unfortunately, Magill's tenure was rife with charges of theft and mismanagement.

By the late 1920s Abbott's declining physical health led to him taking a reduced role at the *Defender*. As a result, Magill began assuming greater levels of control and leadership at the paper. As the temporary head of a paper with significant influence over public opinion, Magill was a failure. For example, he proved unable to maintain a relationship with one of the paper's longtime allies, the fledgling Brotherhood of Sleeping Car Porters (BSCP). As the leader of the BSCP, A. Philip Randolph sought to build the organization, while articles in the *Defender* seemed to support the main employer of BSCP members, the Joseph Pullman Company. Rather than meekly accept this opposition, A. Philip Randolph led a public assault against the previously pro-porter *Defender*, implying that it now bowed to the demands of white corporate owners rather than support the needs of black working men.[30] A competing newspaper, the *Chicago Whip*, launched claims of a sellout by the *Defender* to Pullman Company that stung the latter deeply. This charge of being compliant to the wishes of the Pullman Company in opposing the organizing of porters into the BSCP was a potential public-relations nightmare.

Furthering the challenges of Magill's leadership were charges of massive theft by trusted *Defender* employees (dubbed derisively by the competing *Chicago Whip* as "the Four Horsemen"). The employees were eventually fired, but the combination of charges of pro-corporate sympathy and financial mismanagement led some to question the future of the *Defender*. Fortunately, Abbott returned to an active role in the early 1930s, reversed the anti-unionism immediately, and quelled the charges of the paper having been a puppet of the Pullman Company. Additionally, his presence stabilized the management structure of the company (a stabilization aided by his firing of Magill) and restored confidence in the content and future of the *Defender*.[31]

There were appointments of note through the years, as well. Roscoe Conklin Simmons, nephew through marriage to Booker T. Washington and a skilled orator, was hired as the paper's first road promoter in the East and was even sent to Paris during World War I. In 1923, veteran of the 8th Infantry Regiment (370th), Richard Jones was hired as business manager. He left in 1927 to head the South Center Department Store on Forty-Seventh Street and South Parkway (King Drive). During this decade, writer Henry D. Middleton was even hired as managing editor to elevate the quality of writing. In 1934, Abbott saw fit to rehire early management team player Frank "Fay" Young as managing editor.

The next year, in 1935, a most decisive move was made when Abbott appointed his heir apparent and nephew, John H. H. Sengstacke, as vice president. After Abbott's death in 1940, Sengstacke proved a sterling choice, as he steered the *Defender* upward into a level of prominence. Abbott's early advice to this young aspiring business leader is telling:

> I do hope that you will listen to the things that I try to tell you from time to time. Of course, I don't mean that you shouldn't have any initiative. I want you to have that and plenty of it because in this business if you are going to keep ahead of the other fellow, you must have initiative and guts to push forward. You will find, further, that these requisites every business man should have no matter what business he is in, and yet, it is seldom found in Colored organizations: That is, loyalty to the man from whom you are drawing your pay; a thorough knowledge of your work that you hire yourself out to do; trustworthiness along all lines; knowing how to delve into the intricacies of your business in a businesslike way in order that you can talk about it with the ease and familiarity that a baby talks to its mother about something to eat. When an order is given by the boss to the department head, that order is sacred in the confidence of the man to whom it is given and it should be treated as a sacred trust and not talked all over the streets and to everybody at the firm. As a rule, that is what is done in Negro organizations.[32]

Employing professional printers gave Abbott a unique problem. By necessity, because of the white printers' union strength, the *Defender* workforce was racially divided between a highly paid all-white printers unit and a meagerly paid all-black office force.[33] This unexpected integrated workforce remained in place until the middle of the Depression. Then economic necessity dictated a correction, and all-black printers were hired.

Competitors[34]

The dynamic growth of the *Defender* was challenged nationally as well as locally by events during the 1920s. Despite major and minor competitors, the *Defender* still managed to dominate the publishing field. Its oldest competitor, *The Broad Ax*, suffered the fate of its aging publisher, Julius F. Taylor, and began its fade into obscurity during the early years of the Depression. In years past, it had come alive mostly at election time, when advertising revenue from Democratic contestants was heaviest and the black Republican machine was only in its earliest years of ascendancy. *The Broad Ax* was the only newspaper published outside the Black Metropolis, and that corresponded to its impact during this decade as both a caustic social voice and a channel for the Democratic Party. The Republican Party held sway over the politics of the Black Belt, and the idea of supporting the Democratic Party in any manner remained repugnant.

The *Whip* had yet to distinguish itself but was carving out a niche as a militant voice for job procurement within the Black Metropolis. It was in its ascendancy, in contrast to the declining position of the iconoclastic *Broad Ax*. The newspaper itself was the creation of two Yale University graduates, Joseph D. Bibb and A. C. MacNeal, who started the newspaper in 1919.[35] The paper enjoyed a circulation of 30,000 copies per week during the 1920s. Henry H. Proctor served as city editor, fellow Yale graduate A. Clement MacNeal held the post of business manager, and Harold C. Thompson handled circulation matters. Its offices were located at 3420 South State, a half block north of the epicenter of the Black Metropolis. Advertising itself as an alternative to the *Defender*, the *Whip* heralded its independence with the submast heading "An Independent Weekly." It further touted its reach: "We cover Chicago territory like no other medium among black people" and "Get in Touch with the Whole Negro Race through *The Chicago Whip*." Objecting to the sensationalistic mass approach of the *Defender*, in which violence and notoriety qualified as matters of utmost importance, the *Whip* proclaimed it followed a different path. It advertised: "The One paper that correctly interprets the latest news of interest to black people and which represents the thought of intelligent and right-thinking black people of the country."[36]

The *Whip*, moreover, distinguished itself for its crusade to increase job opportunities on the South Side. Its buying-power campaign attracted notoriety by 1928–30 under the slogan "Don't Spend Your Money Where You Can't Work," a spur-of-the-moment idea of Bibb's.[37] The paper claimed inaccurately to have secured thousands of jobs within the Black Belt by use of organized purchasing power and that the jobs "movement spread throughout the city like wild-fire."[38] Scores of jobs actually were secured, while thousands were needed to end unemployment. The idea of job action to balance black purchasing power with employment needs, of course, was not new and had been promoted in a more subdued form by the *Chicago Defender* as early as 1914 and organizationally by the Chicago Urban League in 1927.

Another publication, business magnate Anthony Overton's *Half-Century Magazine,* was unsuccessful after a decade's effort that focused predominantly on business and women's audiences, with a touch of literary appeal. The *Half-Century Magazine,* established in 1916 with a cultural, business, and racial-uplift outlook, became an economic competitor to the *Defender* (constantly bashing its choice of ads and emphasis on sensationalism) and the *Crisis* (criticizing its highbrow approach to accepting and publishing literary strivings and its assimilationist approach to racial adjustment).[39] In its appeal to the female market, with its interest in personal grooming and improved housekeeping, it preceded its final step toward transformation by January 1921 with its demise and subsequent market reentry as the *Chicago Bee* newspaper in April 1925.

As for the *Chicago Bee,* Black Chicago now had a major weekly newspaper that presented a more middle-class, conservative tone and content aimed at a sedate Sunday's reading. Not unexpectedly, it was also billed as a family enterprise. "The fact that the son and daughters of Mr. Anthony Overton are the principal owners of the *Chicago Sunday Bee* has naturally given this paper the benefit of the wise counsel of his seasoned business genius. This connection at the same time has afforded an adequate financial background." The *Bee* envisioned itself as taking an evolutionary step beyond Abbott's sensationalism, acceptance of fraudulent advertising, and promotion of superstitious, exploitative gimmicks. In promoting what it stood for, the paper mentioned higher education, amicable racial relations, civic and racial improvement, and, accordingly, the promotion of Negro business.[40]

Meanwhile, two other small newspapers reconstituted and renamed themselves—the *Chicago World* was formerly the *Enterprise* until 1926, and the *Heebie Jeebies* was later renamed *The Light.* The *Heebie Jeebies* remained under the control of Claude A. Barnett and his Associated Negro Press (ANP) and concentrated on the news of the theater world with a sprinkling of light literary renderings. This effort was meant to challenge the *Defender's* emphasis on theater life. Overall, the ANP served as a news clipping bureau for other newspapers rather than as a traditional newspaper. Nonetheless, even as a gatherer and distributor of news created by others, the ANP was not without its detractors. For example, in 1919 it suffered heavy criticism for its sensationalistic riot coverage from Overton's *Half-Century Magazine.*[41]

More formidable than the ANP in a political town was the *Chicago World,* the brainchild of Jacob R. Tipper of Bainbridge, Georgia. Another Georgian, who like Abbott reveled in the saga of his family's elevation from bondage to freedom before the Emancipation, Tipper arrived with his wife in Chicago in 1908 in advance of the Great Migration. He prospered, running a grocery store while engaging in Republican Party politics as a protégé of Edward H. Wright in the Second Ward. His initial publication was the *Chicago Enterprise,* in 1918, which was transformed into the *Chicago World.* From 1926 on, circulation grew until it reached 40,000 people each week. From a location a block away from the *Defender* at 3611 South Indiana,

Tipper employed a staff of ten and operated from his plant with equipment valued at $35,000.[42] From New York, Marcus Garvey's *Negro World* offered only token competition; from Pittsburgh, the *Pittsburgh Courier* won a small readership; what African Americans nationally claimed as their own formidable and uncompromising voice was the *Chicago Defender*.

Beyond the *Defender*

Once Abbott had achieved financial stability, both in his private life and in business operations, Abbott promoted high culture after he and his wife traveled abroad to South America, and then to Europe in 1929. Abbott became especially critical of black deportment and supported uplift as a suitably better choice. He called correspondingly for better-educated black mothers, cleanly attired workers appearing in public instead of in their dirty work clothes, and the speeding of blacks' slow pace in assimilating into mainstream culture.[43] This dalliance into the world of mainstream respectability was followed by another shift to reality and outright flamboyance to reattract readers by the Depression year 1935.

Abbott's creativity was at work again when he planned (abortively) to publish a magazine, *Reflexus* (pronounced: Reflects Us), and later, in 1930–33, *Abbott's Monthly* (a forerunner to John H. Johnson's lucrative *Ebony*). The former appeared impressively as a ninety-six-page production and found a ready market with Abbott publishing 100,000 copies.[44]

Yet regardless of the publishing vehicle, the advancement of his race always remained paramount in Abbott's mind, so progress in civil rights was always the ultimate prize. According to his major biographer, Roi Ottley, Abbott revealed his strategy: "I have made an issue of every single situation in which my people were denied their rightful share of participation."[45]

Abbott's growing wealth led some to question his use of money and by extension the proverbial question of whether he had reached the millionaire status.[46] Although popular interest remains high, this essay concentrates on the means used to reach this point in the publisher's business development, where the accumulation of wealth was more dependent on entrepreneurial and business acumen rather than being an objective to be attained in Abbott's mind. What the public witnessed conspicuously on display, without a doubt, was a lavish lifestyle beyond the imagination of many.

This publishing icon spent generously on his two wives, and on his family, particularly the Sengstackes, but also on the Abbotts of Georgia and even the Sengstackes of Germany.[47] When his first trophy wife, Helen (1918–34), sued Abbott for divorce in 1934, he was reported to have $335,000. Significantly, this cash was deposited in two white banks even though his two close community business compatriots, Jesse Binga and Anthony Overton, were bankers.[48] The final divorce decree allotted thousands in cash to Helen in addition to two luxury cars, his home's furnishings, and the services of two household servants. Following financial reverses in 1932 and this divorce, in 1935 Abbott shifted $250,000 of personal funds to save the paper.[49]

Robert S. Abbott was the embodiment of the Black Chicago entrepreneur of the early twentieth century. An unabashed race man, he built an enterprise to support and be supported by the black community in Chicago and throughout the United States. Certainly he sought wealth from his business, but that wealth came as a result of a greater mission and intent: racial uplift. Abbott had not set out to make money; he had set out with a unique racial charge from his father. In completing that charge he certainly became wealthy, and a leading force among blacks. Through the *Defender*, Abbott was fueled by both the mission of the paper and by the unique Chicago spirit of racial uplift. As a result, Abbott built one of the most lasting business and intellectual institutions in American history.

Upon Robert S. Abbott's passing in 1940, his next-door neighbor and eulogist, the Rev. Archibald J. Carey Jr., could speak reverently and profoundly of Abbott because of, and yet beyond, his material success. He reminisced one and a half decades later on the meaning of Abbott's life and accomplishments:

> Thru the *Chicago Defender* . . . he did, in fact, become 'the greatest single force in Negro journalism' and may have had wealth 'thrust upon him.' Nevertheless, the most significant aspect of his life was his dreams. He dreamed of empire, all right, but it wasn't for material things alone he yearned. It was for unlimited freedom of movement and an unshackled life for himself and his people that he had unfailing hope . . . It is easy to perceive that the genius of the man was the dauntless and audacious quality of his dreams.[50]

Notes

Epigraph: Robert Sengstacke Abbott to John H. H. Sengstacke, April 17, 1934, Abbott-Sengstacke Family Papers, Box 8, Folder 33. I have benefited immensely from the public accessibility of the extensive Abbott-Sengstacke Family Papers that have been recently curated as part of the Vivian G. Harsh Research Collection of Afro-American History and Literature at the Carter G. Woodson Library Center of the Chicago Public Library. This essay reflects the influence of this collection and added to my understanding of Robert S. Abbott and the building of the *Chicago Defender*. The story of the *Chicago Defender* through photographic evidence is to be found in Myiti Sengstacke Rice, ed., *Chicago Defender* (Charleston, SC: Arcadia Publishing, 2012).

1. Roi Ottley, *The Lonely Warrior: The Life and Times of Robert S. Abbott* (Chicago: Henry Regnery, 1955), 86, 88.

2. Metz T. P. Lochard, "The Negro Press in Illinois," *Journal of the Illinois State Historical Society* 56 (Autumn 1963): 572, 588. The *Defender* held the distinction of having a foreign

desk manned by an editor, Metz T. P. Lochard, who had earned his first PhD at the Sorbonne of the University of Paris and his second at Oxford University in English literature.

3. Roi Ottley, *The Lonely Warrior*, 2.

4. Ibid., 14–15.

5. Ibid., 42–60.

6. Ibid., 77–78. A recent interpretation at variance with the contention that the core of this rejection was based primarily on complexion is found in Christopher Robert Reed, *Knock at the Door of Opportunity: Black Migration to Chicago, 1900–1919* (Carbondale: Southern Illinois University Press, 2014), 68–69.

7. Carroll Binder, *Chicago and the New Negro* (Chicago: *Chicago Daily News*, 1927), 11. See also Frederick H. H. Robb, *The Negro in Chicago* (Chicago: Washington Intercollegiate Club, 1927) 2 vols., 1:124, "Race Publications in Chicago."

8. Tombstone at the grave of Robert Sengstacke Abbott, Lincoln Cemetery, Alsip, Illinois.

9. Ottley, *The Lonely Warrior*, 73. Robert S. Abbott held the deepest affection for Hampton, an affection lasting to the end of his days. Soon after his success as a publisher, he was elected president of the Hampton Alumni Association and became a strong supporter of the institution. He considered support of his alma mater his "moral duty."

10. St. Clair Drake and Horace R. Cayton, *Black Metropolis: A Study of Negro Life in a Northern City* (New York: Harcourt, Brace and World, 1945), 59–60.

11. Ottley, *The Lonely Warrior*, 113.

12. Ibid., 118.

13. On "the Stroll," see Davarian L. Baldwin, *Chicago's New Negroes: Modernity, the Great Migration, and Black Urban Life* (Chapel Hill: University of North Carolina Press, 2007), 19.

14. Ibid., 86.

15. Ethan Michaeli, *The Defender: How the Legendary Black Newspaper Changed America, from the Age of the Pullman Porters to the Age of Obama* (New York: Houghton Mifflin Harcourt, 2016), 31–32.

16. Carter G. Woodson, "Personal [Remarks on Robert S. Abbott]," *Journal of Negro History* 25 (January 1940): 262.

17. "The Realization of a Dream: An Epic of Negro Business," *Messenger* (September 1923): 871–73; Robb, *The Negro in Chicago*, 1:90, 91. Abbott's original offices were rented from a woman by the name of Henrietta Lee at 3159 State Street, in the historic neighborhood of Bronzeville.

18. Metz T. P. Lochard, "Phylon Profile, XII: Robert S. Abbott—'Race Leader,'" *Phylon* 8 (1947): 124–26; Ottley, *The Lonely Warrior*, 159–71. Also, see Drake and Cayton, *Black Metropolis*, 58–60, as well as Rice, *Chicago Defender*, 31.

19. Rice, *Chicago Defender*, 7.

20. Ottley, *The Lonely Warrior*, 196–97.

21. Ibid., 200.

22. Robb, *The Negro in Chicago*, 1:91; Charles S. Johnson, "These 'Colored United States,' VIII—Illinois: Mecca of the Migrant Mob," *Messenger* 5 (December 1923): 928.

23. *Simms's Blue Book and Business Directory* (Chicago: Simms Publishing, 1923), 79. See also *Black's Blue Book*, 1923–24 (Chicago: Black Printing), 43, and Lochard, "The Negro

Press in Illinois," 573, who wrote of circulation peaking near a quarter of a million copies at the end of World War I.

24. Ottley, *The Lonely Warrior*, 194, 301.

25. William E. Berry, "Robert S. Abbott," in *Encyclopedia of African American Business History*, ed. Juliet E. K. Walker (Westport, CT: Greenwood Press, 1999), 2.

26. Robb, *The Negro in Chicago*, 1:90. See chapters 7 and 8 with Pullman columns.

27. Michaeli, *The Defender*, 30–32. Trying to compile exact figures on the *Chicago Defender*'s circulation proved disappointing despite my intensive examination of the Abbott-Sengstacke Family Papers. Accessibility to and reliance on other sources fortunately has helped close the gap for better understanding of the *Defender*'s rapid growth. These sources include various contemporary ones such as business publishers Simms (*Simms Blue Book and Business Directory* [Chicago: Simms Publishing, 1923]) and Black (*Black's Blue Book*, 1923–24 [Chicago: Black Printing Co.]), and later sources such as authoritative writers Lochard ("The Negro Press in Illinois [1963]," "Phylon Profile, XII: Robert S. Abbott—'Race Leader' [1947]"), and Ottley, *The Lonely Warrior*.

28. Lochard, "The Negro Press in Illinois," 354.

29. On William B. Ziff, see Armistead S. Pride and Clint C. Wilson II, *A History of the Black Press* (Washington, DC: Howard University Press, 2011), 240–41, and Jason Chambers, *Madison Avenue and the Color Line: African Americans in the Advertising Industry* (Philadelphia: University of Pennsylvania Press, 2008), 31–34. On Ziff's views regarding race, see Earl Conrad, "'American Viewpoint'—The Gentlemen Talk of Ziff," *Chicago Defender*, May 5, 1945, 11. Follow-up discussions of Ziff's rather disparaging views on African Americans are to be found in these issues of the *Defender*: Lucius C. Harper, "'Dustin' Off the News,'—W. B. Ziff Shows Negroes How He Feels to Be Rich," May 12, 1945, 1, and Lucius C. Harper, "'Dustin' Off the News,'—Mr. Ziff Gives His Version on Back-to-Africa," June 16, 1945, 1. On Abbott's mastery of the English language as seen by black contemporaries, see Ottley, *The Lonely Warrior*, 86. See also Rice, *Chicago Defender*, 35.

30. Ottley, *The Lonely Warrior*, 260–66.

31. Ibid., 333, 342–44.

32. Abbott's assessment of good business leadership is found in a letter from Robert Sengstacke Abbott to John H. H. Sengstacke, April 17, 1934, Abbott-Sengstacke Family Papers, Box 8, File 33, Vivian G. Harsh Research Collection of Afro-American History and Literature at the Carter G. Woodson Library Center of the Chicago Public Library.

33. Rice, *Chicago Defender*, 27–29. See also Ottley, *The Lonely Warrior*, 194, 301.

34. The work of Christopher Robert Reed of the Black Chicago History Forum on competing newspapers forms the basis of this section. See his *The Rise of Chicago's Black Metropolis, 1920–1929* (Urbana: University of Illinois Press, 2011).

35. Telephone interview between Christopher R. Reed and Mrs. Goldie Bibb of Chicago, Illinois (the widow of *Chicago Whip* editor Joseph B. Bibb), on January 25, 1978. The interview was conducted from the home of Mrs. Lovelynn Evans, who for ten years served as the women's editor of the *Chicago Whip*. See Robb, *The Negro in Chicago*, 2:233, 247. A fourth founder is listed as W. C. Linton—Robb, *The Negro in Chicago*, 1:122. The newspaper is incorrectly described as "socialist-leaning" and "anti-capitalist," no doubt confusing

it with *The Messenger*, in Lizabeth Cohen, *Making a New Deal: Industrial Workers in Chicago, 1919–1939* (Cambridge: Cambridge University Press, 1990), 148, 154.

36. Robb, *The Negro in Chicago*, 2:233; James N. Simms, comp., *Simms' Blue Book and National Negro Business and Professional Directory* (repr., 1977; Chicago: James N. Simms, Publisher, 1923), 115; and Oliver Cromwell Cox, "The Origins of Direct-Action Protest among Negroes," unpublished manuscript, c. 1932, 1933 (microfiche copy), 13f., Kent State University Libraries, Kent, Ohio.

37. Mrs. Goldie Bibb, telephone interview by author, January 25, 1978.

38. Cox, "The Origins of Direct-Action Protest among Negroes," 13f.; John McKinley, "Leaders Endorse the *Chicago Whip*'s New Economic Program"; Robb, *The Negro in Chicago*, 2:233.

39. "Anthony Overton, Born Entrepreneur," *Issues & Views* (Spring 1977), p. 2 of 3. Accessed at http://www.issues-views.com/index.php/sect/1000/article/1006.

40. Robb, *The Negro in Chicago*, 2:214, 215; Davis, "Negro Newspaper in Chicago," 128; "A Modernistic Bit for South State," *Chicago Tribune*, October 27, 1929, 3:9, 10; Cox, "Origins of Direct-Action Protest."

41. "Race Riots and the Press," *Half-Century Magazine* (August 1919): 18.

42. "The Chicago World Fulfills an Ideal," Robb, *The Negro in Chicago*, 2:238.

43. The competing *Chicago Searchlight* of May 22, 1920, shared a similar view. See Lochard, "The Negro Press in Illinois," 578.

44. Ottley, *The Lonely Warrior*, 291.

45. Ibid., epigraph, 355. See the credit given the *Defender* by the Chicago NAACP leadership in Christopher Robert Reed, *The Chicago NAACP and the Rise of Black Professional Leadership, 1910–1966* (Bloomington: Indiana University Press, 1997), 12.

46. Ottley, *The Lonely Warrior*, 219.

47. Ibid., 356–57.

48. Along with Robert S. Abbott, Jesse Binga and Anthony Overton represented the triumvirate of African American business leadership during the 1920s, the heyday of the Black Metropolis. The trio provided the directorship of the Associated Business Clubs (the ABC), a parallel, independent (as expected of Chicagoans), and sometimes cooperating business counterpart to the National Negro Business League. As to individual business enterprises, Binga owned the Binga State Bank and enormous real estate holdings, while Overton owned the Douglass National Bank, the Overton Hygienic Company, the Victory Life Insurance Company, and the *Chicago Bee* newspaper. Together, the Binga and Overton banks held one-third of all black banking assets in America. See Reed, *The Rise of Chicago's Black Metropolis*, chapter 3, "The Golden Decade of Black Business."

49. Ottley, *The Lonely Warrior*, 301.

50. [Rev.] Archibald J. Carey Jr., "A Negro Warrior for Justice," book review of Roi Ottley, *The Lonely Warrior: The Life and Times of Robert S. Abbott*, *Chicago Tribune*, May 29, 1955, pt. 4, B3. There were those occasions when Abbott's dreams became so unrealistic as to need harnessing. His longtime friend Phil Jones assumed that responsibility. See Ottley, *The Lonely Warrior*, 203.

CHAPTER 3

The Rise and Fall of Jesse Binga, a Black Chicago Financial Wizard

ROBERT HOWARD

There is an aphorism that states, "When the American economy catches a cold, the black community catches pneumonia." This chapter will demonstrate how this truism affected the life of Chicago banker Jesse Binga. Binga, a late nineteenth-century migrant to the Windy City, was an extremely self-confident (if not arrogant) individual whose personality helped him evolve from an itinerant street peddler into a powerful real estate mogul and banker. At the same time, Binga became known for his philanthropic interests and intense desire to enhance the economic status of Chicago's African American community. Yet, perhaps ironically, Binga's self-assuredness ultimately contributed to his downfall. Most of Binga's financial interests were located in the historic Thirty-Fifth and South State Street district. However, by the mid-1920s, black Chicago's commercial life increasingly moved southward toward 4700 South Parkway. Undaunted by this development and ignoring the advice of others, Binga, in 1927, purchased more land in the Thirty-Fifth and State Street district to build his five-story Binga Arcade Building. This facility, when completed in 1929, quickly became a community showplace. Yet, with the onset of the Great Depression, it quickly became a proverbial white elephant. Moreover, when a now desperate Jesse Binga apparently embezzled funds from the Binga State Bank to help keep his sinking financial ship afloat, the longtime community icon soon became a convicted felon. In the end, Jesse Binga's mixed historical legacy remains both fascinating and instructive.

Ancestry and Early Life

Jesse Binga, born on April 10, 1865, came from a family lineage of free blacks. His father, William, was born in Amherstburg, Ontario, in 1817. His mother, Adelphia, was born near Rochester, New York, in 1828. While the location and date of William and Adelphia's marriage is unknown, the couple moved to Detroit in the 1840s.[1] Although life in mid-nineteenth-century America was difficult for most blacks, the Bingas, living in the extreme northern part of the United States, experienced a sense of freedom and confidence not enjoyed by their southern brethren. William Binga took up the trade of barbering and opened a shop in Detroit. Adelphia Binga appeared to be the risk-taker in the family. Classified as a mulatto in the 1870 census, she presumably could move freely in and around Detroit because of her skin color. When Jesse was a small boy, she was a food wholesaler, becoming the first person to ship whitefish below the Mason-Dixon Line and sweet potatoes to the Gogebic iron region, located in Michigan's Upper Peninsula. Mrs. Binga also was an accomplished property owner who established, rented, and managed a row of apartment houses in Detroit referred to as "the Binga Row." In fact, one writer has referred to Mrs. Binga as a "serial entrepreneur."[2]

Young Jesse helped around his dad's barbershop by cleaning up and working the cash register. He also tagged along with his mother, helping her collect rents and working as a handyman. This is where he learned many skills, including the ability to cost out repair jobs in an efficient manner. It appears clear that the young Jesse acquired his entrepreneurial bent from both his parents, as well as his grandparents, who owned a farm in Ontario, Canada.[3]

Farming, barbering, food wholesaling, and real estate were ventures that helped inculcate into the young Binga's psyche the importance of property ownership. Consequently, Jesse developed a restless ambition as a young teenager and dropped out of high school after finishing only his first two years. Once he decided not to return to school, Binga's parents provided him with an economic foundation to build upon. His father taught him barbering, and his mother gave him a small piece of real estate to manage. She also required that he study law under Thomas Crispus, the first black law graduate from the University of Michigan, Ann Arbor.[4]

In his personal life, the young Binga met and subsequently married Frances Scott on April 14, 1885. Three months later, on July 16, 1885, Jesse and Frances became parents with the birth of their son Deville Bethune.[5] Shortly afterward, Jesse decided he was not ready for marriage and fatherhood. Thus he abruptly sold his small real estate holding and started a western sojourn with a friend. Significantly, Jesse Binga, later a devout Catholic, never mentioned this first marriage in subsequent interviews.

Jesse Binga's early travels took him briefly to Chicago and then to Kansas City, Missouri, where his traveling companion, who he called his "chum" in the article written about him by Inez Cantey, took ill. Using the skills he learned from his father, Binga worked as a barber in Kansas City until his friend recovered and then continued westward by himself. He initially traveled north through St. Paul, Minnesota, and Missoula, Montana, where his uncle Jordan Binga lived. Jordan had interests in mining, restaurants, and real estate ventures. Jordan was another family risk-taker, which helped affirm the positive aspects of entrepreneurship to the young Jesse. After briefly visiting his uncle, Jesse Binga settled in Tacoma, Washington, and set up shop as a barber for a short period of time. Feeling wanderlust again, Binga sold his stake in the barbershop and moved on to Seattle, Washington, where he established another barbershop on the waterfront as a squatter. Unfortunately, the rainy weather had an adverse effect on his health. Binga subsequently sold his shop along with his squatter's rights and moved on to the San Francisco/Oakland, California area. This would be the last time he set up shop as a barber.[6]

Starting a new chapter in his travels, Jesse Binga became a porter on the Southern Pacific Railroad, working his way up and down the West Coast as well as to Reno and Carson City, Nevada, and finally Ogden, Utah. In Ogden he switched rail companies and started working from Ogden and Pocatello, Idaho, to Butte, Montana. This run is where Binga made his first major real estate investment. He purchased twenty lots of newly opened Indian land for twenty dollars each and quickly sold them at a handsome profit. It's been said that these land sales allowed him to pay off his debts and make his next move.[7]

After eight years of traveling throughout the western part of the United States, in 1893 Jesse, decided to go back east and headed for Chicago, Illinois. Binga later mentioned that his plan was to "give Chicago a try and if it didn't work out he would move to South America and give it a go there."[8] Binga's western travels, family heritage, and entrepreneurial experiences gave him a worldview different from that of the majority of late nineteenth-century African Americans. Moreover, Binga's unique background and mindset assisted him as he experienced the joys and pains offered by the business world over the next thirty-seven years.

First Years in Chicago, 1893–1908

Jesse Binga's second move to Chicago seemingly came at an opportune time. In 1893, a year later than planned, the city hosted the Columbian Exposition. The postponement of this World's Fair, held to celebrate the 400th anniversary of Christopher Columbus's landing in America, actually worked to the city's advantage. This high-profile event helped to temporarily divert Chicago's and the nation's attention from the Panic of 1893, which featured the failure of multiple railroads and banks, a stock market crash, and excessive unemployment.[9] Notwithstanding this negative backdrop, Binga soon discovered many entrepreneurial opportunities in this great midwestern city.

Besides a short biography of Binga written by his personal secretary Inez V. Cantey, there exists little documented information about his early years in Chicago. In Cantey's work, Binga described himself as a "huckster."[10] Yet it remains unclear what Binga did to survive during this during his first years in Chicago. Another Binga biographer, Carl R. Osthaus, has provided the following speculative analysis about this phase of Binga's life: "by some accounts he opened a fruit stand at the corner of 12th and Michigan; by others he became a wagon driver peddling coal oil and gasoline. Perhaps, in truest Horatio Alger heroics, he was a shoeshine boy, as one report stated." Osthaus goes on to state that in either 1896 or 1898, Binga opened up a storefront realtor business at 3331 South State Street.[11]

Binga made his first big deal in 1905 by leasing a small apartment in the formerly white-only Bates Building, located at 3637 South State Street. This is where all the skills he learned from working with his mother came into play. He subsequently subdivided this apartment into smaller kitchenette units to accommodate more than one family. Binga then leased the sliced-up apartment to black newcomers to Chicago seeking to fill jobs created by a now booming economy. He eventually acquired all of the apartments in the Bates Building.[12]

Based upon his success with the Bates Building, Binga boldly convinced investors to back construction of a three-story building on land he had leased at Thirty-Sixth Place and South State, across the street from the Bates location. By 1908, Binga had also leased the newly constructed three-story building and opened up a private bank in this location on September 21, 1908. As John N. Ingham and Lynne B. Feldman have asserted, the new Binga Bank was "the first one owned, managed, directed, or controlled by blacks in the North."[13] Jesse Binga later told the *Chicago Defender* that his financial institution served two important purposes. First, it "furnishes a nucleus around which the business interests of the section can assemble and operate." Second, it "creates a standing fund which is always open to the launching of legitimate new enterprises."[14]

Business Titan, 1909–29

During his first fifteen years in Chicago, Jesse Binga had evolved from a street huckster into a true "up and comer" in the realms of banking and real estate. No doubt influenced by his family and his own personal drive, during the twenty-year period from 1909 to 1929 Binga greatly expanded his economic base in the Windy City. In 1909 he leased a group of apartment buildings located from 2412 to 2428 South Wabash for $21,000. He next agreed to a thirty-year lease on another set of apartment buildings located from 4712 to 4752 South State Street, eventually opening up a branch real estate office in one of the lower units at 4732 South State. His holdings became known as "the Binga Block," reminiscent of his mother's real estate holdings, "the Binga Row" in Detroit.[15]

Binga's February 20, 1912, marriage to Eudora Johnson, the daughter of the deceased gambling kingpin John H. "Mushmouth" Johnson, represents a controversial component of his ascent as a Black Chicago business leader during this period. Eudora, described as physically unattractive, inherited $200,000 when her father died in 1907. Jesse Binga, conversely described as tall and handsome, soon began wooing Eudora. Based upon this scenario, some have argued that Binga ultimately married Eudora Johnson for her money. While this allegation can't be substantiated with certainty, two aspects of Jesse and Eudora's relationship appear crystal clear. First, their wedding, chronicled by all of Chicago's major newspapers as one of the most magnificent events of the year, dramatically enhanced Jesse Binga's status as a member of Chicago's elite. Second, access to his new wife's significant financial assets assisted his quest for even greater commercial prominence.[16]

The World War I "Great Migration" to Chicago magnified the importance of both Jesse Binga's growing real estate business and his pioneering bank. In 1920, Binga announced that his private bank located at Thirty-Sixth Place and State Street would be converted to a state bank. He chose this strategy for a couple of reasons. First, rapidly changing banking laws now encouraged all private banks to become state or federal institutions. Second, and more importantly, by reorganizing as a state bank he would outposition neighborhood competition that did not yet have the imprimatur of a state bank. On April 4, 1921, his bank became the Binga State Bank (BSB), fully sanctioned by the State of Illinois. Concurrently, he became one of the largest minority employers of blacks in the community as his real estate and banking staff reached upward of seventy-five people. The BSB opened with $100,000 in capitalization and a $20,000 reserve fund. Deposits quickly grew to $300,000 by October 1921 and reached $1,153,000 by 1924. The bank's stated mission was, "We cannot succeed if we ignore even the smallest fraction of the nation, if it has resources."[17]

The Binga State Bank served as a happy medium between large white banks in Chicago's downtown business district that were often discriminatory and discourteous toward black customers, and the loan sharks who preyed on working-class people. Moreover, the BSB and Anthony Overton's Douglass National Bank, located down the street, soon possessed over one-third of the combined resources of black-owned and -operated banks in America.[18]

While Binga's financial empire grew, so did his recognition on the local and national scenes. In 1919 he began writing a weekly article in Robert Abbott's *Chicago Defender*. His travels took him to the National Negro Business League meeting in 1920, the inauguration of President Harding in 1921, and Hampton University in 1922. He also joined the Community House board in 1921, and the Metropolitan Community Evening Club and the Chicago Clearing House in 1922. The Clearing House served local banks to guarantee their good faith and credit in case of a sudden downturn in the economy.[19]

Even before his business and personal profile grew after the establishment of the Binga State Bank, Jesse Binga possessed a level of self-confidence that seemingly crossed the border into arrogance. As he told the *Chicago Daily News* in 1916, "I'm an Irishman. You won't find any other colored people like me . . . Few of them aside from the professional men, have got beyond the stage of 'small business.'"[20] This statement may have been summoned from deep within his psyche, as his forgotten first wife was classified as Irish in the 1870 census. Nevertheless, while he acted with the boldness of a fully vested free man in America, he continuously had to defend that position.

In 1917 Jesse and Eudora Binga moved from their original dwelling at 3324 South Vernon to 5922 South Park Avenue, located in an all-white community. As a result, his home and real estate businesses were bombed seven times by 1920.[21] Jesse and Eudora stood their ground through all this turmoil and refused to move. In fact, the Bingas ultimately hired security guards to watch their home twenty-four hours a day. Their move to 5922 South Park Avenue upset not only their immediate neighbors, but also the white community at large. Yet, by refusing to leave, Jesse Binga demonstrated that he would not be intimidated by white hostility. As he told the *Chicago Defender* in 1921, "I have as much right to enjoy my home in Washington Park as anyone else."[22]

Based upon his residential problems, Binga soon became a public spokesperson on the issue of racial discrimination in Chicago. In fact, his personal situation contributed to the establishment of the Protective Circle of Chicago, whose mission was to "oppose segregation, bombing, and the defiance of the Constitution."[23] Besides working with the Protective Circle, Binga also served on a committee of local African Americans who provided information to the commission established to explore the causes of the 1919 race riot in the Windy City. Also, in his capacity as the only African American member of the Illinois Bankers Association, he urged that group to support the fight against racial discrimination.[24]

Although Jesse Binga found himself embroiled in a personal fight for basic human dignity during the early 1920s, he remained mindful of the plight of others less fortunate than he. Consequently, his contributions during this period supported such disparate organizations and causes as the Chicago Urban League, 1921 Tulsa riot victims, the YWCA, the YMCA, Howard University Medical School, and Japanese earthquake victims.[25] As Oliver Zunz has written, most successful businessmen accelerated their philanthropic activities during the late nineteenth and early twentieth centuries. He specifically noted that this phenomenon represented "a capitalist venture in social betterment, not an act of kindness as understood in Christianity."[26] In the case of Jesse Binga, while corporate self-aggrandizement may have partially motivated his generosity, it also appears that he was a confirmed "race man" who felt compelled to financially assist community-uplift efforts. As a successful black man, Jesse Binga wore many hats. He had to fight for the sanctity and safety of his home, ensure his real estate tenants were treated fairly, battle with the downtown financial institutions to obtain the credit he needed to continue building his financial empire, and be continually mindful of the welfare of the black community at large.

After successfully converting the original Binga Bank into a state chartered bank in 1921, Binga didn't rest on his laurels. He immediately went to work on the future expansion of his real estate and banking empire. In 1923 he acquired title to the corner lot at Thirty-Fifth and State Street, located next to the BSB, at a cost of $150,000. The following year, on October 24, 1924, Jesse Binga proudly opened the new Binga State Bank on this site.[27] The new bank featured a state-of-the-art decor and a modern and expanded safe-deposit-box area in the basement. Before opening the new facility, Binga had astutely coestablished the Binga Safe Deposit Company, as a separate entity to monitor safe-deposit-box activity, with his long-time friend Robert Abbott.[28]

In retrospect, given his real estate and financial acumen, Binga's putting of all his financial empire building eggs into one geographic basket appeared shortsighted. Most of his holdings were located in the historic Thirty-Fifth and South State Street district. However, beginning in the mid-1920s, the epicenter of Black Chicago's residential and commercial activities began moving southward toward 4700 South Parkway. The scheduled 1929 opening of the Regal Theater and South Center retail complex seemingly reinforced this important demographic shift. Undaunted by these developments, in 1927 Binga, purchased more land in the Thirty-Fifth and State Street district to build his five-story Binga Arcade office building. When completed in 1929, this facility had a reported total construction cost of $500,000. Moreover, it has been said that "there was no building anything like it south of Van Buren St. in the Loop."[29]

The autocratic component of Jesse Binga's personality seemingly contributed to his questionable decision to build the Binga Arcade building. The self-described "black Irishman" once stated, "Lots of people criticize me. They don't like my methods and they offer me suggestions. I always tell them: Jesse Binga knows what he's doing and he's doing it like Jesse Binga wants it done." This mindset carried over into his interaction with members of the Binga State Bank board of directors. Binga's intransigence resulted in this body having a virtual revolving door, through which he continuously removed directors "who challenged his right to decide matters as he saw fit."[30]

Jesse Binga's business and personal profile, notwithstanding the potential danger associated with his Binga Arcade project, received two huge boosts in 1927. First, on May 8, 1927, the influential *Chicago Tribune* featured him in a front-page story. One month later *The Sphinx*, the official publication of Alpha Phi Alpha

Fraternity, featured a reprint of the *Tribune* article under the title "Brother Jesse Binga: Banker, Builder, Financier."

The *Tribune*'s laudatory work discussed not only Binga's business success, but also his philanthropic impact in the black community and his volunteerism on socially relevant boards.[31]

This article also shared with readers the following Benjamin Franklin and Booker T. Washington–like aphorisms that influenced Binga's business and personal life:

- Learn a business—and then mind it.
- Learn something not so you know about it but so you know it.
- Save, save, save, and when you've got it then give, give, give.
- Nothing is so easy or as wasteful as the work of hating—except hating work. And that goes for races as well as individuals.
- Get a competency. Then the world—white or colored—will concede that you are competent.
- Only business contacts with the community as a whole—white and colored— will educate the colored man in business.
- Learn business: Establish a credit: Provide for your own wants. That is my message to our group.
- You can be a menial or a man of business. But to get out of the menial place requires thrift that produces property. And property enlarges life. Work, then, not for gain alone but for the enlarged life that honest gains create.
- Life is pretty much what you make it—and making it big means using every day of it.[32]

Based upon his business dealings with others, it's not surprising that *humility* failed to make his list of desirable attributes and actions. Yet the additional visibility and recognition Binga received from the 1927 *Chicago Tribune* article seemingly verified, in his mind, the correctness of his approach to life.

Binga no doubt received similar validation when *The Sphinx* reprinted the May 8, 1927, *Tribune* article in its June 1927 issue. Alpha Phi Alpha Fraternity, the first African American intercollegiate Greek-lettered organization established at Cornell University on December 4, 1906, prided itself on the accomplishments of its members. As *The Sphinx* introduction to the *Tribune* reprint asserted: "it is the avowed policy of the staff of the editors of the SPHINX to endeavor to feature and give due publicity to worthy and outstanding achievements of men who are numbered among our Brothers in Alpha Phi Alpha." Moreover, Binga deserved such positive visibility because "through his bank and real estate office, he has done more to elevate the economic status and improve the home life of our group in Chicago than any other one agency."[33]

The year 1929 represented a milestone for Jesse Binga and his empire building. In February he opened the magnificent Arcade building at the aforementioned cost of $500,000. According to the February 16, 1929, issue of the *Chicago Defender*, this "five story edifice of the Tudor Gothic period, constructed of the finest stone of the age and standing on the northwest corner of 3500 South State Street . . . radiates and gives to this corner beauty and distinction that must be seen to be appreciated."[34]

Jesse Binga was clearly committed to promoting business development in the Thirty-Fifth and State Street district. In fact, a year before the completion of the Binga Arcade, he told the *Chicago Defender* that "new investments and new enterprises are being opened by our people in this neighborhood means that 35th Street will always be Colored Chicago's most important commercial center."[35] Nevertheless, in 1929 he announced his plan to establish a new financial institution, the South Park National Bank, in the burgeoning Forty-Seventh Street neighborhood. Significantly, just as Binga's intransigence prompted him to spend most of his investment capital in the Thirty-Fifth and State Street district, a similar mindset prompted him to begin funneling money from the Binga State Bank into this new institution. Moreover, as Christopher Reed has written, "the impracticality of this venture convinced Binga's board of directors for the Binga State Bank to oppose it. His response was to replace them and any others who questioned his quest."[36]

The spring of 1929 seemed to be going particularly well for Jesse Binga. He controlled one of the two largest black banks in America. His real estate holdings were producing an abundance of cash from rentals. The Binga Arcade office building had just opened to rousing acclaim within the black community. Finally, Binga had just purchased a property to begin building his second bank in Chicago. It seemed as if his thirty-year upward business trajectory could not be stopped. Unfortunately, the self-assured Binga had not taken to heart comments he made in a February 16, 1924, *Chicago Defender* article titled "Jesse Binga Gives Points on Real Estate to A.B.C. [Associated Business Clubs]. He prophetically stated, "property purchased by Colored people in Chicago during the last 10 years has advanced $10,000,000 in value. But values are now at their peak and it behooves those who invested to be careful."[37] Ironically, those words would haunt Jesse Binga during the ensuing Great Depression.

The Fall of Jesse Binga, 1930–35

On August 9, 1930, the *Chicago Defender* featured a front-page story detailing how three state banks (including the Binga State Bank) had closed their doors within the past week. Under the subheading "South Side Hit Hard When Institutions Shut Doors," readers were told that "all three banks were the depositories of thousands of South side businessmen, workers and housewives."[38] In seeking to explain the Binga State Bank's closing, the *Defender*, echoing Binga's 1924 speech to the Associated Business Clubs (ABC), noted: "it is reported that the bank invested too heavily in real estate, which following the post-war period, has taken a decline as far as rental and revenues are concerned."[39]

Jesse Binga was not the only person fooled by the 1920s real estate bubble. Yet, as Abram Harris noted in his study of early twentieth-century African American banks: "it is hardly to be doubted that the general financial condition of the country in 1930 and the especially panicky situation in Chicago precipitated the failure of the Binga Bank; [nevertheless,] the dominance of Binga in the affairs of the bank was in a large measure responsible for its financial operations."[40]

The August 9, 1930, *Chicago Defender* elaborated upon how Binga's personal management style contributed to the Binga State Bank's problems. It reported, "Last January when the bank examiners visited the institution they were not satisfied with the methods in which loans were made. The loan committee, authorized by law, is said to have been ignored by Jesse Binga." Moreover, after the State of Illinois demanded that such a committee be formed, the *Defender* continued, "this committee, according to those close to the inner workings of the bank, upon investigation, is said to have discovered the existence of $267,000 of illegally authorized loans." Finally, to make matters worse, "this discovery brought in the bank examiners again and in July the committee is said to have reported the sum much larger than at first stated." Later in the article, the *Chicago Defender* noted that Binga had personally authorized, without committee oversight, loans totaling $430,000.[41]

Later investigations revealed that Binga's control of the Binga State Bank's loan program reflected more than his autocratic nature. By not allowing committee oversight of the loan process, Binga could profit from the issuance of "dummy loans." As Abram Harris described this process, "through pretended loans to the Commercial Burial Association, Henry M. Shackleford, J. Turner, J. A. Slowe, Quinlock King, N. Richardson, Fountain Thurman, and Charles E. Worthington, Binga obtained the following amounts from the bank: $10,000; $4,700; $658; $13,000; $1,000; $9,000; $6,500; and $8,000."[42]

In the short term, before the specifics of Binga's apparent thievery became public knowledge, there were concerted efforts to reopen the Binga State Bank. The September 6, 1930, issue of the *Chicago Defender* reported that the board of directors, minus Binga, had come up with a plan to satisfy the state auditors as well as the depositors. The plan required that the board raise $100,000 in cash to be added to the $156,000 being held by the state auditors. In addition, the depositors would receive 60 percent of their deposit value, with 40 percent held over to help reorganize the bank. The board also insisted that Jesse Binga turn over forty properties to be liquidated and these funds be set aside for future bank use. Finally, board member and local undertaker Charles Jackson would be named new president of the bank, since the plan included the resignation of Mr. Binga.[43]

Independent efforts to save the Binga State Bank were made all the more difficult after a follow-up November 1930 examination of the troubled financial institution. This up-to-date survey of the bank's operations found there was "a shortage in its actual assets over liabilities of over $500,000." The report's conclusion, which called for the appointment of a court-appointed receiver, stated that the "capital stock of the bank has become impaired" and "the business of the bank is being conducted in an unsafe manner."[44]

On November 30, 1930, Edward H. Morris, a prominent local African American attorney, assumed the position of receiver of the Binga State Bank. His subsequent report was damning of Jesse Binga and disheartening to thousands of Black Chicago depositors. Morris revealed that "the given value of the various items of the bank's resources were erroneous and did not reflect the true financial condition of the bank." Moreover, besides finding that the stated worth of the Binga State Bank's resources was "highly inflated," Morris concluded that "the institution had been conducted in an illegal, fraudulent and unsafe manner."[45]

Notwithstanding the extremely bad news in attorney Morris's findings, a number of depositors and their supporters remained hopeful that the former Binga State Bank could be saved. In its February 14, 1931, issue, the *Chicago Defender* featured a front-page story titled "To Reopen Binga Bank." Readers were informed of a February 15, 1931, mass meeting scheduled to be held at Pilgrim Baptist Church, located at Thirty-Third and Indiana Avenue. Among the scheduled speakers at this event were Charles R. Walgreens, the founder of the Walgreens Drug Store chain, and John A. Carroll, president of the Hyde Park–Kenwood Bank. The *Defender* also noted that "the news of the proposed reopening of the Binga State Bank comes at a surprise to the thousands of depositors inasmuch as many had given up hope that the bank would ever open its doors again for business."[46] In the end, the Binga State Bank never reopened its doors. There exists a long-standing historical debate as to why.

W. E. B. DuBois discussed the closing of the Binga State Bank in the December 1930 issue of *Crisis*. First and foremost, DuBois declared "it was not necessary for the Binga Bank to fail." Moreover, he continued, "it was only necessary that the banking world, which means the big white banks of Chicago, should stand behind Mr. Binga." Yet, according to DuBois, for reasons other than purely financial, "the Binga Bank was allowed to fail because owners and masters of the credit facilities of the nation did not care to save it. Binga was not the kind of man they wanted to succeed . . . He could not be bluffed or frightened and not all the bombs in Chicago could keep him from buying and living in a house in one of the best sections of the city . . . He represented the self-assertive Negro and was even at times rough and dictatorial."[47] Although DuBois acknowledged both the positive and negative aspects of Binga's personality, he left no doubt as to which he thought was most important.

Six years after DuBois's assessment of the Binga State Bank's closing, Abram Harris, in his classic 1936 work *The Negro as Capitalist: A Study of Banking and Business among American Negroes*, provided a dramatically different analysis of the Binga State Bank's permanent closure. He acknowledged that "much has been made of the fact that Binga was unable to secure financial aid from white organizations and it has been generally felt that had the white institutions come to his assistance the failure of the bank would have been prevented." Yet, he continued, "the real difficulty was that white institutions in Chicago at this time were in a precarious position and that because of this their apparent discrimination was simply economic precaution." While Harris attempted to disassociate racial animosity from the white banking community's failure to assist the Binga State Bank, he did concede "it must also be remembered that almost $800,000 of the resources of the [Binga State] bank were tied up in mortgages on Negro property. It was reported by one official of the bank that the white bankers refused to handle these mortgages and this was the chief contributing factor to the bank's failure."[48]

Frank Cyril James's authoritative 1938 study *The Growth of Chicago Banks* asserted that the Binga State Bank was one of several local banks that did not receive assistance from the Chicago Clearing House during the early 1930s. While all of Chicago's big downtown banks were protected, many outlying banks, including the Binga State Bank, were allowed to close. As James revealed, according to Chicago Clearing House officials, "an attempt to save every bank would have, it was feared, involved the Loop banks themselves in the common ruin."[49]

Carl R. Osthaus, in his January 1973 *Journal of Negro History* article "The Rise and Fall of Jesse Binga, Black Financier," echoed Abram Harris when he asserted that "prejudice did not defeat Binga. The attempts to reorganize the bank were hindered by his personal demand to remain as president and the financial instability of those people and institutions that normally would have helped him. His white friends had loaned him money before and did so during his troubles."[50]

More recently, Christopher R. Reed, in his 2011 monograph *The Depression Comes to the South Side*, reemphasizes the race-based reasons for the Binga State Bank's demise. Reed asserted that the Binga State Bank, as a member of the Chicago Clearing House Association (CCHA), should have received the funds it needed to reopen from "the city's institutional network for banking protection." Yet when Binga approached the CCHA for assistance, its president Melvin Traylor, "a southerner with true conservative roots, both financially and racially, supposedly referred to Binga's business as a 'little nigger bank that didn't mean anything' in the broader scope of the city's expanding banking operations."[51]

Once it became clear that the Binga State Bank would not reopen, Jesse Binga, along with thousands of distraught former depositors, had to endure the public spectacle associated with his being tried for embezzlement beginning in July 1932. Jesse Binga's first trial lasted a week. It featured the prosecution's presentation of boxes and boxes of evidence and a multitude of witnesses. After the prosecution presented its case, Binga's attorney, James Cashin, stunned the courtroom by waiving a defense and moving for a directed verdict of not guilty on the grounds that the State had not made a strong enough case. Judge Prystalski indicated he would sustain Cashin's motion for direct verdict because the prosecution had not shown that any of the money alleged to have been embezzled from the bank by Binga was ever in the Binga State Bank. He commented that "testimony revealed funds. . . . were held by Binga personally and no listings of them were found on the books of Binga State Bank."[52] Thus the case was dismissed on a technicality because Judge Prystalski deemed that the transfer of money between the subscribers of the new bank and Mr. Binga was a personal matter.[53]

Undeterred by Binga's acquittal in their first case, the prosecution proceeded to charge Binga with embezzlement associated with "dummy loans." Moreover, to increase their likelihood of securing a conviction in a second trial, the prosecution persuaded Inez Cantey, Binga's personal secretary, to turn state's evidence.[54] Significantly, right before Jesse Binga's second trial in May 1933, his wife Eudora passed away. As he dramatically asserted during court proceedings, the stress associated with his legal troubles contributed to her death.

Similar to the first Binga trial, the prosecution, during its second attempt to convict the beleaguered ex-banker, began by presenting a large amount of documentary evidence, along with corroborating testimony. Saving the best for last, the State brought Inez V. Cantey to the stand, where she testified for two full days. Her most damning statement, which she repeated on several occasions, was that the misappropriation of bank funds was done "only with Mr. Binga's permission." "Even under the intense pressure of James Cashin's cross-examination, Cantey never wilted or cringed, but continued to reiterate the statement, "only with Mr. Binga's permission." The prosecution contended that Jesse Binga used a number of people as go-betweens to embezzle $32,500 for his personal use. Moreover, these individuals insisted they knew nothing of the chicanery but signed the loan documents only at his insistence. Cantey's cool and calm testimony seemingly confirmed the prosecution's allegations.[55]

The only witness produced by the defense was Jesse Binga himself. Needless to say, his appearance on the witness stand represented a critical juncture in the proceedings. Binga started out by telling of his Horatio Alger–like rise to power. The whites in the courtroom were amazed at the wealth and power that this now old and seemingly tired black man commanded at the height of his power. After James

Cashin offered friendly, nonthreatening questions to his client, the prosecution began to cross-examine Jesse Binga. Binga immediately sought to evade prosecutor Donald Thompson's questions by repeatedly responding with, "What did you say?" Binga also complained that the prosecutor disrespected him by speaking loudly and roughly. Consequently, the prosecutor lowered his voice and continued his questions with a laserlike precision that seemed to upset the former business icon. To the shock of persons in the courtroom, Binga soon erupted with rage and leaped from the witness stand, shouting, "I can't stand it . . . ! You've killed my wife! You've taken my property and now you are persecuting me." His skin was flushed and his hair seemed to stand on edge as he left the witness stand and headed toward the prosecutor's table. There, he began crying while he pounded on it.[56]

Binga's emotional outburst, predictably, put the courtroom in a state of disarray. Wisely, to calm things down, Judge James F. Fardy called for a ten-minute recess. After all the participants returned to the courtroom, it seemed a mere formality that the all-white jury would find Binga guilty of embezzling $32,500. The contrasting testimonies of Jesse Binga and Inez Cantey, coupled with Cantey's unwavering statement that "only Mr. Binga had the authority to transfer or release funds," seemed to support the validity of the State's assertions against him. At this point, James Cashin pleaded for mercy for his client. He stated "there was no criminal intent; he [Binga] had been a wholesome, inspiring influence on his community." After Cashin's statement, Judge Fardy announced that the case would be continued until June 28, 1933, for sentencing.[57]

Before the sentencing trial took place, Mr. Binga's attorney asked for a new trial. In fact, Cashin's aggressiveness in defending Binga is indicated by the fact that, by November 3, 1933, when Jesse Binga finally received a sentence of one to ten years in prison for embezzlement, the case had generated forty continuances.[58] Still unwilling to give up the fight, Cashin successfully appealed the guilty verdict to the Illinois Supreme Court. However, as the March 2, 1935, *Chicago Defender* reported, Illinois's highest legal body ultimately denied Binga's request for a new trial and by implication ordered him to serve his prison sentence at the Joliet State Penitentiary.[59]

Postscript, 1935–50

As Carl Osthaus has written, once Binga finally began serving his sentence, "the public reaction on the South Side was surprisingly mild and generally sympathetic. The *Defender* emphasized Binga's plight, describing the beaten, aging financier as a victim of the tragic depression." Moreover, as time went along, "people came to associate his imprisonment with the collapse of his bank and not with embezzlement. Other banks had fallen in the Depression, but few bankers had been so punished." Moreover, to a growing number of Black Chicagoans, this seemed grossly unfair because "Binga had given his entire personal fortune in his attempts at [bank] reorganization in 1930." Thus, in the end, "Binga remained a hero to his own group."[60]

Shortly after Binga's imprisonment, his friends and supporters, including the noted attorney Clarence Darrow, began a campaign that sought an early parole for the ex-banker. Their efforts came to fruition in 1938 when "the former financial king, now seventy-three, was paroled to Father Joseph Eckert of St. Anselm's Church and given a job as a handyman and usher at fifteen dollars a week." Three years later, in April 1941, Binga received a full pardon from then-governor of Illinois Dwight Green.[61]

In contrast to Binga's often bombastic behavior during his entrepreneurial heyday, the ex–real estate and banking tycoon spent his final years living quietly with his nephew until he died after an accident on June 13, 1950. Comparative obituaries in white and black publications graphically illustrated his relative insignificance to one group and his profound importance to another.

Chicago's white-owned *Herald-American* summed up Binga's life in a one-sentence, June 14, 1950, summary that included, "Jesse Binga, who rose from a laborer to a millionaire and a power on Chicago's South Side . . . died penniless yesterday in St. Luke's Hospital." By contrast, the Associated Negro Press (ANP) published an extensive June 21, 1950, wire story outlining Binga's life under the title "Jesse Binga Represents Vanishing Race of Self-Made Men." After recounting the highs and lows of Binga's career, the ANP noted that "Binga's death does recall the great days of the past—the day of the self-made man on Chicago's southside."[62]

Notwithstanding his various foibles and idiosyncrasies, Jesse Binga was, indeed, a self-made man. Normally, in the context of American business history, such individuals are lionized. Yet, as a black male in racist early twentieth-century America, his exhibitions of self-assuredness and confidence were sometimes construed as being "uppity." Thus, in this context, Binga had to be reminded of his proper "place." Also, while the evidence indicates that Binga clearly engaged in questionable actions as president of the Binga State Bank, it also indicates that these activities, in and of themselves, were not the only cause for his subsequent demise. For instance, when the Binga State Bank closed in 1930, one of the persons that Binga sought assistance from was Edward Brown, first vice president of the First National Bank of Chicago. To Binga's distinct surprise and shock, Brown began their meeting with the insult, "You are no banker." Moreover, as Binga stated in a later interview, Brown "blocked every effort I made afterward to save the bank."[63]

Circumstantial evidence suggests that the noted Chicago businessman and philanthropist Julius Rosenwald could have influenced Brown's (and other white

Chicago bankers') dismissal of Binga's credentials as a banker. In response to a question from George Woodruff, chairman of Chicago's National Bank of the Republic, regarding the feasibility of black-owned banks in the black community, Rosenwald's June 11, 1930, reply included the following; "*a strictly Negro bank is to my mind a mistake, although I would not care to say so publicly, because so few people think far enough on a subject of this kind. However, I have expressed my views very freely to educators and to some bankers*" (italics added). Rosenwald continued: "in my opinion, there are few, if any successful Negro banks in the country and it is easy to explain. They are offered only the poorer grade of Negro accounts, and as you know the average risk in loaning to a Negro is far less desirable than the average loan to a white man. Even a Negro with any large amount of money to deposit would rarely if ever take it to a Negro bank." Rosenwald concluded by asserting, "*I do not believe the time has come when the Negro should enter the banking business*" (italics added).[64]

Considering Rosenwald's prominence in Chicago during this period, along with his admission that he had expressed these views "to some bankers," it is not unreasonable to assume that Edward Brown and other white Chicago bankers were influenced by Rosenwald's beliefs. Thus it appears that not *all* of Binga's problems as a banker were self-induced.

In the end, Jesse Binga, from a business standpoint, died a failure in 1950. Yet the passage of time has placed his entrepreneurial career in clearer perspective. For instance, while Julius Rosenwald did not believe that blacks were capable of running banks, Binga possessed the audacious belief that *he could*. Moreover, at a time when blacks were expected to assume a servile ambience in American society, Binga's unabashed self-confidence appeared to be out of place. While Jesse Binga's supreme belief in his capabilities sometimes manifested itself in autocratic behavior, his numerous charitable endeavors suggest he was much more than a self-centered boor. Thus this complex individual should be remembered for the totality of his extraordinary business career: successes, as well as setbacks.

Notes

1. Genealogy chart produced by Anthony J. Binga Sr., December 1979, Binga notes, section 14, located in Dr. Christopher Reed Papers, Roosevelt University, Chicago, Illinois; 1870 United States Federal Census, Ancestry.com; Michigan, Deaths and Burial Index 1867–1995, Ancestry.com; State of Illinois Coroner's Certificate of Death (Jesse Binga), #41387, June 20, 1950; John N. Ingham and Lynne B. Feldman, *African-American Business Leaders: A Biographical Dictionary* (Westport, CT: Greenwood Press, 1994), 75.

2. Carl R. Osthaus, "The Rise and Fall of Jesse Binga, Black Financier" *Journal of Negro History* 58 (January 1973): 40; accessed December 6, 2016, at www.chicagocrimescenes .blogspot.com/2009/07/saga-of-jesse-binga.html.

3. Ibid., 40; Binga genealogy chart.

4. Osthaus, "The Rise and Fall of Jesse Binga, 40; Inez V. Cantey, "Jesse Binga," *Crisis Magazine* 34 (December 1927): 329; Ingham and Feldman, *African-American Business Leaders*, 75.

5. Michigan, Marriages, 1868–1925, Frances Scott, 1865, Ancestry.com; Binga genealogy chart; Anthony J. Binga Sr., "Jesse Binga: Founder and President, Binga State Bank, Chicago, Illinois," *The Journal of the Afro-American Historical and Genealogical Society* 2 (1981): 148. Anthony Binga was a nephew of Jesse Binga.

6. Cantey, "Jesse Binga," 329.

7. Ibid.

8. James O'Donnell Bennett, "Plans, Work, Binga's Secret for Success," *Chicago Tribune*, May 8, 1927, 20.

9. https://www.chicagohs.org/history/expo.html http://www.historycentral.com/Industrialage/Panic1893,html.

10. Cantey, "Jesse Binga," 329.

11. Osthaus, "The Rise and Fall of Jesse Binga," 41.

12. Ibid., 42.

13. Ibid.; Ingham and Feldman, *African-American Business Leaders*, 77.

14. "Bank's Great Business Shows It Growing Fast," *Chicago Defender*, November 23, 1912, 8.

15. Osthaus, "The Rise and Fall of Jesse Binga," 40.

16. "Mrs. Binga, Wife of Ex-Banker, Is Dead," *Chicago Defender*, April 1, 1933, 1; Ingham and Feldman, *African-American Business Leaders*, 75, 78; "Binga-Johnson Wedding: The Most Brilliant Ever Held in Chicago, *Chicago Defender*, February 24, 1912, 1.

17. "History of the Binga Bank," *Chicago Defender*, April 3, 1926, 4.

18. Osthaus, "The Rise and Fall of Jesse Binga," 44; Abram Harris, *The Negro as Capitalist: A Study of Banking and Business among American Negroes* (Chicago: Urban Research Press, 1992; orig. pub. 1936), 195.

19. "History of the Binga Bank," *Chicago Defender*, April 3, 1926, 4.

20. Ingham and Feldman, *African-American Business Leaders*, 78.

21. "Bombing Binga," *Chicago Defender* (National Edition), September 3, 1921, 16.

22. "Bomb Rips Front Porch from Jesse Binga's Dwelling," *Chicago Defender*, September 3, 1921, 3.

23. Chicago Commission on Race Relations, *The Negro in Chicago: A Study of Race Relations and a Race Riot* (Chicago: University of Chicago Press, 1922), 593.

24. "Seeks to Create Stronger Ties in Financial World," *The Chicago Defender*, June 24, 1922, 2.

25. *Chicago Defender*, September 18, 1920, 8; April 2, 1921, 3; June 11, 1921, 2; May 2, 1922, 4; March 24, 1923, 2; September 8, 1923, 1.

26. Oliver Zunz, *Philanthropy in America: A History* (Princeton, NJ: Princeton University Press, 2012), 2.

27. "Binga State Bank to Move into New Quarters Monday," *Chicago Defender*, October 18, 1924, 2.

28. "Jesse Binga, Who Worked Way Up from Ranks Now Looms as a Financial Colossus," *Pittsburgh Courier*, December 13, 1924, 3.

29. "The Saga of Jesse Binga," Chicago Crime Scenes, accessed December 19, 2016, at http://www.chicagocrimescenes.blogspot.com/2009/07/saga-of-jesse-binga.html.

30. Osthaus, "The Rise and Fall of Jesse Binga," 50.

31. James O'Donnell Bennett, "Plans, Work, Binga's Secret for Success," *Chicago Tribune*, May 8, 1927, 1.

32. Ibid.

33. B. T. McGraw, "Brother Jesse Binga: Banker, Builder, Financier," *The Sphinx* 13 (June 1927): 3. The evidence suggests that Binga, who did not have a college degree, entered the fraternity as an honorary member (based upon his professional accomplishments). Significantly, Anthony Overton, a fellow Black Chicago banker, also became a member of Alpha Phi Alpha through the honorary member process. See "Brother Anthony Overton," *The Sphinx* 9 (October 1923): 23.

34. "Jesse Binga Adds New Land Mark to City's South Side," *Chicago Defender*, February 16, 1929, 2.

35. Ingham and Feldman, *African-American Business Leaders*, 78.

36. Christopher R. Reed, *The Rise of Chicago's Black Metropolis, 1920–1929* (Urbana: University of Illinois Press, 2011), 117.

37. "Jesse Binga Gives Points on Real Estate to A.B.C.," *Chicago Defender*, February 16, 1924, 4.

38. "3 Chicago Banks Closed," *Chicago Defender*, August 9, 1930, 1.

39. Ibid., 3.

40. Harris, *The Negro as Capitalist*, 192.

41. "3 Chicago Banks Closed," 3.

42. Harris, *The Negro as Capitalist*, 194.

43. "Binga Bank Depositors Meet," *Chicago Defender*, September 6, 1930, 13.

44. Harris, *The Negro as Capitalist*, 190–91.

45. Ibid., 191.

46. "To Reopen Binga Bank," *Chicago Defender*, February 14, 1931, 1.

47. W. E. B. DuBois, "Postscript," *Crisis* 37 (December 1930): 425.

48. Harris, *The Negro as Capitalist*, 194–95.

49. Frank Cyril James, *The Growth of Chicago Banks, Vol. 2* (New York: Harper and Row, 1938; 1969), 1,000.

50. Osthaus, "The Rise and Fall of Jesse Binga," 57–58.

51. Christopher R. Reed, *The Depression Comes to the South Side: Protest and Politics in the Black Metropolis, 1930–1933* (Bloomington: Indiana University Press, 2011), 18–19.

52. "Binga Jury Disagrees," *Chicago Defender*, July 23, 1932, 1.

53. Osthaus, "The Rise and Fall of Jesse Binga," 58.

54. Ibid., 58.

55. "High Lights of the Binga Trial," *Chicago Defender*, June 3, 1933, 2.

56. Ibid.

57. "Chicago Banker Faces One to Ten Year Sentence," *Pittsburgh Courier*, June 8, 1933, 1.

58. "Jesse Binga Has Won Forty Continuances," *Pittsburgh Courier*, November 4, 1933, 3; "Binga Denied New Trial," *Chicago Defender*, March 2, 1935, 13.

59. Ibid.

60. Osthaus, "The Rise and Fall of Jesse Binga," 59.

61. Ibid., 60; "Saga of Jesse Binga."

62. Osthaus, "The Rise and Fall of Jesse Binga," 60; Luix Virgil Overbea, "Jesse Binga Represents Vanishing Race of Self-Made Men," Associated Negro Press wire story, June 21, 1950, Claude A. Barnett Papers, Box 261, Folder 3, Chicago Historical Museum.

63. Harris, *The Negro as Capitalist*, 193.

64. Letter, Julius Rosenwald to George Woodruff, June 11, 1930, the Julius Rosenwald Papers, Box 52, Folder 11, Special Collections, Regenstein Library, University of Chicago.

CHAPTER 4

Contested Terrain

P. W. Chavers, Anthony Overton, and the Founding of the Douglass National Bank

ROBERT E. WEEMS JR.

Anthony Overton is widely regarded as one of the most significant African American entrepreneurs of the early twentieth century. For instance, the Harvard University Business School's database of "American Business Leaders of the Twentieth Century" lists him as the first African American to head a major business conglomerate.[1] Traditionally, Anthony Overton has been credited with starting the Douglass National Bank, one of the cornerstones of his Chicago-based financial empire. Yet Madrue Chavers-Wright, in her 1985 book *The Guarantee: P. W. Chavers: Banker, Entrepreneur, Philanthropist in Chicago's Black Belt of the Twenties,* declares her father, P. W. Chavers, was the Douglass National Bank's actual founder. This chapter will examine the contested terrain regarding the establishment of the second national bank chartered by African Americans.[2] Among other things, the story of the Douglass National Bank reveals the limitations of *both* group and individual entrepreneur–based strategies for African American economic development.

A variety of sources explicitly identify Anthony Overton as the organizer and founder of the Douglass National Bank.[3] For instance, a March 1929 article in *Opportunity: A Journal of Negro Life* noted: "at first he [Overton] had his Hygienic plant, turning out cosmetics and hair preparations. Then, because he saw the great need for a banking institution which would take care of certain developments, he founded his National Bank."[4] Similarly, an extended obituary of Overton, published

in the July 1947 issue of *The Journal of Negro History*, included the following assertion: "as a manufacturer he was eminently successful, and he became ambitious
to invade other fields. Negroes had never before conducted a national bank, and
he decided that he would make the step beyond the small private banking firms
which Negroes as a rule operated."[5] Decades later, John N. Ingham and Lynne B.
Feldman's 1994 *African-American Business Leaders: A Biographical Dictionary* and Juliet
E. K. Walker's 1999 *Encyclopedia of African American Business History* likewise situated
Overton as the organizer of the Douglass National Bank.[6]

Notwithstanding long-held beliefs regarding Overton and the founding of the
Douglass National Bank, Madrue Chavers-Wright, as well as corroborating contemporary newspapers, provides indisputable evidence that her father, Pearl W.
Chavers, should be credited with this historical distinction. Moreover, in her book
The Guarantee, Chavers-Wright insinuates that Overton was part of a conspiracy that
ultimately resulted in Chavers being administratively removed from the institution
he organized.

Despite its provocative thesis, *The Guarantee* remains a fairly obscure work. The
apparent cause for its marginality, as a truly reputable historical source, is that it
combines historical narrative with historical fiction. In the book's acknowledg-
ments section, Chavers-Wright explains:

> I have used a semi-autobiographical format to present the intimate family portrait
> of the life and works of Pearl William Chavers, or P. W., as he was known to his fam-
> ily, friends, and close associates. This book is based on a true story of his life—as I
> knew him—and the Chicago Black Belt, as I knew it. *I have fictionalized some names,
> certain incidents and details, and much of the dialogue, for the purposes of drama, and at times
> anonymity.*[7] (italics added)

Chavers-Wright's admission that she developed some of her book's incidents and
dialogue for the purpose of enhancing its dramatic effect has to be taken into consideration when assessing the words and actions of "Richard Owens," the apparent
fictionalized name given to Anthony Overton. Also, Chavers-Wright was a five-
year-old girl when the Douglass National Bank commenced operations in 1922.
Thus it is highly unlikely that she could provide a credible first-hand recollection
of this event and what preceded it.

Although some of *The Guarantee* is a manifestation of Chavers-Wright's imagination, to her distinct credit, this book also includes corroborating documentary evidence to support her claims regarding the establishment of the Douglass National
Bank. In fact, the most important contribution this book makes is to bring the life
of Pearl William Chavers into the narrative of recorded African American history.

Pearl William "P. W." Chavers was born in Columbus, Ohio, in 1876. His father
died when P. W. was a boy, and to help buttress the family's finances, the young P.

W. became an entrepreneur. Chavers-Wright describes this phenomenon as follows: "At an early age, P. W. worked to help his mother with family expenses by selling newspapers . . . He would invest in a large supply of newspapers and set up routes for other boys to deliver them, making a profit on his investment."[8]

Later, as a student at Hudson College, a local business school in Columbus, he sought to learn all he could about the structure of business. When he graduated, his business expertise included knowing how to form a corporation, as well as how to market and use stocks and bonds. The ambitious young Chavers also became involved in Republican politics and in 1900 attended the G.O.P. national convention, where he met Booker T. Washington.[9]

P. W. Chavers's first enterprise after graduation was *The Columbus Standard* newspaper, established in 1901. This periodical, later renamed *The Ohio Standard World*, expanded to include supplements in Dayton, Cincinnati, Toledo, and Springfield, Ohio. As editor, Chavers not only advocated the effective use of black voting power, but also promoted Booker T. Washington's ideas about the importance of black business development.[10]

Based upon his long-standing entrepreneurial inclinations, Chavers soon expanded his financial interests into other spheres. Besides being involved in a real estate partnership, Chavers, in 1905, established a women's garment factory. Moreover, while he was interested in increasing his personal wealth, the idealistic Chavers was also interested in helping other blacks succeed. In 1907 he organized the Lincoln Ohio Industrial Training School for Colored Youth. This institution "provided employment opportunities to countless black youngsters with special emphasis on the needs of the poor, unskilled young migrant black women pouring into Columbus from the rural South. The students were taught the practical skills of dressmaking, shorthand, typing, cooking, and domestic service free of charge." Moreover, this institution, which received moral and financial support from both prominent blacks and whites in Columbus, included an employment bureau that placed its students in jobs upon their graduation.[11]

Significantly, while P. W. Chavers was building a positive public reputation, his private life was much less fulfilling. His first wife apparently did not share Chavers's commitment to racial uplift, which ultimately led to a divorce and "many years of loneliness" for him. That aspect of his life improved dramatically in 1912 when he went to Chicago for the Republican National Convention as a delegate. While in the city, he met the woman who later became his second wife. Yet Chavers's new-found marital bliss soon generated a complication that would dramatically change his life. During their first years of marriage, Chavers and his new bride, Minnie, lived in Columbus. However, Minnie "found life [in Columbus] very insulated and uninspiring compared to life in Chicago, where she had lived and worked as a dressmaker for many years." In the end, besides seeking to satisfy his wife, the pragmatic Chavers decided to move his women's garment factory to Chicago in 1917 because the Windy City represented a bigger potential market for this enterprise's products.[12]

Within a short period of time, Chavers's decision to relocate his women's garment factory to Chicago proved to be very lucrative. This enterprise, located at 534 East Forty-Third Street, subsequently generated profits from its relationship with a variety of wholesale and retail outlets. For instance, Chavers-Wright asserts, "several times a year, some merchandise was made specifically for Marshall Field's basement sales. Business thrived, even during the race riots."[13]

Besides transplanting his business acumen from Columbus to Chicago, P. W. Chavers also brought his sense of social responsibility to the Windy City. Within his company, Chavers quickly gained a reputation as a benevolent employer who was concerned with both the work- and home-related problems of his employees. Moreover, word of his commitment to racial uplift spread outside the walls of his Forty-Third Street facility. As Chavers-Wright contended, "in the ghetto, one's reputation travels fast. People brought troubles of all types to him at all hours; he found the time to see, hear, and help, somehow."[14]

During early 1920, one of the problems brought to Chavers's attention was the financial difficulties of the black-owned R. W. Woodford Bank. Before 1921, when the state of Illinois made individual ownership of banks illegal, the R. W. Woodford Bank, similar to the more famous Binga Bank (established by Jesse Binga in 1908), was a privately owned enterprise that served Chicago's growing African American community.[15] Because the R. W. Woodford Bank operated outside the realm of governmental regulation, its depositors were justifiably concerned that the bank's problems would result in totally uncompensated losses.

Chavers, after attending several meetings of worried Woodford Bank depositors, agreed to become the trustee of the ailing institution during the spring of 1920. Later, with advice and encouragement from Jesse Binga and J. Gray Lucas (the attorney representing the interests of Woodford Bank depositors), Chavers worked out a deal with the Woodford Bank's court-appointed receiver whereby its assets would be transferred to a new institution, the Merchants and Peoples Bank. Moreover, to maintain a positive sense of continuity, the proposed Merchants and Peoples Bank would be housed at 3201 South State Street (the site of the old R. W. Woodford Bank).[16]

In 1921, when a new Illinois law that prohibited individual ownership of banks went into effect, Chavers dramatically enhanced his visibility in the realm of banking. Unlike Jesse Binga, who secured a state charter for his previously privately owned Binga Bank, Chavers announced his intent to seek a federal charter for the Merchants and Peoples Bank. While there existed few substantive differences between federal and state banks, Chavers apparently believed that securing a national charter, instead of a state charter, would enhance the reorganized bank's stature in the eyes of its potential depositors. This, in fact, was the first time that a black-controlled institution sought to become a national bank.[17]

More important than the issue of a federal versus state charter for the reorganized Merchants and Peoples Bank was P. W. Chavers's vision for the proposed new financial institution. As he reportedly told his brother-in-law, "after the bank is reorganized and operating on a sound basis, it will become a mighty force on the South Side making money available for mortgages. We will be able to buy property, build factories, provide steady employment, broaden the base of a Negro entrepreneurship and help Negro families improve and maintain properties they own."[18]

Significantly, Chavers's brother-in-law cautioned him that, despite his idealistic vision about the reorganized bank's impact, he would run into opposition. Chavers-Wright described this warning to her father as follows: "As I see it, by going into the banking business you are flirting with something quite dangerous . . . the envy of others around you . . . These Chicago people, white, black, and in-between, are jealous people. I know, I lived here many years before you came."[19]

Based upon Chavers-Wright's admissions regarding embellishments in *The Guarantee*, it remains questionable whether the above conversations took place as depicted. Also, additional research definitively indicates that Chavers-Wright's chronology of how the Merchants and Peoples Bank became the Douglass National Bank is incorrect.

In *The Guarantee*, Chavers-Wright states that her father, beginning in November 1921, began drafting speeches where, among other things, he suggested that the national bank be named after the venerable Frederick Douglass. Moreover, the following month, when questioned by his wife as to why he didn't the name the bank after himself, he allegedly replied: "I've been warned many times about fanning jealousy in Chicago. Remember what your brother George kept telling me? There is too much infighting among our people already; I don't want to incite any more." In addition, on that same December 1921 evening, P. W. Chavers reportedly told his wife: "I'm sure we'll get the permit Minnie. The Douglass National Bank will be the first of its kind, owned and operated by our people."[20]

An examination of contemporary newspapers indicates that the evolution from the Merchants and Peoples Bank to the Douglass National Bank took place much earlier in 1921. For example, the April 30, 1921, issue of the Chicago *Broad Ax* featured a small front-page article titled "The 1st National Bank among Colored People in the United States Opens in Chicago." Although the Douglass National Bank was not actually open for business in April 1921, the *Broad Ax* did inform its readers that the institution received its federal charter on April 27, 1921, and listed P. W. Chavers as its president.[21] This, among other things, indicates that Chavers, well before November 1921, had decided to name his proposed national bank after Frederick Douglass.

Two weeks later, in its May 14, 1921, issue, the *Broad Ax* listed the officers of this fledgling financial institution. Besides Chavers, Major Robert R. Jackson, alderman of Chicago's Third Ward, was cited as Douglass National Bank's vice president. Its board of directors included, as chairman, O. F. Smith, president of Citizens' Trust Bank (the only non–African American in the group); Rev. John W. Robinson, pastor of St. Mark's Methodist Episcopal Church; and physician Dr. Edward S. Miller. Significantly, Anthony Overton was not among the original officers of this bank.[22]

Chavers, by early 1921, had been successful in getting the federal charter for the Douglass National Bank. Nevertheless, he soon faced the even more daunting task of raising the $200,000 necessary for the bank to actually commence operations. Moreover, as Christopher Reed has cogently observed, while Chavers did receive the bank charter, the U.S. Office of the Comptroller of the Currency began raising "legitimate questions about the capabilities of the board of directors Chavers had assembled. These were basically inexperienced men in the world of banking who desired to operate an institution authorized under federal auspices."[23]

To address the issue of raising the necessary capitalization for the Douglass National Bank, Chavers undertook a grassroots stock-selling campaign. Chavers's plan to fund this institution, based upon stock sales to numerous smaller investors, reflected what Madrue Chavers-Wright has called her father's desire to create "a People's National Bank!"[24]

One of the techniques used by the embryonic Douglass National Bank to attract potential stockholders was featuring an informational booth at various community events. For example, as the June 11, 1921, issue of the *Broad Ax* noted, the Douglass National Bank's exhibit attracted the largest crowds at a festival held at the Eighth Regiment Armory. The visually striking display featured a poster outlining the history of African Americans surrounded by three portraits. According to the *Broad Ax*, "on the left of the sign appears a picture of the Sainted Frederick Douglass, 'typifying physical freedom,' in the center Booker T. Washington representing 'industrial freedom' and on the right a portrait of P. W. Chavers, president of the bank showing 'economic freedom,' the three great steps in the upward development of the race."[25]

In the short term, Chavers's attempts to generate grassroots interest in the Douglass National Bank appeared to be working. As the July 30, 1921, issue of the *Broad Ax* reported, at the bank's well-attended July 26 meeting of stockholders, Chavers, to stimulate even more stock sales, offered prizes to those that recruited additional investors. Also, while the Douglass National Bank would be housed in Chicago's South Side black enclave, Chavers did not ignore African Americans who resided in the city's West Side black community. As the September 10, 1921, issue of the

Broad Ax revealed, a recent bank-sponsored meeting held at the Friendship Baptist Church, located at Lake and Ada Streets, attracted a large crowd that "listened to several well delivered addresses on the most vital subject: 'the economic development of our group.'"[26]

By December 1921, according to the *Broad Ax*, interest in the Douglass National Bank had reached a fever pitch. In a December 3, 1921, article, titled "The Douglass National Bank," readers were informed that the bank's officers had just returned from a recent stock-selling campaign in Indianapolis where "the population turned out 'en masse' to welcome the bank representatives and indicated their interest by subscribing and paying for a large number of shares." Moreover, the *Broad Ax* continued by noting "similar meetings have been held in St. Louis and Detroit and Mr. Chavers and the board are much elated with the evident awakening of the race to its industrial and commercial needs and predict that within a short time we will obtain REAL freedom: That of economic emancipation." The *Broad Ax* concluded this upbeat assessment of the Douglass National Bank's progress by declaring that "all necessary equipment, such as pass books, check books, etc., have been ordered and will be installed as soon as the contractor completes the renovation of the building [at 3201 South State Street] and makes it ready for the formal opening early in January, 1922."[27]

By late 1921, national media, as well as local African American newspapers, were following the Douglass National Bank story. On December 7, 1921, the *New York Times* featured an article on the soon-to-be-opened institution. Citing a December 6, 1921, announcement by Chavers, Douglass National Bank's grand opening, scheduled for January 2, 1921, would include "a parade of more than 5,000 negro school children, members of churches and business organizations." Moreover, "store fronts and electric lamp posts along South State Street" would "be decorated with flags and bunting."[28]

Despite the growing hoopla surrounding what the December 10, 1921, issue of the *Chicago Defender* called "this huge move in the financial world,"[29] there existed growing discord within the Douglass National Bank's board of directors. While Chavers had promoted a democratic strategy of raising the $200,000 needed for capitalization, others, most notably Rev. John Robinson, sought to attract fewer, more financially established investors. Notwithstanding positive newspaper articles to the contrary, Chavers's preferred capitalization process had proceeded slowly, and by December 1921 the bank was still short of the money needed to officially open its doors. Moreover, Chavers's December 6, 1921, announcement regarding a January 2, 1922, grand opening parade further complicated the situation. Thus, to help avert both public embarrassment and financial disaster, Reverend Robinson approached Anthony Overton about joining the Douglass National Bank's board and being the institution's chief investor.[30]

Chavers's apparent failure to raise the capital necessary for the Douglass National Bank to open had implications that remain relevant to this day. One of the historic questions about African American business and economic development is whether it should be an inclusive process involving a large number of individuals pooling their resources, or a process dominated by a few entrepreneurially minded individuals. In this particular instance, since Chavers's democratic model of capital accumulation was not achieving the desired result, the recruitment of Anthony Overton to join the Douglass National Bank's board appeared eminently pragmatic.

Anthony Overton, by late 1921, had positioned himself as the leading African American entrepreneur in the Windy City. After moving to Chicago in 1911, he successfully expanded the operations of the Overton Hygienic Manufacturing Company. Also, in 1913 Overton assumed the presidency of the Chicago Negro Business League. Under his leadership, the Chicago Negro Business League became affiliated with the Chicago Chamber of Commerce. This prompted the *Chicago Defender* to declare in its March 7, 1914, issue that "the Chicago league is now one of the strongest branches of the nation's Negro Business League."[31] In addition, Overton's skillful use of *The Half-Century Magazine*, which he established in 1916 to promote various Overton Hygienic Manufacturing Company products, represented another catalyst for his commercial success and visibility.

Unfortunately, the business records of Overton Hygienic are not extant. However, Dun & Bradstreet, the preeminent business financial reporting agency, provides an important alternative way to assess the growing profitability of Overton's cornerstone enterprise.

Before the appearance of *Half-Century*, relevant Dun & Bradstreet reports reveal that Overton Hygienic was a moderately successful enterprise. In 1912, the year of the company's first appearance in the *Dun & Bradstreet Reference Book*, Overton Hygienic received a financial strength rating of E (signifying company assets in the range of $20,000–$35,000) and a credit rating of 2½, or "good." Three years later, in 1915, Overton Hygienic received a financial strength rating of D+ (reflecting company assets in the range of $50,000–$75,000) and a credit rating of 2, or "good."[32]

After the 1916 appearance of *The Half-Century Magazine*, subsequent editions of the *Dun & Bradstreet Reference Book* revealed Overton Hygienic's steady ascent as a commercial enterprise. In 1917 Dun & Bradstreet gave Overton Hygienic a financial strength rating of C+ (conveying company assets in the range of $125,000–$200,000) and a credit rating of 1, or "high" (the top rating). Three years later, in 1920, Overton Hygienic received a financial strength rating of B (reflecting company assets in the range of $200,000–$300,000) and a credit rating of 1, or "high." In 1922 the *Dun & Bradstreet Reference Book* gave the Overton Hygienic Manufacturing

Company a financial strength rating of B+ (signifying company assets in the range of $300,000–$500,000) and a credit rating of 1, or "high."[33]

Besides Overton's growing stature as an entrepreneur, which prompted Rev. John W. Robinson to approach him about joining the Douglass National Bank board, Overton accepted the invitation because he had a long-standing interest in banking. Notwithstanding an unsubstantiated personal claim that he founded the Bank of Wanamaker in the Oklahoma territory in 1892,[34] Overton and other local Black Chicago entrepreneurs took over the affairs of the Home Security Savings Bank in 1913. According to the June 21, 1913, issue of the *Chicago Defender*, Overton and his colleagues served as trustees of this institution, previously the South Side branch of a white-controlled bank, "to protect the interests of the colored subscribers and depositors."[35]

Besides Overton's direct involvement with Home Security Savings, he indirectly expressed his interest in banking through *The Half-Century Magazine*. Along with using this periodical to promote his various commercial products, Overton, employing the pseudonym "McAdoo Baker," also used this periodical to promote his beliefs regarding African American economic development. One of his contributions in this genre was an article titled "Banks," which appeared in the January 1919 issue of *The Half-Century Magazine*. This essay not only educated readers on how banks operated, but also stressed the need for "a bank in Chicago under Colored ownership and management."[36]

To Baker, it made absolutely no sense for blacks in Chicago to have millions of dollars in the city's white-owned banks, when "very rarely can a loan be secured from any of the [white] banks of our city, by any of our people."[37] In addition, Baker decried white banks' concurrent acceptance of black deposits and their refusal "to give any of our people employment." Finally, to make matters worse, Baker asserted that "these same Negro funds are *loaned to white* business institutions, that likewise would not give employment to one of our race in any capacity. The Negro's money is used to close the door of opportunity in his own face."[38] Significantly, Baker's assessment of Black Chicago's relationship with white-owned banks, as analogous with economic suicide, would be echoed by later observers of African American economic history.[39]

Baker concluded his article on banks by asserting that black Chicagoans needed a financial institution where they could "gather into large workable funds, the deposits of our people so that the same can likewise be loaned in turn to our people at a *reasonable* rate on their real estate by mortgage securities or to our business people to encourage their race business development."[40]

Besides Overton's financial stature and long-standing interest in banking, Reverend Robinson sought Overton's involvement with the Douglass National Bank because he had been informed that "Washington officials wanted someone who was either Caucasian or an African American of Anthony Overton's financial stature to head the bank."[41] When Robinson shared this information with Chavers, Chavers dismissed it. After his enormous investment of time and energy, Chavers apparently could not accept the fact that the bank could not open with him as its president.

In February 1922, Chavers requested an extension from the deputy comptroller of the currency, hoping that he could both generate the funding necessary to open the Douglass National Bank and regain the confidence of Reverend Robinson and other recalcitrant board members. Unfortunately for Chavers, this strategy failed and in April he reluctantly agreed to accept Anthony Overton as a bank board member.[42]

In a last-ditch effort to salvage his weakening stature within the embryonic Douglass National Bank, in June Chavers decided to circumvent Chicago obstacles and use his Ohio political contacts to secure the sought-after federal bank charter. In fact, with the assistance of fellow Ohioan President Warren G. Harding, during a trip to Washington, D.C., Chavers, did indeed secure a finalized federal charter for the Douglass National Bank on June 27, 1922.[43]

On the surface, it appeared that P. W. Chavers's trip to Washington, D.C., had generated a major personal victory. Against all odds, including the opposition of some Douglass National Bank board members, he had persevered and won. Yet, upon his return to Chicago, Chavers's exhilaration and sense of vindication turned to dismay and shock.

According to Chavers-Wright, the Douglass National Bank opened its doors for business on June 29, 1922.[44] Moreover, she asserts that on July 10, 1922, at the Douglass National Bank's initial board meeting after officially commencing operations, the first order of business was a motion for Chavers to resign from the presidency and to accept a noncompensated vice president position. Apparently, while Chavers was in Washington, the board had elected Anthony Overton as the bank's new president. In recounting this episode, in a chapter titled "The Coup," Chavers-Wright contended that the Douglass board of directors, who wanted to be rid of Chavers, offered him an insulting proposal "that they knew he would be too embarrassed to accept." Their strategy seemingly worked when Chavers stormed out of the meeting.[45]

While there is no doubt that the Douglass National Bank board of directors sought to remove Pearl William Chavers as its president, the evidence suggests that Chavers was not as totally unaware of their intentions as *The Guarantee* implies. In fact, Chavers-Wright's depiction of what took place on July 10, 1922, apparently represents an instance where she "fictionalized . . . certain incidents and details, and much of the dialogue, for the purpose of drama."[46]

On Saturday, July 8, 1922, the *Chicago Defender* featured a story headlined "National Bank to Open Soon on South Side," which included the subheadline

"Pioneer Institution to Have Formal Opening July 12, Overton Is Head." Moreover, the article, besides explicitly citing Anthony Overton as the bank's president, listed P. W. Chavers as simply a member of the board of directors.[47] Considering the hoopla surrounding the opening of the Douglass National Bank and the *Chicago Defender*'s role as the top black newspaper in the city, it appears *highly unlikely* that P. W. Chavers was *not* aware of this article before he attended the Monday, July 10, 1922, board meeting.

In her book *The Guarantee*, Madrue Chavers-Wright focused upon the treachery of the Douglass National Bank's board of directors in its ouster of her father from the bank's leadership. While the board's summary dismissal of her father was indeed stunning, the evidence suggests that they may have been emboldened by the U.S. government's tacit approval of this action. In recounting her father's reaction to the July 10, 1922, Douglass National Bank board of directors meeting, Wright-Chavers asserted that the other board members' attitude toward P. W. Chavers was "that he had acted for the bank in securing the charter like an ordinary political emissary."[48] Considering long-standing government concerns about the original constitution of the bank's board of directors, it is not implausible to suggest that, at the very time Chavers was in Washington securing the charter, the Douglass National Bank board of directors informed the comptroller of the currency that Anthony Overton would assume the leadership of this historic African American financial institution. Moreover, the government's response to a subsequent lawsuit filed by P. W. Chavers against the Douglass National Bank insinuates that it approved of the simultaneous ascent and descent of Anthony Overton and Pearl William Chavers, respectively, within the Douglass National Bank's administrative hierarchy.

On November 22, 1922, Chavers filed a suit in federal court against the Douglass National Bank claiming that "the bank is insolvent, that its charter was fraudulently obtained, and a move is on to unfairly and illegally dispose of its assets." Specifically, Chavers's lawsuit contended that "the officers of the bank are planning to float a bond issue totaling some $175,000, practically all of the bank's capital, for the construction of a building at 36th Place and State Street for the Overton Building Company whose head is Anthony Overton. Mr. Overton is also president of the Douglass bank."[49]

For his part, Overton told the *Chicago Defender* that he had been asked to take charge of the Douglass National Bank after "Chavers had struggled for a year." Moreover, he declared: "the charge that the bank is insolvent is absurd. The National bank department would not permit us to run a day if we were insolvent." Finally, Overton responded to Chavers's charge that the bank charter had been secured through fraudulent means by reminding the former president that Chavers himself had singularly undertaken that task. [50]

Chavers received a crushing defeat a month after filing his lawsuit, when the case was thrown out of court. As the *Chicago Defender* reported in its December 23, 1922, article "Bank O.K.; Court Suit Is Stopped," the Douglass National Bank had been thoroughly examined by the comptroller of the currency and was found "to be solvent and in splendid condition." Moreover, to the embarrassment of P. W. Chavers, the *Defender* continued, "Comptroller Crissinger complimented Anthony Overton, president of the bank, and the officers upon the wonderful showing the institution had made during the first six months of business."[51]

Even before the administratively reconfigured Douglass National Bank received legal vindication in late 1922, Overton used *The Half-Century Magazine* to extol his rise to the institution's presidency. For instance, beginning with the July–August 1922 issue of *The Half-Century Magazine* and continuing until the magazine's (final) January–February 1925 issue, the inside cover of the periodical featured a prominent full-page advertisement of the Overton-led Douglass National Bank.[52] Moreover, the July–August 1922 issue of *Half-Century* contained a full-page article on the newly formed Douglass Bank that included this favorable assessment of its president: "The same wisdom and commercial ability that popularized and made profitable the sale of High Brown Toilet Preparations and the same sound judgment and integrity that placed the Overton Hygienic Company in the first rank among commercial institutions, regardless of color, is guiding the Douglass National Bank to its rightful place among the foremost banking institutions of the world."[53] This, among other things, conveyed the notion that, unlike Chavers's previous vision of "the People's National Bank," the newly opened financial institution would be intrinsically linked with the business persona of Anthony Overton.

In its September–October 1922 issue, *The Half-Century Magazine* featured a short editorial, "Have You Seen Them?," which declared "there are some new bank notes in circulation that should attract and hold the attention of the entire race." With undisguised pride, the *Half-Century* continued, "these bright, new, crispy banknotes are being issued by the United States government through the Douglass National Bank of Chicago in denominations of $5.00 and more. These bills are worthless unless they bear the signature of Anthony Overton, the president of the bank. The Douglass National Bank is the first Colored Organization ever granted the privilege of putting money into circulation."[54]

The Half-Century Magazine's November–December 1922 issue provided readers with even more encouraging news about the newly opened Douglass National Bank. In an editorial called "A Monument to Racial Industry," it announced that ground had been broken for a new commercial structure that would house several African American enterprises, including the Douglass National Bank and the Overton Hygienic Manufacturing Company. Moreover, to help minimize negative publicity associated with P. W. Chavers's then pending lawsuit against the Douglass

National Bank, *Half-Century* presented this construction project as a racial victory. Besides contending that the new Overton Building, when completed, would be "the finest structure of its kind owned by Negroes," the magazine claimed that "it is impossible to place a monetary value on this very interesting building project—for its value to the race is immeasurable."[55]

Ironically, although P. W. Chavers had literally been removed from the Douglass National Bank's administrative team after the July 10, 1922, board of directors meeting, his name still appeared (as a vice president) in full-page bank advertisements that appeared in the July–August and September–October issues of *The Half-Century Magazine*. However, his name disappeared from the ad in the November–December issue, which, not coincidentally, occurred at the time he filed his lawsuit against the institution.[56] In the final analysis, by the end of 1922 the Douglass National Bank had become an integral part of Anthony Overton's growing financial empire and an embittered P. W. Chavers had to reorganize his commercial and personal life.

Notwithstanding his harsh experience with the Douglass National Bank, which caused him to reflect that maybe his wife had been right in suggesting that he name the fledgling institution after himself,[57] a later Chavers project, the establishment of a campsite and resort in rural Wisconsin for blacks, represented another instance where his strong commitment to racial uplift worked to his financial detriment.

In 1926 Chavers assumed a mortgage to purchase six thousand acres of land in Langland County, Wisconsin, which he subsequently named Camp Madrue (after his daughter). Wright-Chavers recalled her father's motivation for this project: "P. W. thought of the thousands of black children playing in the dingy alleys of Chicago and how this camp, with its clean, unspoiled environment, beautiful acreage, mineral water, pure air, and plenty of sunshine, which were sorely needed by many, would provide a respite from the harsh reality of the urban slums."[58]

Regardless of Chavers's laudable intentions regarding Camp Madrue, he, similar to his earlier efforts with the Douglass National Bank, experienced difficulty in raising money to fully develop the campsite. Although Chavers charged fees for the youth campers and offered lots for sale to adults, the rates were extremely low. Chavers's actions in this regard allegedly prompted his wife to assert that "she spent as much for a single dancing lesson for one of her children as he was charging for a full week of room and board at the camp."[59]

Despite his wife's misgivings, Chavers continued in his quest to keep "his life-long promise to himself to do something really important for colored children and to bring happiness in their lives."[60] During the economic boom period of the late 1920s, Chavers, through his contacts, was able to keep Camp Madrue financially afloat. However, the Wall Street crash of October 1929 would have a negative effect not only on P. W. Chavers and Camp Madrue, but also on Anthony Overton and the Douglass National Bank.

By June 1930, in the midst of worsening economic conditions, P. W. reluctantly accepted the fact that his vision of a "Camp for Colored Children" would not come to pass. On August 5, 1930, that realization became confirmed when the Citizens Trust and Savings Bank, which funded Chavers's land purchase in Wisconsin, closed after a run on the bank by worried depositors depleted its reserves. As Wright-Chavers noted, "with this, Daddy's equity in most of his real estate was wiped out."[61]

While the demise of P. W. Chavers's Camp Madrue was a relatively obscure consequence of the Great Depression, the concurrent failure of Overton's Douglass National Bank sent shockwaves throughout Chicago and the country. On the eve of Wall Street's collapse, some commentators began referring to Overton as "the Merchant Prince of His Race."[62] In fact, from a business standpoint, he appeared to have the proverbial Midas touch. Besides presiding over a national bank and a thriving personal-care-products manufacturing company, he had added the Victory Life Insurance Company to his business conglomerate. Moreover, in 1927 Victory Life made history by becoming the first black insurer qualified to do business in the state of New York.[63]

Ironically, considering his business savvy, Overton's missteps regarding both the Douglass National Bank and the Victory Life Insurance Company contributed to both enterprises' problems. When the Douglass National Bank commenced operations in 1922 and Victory Life began two years later, both institutions directed a significant amount of money (in the form of bank loans and investment capital) toward real estate in the African American community. At the time, this appeared to be a profitable strategy, because the 1920s represented a boom period for the real estate market. However, when real estate values plummeted with the onset of the Great Depression, both Douglass National and Victory Life possessed dramatically depreciated assets.[64] Moreover, in the case of the Douglass National Bank, some of its now cash-strapped borrowers were unable to make payments on their mortgages. For instance, as Abram Harris noted in his classic 1936 study of African American banks, *The Negro as Capitalist*, several black churches and lodges defaulted on substantial loans they had received.[65]

In all fairness to Anthony Overton, he was not the only person fooled by the 1920s real estate bubble. However, his funneling of Victory Life Insurance Company funds into the Douglass National Bank reflected what Merah S. Stuart referred to as Overton's "perplexing entanglements of the affairs of the two institutions."[66] Moreover, the subsequent negative public reaction to Overton's machinations no doubt provided P. W. Chavers with a sense of vindication regarding his earlier, albeit unsubstantiated, critique of Anthony Overton's business practices.

Although the Douglass National Bank and the Victory Life Insurance Company were two separate business entities, Overton clearly felt compelled to use Victory Life funds to support not just the Douglass National Bank, but also family members. In January 1927, Overton took $70,000 from Victory Life to invest in Douglass National Bank stock. Although the New York Department of Insurance expressed their displeasure with this transaction, Overton disregarded this concern and orchestrated another $60,000 Victory Life investment in the Douglass National Bank. To make matters worse, a June 30, 1931, examination of the Victory Life Insurance Company not only revealed its possession of diminished-in-value Douglass National Bank stock, but also two personal loans that used Douglass National Bank stock as collateral: "one for $40,000 to Overton's daughters, and a personal loan of $15,000 in the name of George A. Gaughn, who was subsequently found to be Overton himself."[67]

In an interesting twist of circumstance, Overton, who assumed the presidency of the Douglass National Bank through an apparent coup against P. W. Chavers in 1922, suffered a similar fate ten years later when the New York directors of Victory Life coordinated his ouster as president. Later, on April 5, 1933, the firm was reorganized as the Victory Mutual Life Insurance Company.[68]

Besides suffering the public humiliation of being removed from the presidency of Victory Life in 1932, Overton, during that same year, witnessed the closing of the Douglass National Bank. Despite a $200,000 loan from the Hoover administration's Reconstruction Finance Corporation, problems with the institution's troubled loan portfolio prompted it to close its doors on May 23, 1932. The bright spot in this bleak scenario was the fact that the Douglass National Bank did not cease operations as a totally insolvent institution. Thus subsequent court-appointed receivers were able to protect the bank's remaining assets and, "upon completing a series of liquidations, depositors received almost all of their original savings."[69]

An apparent irony associated with the demise of the Douglass National Bank was that a 1924 legislative initiative, originated by Pearl W. Chavers, could have theoretically help saved the bank from disaster.

In the wake of being dismissed from the Douglass National Bank presidency in 1922, Chavers drafted a document he called "The Chavers Plan for Guaranteeing Bank Deposits." In this proposal, he called for federal legislation that required national banks to "furnish surety bonds for the protection of depositors." According to Chavers, this would guarantee the safety of bank deposits by requiring banks to secure "a bond in the amount equal to the total amount of capital stock." The apparent motivation for Chavers's efforts in this regard, as reflected in his ill-fated November 1922 suit against the Douglass National Bank, was his belief that Overton sought to misuse bank funds.[70]

With the support of Illinois congressman Thomas A. Doyle, "The Chavers Plan for Guaranteeing Bank Deposits" formed the basis of H.R. Bill 8977 submitted to Congress on April 30, 1924.[71] During the prosperous 1920s, "deposit guaranty legislation was unpopular for political reasons" and H.R. Bill 8977 languished in the House subcommittee on Banking and Currency. However, during the early 1930s, in the midst of a worsening economic situation, Chavers's brainchild and later similar bills were melded together to form the cornerstone of the Banking Act of 1933. Thus Chavers's efforts played a contributing role in the subsequent establishment of the Federal Deposit Insurance Corporation (FDIC).[72]

In the end, the roles of Pearl W. Chavers and Anthony Overton in the founding of the Douglass National Bank remain in the realm of contested terrain. On one hand, Chavers clearly was the originator of the *idea* of a black national bank in Chicago and worked tirelessly to bring his vision to fruition. Yet a bank is more than an intellectual creation; it is also a physical entity that engages in a variety of commercial transactions. Thus, based upon the apparent limitations of Chavers's capitalization plan, as well as concerns about his credentials to head a major financial institution, Douglass's board of directors, as well as the U.S. comptroller of the currency, concluded that Anthony Overton was better suited to preside over this historic African American enterprise. Consequently, when the bank *actually* opened its doors for business, Overton and not Chavers stood as its president. Nevertheless, Overton's ascension to the bank's presidency later proved to be a dual-edged sword. When the Douglass National Bank unceremoniously closed its doors in 1932, Overton, the former "Merchant Prince of His Race," became directly associated with business failure. Thus Chavers's initial vision of a democratically owned black national bank and Overton's later quest to expand his personal business empire were both short-lived.

Notes

1. "American Business Leaders of the Twentieth Century," accessed December 19, 2016, at http://www.hbs.edu/leadership/database/leaders/Anthony_Overton.html.

2. Abram L. Harris, *The Negro as Capitalist: A Study of Banking and Business among American Negroes* (Chicago: Urban Research Institute, 1992; orig. pub. 1936), 173. According to Harris's definitive study of the history of African American banks, the first black-controlled national bank was the First National Bank of Boley (Oklahoma).

3. Some of the works that cite Overton as the organizer and founder of the Douglass National Bank include Dewey R. Jones, "Chicago Claims Supremacy," *Opportunity: A Journal of Negro Life* 7 (March 1929): 93; Deton J. Brooks Jr., "From Slave to Wealth Is Story of Overton," *Chicago Defender*, December 26, 1942, 13; "Anthony Overton," obituary, *The Journal of Negro History* 32 (July 1947): 394–96; John N. Ingham and Lynne B. Feldman, *African-American Business Leaders: A Biographical Dictionary* (Westport, CT: Greenwood

Press, 1994), 495; Juliet E. K. Walker, ed., *Encyclopedia of African American Business History* (Westport, CT: Greenwood Press, 1999), n.p.

4. Jones, "Chicago Claims Supremacy," 93.

5. "Anthony Overton," obituary, 394. This obituary provided an incorrect (1923) opening date for the Douglass National Bank; it commenced business in 1922.

6. Ingham and Feldman, *African-American Business Leaders*, 495; Walker, *Encyclopedia of African American Business History*, n.p.

7. Madrue Chavers-Wright, *The Guarantee: P. W. Chavers: Banker, Entrepreneur, Philanthropist in Chicago's Black Belt of the Twenties* (New York: Wright-Armstead Associates, 1985), xviii.

8. Ibid., 13.

9. Ibid., 14, 19.

10. Ibid., 19–20.

11. Ibid., 20, 22.

12. Ibid., 25, 27.

13. Ibid., 39.

14. Ibid., 40.

15. Harris, *The Negro as Capitalist*, 173.

16. Christopher Robert Reed, *The Rise of Chicago's Black Metropolis, 1920–1929* (Urbana: University of Illinois Press, 2011), 88.

17. Ibid., 89.

18. Chavers-Wright, *The Guarantee*, 54.

19. Ibid., 53.

20. Ibid., 74–77. This incorrect chronology also appears in Christopher Reed's important study *The Rise of Chicago's Black Metropolis, 1920–1929*, 89.

21. "The 1st National Bank among Colored People in the United States Opens in Chicago," *Broad Ax*, April 30, 1921, 1.

22. "The Douglass National Bank: Will Soon Throw Its Doors Open for Business at Thirty-Second and State Streets," *Broad Ax*, May 14, 1921, 1.

23. Reed, *The Rise of Chicago's Black Metropolis*, 89–90.

24. Chavers-Wright, *The Guarantee*, 74.

25. "The Douglass National Bank," *Broad Ax*, June 11, 1921, 3.

26. "The First Stockholders Meeting of the Douglass National Bank," *Broad Ax*, July 30, 1921, 2; "Big Meetings Are Being Held in the Interest of the Douglass National Bank," *Broad Ax*, September 10, 1921, 1.

27. "The Douglass National Bank," *Broad Ax*, December 3, 1921, 2.

28. "Negroes to Open Bank," *New York Times*, December 7, 1921, 19.

29. "Douglass Bank to Open with Big Street Parade," *Chicago Defender*, December 10, 1921, 4.

30. Reed, *The Rise of Chicago's Black Metropolis*, 90.

31. "Business League Banquets at Pullman Club," *Chicago Defender*, March 7, 1914, 4.

32. *Dun & Bradstreet Reference Book*, vol. 177, 1912, part 1, 62 (Illinois listing); ibid., vol. 187, 1915, part 1, 46 (Illinois listing).

33. Ibid., vol. 197, July 1917, part 1, 49 (Illinois listing); vol. 207, January 1920, part 1, 53 (Illinois listing); vol. 218, September 1922, part 1, 53 (Illinois listing).

34. John McKinley, "Anthony Overton: A Man Who Planned for Success," *Reflexus* 1 (April 1925): 14. Wanamaker was a small boomtown associated with the Oklahoma Territory land rush of 1889. Notwithstanding Overton's later declarations, the fact that Jimmie Franklin did not even mention Overton in *Journey toward Hope: A History of Blacks in Oklahoma* (his definitive study of the subject) suggests Overton's lack of veracity regarding this issue.

35. "The Home Bank Has Money to Pay Creditors," *Chicago Defender*, June 21, 1913, 1.

36. McAdoo Baker, "Banks," *The Half-Century Magazine* 6 (January 1919): 9.

37. Ibid.

38. Ibid.

39. A classic example of this genre is Merah S. Stuart's 1940 book *An Economic Detour: A History of Insurance in the Lives of American Negroes*. On pages 37–38, he discussed what happens when African Americans buy insurance from white companies versus black ones. "Every one of the $248, 910 paid [weekly] into Negro companies is free to perform its natural function of helping to create employment to which the qualified among the group that spends it is eligible. Every one of the $995,640 paid [weekly] by Negroes into white companies, as soon as paid over the line, becomes earmarked for discrimination against employment of the group that spends it; and the employment these dollars help create is forbidden fruit to the sons and daughters of those who each week unthoughtfully pay this price to keep the doors of opportunity closed against their own."

40. Ibid.

41. Reed, *The Rise of Chicago's Black Metropolis*, 90–91.

42. Chavers-Wright, *The Guarantee*, 136, 141.

43. Ibid., 154.

44. Ibid., 154–55.

45. Ibid., 157–59.

46. Ibid., xviii.

47. "National Bank to Open Soon on South Side," *Chicago Defender*, July 8, 1922, 2.

48. Ibid., 158.

49. "Douglass Bank's Affairs Thrown into U.S. Court," *Chicago Defender*, November 25, 1922, 2.

50. Ibid.

51. "Bank O.K.; Court Suit Is Stopped," *Chicago Defender*, December 23, 1922, 3.

52. *The Half-Century Magazine*. Volumes 13–18 (July–August 1917 through January–February 1925) of the magazine each featured a full-page advertisement for the Overton-led Douglass National Bank.

53. "The Douglass National Bank," *The Half-Century Magazine* 13 (July–August 1922): 6.

54. "Have You Seen Them?" *The Half-Century Century Magazine* 13 (September–October 1922): 3.

55. "A Monument to Racial Industry," *The Half-Century Magazine* 13 (November–December 1922): 3.

56. Advertisement for the Douglass National Bank, *The Half-Century Magazine* 13 (July–August 1922): 2; (September–October 1922): 2; (November–December 1922): 2.

57. Chavers-Wright, *The Guarantee,* 164–65.

58. Ibid., 299.

59. Ibid., 307.

60. Ibid., 301.

61. Ibid., 355.

62. "From Clerk in His Dad's Store to the Topmost Rung of Success," *Pittsburgh Courier*, August 10, 1929, A8.

63. Merah S. Stuart, *An Economic Detour: A History of Insurance in the Lives of American Negroes* (College Park, MD: McGrath, 1969; orig. pub. 1940), 94–95.

64. Ingham and Feldman, *African-American Business Leaders*, 497.

65. Harris, *The Negro as Capitalist*, 181.

66. Stuart, *An Economic Detour*, 96.

67. Ingham and Feldman, *African-American Business Leaders*, 497.

68. Ibid.; Stuart, *An Economic Detour*, 97.

69. Christopher Robert Reed, *The Depression Comes to the South Side: Protest and Politics in the Black Metropolis, 1930–1933* (Bloomington: Indiana University Press, 2011), 21.

70. Chavers-Wright, *The Guarantee*, 167. The title of this book was derived from Chavers's plan to guarantee the safety of bank deposits.

71. Ibid., 281.

72. Ibid., 392–93, 409.

CHAPTER 5

King of Selling

The Rise and Fall of S. B. Fuller

CLOVIS E. SEMMES

S. B. Fuller was one of the most successful African American businessmen of the twentieth century, basing his commercial empire in Chicago's historic Bronzeville community on the South Side. Fuller's business model was door-to-door/direct sales of personal and beauty care items. Initially, a racially segregated political, social, and economic structure restricted Fuller's markets to black consumers. However, from his core business of direct sales to blacks, Fuller generated the cash to purchase and invest in other companies, which included franchisee relationships. This enabled Fuller to diversify his product line and expand his core businesses to reach the white consumer market. Fuller's unprecedented business success influenced his philosophy of how African American entrepreneurship should evolve. Specifically, he became an outspoken critic of race-focused business organizations and enterprises. However, white racism, existing structures of inequality, and the declining effectiveness of direct sales ultimately eroded Fuller's competitive and profitable position in the marketplace. His story reveals historic challenges to black entrepreneurship in black communities and in American society generally. Because of his unique and pioneering accomplishments, S. B. Fuller remains a central figure in the history of black business development and the entrepreneurial legacy of Chicago's African American community.[1]

The Rise of S. B. Fuller

S. B. Fuller was born June 4, 1905, in Ouachita Parish in the northeastern section of Louisiana, about six miles from Monroe.[2] Fuller's mother, Ethel Johnson, and father, William Fuller, had eight children, including S. B. Their last child died at birth.[3] The Fullers were tenant farmers, and father William later became involved in commercial fishing. S. B. saw his father engage in farming, hunting, fishing, and bartering to sell syrup, vegetables, fresh eggs, and fish at market. Seeing his father's independence in a segregated and racially oppressive South probably contributed to S. B.'s drive to become an independent businessman. Fuller's eldest daughter, Mary, explained that S. B. was mostly known by the two initials S. B., but was at times called Sexton, sometimes pronounced Session, and his mother called him Buddy.[4] Writers and scholars have referred to Fuller as S. B. or Samuel B. Fuller.

William and Ethel Fuller moved their family to Memphis, Tennessee, in 1920. When Ethel died and William left the family, S. B., the oldest child, took on the responsibility of caring for his younger siblings. It was during this period that S. B. started selling household items (Keystone Products) door-to-door, which he purchased via mail order. It was through door-to-door sales that S. B. met Lorena Elizabeth Whitfield. She was one of nine children that had grown up in Hernando, Mississippi, but her parents, Oliver Whitfield and Mary Dockery Whitfield, moved the family to Memphis. S. B. and Lorena married in 1923; both were eighteen years old, and Lorena was willing to help S. B. care for his siblings.[5]

Fuller continued to sell Keystone Products but added selling women's dresses directly to his customers. S. B. provided his clients with a layaway plan and created a thriving business. However, white merchants began to complain, and the white sheriff told S. B. that blacks should not try to do business and that he could go to the lumberyard and take a job as a lumber inspector. At this point, S. B. decided to leave Memphis and go to Chicago, one of many urban areas in the North that had become attractive to southern migrants attempting to escape the economic degradation and racial oppression of the South. S. B. started out walking to Chicago but was able to hitch a ride most of the way. He left the money he had saved with his wife, who was expecting their third child, a son, McKinley, who would later die at the age of three. S. B. arrived in Chicago on May 12, 1928. At first he tried working in the steel mills of Gary, Indiana, but soon left to take a job delivering coal. This job enabled S. B. to bring his family to Chicago by September. However, the family struggled and moved frequently during the Depression.[6] Later, selling would become S. B.'s saving grace.

By 1932, S. B. and Lorena had four daughters when S. B. became manager of the coal yard where he had delivered coal. His new position gave him some additional time to reflect. S. B. began to read and seriously study a set of books on *The Art and*

Science of Selling. The white owner of the coal yard learned that S. B. had a dream of becoming a salesman and expressed to S. B. that he did not want him to become frustrated since such a position, he felt, was not suited for a "colored man." S. B. reacted by quitting his job at the coal yard but stayed on without pay until his boss could find a replacement. S. B. explained that he did not want security, because "Where there is security there can be no freedom."[7] Subsequently, S. B. worked various jobs until he landed employment as a salesman for the black-owned Commonwealth Burial Association Insurance Company. Here S. B. began to apply his ideas about increasing the size and effectiveness of the sales force to increase profits. It was also during this period that S. B. overcame his poor speaking abilities. He had a limited vocabulary, stammered, and had a lisp. With hard work and self-study, S. B. became an adept motivational speaker. He also met the woman who would become his second wife and business partner, Lestine (Lesterine) Thornton, a native of Pittsburgh, Pennsylvania. Notably, S. B. routinely researched the salaries of corporate presidents and found that of the group he was studying, the president of a soap company made the most money. Consequently, S. B. decided to leave the insurance business to sell soap.[8] His life would change dramatically.

In 1935 Fuller invested his meager bankroll of $25, as the *Chicago Defender* newspaper explained, "in a pitifully small, and relatively unknown stock of powders, face creams and lotions." Fuller found a soap company that was going out of business and purchased what he could of its inventory at a discount. His assistant and future wife helped him to remove the company's name from the soap with sandpaper. S. B. had new wrappers printed with the name "Fuller's Quality Soap." He had the foresight to copyright the name "Fuller's Quality," which helped him to win a legal battle over it with a competitor at a later date. During this venture, S. B. sold soap so fast that he could hardly keep up with demand. S. B. wanted to expand into additional commodities and found another company that sold cosmetics and other goods, Hindu Products Company, that wasn't doing well. S. B. packaged and sold only the cosmetics. He saved the profits from his door-to-door sales and within a year established the Fuller Products Company.[9]

S. B. wanted to manufacture his own products and began to do so by hand with the help of several workers that he had hired, including Lestine. Fuller first located his business in the *Chicago Defender* building at 3441–3443 South Indiana in 1936 (the *Defender* later moved to 2400 South Michigan Avenue). S. B. made subsequent moves to 428 East Thirty-Fifth Street and to 6245 South Cottage Grove, which provided more space for machinery to manufacture Fuller's products. When shopping for machinery, S. B. learned that Boyer International Laboratories was available for purchase. Boyer, a white-owned company with white employees, sold Jean Nadal cosmetics for women, a hair dressing called Hair Arranger, the Alden Scott men's line, and other merchandise distributed to beauty supply houses and beauty shops and barbershops. Boyer's clientele were primarily white and in the South. S. B. handled the sale with discretion, and not many whites knew that a black man owned the company. When Fuller purchased Boyer, its building, machinery, and employees became his. Thus Fuller was able to operate his business enterprises from Boyer's seven-story, 91,000-square-foot building located at 2700–2710 South Wabash. The Boyer building became the Fuller building. S. B. kept the Boyer operation separate from his existing enterprise, maintaining them as two distinct companies. After the acquisition of Boyer, Fuller's product line and market expanded significantly.[10] Moreover, Fuller's early relationship with the *Chicago Defender* would continue at critical points in his career. John Sengstacke, editor and publisher of the *Defender*, would become a business partner and investor in Fuller enterprises, as well as a vocal and consistent supporter.[11]

By 1948, Fuller had established a convention to bring his employees together. He became widely recognized for his ability to recruit, maintain, and motivate an efficient and effective sales force. Fuller was lauded for giving blacks and whites the opportunity to become entrepreneurs and to make a good living.[12] Reportedly, Fuller Products had twenty-four branches across the country in 1949 and 1,000 dealers who sold door-to-door. At the Fuller Products convention in 1949, top producers divided prizes totaling $2,500. At Fuller's 1951 convention, an estimated 1,700 salesmen attended and branches competed for a huge gold-and-marble trophy. At this convention, Fuller awarded prizes that included trips to Paris, Hawaii, and Los Angeles. Meetings took on the character of pep rallies and religious revivals, and the company claimed a nationwide sales force of nearly 5,000. The pep meeting and banquet for the convention in 1951 were held at the Gold Room of the Congress Hotel in Chicago, and individual sessions were held at Fuller headquarters, 2700 South Wabash. The banquet for the 1951 convention featured the original creations of Mrs. Oteal Sharpe Elliott, founder of the Oteal School of Dressmaking and Design in Chicago. Fuller had recently added the Oteal line to his door-to-door sales. Oteal Sharpe Elliot was subsequently cited at the Eighth Conference on the Negro in Business in Washington, D.C., April 16–18, 1953, for her outstanding achievement in designing and manufacturing. Fuller also acquired Rose Meta cosmetics company and added its products to his door-to-door sales. Subsequent convention banquets were held at the Grand Ballroom of the Palmer House Hotel. At the 1955 convention, eighty-five branch managers from nearly a dozen states read reports; there were approximately 1,500 attendees, and top salespeople received prizes of fine jewelry and household items.[13]

Reports from successive conventions and meetings, new acquisitions, and new appointments illustrated the steady growth and prominence of the Fuller Products conglomerate throughout the 1950s. White millionaire W. Clement Stone, the positive-thought guru and philanthropist, was a featured speaker at the 1956 convention; Fuller, however, gave the keynote address. By 1957, Fuller Products claimed one hundred branches in thirty-eight states and more than 6,000 dealers, managers, and distributors. At his 1957 convention, Fuller presented a Fleetwood Cadillac to his top salesman. He awarded the number-two salesman a Ford and the number-three salesman a Plymouth. At the 1959 convention, twenty-six top salesmen received $5,600 in cash prizes. Reportedly Fuller began to pick up the tab for his employees who attended the annual conventions. Continuing through the 1950s, Fuller Products' presence in thirty-eight states held steady. S. B. Fuller also acquired the *New York Age*, the nation's oldest black-owned newspaper, and while owned by Fuller, the National Newspaper Publishers Association cited the *Age* at its annual awards banquet for winning first place under the Original Column category. Great fanfare followed Fuller's appointment of Dr. Theodore R. Mason Howard, a noted physician and surgeon, as his medical director. Similar publicity surrounded Fuller's hiring of Mrs. Ann Arnold Hedgeman, who had been a highly paid assistant to New York mayor Robert Wagner, as associate editor of the *Age*. Later, Fuller became chairman of the board of the *Courier* newspapers, which had twelve branch offices in major cities nationwide. Pittsburgh was the flagship location for the newspaper. Fuller reportedly did not have controlling interest, but Mrs. Jessie M. Vann, wife of the late founder of the *Pittsburgh Courier*, had come to Fuller on multiple occasions for loans totaling $500,000 to assist her newspaper. In the 1960s Fuller would take over the newspaper to save his investment.[14]

Accolades

Fuller's humble beginnings and phenomenal rise to success led to the many accolades that he would receive throughout his life. Fuller rose from intense poverty and racism and, with only a sixth-grade education, transformed a $25 investment into a multimillion-dollar business, the foundation of which was the door-to-door selling of cosmetics and personal care products. Fuller began his business in Chicago in 1934, incorporating in 1936. Three years later nearly five thousand people from over fifty black-owned businesses in Chicago participated in the first annual parade sponsored by the Chicago Negro Chamber of Commerce. The parade, which began at Thirty-First and South Parkway (now Martin Luther King Jr. Drive), moved south to Fifty-First Street and into Washington Park. At a ceremony in the park, several prominent black businessmen received awards. Currency exchanges, locksmiths, pie bakers, cosmetic manufacturers, insurance companies, newspapers, beauty schools, shirt manufacturers, grocery stores, tailors, food distributors, candy makers, shoe stores, clothiers, radio experts, dairies, mechanics, florists, photographers, printers, sign painters, mattress makers, venetian blind makers, and more were among the enterprises represented in the parade. Fuller earned recognition for the best float, but his success at business was already gaining notice. Parade chairman John B. Knight Jr. said of Fuller as he presented him with his award: "This young man who three years ago started this organization, which now employs more than 200 people, is rapidly becoming one of our great industrial leaders."[15]

More accolades would follow. From 1942 to 1946, Fuller served as president of the Chicago Negro Chamber of Commerce. During the first year of his presidency, the chamber hosted the annual convention of the National Negro Business League. At the convention, Fuller won the Robert S. Abbott Award, given to the person making the most outstanding business achievement during the year. Upon retiring from the chamber presidency, Fuller received additional public recognition. Reportedly, over five hundred leading citizens of Chicago's South Side community attended the retirement banquet in his honor. The event was held at Corpus Christi auditorium; attorney Oscar Brown was master of ceremonies, and John H. Johnson, editor and publisher of *Negro Digest* and *Ebony*, was the main speaker.[16] In 1951 John Sengstacke, editor and publisher of the *Chicago Defender*, publicly congratulated Fuller for his work in stimulating black-owned businesses nationally, and in 1953 the National Negro Business League, the venerable organization founded by Booker T. Washington, gave Fuller its Outstanding Businessman Award. It was at this time that Fuller began to publicly decry the idea of a separate black economy, urging his audience of black businessmen and businesswomen to move beyond the idea of catering to a black market and strive to compete with all businesses at the highest level.[17] The decline of commercial segregation and the need to gain access to white consumers posed a major challenge to black businesses seeking to move forward. However, Fuller, who sold to a substantial white market, seemed to have met this challenge, and one writer noted that *Fortune* magazine had identified Fuller's Chicago enterprises as grossing $18 million in 1956.[18] Following the lead of the National Negro Business League, the National Association of Market Developers cited Fuller as Businessman of the Year in 1957.[19] Moreover, Fuller was the first black member of the National Association of Manufacturers and had membership in the Illinois Chamber of Commerce, the Toilet Goods Association, and the Chicago Association of Commerce and Industry.[20] Active in Republican affairs, Fuller won the Distinguished Service Award from the United Republican Fund of Illinois in 1965. Former vice president Richard Nixon was the principal speaker at the annual fund-raising dinner where Fuller received his award.[21]

Public Service

From a very early period, Fuller committed considerable time to service on boards and substantial time and money to civic and charitable causes. For example, in 1938, two years after launching Fuller Products Company, S. B. Fuller became chairman of the board of the Chicago Negro Chamber of Commerce, which was organized in 1933.[22] Subsequently he was elected to the executive committee of the National Negro Business League in 1940 at the league's annual convention held in Detroit.[23] Fuller became president of the Chicago Negro Chamber of Commerce in 1942. During his tenure as president, Fuller led the chamber to sponsor the purchase of $1 million in war bonds and stamps, joining other African American civic groups in Chicago that supported the war effort. Between September of 1942 and March of 1943, Black Chicagoans purchased $3.5 million in war bonds through a series of bond rallies. This figure did not include money raised through payroll deductions. One of the largest purchases came from a dinner at the black-owned Parkway Ballroom sponsored by the American Women's Volunteer Service, which raised $453,406.[24] In 1961 Fuller served on the board of the newly created Consolidated Publishers, an organization that represented 150 black-owned newspapers with a combined circulation of over one million, which had the purpose of connecting potential advertisers with a growing black consumer market.[25] Fuller served for many years as chairman of the executive committee of the board of trustees for the Chicago Baptist Institute. Under Fuller's stewardship, the Institute built an eighteen-story apartment complex, named Baptist Towers, to serve lower-middle-income families. Planning for the project began in 1965. The facility, located at 5110 King Drive (formerly South Parkway), opened in June of 1970.[26] Fuller served on the board of the Chicago Urban League and donated money to this organization as well as the NAACP.[27] Fuller would serve on additional boards and be asked to lead other organizations and groups, which are too numerous to list.

Obviously Fuller could not meet every request for his services, but one rejection is notable for its embodiment of Fuller's evolving philosophy of business and his influence in local and national organizations concerned with black business development. Fuller's rapid and phenomenal success and the fact that he sold to a substantial white market and employed a significant number of whites convinced him that being defined as a Negro or black business was limiting. For him, the implication was that you were something less. In 1954, when the annual convention of the National Negro Business League met again in Chicago, Fuller rejected a nomination to become president of the organization. He was not happy that a motion on the floor to remove the word "Negro" from the league's name was defeated by a vote of 23 to 21. Fuller also asked that his name be removed as a board member of the league.[28] However, Fuller must have been pleased when the membership of the Chicago Negro Chamber of Commerce elected to change its bylaws in 1954 to accept non-black-owned businesses. The rationale was that initially the organization was needed to address the peculiar problems of black-owned businesses, but this period had passed. The broader concern was to address business development in black areas, which included opening new businesses and halting the flight of old businesses. White-owned businesses became members of the Chicago Negro Chamber of Commerce for the first time in January 1957, and later in the same year the new name for the organization became the Cosmopolitan Chamber of Commerce.[29]

Fuller's charitable and civic activities were similarly eclectic and broad-based. Fuller served on the Citizens Committee to save Poro College, an enterprise of legendary entrepreneur Annie Malone, as she struggled with federal tax problems.[30] He donated large numbers of toys to the *Defender* Charities for Christmas distribution and financed uniforms and equipment for a newly formed little-league team. Fuller provided the awards for a citywide essay contest in African American history for elementary and high school students.[31] He also held a "Boy Scout Day" and an African American history art exhibit at his department store.[32] An economic conservative, Fuller was an active fund-raiser for the Illinois Republican Party, but he also donated to Democrats and supported progressive causes. Fuller, for example, wrote a check to the Democratic Party at an event sponsored by the Women's Auxiliary of the Second Ward Regular Democratic Organization. He also served on a committee to honor black congressman William L. Dawson, even though Fuller had previously raised funds to support a Republican opponent to Dawson. Additionally, Fuller was a signer with other prominent citizens of an open position statement challenging segregation policies in Chicago's public schools.[33] Among his humanitarian endeavors, Fuller was a major part of a foundation formed to assist an impoverished mother who gave birth to quadruplets.[34] He also led efforts to send needy girls and boys to summer camp, and he was behind multiple endeavors to provide job training and job opportunities to the unemployed.[35]

Ambassador

Fuller received invitations to many prominent events because of his success as a businessman, his respected standing in the community, and his speaking abilities. He was one of a number of dignitaries invited to greet Kwame Nkrumah, prime minister of Ghana, at Midway Airport, when Nkrumah visited Chicago. Fuller and his wife Lestine attended the luncheon hosted by Governor Stratton and Mayor Daley for Queen Elizabeth II and Prince Phillip when the royal couple visited Chicago. Fuller also attended a dinner for President Eisenhower and sat at the presidential table when Eisenhower came to Chicago in support of the Illinois Republican Party.[36] Fuller, a member of Pilgrim Baptist Church, was a favorite speaker for religious groups and churches. Examples were the Baptist State Convention of Illinois, Metropolitan Community Church, Beth Eden Baptist Church, Emmanuel Baptist Church, the Fifteenth Annual Midwest Youth Conference at Antioch Missionary Baptist Church, Greater Union Missionary Baptist

Church, New Mozart Missionary Baptist Church, New Covenant Baptist Church, the Baptist Ministers Conference of Chicago and Vicinity, Olivet Baptist Church, St. Mary's AME Church, Woodlawn AME Church, and the National Convention of Gospel Choirs, held at Pilgrim Baptist Church.[37] Fuller also spoke to numerous clubs, schools, and business groups.[38]

Wives and Family

When S. B. Fuller started his business in 1934 and incorporated in 1936, he was married to his first wife, Lorena Elizabeth Whitfield. The two separated in 1936 and were divorced in 1945. Lorena bore all five of S. B.'s daughters (Mary, Jessie, Ethel, Luella, and Geraldine), and it appears that Lestine, S. B.'s second wife, did not have any children by S. B.[39] In fact, discussions of the Fuller family most always gave the impression that S. B.'s five daughters were also Lestine's daughters. Additionally, hundreds of articles written on S. B. Fuller failed to mention Lorena as S. B.'s first wife. For example, an obituary in *Jet* magazine for Lestine Fuller read, "When the couple decided to start Fuller Products in 1935, Mrs. Fuller [Lestine] was right by her husband's side to guide and support him." Similarly, an obituary for S. B. Fuller published by the *Chicago Sun-Times* reported, "He [Fuller] worked for several years as an insurance representative for Commonwealth Burial Association Insurance Co. before starting Fuller Products, with his wife Lestine's assistance, in 1935."[40] In 1945, when Lorena and S. B. divorced, S. B. had already made a name for himself in business. He was president of the Chicago Negro Chamber of Commerce and served on the board of the Chicago Urban League. Born in Pittsburgh, Lestine Thornton moved to Chicago in 1932 and, no doubt, became the backbone of Fuller Products, working in every conceivable position while assisting S. B. to launch the fledgling enterprise. However, Lorena was S. B.'s wife at the time and the person bearing and raising their children. She cared for S. B.'s younger siblings, bore the excruciating pain of the early death of son McKinley at three years of age, and supported the family through its most financially challenging period.

Interviews with several members of the Fuller family did not reveal the existence of Lorena, but elder daughter Mary attempted to explain this anomaly in the book she published on her father. She stated: "Lorena was a warm-hearted and caring person, but she had difficulty understanding SB. . . . Lorena was concerned about the lack of money to pay bills and buy family necessities. She wanted her husband to get a job and bring home a pay check." Mary went on to explain that Lorena never believed that S. B. would reach the goals that he had set for himself and that they lived in separate worlds. When the two divorced in 1945, Mary said, S. B. bought Lorena a home and gave her a new car, a cash settlement, alimony, and child support. Lestine and S. B. were married without ceremony on November 20, 1946.[41]

The couple settled into a small apartment on the South Side of Chicago and then a small home in the all-black suburb of Robbins, Illinois. By 1958, however, S. B. and Lestine had built their dream home at 13500 South Kedzie in Robbins, Illinois, a twelve-room, four-thousand-square-foot (excluding the basement) ranch-style structure with circular interior rooms. The grounds included a private park and a small lake. The couple resided in the new home by themselves. Chicago architect Richard E. Carlson designed the home, which took two years to build at a cost of $250,000. Some were critical of Fuller for building the home in a poor suburb that lacked development. Fuller, however, believed that his home would stimulate development in the lowly suburb and improve housing conditions there. The suburb had evolved from a history of African American self-help and self-determination. The first black-owned airport was built in Robbins in 1930 (opening in 1931) but was destroyed by a violent storm in 1933. Fuller's presence stimulated significant improvements in the suburb, but over the years, development of the community was not sustainable.[42]

On Top: The Beginning of the End

The 1960s would usher in a new set of accomplishments by S. B. Fuller but would also plant the seeds of his downfall. Perhaps the first sign of trouble was the *New York Age*. It ceased publication in March 1960. Fuller first purchased the paper in 1957 from the Robert S. Abbott Publishing Company. At the time, the *Age*, founded in 1880, had been part of the *Chicago Defender* chain for two years.[43] Also, by 1963, Fuller clearly had controlling interest of the *Courier* papers, but not for long.[44]

Notably, Fuller had built the core of his business on door-to-door selling, which precluded significant investments in retail outlets and the attendant overhead. He quickly moved to manufacture his own products and bought and invested in companies that could produce products for his national sales force to hawk. However, door-to-door sales were a declining phenomenon in the 1960s, and Fuller began to move into retail and business enterprises that required significant capital investments and overhead costs to maintain. Financing these ventures would become challenging, as major banks resisted making loans to black-owned businesses. A brief mention in the February 24, 1962, *Chicago Defender*'s business column stating that one could now buy stock in the Fuller Products Company revealed this emerging challenge for S. B. Fuller. He needed access to cash.[45] S. B. went directly to investors for help, which often meant churches and their congregants. Fuller was well known among black churches and, as noted previously, was often a featured speaker at their events. Fuller, a religious man, was active in religious affairs and chaired the executive committee of the Chicago Baptist Institute.

Sylvia Sims-Gray remembered her family's relationship with S. B. Fuller. Sylvia was the daughter of the late Reverend Frank Sims, pastor of Ebenezer Missionary Baptist Church between 1959 and 1989. Ebenezer, located at 4501 South Vincennes, was a very prominent church in the black community and had an important history in the civil-rights movement as well as in the growth and development of gospel music. Reverend Sims was a similarly prominent figure in Chicago. It was not clear if his church purchased stock from S. B. Fuller, but Reverend Sims and his wife, Eunice, did. Reverend Sims was consistently vocal to his congregation about supporting black businesses and causes. He was an advocate for racial and social justice who believed that blacks had to uplift themselves. Frank and Eunice made a point of purchasing goods from black-owned businesses. Reverend Sims showed great admiration, like many others, for Fuller's accomplishments, and Fuller encouraged the family to invest in his business ventures. Initially the Sims' purchased $5,000 worth of stock from Fuller. S. B. returned later and successfully convinced the family to invest another $5,000. Ten thousand dollars was a very significant investment for a family in the early 1960s. Frank and Eunice subsequently lost their investment and were extremely disappointed for the remainder of their lives. They wanted to have faith in Fuller, who symbolized an important strategy for uplifting the black community.[46]

Nonetheless, for S. B. Fuller, despite the demise of the *New York Age* newspaper, and the subsequent loss of investors' money, the 1960s opened with a typical stream of accolades and accomplishments. The Fuller Products Company won a suit against the Fuller Brush Company, a white-owned business, for using the name "Fuller's" on its vitamins, and the ruling entitled the Fuller Products Company to damages.[47] Winning the lawsuit further convinced a loyal black following that S. B. Fuller could do no wrong when it came to business. Moreover, in 1963 Guaranty Bank and Trust Company at 6760 South Stony Island elected Fuller to its board of directors.[48] Consequently, S. B. Fuller's reputation continued to grow. He embodied the idea that blacks could become major players in the business world. Fuller's achievements appeared even more significant in the midst of the civil-rights, Black Power, and Black Consciousness movements of the 1960s. Acquiring ownership, which meant self-determination, fit the aspirations of a black community that was circumscribed by multiple and profound levels of inequality, some visible, some invisible. Fuller, however, would argue that a lack of hard work and motivation were the only factors standing in the way of success in business for the black community, not racism.

Fuller's own experiences ultimately proved him wrong, but for the moment, he attempted to transform his core business from door-to-door sales to sales through brick-and-mortar retail outlets. Rumors began to surface that Fuller had purchased the South Center Department Store, which was positioned in a prime commercial location on Chicago's South Side. He denied the purchase initially, but admitted to negotiations with Morris Berman, the current president of South Center Department Store.[49] A short time later the *Pittsburgh Courier* announced:

> South Center Department Store, for years a fixture in the 47th St. shopping area, has been purchased for an undisclosed sum by a group of Negroes headed by S. B. Fuller and John H. Sengstacke. Mr. Fuller is president of Fuller Products Company, publisher of *The Pittsburgh Courier* and chairman of the Courier's board of directors. Mr. Sengstacke is editor of *The Chicago Daily Defender* and president of *Defender* Publications.[50]

Another prominent investor with Fuller was Marva Louis Spaulding (a former wife of boxer Joe Louis), who resided at 4320 South Michigan.[51] However, there were hundreds of smaller investors who backed Fuller. Moreover, even though the initial announcement focused on the South Center Department Store, Fuller also purchased the commercial property that housed the store. This commercial property included the historic Regal Theater, the largest movie house and live-show entertainment venue ever constructed specifically to serve a black community.[52]

Many believed that the South Center Building was the prime black-owned commercial property in the country. Located at 4701–4759 South Parkway (now Martin Luther King Jr. Drive), Fuller purchased the property for $1,157,000. His Fuller Products Company was still based at 2700–2710 South Wabash. The South Center Building contained 250,000 square feet of commercial space and was first conceived as a commercial center for a growing black population in 1926. The South Parkway Building Corporation under Louis Englestein, president, sold the building to Fuller. McKey and Pogue was the real estate broker. At the time, the building contained seven stores, fifty-four office units, and fifteen thousand square feet of loft space. South Center Department Store occupied eighty thousand square feet of space and opened in 1928. Among its residents, the South Center Building housed the Regal Theater, a three-thousand-seat house, which also opened in 1928; Neisner Brothers, a general merchandise store; Terry's, a general department store; Vito's Supermarket; and branch offices for the Department of Welfare, the Social Security Administration, and the Illinois Department of Labor—Unemployment Compensation Division. The building also included Chicago's historic Savoy Ballroom, which by 1963 had long been converted to office space. The South Center Department Store, now owned and operated by Fuller, had 110 employees and 76 departments. Besides this new acquisition, Fuller's financial empire included the Fuller Products Company, the *Pittsburgh Courier*, J. E. McBrady Cosmetics, Rose Meta Beauty Products Company, Lipsey Printing Company, Chez O'Teal Hosiery Company, Boyer International Laboratories, the Patricia Stevens Cosmetic Company, and the Jean Nadal Cosmetic Company.[53]

It was not always clear what relationship Fuller had with these various enterprises. Some he fully owned, and others were investments where the Fuller Products Company functioned as a distributor, retailer, or franchisee. Rose Meta Beauty
Products, for example, was a subsidiary of the Rose Meta House of Beauty in Harlem, reportedly the largest and most exclusive black-owned beauty salon in the
country.[54] Fuller also established the Fuller Guaranty Corporation and acquired a
$3 million New York real estate trust, a large cattle ranch, and commercial farms.[55]

Fuller's purchase of the South Center Department Store had significant historical import that did not escape the news coverage of the event—or Fuller himself.
Fuller hired Brigadier General Richard L. Jones (retired) as vice president of South
Center Department Store. Jones had formerly been associated with South Center
for twenty-three years and had pioneered integration at the store when it first
opened in 1928. At that time Jones became general superintendent of the store
and was widely recognized as the first black person in the country to occupy such
a position. Jones was thirty-four when he accepted the job. He had served as a
second lieutenant in the U.S. Army during World War I and was a military police
commander from 1917 to 1919. Jones worked in various capacities for the *Chicago
Defender* after the war before taking the position at South Center. He reentered military service during World War II and earned the Legion of Merit for his outstanding
war service. Jones attained the rank of brigadier general in the Illinois National
Guard before retiring in 1953. He continued his position at South Center after the
war and was active in civic life. Jones later became ambassador to Liberia and was
an alternate delegate to the eleventh General Assembly of the United Nations.
After this service Jones returned to South Center until he accepted a position as
executive vice president of the Victory Mutual Life Insurance Company. Fuller, of
course, brought Jones back to South Center Department Store in 1963.[56]

The *Pittsburgh Courier* explained that South Center was the nation's first department store to integrate its personnel and advance the position of African Americans in executive positions in retail and marketing. Moreover, its purchase by Fuller
reportedly made South Center Department Store the largest black-owned department store in the country. For Fuller, purchase of the South Center complex was to
be the first step in a complete rehabilitation of the Forty-Seventh-Street shopping
district. Public announcement of the South Center purchase also gave Fuller the
opportunity to advance his philosophy that blacks must expand into the business
field if they were to make real progress in racial integration. Blacks, he felt, must
become employers instead of asking for job opportunities.[57]

After his purchase of South Center, Fuller, seeing business development as
the key to substantive civil rights, sought other retail opportunities for himself
and others. Fuller surmised that black unemployment would go down if blacks
got involved in the distribution of consumer goods. He saw that demand for such

items as televisions, air conditioners, stereos, washing machines, and deep freezers was high. This prompted Fuller to open a Philco Home Appliance Center at 8605 South Cottage Grove. The venture, which was essentially a franchise, was in cooperation with the Philco Company, a subsidiary of Ford Motor Company. Fuller envisioned a national chain of home-appliance stores and anticipated training scores of men and women to sell home-appliance products. The grand opening for his first and only appliance store was August 15–17, 1963.[58] The next year the Cosmopolitan Chamber of Commerce moved into the South Center Building, which also housed Fuller's Free Employment Service. There were plans for the *Chicago Courier* newspaper to move in as well, and S. B. Fuller continued to lead the way in improving the Forty-Seventh Street shopping area. Following Fuller's lead, a number of Forty-Seventh Street merchants made interior and exterior improvements to their businesses and participated in efforts to improve the neighborhood, including eliminating houses of prostitution and dope peddling. The Cosmopolitan Chamber of Commerce actively encouraged blacks to shop in their own neighborhoods in order to sustain support for the Forty-Seventh Street commercial district.[59]

Through his success, S. B. Fuller provided many in the black community with a sense of pride and inspiration, but he also angered many blacks, including prominent civil-rights leaders. His remarks before a New York meeting of the Sixty-Eighth Annual Congress of American Industry, sponsored by the National Association of Manufacturers, upset many. Reportedly, Fuller asserted that the black man "thinks that there is a racial barrier that keeps him from making progress." Consequently, according to Fuller, the black man "asks for legislation to remove the barrier which he automatically created himself, due to the lack of action on his own behalf." Fuller's remarks occurred at the height of the civil-rights movement and the struggle against racial oppression. African Americans and others committed to social justice had been thrown in jail, beaten, and murdered for challenging a corrupt and racist system. Fuller appeared to be blaming blacks for their subordinate position in American society, ignoring centuries of racial inequality and oppression. The press quoted Dr. Martin Luther King Jr. as saying, "It is most unfortunate that a man who has risen to such heights financially could reveal himself so insensitive to the plight of the very people who have helped make his success possible." Whitney Young, executive director of the National Urban League, similarly declared, "Every group has its Benedict Arnolds." James Farmer, executive director of CORE (Congress of Racial Equality), stated that Fuller "reveals a shocking ignorance of the Negro position and problem in American life." Some leaders in the black community talked of boycotting Fuller.[60] No boycott of any significance materialized from the black community, but Fuller soon faced serious backlash from white southerners.

The Fall

Fuller's financial success, which peaked in the early 1960s, had a lot to do with having the opportunity to sell to a white or general market. As mentioned previously, S. B. Fuller discreetly purchased Boyer International Laboratories, a white-owned manufacturer of cosmetics and personal care products. The firm had a largely white and southern clientele. Two of the firm's major product lines were Jean Nadal cosmetics and H. A. Hair Arranger. In the midst of an intense struggle by blacks to end racial segregation and oppression in the South, white southerners did not know a black man owned the company that produced some of their favored consumer products. Fuller employed black and white agents to sell his goods, and over time white southerners became aware that he owned Boyer International Laboratories. In the end, the White Citizens Council organized a 100 percent boycott of Boyer products, which accounted for over 60 percent of Fuller's annual sales.[61]

Fuller subsequently secured a letter of intent from a prominent white-owned firm to purchase Jean Nadal for $1 million and $600,000 in royalties over a fourteen-year period. With a letter from the company stating its intent to buy, Fuller borrowed $500,000 to purchase the South Center commercial complex, which included the Regal Theater. The company reneged on its promise, and Fuller was forced to liquidate his New York real estate trust worth $3,000,000, his cattle ranch, and his newspaper in order to meet his debts.[62]

Meanwhile, Fuller attempted to follow through with his plans to improve the visual appeal of South Center Department Store, the South Center Building, and the Forty-Seventh Street commercial district. A. L. Foster, executive director of the Cosmopolitan Chamber of Commerce, noted, "Since acquiring the property housing the South Center Department Store, Regal Theatre, Terry's, Neisner's and professional offices, S. B. Fuller has spent a small fortune in restoring the exterior of the building to its former attractiveness. . . . Fuller has also completely renovated the interior of the South Center and established a modern grocery in the basement."[63] Other businesses in proximity to South Center followed suit, but there were limits to what Fuller could do. He could not require all businesses in the neighborhood to upgrade, and he could not stop residents from leaving the neighborhood to shop elsewhere.[64] Additionally, there was the problem of the aging infrastructure of the Regal Theatre, which was an exceptionally large and ornate structure that was expensive to maintain. The former owners had made cosmetic improvements, but expensive repairs to the roof and to the cooling and heating systems still needed to be done. From the previous ownership, Fuller retained the building manager and the managing director of the Regal, who controlled bookings and film acquisitions. Both men, who were white, apparently had little loyalty to Fuller and took advantage of him.[65]

Moreover, the Regal Theater, when sold to Fuller, was no longer part of a major theater chain. For most of its existence the Regal was managed by the Balaban and Katz theater chain, which was owned by Paramount, the largest motion-picture production, distribution, and exhibition company in the country. Because of anti-trust suits, Paramount and other major motion-picture companies had to divest themselves of much of their theater holdings and cease monopolistic practices governing film exhibition. Fuller, who now owned a very expensive theater, could not benefit from the economies of scale enjoyed by large chains, and he could not profit from the monopolistic practices that supported the previous Regal Theater management.[66]

Additionally, white-owned businesses were more and more actively engaged in seeking black consumer dollars, and commercial segregation as Fuller knew it was breaking down. For example, movie attendance was on the decline, and downtown theaters increased their efforts to attract youthful black moviegoers. Also, between 1960 and 1968, numerous venues emerged that regularly booked the kind of talent traditionally found at the Regal. The market and population surrounding the South Center commercial complex and the Forty-Seventh Street business district was in decline as residents began to move away as a result of deindustrialization, increasing joblessness, and underdevelopment resulting from previous structural inequalities that isolated and exploited black communities.[67] Indeed, the fact that Fuller was able to purchase South Center reflected the reality that commercial segregation was no longer profitable to white/mainstream business establishments. Blacks as consumers would now be required to leave their communities to meet their consumer needs at commercial complexes embedded in white-dominated communities.

The southern white boycott of Fuller's most lucrative business, his subsequent debt management problems, and the costliness of the Regal led to a series of poor decisions by Fuller. He reportedly lowered the quality of merchandise in South Center Department Store and tried to increase patronage by attracting welfare recipients. Fuller gave customers on welfare the opportunity to charge $100 worth of goods for only $30. He subsequently learned that it was unlawful to extend credit for retail purchases to welfare recipients, and social service administrators advised their welfare clients not to honor their debts with Fuller. As a consequence, Fuller was left with over $1 million in unpaid bills.[68]

Fuller went bankrupt in 1968, but there was some hope when he regained control of his basic cosmetic business and emerged from bankruptcy with a court-ordered plan to repay all unsecured creditors 100 percent over a five-year period. However, South Center, which included the Regal Theater, could not be saved, and Talman Federal Savings and Loan foreclosed on the property. In an effort to address his earlier cash-flow problems, Fuller had divested himself of his stake in the *Pittsburgh Courier* by 1967, selling it to Sengstacke Enterprises, which owned the *Chicago Defender*.[69]

Earlier, in 1965, S. B. Fuller made an ill-advised effort to address his financial woes. To raise needed cash, he sold promissory notes between 1965 and 1967 issued from his Fuller Products Company. The notes had nine-month maturity dates at annual interest rates of 10 to 25 percent. Fuller personally guaranteed the notes, and investors ranged from individuals who purchased a few hundred dollars' worth of the notes to institutional investors like Chicago's Antioch Missionary Baptist Church, which bought $100,000 of the notes. S. B. Fuller failed to redeem the short-term notes that he had issued between 1965 and 1967. As a consequence, these short-term notes became long-term obligations, which the Securities and Exchange Commission required to be registered. Fuller had not done this. Moreover, Fuller unlawfully failed to disclose the financial condition of his company.[70]

In 1971 the federal government issued a six-count indictment charging Fuller with violating the Federal Securities Act from 1965 through 1967. Fuller faced up to $5,000 in fines and up to five years in prison for each count. At the time, $1.62 million in notes was still outstanding. In 1972 Fuller pleaded guilty before U.S. District Court Judge Alexander J. Napoli to one count of the six-count indictment, for "fraudulent sale and material misstatements to purchasers of promissory notes that lacked registration with the Securities and Exchange Commission." The remaining counts were dismissed. Assistant U.S. Attorney Howard M. Hoffman recommended that Judge Napoli grant probation to Fuller in order for him to carry out an agreement under a separate court action to reorganize his cosmetic company and pay creditors. Consequently, Napoli sentenced Fuller to five years' probation. Under this prior agreement, the court required Fuller to pay note holders over a three-year period 10 percent a year of what they were owed. It then required Fuller to pay 20 percent of his debt the fourth year and the remaining 50 percent of his debt the fifth year. By 1970 Fuller Products had a net profit of $70,000 and by 1971 a net profit of $101,000. The projected profit for 1972 was $300,000.[71]

There was great public resentment over the Fuller bankruptcy and indictment. Black sentiment resided with Fuller, and many laypersons blamed Fuller's problems on his inability to borrow money for his business through normal banking channels. An array of prominent black businessmen also collectively and publicly blamed Fuller's troubles on the racism of large financial institutions. Large, white-owned financial institutions, they said, wouldn't support black enterprises, even while simultaneously writing off bad loans to white-owned companies and then loaning them money again. Blacks, they felt, can overcome only when they are strong enough to support their own. In 1968, when Fuller's financial woes were revealed in bankruptcy court, civil-rights leader Jesse Jackson, who headed Operation Breadbasket, the economic arm of the Southern Christian Leadership Conference, vowed to support Fuller to keep him from losing control of the South Center commercial complex. Fuller had purchased the building using seven hundred African American investors, and Jackson wanted to preserve their ownership.[72] However, the Fuller Products Company never regained its prior prominence.

After the Fall

On June 4, 1975, over two thousand guests gathered for dinner in the Grand Ballroom of Chicago's Conrad Hilton Hotel to pay tribute to S. B. Fuller on the occasion of his seventieth birthday. Dan Walker, governor of Illinois, who also attended the event, proclaimed June 4 S. B. Fuller Day. Two giants of the black business community, George E. Johnson of Johnson Products and John H. Johnson of Johnson Publications (no relationship to each other), planned the tribute. At the testimonial dinner, the two Johnsons presented Fuller with a check for $70,000 from the dinner's proceeds and $50,000 worth of stock certificates. George E. Johnson contributed the stock from his own company. Testimonials cited Fuller as a business pioneer, a motivational genius, an entrepreneurial role model, and much more.[73] John H. Johnson had looked to Fuller for inspiration in developing his own business, and when Johnson first published *Ebony* magazine, Fuller supported the publication by purchasing full-page ads and directing his branches across the country to sell subscriptions to the periodical. However, Fuller had even greater significance for George E. Johnson, who remembered standing outside of Fuller's factory at seventeen years of age and listening to Fuller motivate his employees. George E. Johnson worked for Fuller for ten years (1944–54) and, with Fuller's encouragement, opened his own cosmetic firm in 1954. Though competitors, when George E. Johnson was threatened with ruin after a plant fire in 1964, Fuller provided space and manufacturing capacity for his former employee so that Johnson could meet his obligations and remain solvent.[74] Some weeks after the Conrad Hilton tribute and testimonial, George E. Johnson presented a bronze bust of S. B. Fuller to Chicago's DuSable Museum of African American History. Jimmie Lou (Jimilu) Mason of Alexandria, Virginia, sculpted the bust. S. B. Fuller and his second wife, Lestine, attended the presentation.[75] S. B. Fuller died in 1988 at the age of eighty-three, and Lestine Fuller died in 1999 at the age of ninety-one.

The Fuller saga was filled with irony. S. B. downplayed the role of white racism on black aspirations, but white racism played a critical role in his own financial downturn. The boycott by southern whites of some of their favorite consumer products because they discovered that Fuller, an African American, produced these products is an example of this racism. Also, as the black lay and business community argued, white-owned banks, which controlled the resources needed for business development and expansion, refused to provide loans to deserving black-owned businesses. Fuller understood this and pursued unorthodox methods of obtaining capital that ultimately contributed to his downfall. Nevertheless, Fuller excused the discriminatory practices of white bankers by explaining that they had never known a black man to own what he owned.[76] Moreover, Fuller was committed to the idea that racism would fall when blacks became integrated into the economic life of the community. Blacks, Fuller said, "are not discriminated against because of the color of their skin. They are discriminated against because they have nothing to offer that people want to buy."[77] Fuller lacked a comprehensive understanding of the complexity of white racism in American society, but his belief that black business development is critical to black advancement remains timely.

Notes

1. See, for example, Juliet E. K. Walker, *The History of Black Business in America: Capitalism, Race, Entrepreneurship* (New York: Macmillan, 1998), 296.

2. Mary Fuller Casey, *S. B. Fuller: Pioneer in Black Economic Development* (Jamestown, NC: BridgeMaster Press, 2003), 9.

3. Ibid.

4. Ibid., 13, 15.

5. Ibid., 17, 20.

6. Ibid., 21–25.

7. Ibid., 27.

8. Ibid., 27–28.

9. Marion B. Campfield, "Fuller Brings It to Your Door," *Chicago Defender*, May 26, 1951, 13, cols. 3–4; Casey, *S. B. Fuller*, 39–40.

10. Campfield, "Fuller Brings It to Your Door"; Casey, *S. B. Fuller*, 43, 49–51.

11. When the *Chicago Defender* shifted from a weekly newspaper to a daily newspaper, S. B. Fuller joined with other prominent citizens to take out charter subscriptions to the newspaper. He also sent a letter to the newspaper praising the first issue of the *Daily Defender*. See "Charter Boosters of *Daily Defender*," *Chicago Defender*, January 7, 1956, p. 1, col. 8; "The People Speak," ibid., February 8, 1956, p. 11, col. 1.

12. "Genius of Direct Selling," *Ebony*, November 1957, 119–22, 124; "Fuller Managers Meet in Chicago, Divide $2,500 Jackpot," *Chicago Defender*, July 16, 1949, p. 5, cols. 2–5; "Mississippi Woman Sidetracked Up Ladder of 'Fuller' Success," ibid., April 14, 1951, p. 2, cols. 3–5.

13. "Fuller Managers Meet in Chicago, Divide $2,500 Jackpot," p. 5, col. 2; Marion B. Campfield, "Mostly about Women," ibid., October 27, 1951, p. 6, cols. 7–8; "1,700 Attend Fuller Products Banquet Confab," ibid., October 27, 1951, p. 7, cols. 3–4; Marion B. Campfield, "Mostly about Women," ibid., April 25, 1953, p. 14, col.1; "Fuller Presents Memphis Salesman with Top Award," ibid., September 3, 1955, p. 2, cols. 6–8; "1,000 Fuller Products Workers Meet in Chicago," ibid., August 27, 1955, p. 4, cols. 1–3. Tragically Mrs. Oteal Sharpe Elliot, the promising dress designer that had signed on with Fuller, was murdered near her home at 4818 South Drexel. Fuller pledged a reward for information leading to the arrest and conviction of the murderer. See "$5,000 Reward for Slayer," *Chicago Defender*, September 3, 1957, p. 1, cols. 1–2; "$1,200 Reward for Society Death," ibid., September 7, 1957, p. 1, cols. 7–8.

14. "Palmer House Lush Setting for Fuller Banquet," *Chicago Defender*, August 11, 1956, p. 11, cols. 1–3; "Fuller Products," ibid., April 20, 1957, p. 7, cols. 2–7; "Fuller Salesmen Trooping Here for Big Convention," ibid., July 24, 1957, p. 6, cols. 1–2; "Top Salesman," ibid., July 29, 1957, p. 5, cols. 2–4; "Fuller to Pick Up Tab for 1,000 Aides," ibid., August 3, 1957, p. 1, cols. 3–6; "Another Top Salesman," ibid., August 10, 1957, p. 14, cols. 2–4; "1,000 to Attend Fuller Convention," ibid., August 11, 1958, p. 5, cols. 3–4; "Awards Banquet Highlights of Fuller Products Confab, Over 1,000 Attend," ibid., August 30, 1958, p. 13, cols. 1–4; "26 Top Salesmen Given $5,600 in Prizes," ibid., August 29, 1959, p. 29, cols. 1–5; "Howard Joins Ida Mae Scott Surgical Staff," ibid., January 19, 1957, p. 8, cols. 1–8; "Ann Hedgeman Quits N.Y. Job to Join Fuller," ibid., September 29, 1958, p. A3, col. 1; "Deny Fuller Purchased Courier," ibid., July 18, 1959, p. 1, col. 8; "Fuller Named Head of Courier Board," ibid., July 25, 1959, p. 12, cols. 2–3; Casey, *S. B. Fuller*, 79–81.

15. Quoted in "50 Businesses Take Part in Huge Parade," *Chicago Defender*, October 21, 1939, p. 3, col. 5.

16. "Chamber of Commerce Banquet and Installation Has Patriotic Theme," ibid., May 2, 1942, p. 6, cols. 6–7; "Business Men Gather Here for Meeting," ibid., September 5, 1942, p. 8, cols. 2–3; "Notables Attend Fuller Banquet," ibid., April 6, 1946, p. 2, col. 7.

17. "Congratulations," ibid., February 3, 1951, p. 2, col. 4; "Chicagoan Wins Business Award," ibid., October 10, 1953, p. 1, col. 1; Lewis A. H. Caldwell, "Businessmen Cite Fuller at Meet: Blasts False Limits of 'Negro Business,'" ibid., November 21, 1953, p. 2, cols. 3–4.

18. "S. B. Fuller Thinks Positively," ibid., June 8, 1963, p. 8, cols. 3–5.

19. "TSU Makes Plans for Marketing Discussion," ibid., March 30, 1957, p. 4, cols. 3–5.

20. Marion B. Campfield, "Fuller Brings It to Your Door," ibid., May 26, 1951, p. 13, cols. 3–4.

21. "Illinois GOP Honors Fuller," ibid. March 2, 1965, p. 21, col. 1.

22. "W. L. Marshall New Head of Business Body," ibid., May 28, 1938, p. 10, col. 6.

23. "Announce New Officers of Business League," ibid., September 14, 1940, p. 7, cols. 7–8.

24. "Chamber of Commerce Banquet and Installation Has Patriotic Theme," ibid., p. 6; Nahum Daniel Brascher, "Thoughts To-Day," ibid., June 20, 1942, p. 15, col. 1; "$3,500,000 War Bond Sales Is Chicago's Proud Boast," ibid., March 6, 1943, p. 1, cols. 1–2.

25. "Publishers Effect Merger, Usher in New Era," ibid., August 26, 1961, p. 1, cols. 1–2.

26. "Chicago Baptist Institute News," ibid., October 7, 1961, p. 18, col. 8; "CBI Makes Plans for New Project," ibid., September 25, 1965, p. 13, col. 3; "Baptist Tower Is Washington Park High Rise," ibid., January 17, 1966, p. 4, col. 3; "Dignitaries to Dedicate Baptist Towers Saturday," ibid., June 13, 1970, p. 28, cols. 1–3; "Dedicatorial Program Features Baptist Towers Open House," ibid., June 20, 1970, p. 24, cols. 1–3.

27. "New Approach to Racial Problems Seen by League," ibid., March 4, 1944, p. 2, col. 2; "10 Businessmen Pledge $1,000 to Current Urban League Drive," ibid., June 27, 1961, p. 16, col. 1; A. L. Foster, "Other People's Business," ibid., July 8, 1961, p. 6, cols. 1–2.

28. "Fuller Quits NNBL Over Name; Reelect Sudduth," ibid., October 30, 1954, p. 1, cols. 6–8.

29. "CNCC Decides on New Name," ibid., January 17, 1957, p. 5, col. 3; "Chamber Unit Will Meet Wednesday," ibid., January 15, 1957, p. 4, col. 5; "Cosmopolitan Chamber of Comm. Plays Vital Role in Community, ibid., January 6, 1962, p. 18, cols. 1–3; A. L. Foster, "Other People's Business," ibid., January 2, 1965, p. 7, cols. 1–2.

30. "U.S. Gives Poro New Date on Tax Claim," ibid., June 7, 1941, p. 6, col. 1.

31. "It's Dolls for the Kids at Yule," ibid., December 21, 1968, p. 5, col. 1; "Babe Ruth Baseball—Just a Game, or Is It?" ibid., June 10, 1972, p. 29, cols. 1–4; "Roundtable launches Negro History Context," ibid., February 6, 1965, p. 3, cols. 3–4.

32. "South Center Promotes Scouts Day," ibid., February 24, 1964, p. 16, col. 2; "Fuller's Store Presents Afro-American Exhibit," ibid., February 7, 1968, p. 2, cols. 3–4.

33. "New Aide, Author of Ike's 'Go Slow' Policy on Mixing," ibid., October 13, 1958, p. 6, cols. 1–5; "To Salute Rep. Dawson for Service Sat. Nite," ibid., September 9, 1964, p. 2, cols. 4–5; "A Position Statement," ibid., June 30, 1965, p. 17, cols. 1–2; "Second Ward Demo Women Sponsor Gala, Colorful Tea," ibid., June 4, 1966, p. 23, cols. 1–4.

34. "'Fairy Godmother' Is Savior to Poverty-Stricken Harris Quads," ibid., September 24, 1963, p. 9, cols. 2–4; "Dec. 9 Benefit to Give Home for Christmas to Harris Quads," ibid., December 4, 1963, p. 5, cols. 3–5; "Harris Quads Move in New Home Today," ibid., September 22, 1964, p. 3, cols. 1–2.

35. "Summer Camp Program Set," ibid., July 1, 1944, p. 16, col. 8; "Southside Group Plans a Unique Civic Center," ibid., October 17, 1964, p. 2, cols. 5–6; "Abernathy Guest of Training School Drive," ibid., October 29, 1964, p. 2, cols. 1–3; A. L. Foster, "Other People's Business," ibid., August 15, 1964, p. 5, col. 1.

36. "City Hails Ghana Prime Minister," ibid., July 30, 1958, p. 1, col. 1; Marion B. Campfield, "Day by Day," ibid., July 6, 1959, p. 14, cols. 1–4; "Chi Warm Host to Ike at Spectacular Dinner Rally," ibid., October 15, 1960, p. 16, cols. 1–8.

37. "Church Group Holds Its Grand Banquet Testimonial," ibid., May 5, 1962, p. 15, cols. 5–6; "S. B. Fuller to Speak at Church Guild Banquet," ibid., February 27, 1958, p. 9, col. 1; "S. B. Fuller to Speak at Metropolitan," ibid., September 22, 1962, p. 7, col. 1; "Fuller Men's Day Speaker at Beth Eden of Morgan Pk," ibid., September 29, 1962, p. 19, cols. 7–8; "Fuller to Speak at Men's Day," ibid., November 10, 1962, p. 15, col. 5; "Baptist Youth Hear Chicagoland Leaders," ibid., December 8, 1962, p. 15, cols. 5–6; "Greater Union to Observe Pastor's 16th Anniversary," ibid., March 23, 1963, p. 5, cols. 4–5; "Fuller, Banquet Speaker for New Mozart Church," ibid., November 7, 1964, p. 15, col. 7; "New Covenant Choirs," ibid., March 27, 1965, p. 4, col. 7; "Clerics to Honor CBI," ibid., May 8, 1965, p. 15, col. 1; "S. B. Fuller Slated to Speak at Sunday Meeting," ibid., July 25, 1964, p. 3, cols. 3–4; "To Speak Sunday," ibid., July 31, 1965, p. 12, col. 8; "Speaker," ibid., September 18, 1965, p. 12, col. 4; "Expects Thousands to Attend Annual Confab," ibid., July 31, 1965, p. 12, cols. 1–2.

38. See, for example, "The Constant Climbers Arrange Clever Program," ibid., February 6, 1937, p. 7, col. 4; "S. B. Fuller to Speak at Sports Club Tea," ibid., July 6, 1940, p. 17, col. 4; "Tour of School Sponsored by DuSable P. T. A.," ibid., April 5, 1941, p. 18, col. 3; "S. B. Fuller to Speak in Milwaukee, Friday," ibid., January 23, 1943, p. 4, col. 7; "Businessmen Attend Mortgage Workshop," ibid., March 17, 1964, p. 8, cols. 1–2.

39. Casey, *S. B. Fuller*, p. 59; "Pictorial Review Shows Highlights of Three-Day Newspaper Publishers Meeting in Chicago," *Chicago Defender*, June 28, 1960, p. 12, cols. 1–3.

40. "Lestine Fuller, Wife of Cosmetic Pioneer S. B. Fuller, Succumbs at 91 in Chicago," *Jet*, November 8, 1999, p. 51; "S. B. Fuller, 83, President, Founder of Cosmetics Firm," *Chicago Sun-Times*, October 29, 1988. The author reviewed over four hundred articles on S. B. Fuller, and none mentioned his first wife, Lorena Elizabeth Whitfield.

41. Casey, *S. B. Fuller*, p. 59, 63.

42. "Motivating Force Behind Fuller Home: The Mrs.," *Chicago Defender*, November 8, 1958, p. 13, cols. 1–4; "Suburban Showplace," *Ebony*, February 1959, 36–38, 40, 42; Casey, *S. B. Fuller*, 63, 83–85.

43. "Race's Oldest Paper Closes Doors Mar. 15," *Chicago Defender*, March 5, 1960, p. 1, col. 5.

44. "Mrs. Vann Retires as President of Courier," ibid., October 17, 1963, p. 6, cols. 1–2.

45. A. L. Foster, "Other People's Business," ibid., February 24, 1962, p. 6, cols. 1–2.

46. Sylvia Sims-Gray, interview by author, May 11, 2012.

47. "S. B. Fuller Wins Slice of $13,000,000," *Chicago Defender*, February 2, 1961, p. 1, col. 1.

48. "S. B. Fuller Elected to Bank's Board," ibid., January 19, 1963, p. 10, cols. 1–2.

49. "Rumor Fuller Buys S. Center Store," ibid., May 29, 1963, p. 4, cols. 1–2.

50. "Chicago Combine Buys Large Department Store," *Pittsburgh Courier*, June 29, 1963, p. 1, 4.

51. Mary Lawrence, interview by author, June 7, 1999, Chicago; also see "Marva Making Fashion Tour across Country," *Chicago Defender*, December 3, 1949, p. 26, cols. 7–8; Joe Louis Barrow Jr., email correspondence, February 7, 2005; Joe Louis Barrow Jr., phone interview by author, February 8, 2005.

52. Clovis E. Semmes, *The Regal Theater and Black Culture* (New York: Palgrave Macmillan, 2006).

53. "Chicago Combine," *Pittsburgh Courier*, p. 4.

54. See "House of Beauty: Rose-Meta Salon Is Biggest Negro Beauty Parlor in World," *Ebony*, 25–29.

55. See Walker, *History of Black Business in America*, 297.

56. "Integration Pioneer Back at South Center," *Chicago Defender*, July 17, 1963, p. 3, cols. 4–5; "Gen. Jones, Soldier-Diplomat, Returns to South Center Store," ibid., August 7, 1963, p. 20, cols. 1–3; Semmes, *Regal Theater*, 19.

57. "Chicago Combine," *Pittsburgh Courier*, p. 4; Semmes, *Regal Theater*, 17, 193–94.

58. "Fuller Opens First Home Appliance Unit," *Chicago Defender*, August 17, 1963, p. 19, cols. 5–6; Casey, *S. B. Fuller*, 132.

59. "New, Bright Lights Add Sparkle to So. Center," *Chicago Defender*, November 21, 1963, p. 10, cols. 1–2; A. L. Foster, "Other People's Business," ibid., April 4, 1964, p. 6, cols. 1–2; May 9, 1964, p. 6, cols. 1–2; and November 21, 1964, p. 6, cols. 1–2.

60. Jackie Robinson, "Jackie Robinson to S. B. Fuller: 'I'm in Total Disagreement,'" ibid., December 21, 1963, p. 5, cols. 1–4.

61. See John N. Ingham and Lynne B. Feldman, *African-American Business Leaders: A Biographical Dictionary* (Westport, CT: Greenwood Press, 1994), 245–46; Walker, *History of Black Business in America*, 297.

62. Ingham and Feldman, *African-American Business Leaders*, 246; Casey, *S. B. Fuller*, 133.

63. A. L. Foster, "Other People's Business," *Chicago Defender*, November 21, 1964, p. 6, cols. 1–2.

64. Ibid.

65. Bill Jefferson, interview by author, August 19, 1986, Chicago. Jefferson was a long-time movie projectionist who had worked at the Regal Theater under S. B. Fuller.

66. See Semmes, *Regal Theater*, 93–95.

67. Ibid., p. 173–74, 195–96. Also see Robert E. Weems Jr., *Desegregating the Dollar: African American Consumerism in the Twentieth Century* (New York: New York University Press, 1998), and William J. Wilson, *When Work Disappears: The World of the New Urban Poor* (New York: Knopf, 1996).

68. Ingham and Feldman, *African-American Business Leaders*, 246–47; "At 70, Fuller Buffeted, Unbowed," *Chicago Sun-Times*, September 8, 1975; Mary Lawrence, interview by author, June 7, 1999, Chicago; Sylvia Sims-Gray, interview by author, May 11, 2012.

69. See "S. B. Fuller Comeback as Case Nears End," *Chicago Defender*, October 23, 1969, p. 2, cols. 2–3; "S. B. Fuller Wins Fight, Restrictions Lifted," ibid., June 4, 1970, p. 12, cols. 2–3; Ingham and Feldman, *African-American Business Leaders*, 247; "Mrs. Jessie Vann Dies in Pittsburgh," *Chicago Defender*, June 8, 1967, p. 4, col. 3.

70. "Federal Grand Jury Indicts a Leading Black Businessman," *Chicago Tribune*, October 1, 1971; "S. B. Fuller Pleads Guilty to Fraud," *Chicago Sun-Times*, May 20, 1972; "S. B. Fuller: The Dean of Black Entrepreneurs," *Chicago Tribune*, June, 1987, sec. 3, p. 1, 14.

71. "Federal Grand Jury Indicts a Leading Black Businessman," *Chicago Tribune*; "S. B. Fuller Pleads Guilty to Fraud," *Chicago Sun-Times*; "Fuller Pleads Guilty on Rap," *Chicago Defender*, May 22, 1972, p. 2, cols. 3–4; "S. B. Fuller: The Dean of Black Entrepreneurs," *Chicago Tribune*.

72. "Breadbasket Backs Fuller in Mortgage Fight," *Chicago Defender*, March 20, 1968, p. 3, cols. 2–5; "Charlie Cherokee Says," ibid., October 5, 1971, p. 5, col. 1; "Leaders Move to Back S. B. Fuller," ibid., October 6, 1971, p. 1, cols.1–4.

73. "Tribute for S. B. Fuller," ibid., May 14, 1975, p. 5, cols. 1–3; "Walker Proclaims Fuller Day," ibid., June 3, 1975, p. 6, cols. 1; "Top Tribute . . .," ibid., June 7, 1975, p. 1, col. 3; "A Tribute to a Black Business Pioneer," *Ebony*, September 1975, 118–20, 122; Casey, *S. B. Fuller*, 54, 138–41.

74. A. L. Foster, "Other People's Business," *Chicago Defender*, November 18, 1961, p. 6, cols. 1–2; Betty Washington, "Johnson Products: A Giant among Giants," ibid., February 21, 1966, p. 50, cols. 1–4; "S. B. Fuller: Accomplishments of a Black Business Pioneer," ibid., June 14, 1975, p. 5, col. 5; Casey, *S. B. Fuller*, 57, 130–31.

75. "Businessman in Bronze," *Chicago Defender*, July 2, 1975, p. 1, cols. 1–2.

76. Casey, *S. B. Fuller*, 135.

77. Ibid., 98, 148.

CHAPTER 6

A Master Strategist

John H. Johnson and the Development of Chicago as a Center for Black Business Enterprise

JASON P. CHAMBERS

If you used a list of someone's youth experiences to predict future millionaires, John Harold Johnson would not have made the cut. He and his mother arrived in Chicago having fled the life limitations in their home state of Arkansas for the possibilities exhibited in the new city. Although opportunities for blacks were not necessarily overflowing in Chicago, there were certainly more there than in Arkansas. So they went. Recalling his departure from the train that brought him as a fifteen-year-old boy to the city with his mother, John Johnson said that he "stood transfixed on the street. I had never seen so many Black people before. I had never seen so many tall buildings and so much traffic."[1] Although it would have appeared only in the realm of his most fanciful dreams, their new city eventually became the home of one of the most successful companies in media history, Johnson Publications.

Perhaps like other rich and powerful men, John H. Johnson was not used to having others tell his story without his direct input. Moreover, Johnson was a publisher, someone well versed and experienced in the power of the written word, something he was used to having control over. As a result, we know little about Johnson that he did not want us to know. His autobiography, *Succeeding against the Odds*, provides substantial information about his life and experiences but is clearly a guarded account (perhaps as are most) and sticks close to the existing information about his life while revealing precious few unknown details. While he was quite a visible figure both in Chicago and nationally, by the time of his death in 2005, Johnson's Horatio Alger–like story was the one told and retold so often that it became part of his legend. The outline is well known: boy and his mother join millions of other southern blacks and migrate north to Chicago, boy catches the eye of powerful mentor, young man puts mother's furniture up as collateral to secure loan for an idea most told him was doomed to failure, young man succeeds wildly and moves from welfare recipient to multimillionaire.[2]

The aforementioned is the legend. But in the process of the legend becoming the story, what has been left out is the day-to-day reality of developing the Johnson Publishing Company (JPC). In fact, given the journey from his humble beginnings in Arkansas to membership on lists of the richest Americans, some of that journey has been treated almost as having been the result of luck, inevitability, or merely being in the right place at the right time. In the process, rather than seeing Johnson's vision and strategic thinking, his bending when the demands of the marketplace said bend and standing firm when they said the same, have gone overlooked. Yes, luck, preparation, and location were truly important in Johnson's success. Still, as Johnson himself said, also true is that his success resulted from a business vision and entrepreneurial drive that allowed him to surmount obstacles that others could not and to recognize opportunities that others did not. This gap in Johnson's story, the strategic thinking and entrepreneurial zeal that pushed him to surmount obstacles that drove many of his competitors from the field, along with the unique advantages that living in Chicago afforded him, are what this chapter examines.

John H. Johnson did not come of age and develop his business enterprises in just any city. He did so in Chicago, the capital of the Midwest, which had been destroyed and then completely rebuilt in the late nineteenth century. So this somewhat new city offered opportunity to those with the courage to reach out and take it, to make, ofttimes with the help of powerful sponsors or mentors, their own fortunes. For blacks in the city there was a unique combination of geographic proximity and a level of prejudice that engendered an "us against them" kind of self-help philosophy. As Allan Spear put it in his 1967 work *Black Chicago: The Making of a Negro Ghetto*: "Whatever the real achievements of Negro businessman, politicians, and civic leaders, the sight of Negroes participating independently in fields that had previously been monopolized by whites became a source of race pride. Jesse Binga, Oscar De Priest, and George Cleveland Hall were more than Negro leaders; they became race heroes. Their accomplishments seemed to prove that Negroes could succeed, just as whites had succeeded, even with the odds arrayed against them."[3]

Thus migrants like young Johnson, who arrived in Chicago in 1933, found a grounded community that encouraged the development of enterprises and organizations primarily to aid and support African Americans.

Finding a Mentor

After graduating from DuSable High School, Johnson went to work for Supreme Liberty Life Insurance. The company was led by Harry Pace, one of the leading black businessmen in Chicago. Working as Pace's assistant, and later for politician and public gadfly Earl Dickerson, put Johnson in the power center of black economic and political life in the city. As a result, he developed a professional network that positioned him to begin some type of business enterprise, the only question being what kind. It was after an assignment from Pace that he made his decision. Pace had tasked him to gather and summarize news related to African Americans so that Pace had an understanding of potential issues facing his clients and company. Glimpsing the possibility that other blacks might be interested in a similar kind of news summary, Johnson decided to go into publishing.

Harry Pace provided Johnson with important access to office space, information, and the support of printing services that few other neophyte entrepreneurs could match. The older man also provided him with important advice, namely to strike out on his own without enlisting the aid of others. While developing plans for his publishing venture, Johnson approached Pace with a list (including Pace) of several prominent blacks whom he planned to ask to join his editorial board. He hoped the list of black luminaries would give the new magazine a measure of instant credibility. Pace advised against the move. His reasoning was sound: Pace and the others on Johnson's list were well known, yes, but that also meant that they had enemies that might array themselves against Johnson's venture. As a young man and relative unknown, Johnson had not yet amassed a similar caliber of enemies. Therefore, Pace argued, it would be better if Johnson's were the only name on the issue.[4] This company or board of one, while at times a difficult arrangement for Johnson, in the long run forced him to rely upon (and listen) only to himself. Throughout his lifetime, Johnson did not have to assuage a board of directors, or even advisors, nor did he have to bend to the whims of investors or partners. Instead he could do largely as he pleased with his company.

Yet beyond Pace, one central question remains, and it is one that Johnson never conclusively answered: Whom did he go to for his initial business advice? Consider that, as a business neophyte he maneuvered a magazine distributor into carrying his first publication, *Negro Digest*, by having friends appear at newsstands and ask for the magazine; and he used his meager budget to have people buy the magazines so that they did not stay on the shelf but instead had the appearance of popularity. Who gave him this advice to do these things? After all, he had no prior experience in running a publishing business and had at best only rudimentary financial knowledge. For example, when he went to secure his first business loan, he admitted that he did not know the meaning of the term "collateral." So where did the ideas come from? In his biography he routinely used the word "I" when describing his successes, but if longtime *Ebony* editor and employee Ben Burns is to be believed, others often had more input than Johnson was willing to credit in later life. Still, it is possible that although he did not have business knowledge (at least in the textbook definition of the term), he had good business instincts that enabled him to make the right strategic decisions.

At a minimum, Johnson's presence in Chicago exposed him to other successful black entrepreneurs. He interacted with Samuel B. (S. B.) Fuller, one of the leading entrepreneurs in the city, attended Fuller's sales meetings, and sometimes went to meetings held by the Negro Chamber of Commerce (NCC).[5] The organization was forward-thinking and focused on "breaking away from the usual concept of Negro business, pointing out new commercial avenues and giving advice to members and non-members alike."[6] So this organization may have served as a source of information for Johnson in the development of his business techniques and strategies. Further, a stated goal of the NCC was for its members to be "cooperative [and to] . . . deal commercially with each other as much as possible."[7] After having met Fuller at a meeting of the NCC, Johnson said, "Mr. Fuller invited me to come by his office. We developed an ongoing relationship. I attended the Fuller morning meetings and they would give me the incentive to go out and sell advertising and reconfirm my commitment to succeed. Seeing that Mr. Fuller could do what he had set out to do, I gained inspiration and motivation and belief in myself."[8] So whether through his attendance at the NCC or through personal interactions with Fuller himself, Johnson undoubtedly gained a measure of insight from the business experience of Fuller and others in the organization. Thus Johnson was able to learn some business techniques (or at least gain inspiration) even though he had never gone to business school. Business history is filled with success stories (and failures, as well, of course) of people who had not been to business school but had the necessary instincts for success.

With Pace's advice; Fuller's inspiration; the input and support of his wife, Eunice; and the publishing knowledge of editor Ben Burns, Johnson made *Negro Digest* a success. Although the magazine was merely an aggregation of news items already printed in other magazines and newspapers, like its inspiration, *Reader's Digest*, the format proved successful. After some early struggles, within a few years *Negro Digest* provided Johnson with a livelihood and comfortable financial status. Another publication, however, would be the one that vaulted him to worldwide fame and a level of wealth he could scarcely believe.

Creating *Ebony* Magazine

Ironically the most financially successful of all Johnson's business ventures, *Ebony* magazine, was not originally his idea. The catalyst for *Ebony* came from two Johnson company employees, Jay Jackson and Ben Burns. The two men proposed a magazine called *Jive*, aimed at musicians and others interested in hip, cool topics. Johnson agreed to partner with the two men, with each putting up $1,000 for the venture. The other men could not come up with the funds, so Johnson became the sole owner. As the owner he decided to reshape the men's original magazine idea into the picture magazine that became *Ebony*. In fact, had it not been for the two freelancers, *Ebony* might not have seen the light of day. Johnson had just come off of a successful fight with the War Production Board, and with the future of *Negro Digest* set, he had no interest in a new publishing venture.[9] Had he waited, Johnson might have been undone. He was not the only one who saw the potential in a picture-based magazine for African Americans. Photojournalism had grown in popularity, but images of African Americans were absent from the periodicals most success-ful with the genre. Further, when it came to photojournalism, blacks were absent from the other periodicals that practiced the craft. Ben Burns recalled visiting the office of Earl Brown, the only black editor at *Life* magazine, as Brown showed him a "three-foot-high stack of rejected picture stories on Negro subjects."[10] A poten-tial rival, John P. Davis, also saw the possibilities of a photo-based magazine and in 1946 began publishing *Our World*, which, for a time, was a strong competitor to *Ebony*. Had *Ebony* not been there as a competitor, perhaps Davis would have been the one to control the segment. Writing in his autobiography, Johnson admitted, "if I had continued to rely on *Negro Digest* alone, I would be out of business today."[11]

While he may not have read every academic treatise on African American con-sumers, envisioned the creation of a magazine, or been able to expressly compare the economic value of the African American market to that of Canada, Johnson had the personal experience to know that there were millions of blacks like him-self—educated men and women who were hardworking professionals in their industries. Like Johnson, they were aware of the ever-present problems of race in America, but they also took time to enjoy material comforts in their lives with their families. In other words, they were blacks who were interested in addressing the challenges of racism and discrimination but who also liked indulging in the leisure and consumer-based pursuits their incomes allowed. Further, Johnson was keenly aware of the growing interest in the African American consumer market, and he knew that if the right marketing vehicle were available (e.g., a magazine), advertisers might be convinced to use it to reach black consumers.

As was the case with *Negro Digest*, Johnson and editor Ben Burns collaborated on the development of *Ebony*. Therefore, it is impossible to say just who was most responsible for the editorial development of *Ebony* during its initial years. Both Johnson and Burns claim a primary role for the development of the magazine. Yet for all that can be said of the young Johnson, he had a clarity of purpose for his magazine: to provide blacks with stories and images of themselves about which they could be proud. He said, "In 1942, Black men and women were struggling all over America for the right to be called 'Mr.' And 'Mrs.' In that year, we couldn't try on shoes and dresses in Atlanta. We couldn't live in hotels in downtown Chicago, then, and the only public place a Black could get a meal in the downtown section of the nation's capital was the railroad station . . . It was a world where the primary need, almost as demanding as oxygen, was recognition and respect."[12]

With this central guiding vision—respect—the content of the magazine undeniably bore Johnson's stamp. Burns recalled that Johnson "checked every article and caption, every photo and title, often revising or cutting entirely anything he did not approve of."[13] The two men did not always get along. In his autobiography Burns said, "My Communist and *Defender* training in protest proved a source of continual acrimony between Johnson and me for almost all the years I worked for him."[14] Yet Johnson did not fire Burns until a final disagreement over the content of the magazine in which he felt Burns "defied" his directions and undermined his leadership.[15] Nonetheless, in the all-important early years of *Ebony*'s existence, Burns's editorial skill and Johnson's racial understanding made a potent combination for developing the first commercially successful African American magazine in history.

But in addition to the aforementioned skill and vision of Burns and Johnson, something must be said about the timing of *Ebony*'s initial publication. In the years following World War II, a series of factors came together that provided more support to the viability of an African American consumer market than had ever existed. First a consistent array of articles, both academic and industry-based, were published that evaluated the consumer power of African Americans in flattering ways. For example, readers of advertising-industry trade journals like *Tide* or *Printer's Ink* were offered repeated descriptions of an "internal market" in the United States that dwarfed that of the external markets in places like Canada and Australia. Additionally, a number of articles detailed the experiences of companies like Pepsi-Cola and Standard Oil, which developed successful and profitable marketing programs among black consumers. This information dovetailed nicely with the anecdotal experience of nearly all Americans during World War II: increased salaries followed by a rapid return to consumer spending once wartime rationing ended. Further, the medium of the photograph offered the chance to show blacks, rather than merely tell them, about the activities of their race. Johnson said: "We wanted to *see* Dr. Charles Drew and Ralph Bunche and Jackie Robinson and the other men and women who were building the campfires of tomorrow. We wanted to know where they lived, what their families looked like, and what they did when they weren't onstage [emphasis in original]."[16] The realities of segregation in America were such that few whites knew of the African American world to which Johnson introduced them, a world of blacks who owned their own homes, drove new automobiles, were educated, had families, took vacations, and bought consumer goods. These factors, combined with Johnson's indefatigable promotion of black consumers and his magazine, *Ebony*, in reaching them, meant that corporate executives interested in wringing the maximum profits available could no longer ignore black consumers.[17]

Nonetheless, viewed objectively, there was little reason for Johnson to expect to succeed at publishing an advertiser-supported general-interest magazine for African Americans. Many had come before him and had failed. Other publishers found limited advertiser interest in supporting a magazine for blacks via advertisements whose very existence might offend their white consumer base. And while Johnson himself noted his own hard work and good luck, and being in the right place at the right time, it is clear that another factor belongs on the list: fear. Fear is an undeniable motivator. It encourages the taking of chances, stretches one's limits. For Johnson, a migrant from the South who had known both rivers and poverty, fear of returning to either led him to doggedly pursue a path toward a goal many others with more experience and contacts had failed to reach. Thus, since in his mind he could not go back, the only way to go was forward. So he bullied and bribed, threatened and cajoled, all the while driven by an almost unrelenting fear of failure or of losing his still-tenuous place at the head of the black publishers table.[18]

One has to differentiate between the content of *Negro Digest* and *Ebony*. The *Negro Digest* was a source of aggregated news about blacks, rather than one made up of articles with original content. Therefore, its stories were often about topics that dominated African American newspapers, such as discrimination, racism, and violence against blacks. These were important topics, to be sure, but it was not the kind of content that differed from that of the black newspapers that often provided its source material. Nor was it the kind of content that would attract advertisers. As a result, for *Ebony*, Johnson focused on developing original content of a kind that advertisers would not find objectionable.

The early years of *Ebony* were tumultuous, as Johnson worked to gather both readers and advertisers. It began as a relatively tame picture magazine, but to entice Johnson spiced up the magazine with articles rife with sexual innuendo and pictures of attractive women. This editorial move catalyzed newsstand sales but did little to increase either subscriptions or advertising schedules. Readership spiked and crested the half-million monthly circulation mark, but advertiser support proceeded slowly.[19] Then, when a mild recession came in the mid-1950s, readership of *Ebony* fell by 20 percent. The drop in circulation was nearly disastrous. The loss of readers meant that *Ebony* fell below its guarantee to advertisers and Johnson had to return $50,000, money he could ill afford to lose, to advertisers. Consequently, Johnson toned down the sexualized content of the magazine and developed a successful subscription program that allowed *Ebony* to grow more consistently. Focused on strengthening the subscription base of *Ebony*, Johnson crafted a program that enabled churches and schools to earn money from selling subscriptions to the magazine. Additionally, he launched an aggressive direct-mail campaign to potential subscribers, as well as a consistent advertising program for *Ebony* in black newspapers. Fellow black entrepreneur S. B. Fuller aided Johnson's subscription program by instructing his door-to-door sales representatives to sell Fuller company products as well as *Ebony* subscriptions.[20]

Still, although subscriptions were vital, Johnson knew that he could not make *Ebony* into the kind of publication he envisioned without consistent national advertising schedules. For he did not want just *any* kind of magazine. Instead he wanted a magazine that rivaled *Life*, the most popular photojournalism magazine of the period. He wanted *Ebony* to present blacks with images from the full range of the African American experience, with particular emphasis on success and the acquisition of material goods. The kind of magazine he had in mind, the kind that had never existed in the history of African American publishing, demanded advertising. And not just any advertising—he wanted advertisements from major national advertisers whose products graced shelves in department stores and automotive showrooms around the country.

Also, as Ben Burns noted, the publishing model for *Ebony* could not be sustained in the manner of that normally done by black periodicals. Whereas black newspapers traditionally relied on newsstand sales for their revenue, the higher costs of assembling *Ebony* meant that without regular advertising schedules, the magazine would either need to be drastically changed or it would fail.[21] Johnson therefore had to convince corporate executives that blacks had value as consumers. To do so did not mean that he had to convince them of blacks' value as a people, but merely that they were a potential source of profit to be respectfully approached via advertisements. Unfortunately, regardless of the number of advertising salesmen deployed, his advertising revenues remained limited. Burns said, "Our advertising sales representatives received cordial receptions at top advertising agencies, but the cordiality did not extend to placing ads in *Ebony*."[22]

Johnson's Gambit

John Johnson's approach to advertising was strategic. Rather than approach advertisers with the initial publication of the magazine, he waited. In fact, Johnson published *Ebony* without significant advertising until reaching 400,000 copies per month, with the hope that such a number would by itself convince advertisers of *Ebony*'s value. His problem was that his success was quickly dooming his magazine to extinction.

For magazine publishers, circulation is not always their most pressing concern. In terms of revenue, a careful balance must be struck between the production costs of magazines published and the amount of income generated from advertisements. It is quite possible for a publisher, as Johnson did, to lose more money the more copies that he sells. Magazines must be printed and distributed and their accompanying costs recovered. The most lucrative means to recovery (and revenue) is advertising. A logical point of comparison is black newspapers, but there are significant differences in creating a weekly versus a monthly periodical. In terms of the advertising in their pages, many black newspapers faced a destructive cycle. Newspaper publishers could not attract many of the major advertisers and their blue-chip ads and instead relied upon smaller merchants who were willing to buy the space. Yet because there were so few national advertisers, agencies resisted placing advertising in black-owned newspapers (beyond fear of white backlash or reprisals) because they did not want their clients' ads associated with the ads for fortune tellers, sex magazines, skin lighteners, and lucky numbers that were part of the black press. As a result, in their search for revenue, black publishers had to continue to accept the kinds of ads that paid the bills, but at the same time prevented their growth in the form of blue-chip advertisers.

The early success of *Ebony* demonstrated that Johnson had the support of readers. Analysis of the magazine by writers in the trade press was also supportive. As one observer said, "*Ebony* is edited with taste, intelligence, and a shrewd understanding of *what its public wants*" (emphasis mine).[23] Johnson was also careful to tell his readers of their responsibility in making *Ebony* a success. In the April 1946 issue, he announced that advertisements would soon be present in the magazine:

> You may be sure that we intend to be particular about the character of the "company" we introduce to the privacy of your home or office or study or wherever you enjoy your copy of *Ebony*. The editors of *Ebony* are determined that the standards of advertising in its pages will be up to the merits of its editorial material. You have our promise that our advertisers shall come a-calling with only the best.... But we will be selective in rejecting advertisements which are of a doubtful nature. In so doing, we wish to encourage your support of the products advertised in *Ebony*, since income from advertisements means your enjoyment of each issue will increase as our editorial department has more funds to bring you the best in photo stor[i]es on Negro life.[24]

Beyond the articles in the trade press, Johnson also regularly advertised *Ebony* in advertising and marketing trade journals. *Ebony* sales literature hawked its role in developing the black consumer market. A brochure was illustrated with the headline "We've opened the door," with a picture of a door through which were walking scores of white salesmen.[25]

"My problem was not the editorial content of the magazine—the readers were yelling for more. My problem was not circulation—I couldn't print enough copies.

My problem was advertising or, to come right out with it, the lack of advertising."[26] This was the final hurdle for Johnson, and perhaps every other black popular periodical that was his antecedent. It was not that blacks did not read or would not support a magazine, it was that every periodical reached a stage when it needed advertising to thrive. None had effectively obtained it before, and how Johnson could do so in the face of both resistance and disinterest from advertising-agency executives was the central question. Even if they were aware of *Ebony* or the potential of the Negro market, it was unlikely in the climate of the mid-1940s that many advertising executives had the temerity to suggest that their clients advertise in the magazine. Such a revolutionary suggestion or recommendation might be followed by a withdrawal of the account from the agency that was so foolish as to hire a man with such obviously poor judgment. So, rather than go to advertising executives, the people that recommended how advertising budgets should be spent, Johnson went to the clients, the ones who established the budgets in the first place. And when they agreed that spending money in *Ebony* was an acceptable choice, advertising executives no longer had to fear the results of suggesting an advertising schedule in *Ebony*. However, in going to the advertising managers of advertisers, he faced a similar problem: people unwilling to put their own jobs on the line by recommending placing advertisements in a black periodical.

When Johnson could not find advertisers for *Ebony*, he created them. As a stopgap measure he created his own mail-order companies like Beauty Star Cosmetics, marketer of hair products, Linda Fashions, purveyor of clothing, and a number of other ventures that sold books and vitamins. He then used *Ebony* to advertise the products of his own company. It was an ingenious move that provided him the money to keep going and the time to continue to press his case with large advertisers.[27]

Finally, nearing a financial breaking point, Johnson decided on an even more aggressive sales strategy. He concluded that he did not just have to speak to the advertising managers of the potential advertisers, but that he had to go even higher in the company. For example, the advertising manager at the Zenith corporation had told Johnson "no, a thousand times no" in his response to Johnson's appeals.[28] Johnson clearly needed a new plan. In order to succeed in the face of such resistance, Johnson decided to go to the very top. For example, in the case of Zenith, it was not until Johnson reached the head of the company, Commander Eugene F. MacDonald, the one who made the policies of the company, that the advertising schedules finally appeared. MacDonald then called the chairmen of the Swift Packing, Elgin Watch, Armour Foods, and Quaker Oats companies and asked them to meet with Johnson and discuss the possibility of advertising in *Ebony*. So it was not just that Johnson went to the clients, it is that he went to the heads of the various companies and got them to agree to change their policies on advertising in *Ebony*.[29]

As in the case of other matters related to Johnson Publishing, Johnson and Burns have a different recollection of the catalyst for the new advertising strategy. Both men claim credit. Johnson argued that using his position as a CEO to reach out to other CEOs was his idea, while Burns claims the idea was his own. Regardless, both men agree on one central point, the one on which the whole strategy depended: Johnson was an "excellent advertising salesman."[30]

To properly appreciate Johnson's growth and success as a salesman, it must be recognized that prior to *Ebony*, he had no limited sales experience and never worked directly for whites. In other words, he never faced the psychological hurdle of trying to advance within a white corporate structure. He had no experience in corporate America and office politics other than those he had learned working at Supreme Life, a black-owned company. Further, we must keep in mind that in his sales calls, Johnson went alone. He went without the comfort and familiarity of *Ebony* staffers and instead walked into various corporate headquarters alone and had to accept the "What's he doing here" stares that were part of the segregated corporate America he operated within. After cresting the hurdles successfully, Johnson often found himself invited to luncheons and other events with whites. But that also meant that as a southern black man he had to overcome the challenges that came from interacting with whites. Not that he was scared, but he was not necessarily comfortable around them. As he said to Burns once, "I never feel comfortable eating with white people. I can't relax."[31] Fearful of appearing to conform to racial stereotypes, Johnson either ate before he attended events with whites or, for much of his professional life, abstained from publicly eating dishes like fried chicken, pork chops, or watermelon. Johnson had to keep up a specific public face, that of the conservative publisher. While former employees often remembered him as personable and gregarious with them, often noted for his willingness to eat with them, meet their family members, and inquire about their personal lives, he was long wary in his contact with whites.[32] He did not want to do anything that might confirm their prejudices and stereotypes about African Americans for fear of what it might do to their perceptions of his businesses.

To his credit, Johnson also understood that his own discomfort in dealing with the effects of race and prejudice might impact his sales representatives, as well. Consequently, he selected them carefully. Ron Sampson, a former *Ebony* advertising salesman, recalled that "he assessed their capabilities on the basis of what their background and experience had been and their ability to present themselves, the ability to believe in the product and *to represent the race*" (emphasis mine).[33] Also, Johnson understood the limitations that his advertising representatives faced, in contrast to their competitors from white-oriented magazines, radio stations, and any other source competing for the advertising spending of agencies and manufacturers. He knew that, beyond the qualities of the product or service being sold, sales were often a personal, relationship-based interaction. Salesmen had to inter-act with clients and decision makers, get to know them, take them to lunch or the occasional ballgame. But the limitations of race and ever-present possibility of racial incidents or embarrassments (even in Chicago) meant that his representa-tives were at a disadvantage. They did not live in the same neighborhoods as their clients, attend the same churches, or belong to the same country clubs. There-fore, to create a "comfort zone" in which his representatives could interact with potential clients, he created a stellar cafeteria and executive dining room at his company headquarters. Sampson said that he and other representatives "brought them [white sales clients] on our turf, invited them to come down and see how this business worked, meet some professional people, and see some folks that they would understand were as professional as they were in terms of how we did our work."[34]

Beyond his employees and readers, keeping his advertisers happy was John-son's priority throughout his career. He had to be wary of offending them and hav-ing them pull their advertising schedules. For example, one advertising executive asked that *Ebony* be sent to his office rather than his home lest his "wife and kids see all that mixed marriage stuff."[35] Additionally, since his circulation was largely dependent on newspaper sales, he had to balance the kinds of stimulating (and sometimes sex-related) stories that drove newsstand sales, but had the potential to offend his advertisers. The content of *Ebony* walked an ongoing tightrope between the kinds of material that would catalyze readership, but also not drive advertisers away from the magazine. Hence Johnson simply was not free to produce just any kind of magazine he may have wanted or his critics may have demanded. In the case of his advertisers, he was beholden to them, and if he offended them too gravely he might be out of business. So he had to carefully balance the content sought by his readers with the content acceptable to his advertisers.

The final step in Johnson's strategic gambit came in the early 1950s. Selling more advertising space can involve the simple process of merely adding more pages to the periodical in question. But Johnson had a different problem. He recognized that to get contracts with some of the key blue-chip national advertisers, he had to get rid of some of *Ebony*'s smaller advertisers. In the early, financially lean years of the magazine, those small advertisers had enabled him to survive, but they now were a liability. Therefore, he had to eliminate the profitable but lowbrow lucky-charm, astrology, and sex-book advertisements present on the back pages of the magazine. Removing the aforementioned offenders would not guarantee blue-chip advertisers, but it would at least forestall one routine justification for avoiding the black press: that they accepted the kinds of product advertising that no national advertisers wanted their brand displayed alongside. It was a strategic risk, but it was a move that ultimately paid off. After eliminating these ads, *Ebony*'s advertising pages steadily grew. Further, a few years later Johnson secured the first advertisements from a major automobile company, Chrysler. Getting Chrysler and other automobile advertisements (some of the most lucrative advertising in the country) was an indication that *Ebony* was finally recognized as a first-rate advertising source by agencies and advertisers alike.[36]

With the final step of Johnson's advertising strategy complete, here at last was the magazine he'd envisioned and that advertisers and agencies had to at least begrudgingly accept. It had a large, independently verified circulation, editorial content that could hardly be called radical, and was unlikely to be a spot for criticizing the policies of its advertisers. Instead writers lauded Johnson and *Ebony* for showing "taste and restraint to avoid the taint that afflicts so much of the Negro press."[37] Johnson was even the subject of a kind of reverse-racism insult when his publications were viewed to be of such quality that some critics argued they could not be produced by blacks. Instead, critics charged that they must have been the product of an invisible white owner like Henry Luce, publisher of *Time* and *Life*, or of the newspaper magnate William Randolph Hearst.[38]

Beyond the advertising in the pages of *Ebony*, Johnson developed a merchandising service to help advertisers address in-store problems in reaching African American consumers. Moreover, the *Ebony* merchandising program included a series of stickers and tags that included some variation on the theme that the product was advertised in *Ebony*. Phrases like "This brand is advertised in *Ebony* because we want you to try it," and "An *Ebony* advertised product," and "You saw this advertised in *Ebony*" were used. This program provided advice on marketing techniques, market research, in-store guidance that included industry-specific dos and don'ts for reaching black consumers, and an array of ongoing surveys of information related to blacks as consumers.[39] Further, over the years, Johnson's staff tracked the social and cultural changes ongoing among African Americans. Beyond merely relaying that blacks had changed their preferences from accepting being called "Negro" to that of "Afro-American," "Black," or "African American," they informed advertisers as to the meaning of those changes for blacks' expectations from advertising and their activity as consumers. Thus in the 1960s, blacks transitioned from merely expecting and welcoming an "invitation" to purchase as evidenced by an advertisement in *Ebony*. Instead they had shifted to expecting that those ads would feature African American models (e.g., people who looked like them) and would include culturally relevant and respectful cues.[40]

The Criticism

Johnson's focus on being "cheerful" and on African American success stories earned him a number of critics. Many, including editor Burns, decried the fact that the magazine did not focus more attention on racism and discrimination.[41] If only because he became the largest and most visible black publisher, Johnson naturally received the most criticism. No matter the content of his periodicals, his presence at the top of the pyramid meant that nearly everyone concerned enough to yield an opinion believed they knew better how to deliver the content of the leading periodical of the race than did Johnson. Some said *Ebony* should be more critical, while others said the opposite. Some said the magazine should analyze racial issues more actively and critically, and others said the opposite.

Even among the staff, opinions as to the magazine's content wavered. For his part, at least editor Burns recognized that his beliefs as a communist colored his ideals about what the content of any black periodical should be, namely a lightning rod of radical polemics and racial protest. But he seemed to have overlooked Johnson's mantra: Give the people what they want. For Johnson it was the *Ebony* reader who determined the content of *Ebony*, as they could have chosen not to purchase it as a result of its "cheerful" outlook. Regardless of the opinion, however, Johnson's editorial practicality was not without merit. Black newspapers were already actively covering topics of racism, discrimination, and segregation. If he had simply delivered a picture version of the existing print content (and replicated the content of *Negro Digest* in the process), *Ebony* would not have been unique on the newsstand. Further, as a monthly magazine, *Ebony* would have been in the position of delivering pictures for stories that were no longer relevant. But Johnson recognized that African Americans, "in addition to being members of the NAACP and Urban League, were also members of sororities and fraternities and lodges. They marched and raised hell but they also raised children and gave debutante balls and watched baseball and football games," and thereby created an irresistible hook for readers and filled a content void in the African American press.[42] As editor Hans Massaquoi said, "*Ebony* is first of all a moneymaking venture. It's a business just as are many other magazines. We can only do the things to advance the black cause if we are solvent. *Ebony* is edited to appeal to as broad an audience as possible. So we have a variety of articles. We feel we have material in the magazine that appeals to young people, old people, intellectuals and perhaps to illiterates."[43]

Massaquoi alluded to three other points that need further exploration. First, the rest of the black press was filled with the kinds of news material Burns and others pressed *Ebony* to include. Further, as he himself admitted, as a monthly magazine *Ebony* was placed in the position of reporting on stories that had already been covered by other, daily and weekly periodicals. Second, Burns clearly never appreciated the lengths Johnson had to go to in order to run a successful company. He never felt sting of not being able to purchase a property simply because he was black, rather than that he lacked the money. Further, he never seemed to appreciate that, while Johnson was the publisher and his boss, Johnson was beholden to the whims of his advertisers whose support he needed to run a successful company. *Ebony* was something new in the black publishing arena. And given the rapid growth of *Ebony's* circulation and advertising revenue and its position as the dominant black-owned magazine of the twentieth century, it is hard to argue with Johnson's development of *Ebony*. Third, magazines that promoted a consumer lifestyle of cars, clothes, homes, and food, like *Ebony*, were much more likely to get advertisements from the companies making products that were part of that lifestyle than magazines that did not.[44]

In order to build his business, Johnson had to bend to insults, slurs, and control that came only as a result of his being African American. For example, in the mid-1940s, when the circulation needs of *Ebony* necessitated a move to a printer who could better handle the quantity of work required, Johnson hired one of the largest printers in the city. At that time the printer was the one with the power. The backlog of print material resulting from the limits imposed by the paper rationing connected to World War II meant that printers could turn down accounts and still have a full load of work. Although the printer, W. F. Hall, agreed to handle the Johnson Publishing accounts, there were some occasions where the company refused to print some material for the magazine. For example, a story on interracial dating among black servicemen and white European women was to be illustrated with photos of blacks and whites mixing at parties and nightclubs, and in physically intimate embraces. After seeing the photos, the printer phoned Johnson and informed him that his workmen did not like the photos and that it would be best if the material were taken out of the story rather than printed, which Johnson accepted.[45]

In the early 1950s, Johnson sought ways to expand his empire. He continued his practice of developing black versions of popular general-audience magazines: the monthly *Tan Confessions* mirrored *True Confessions*, and a new weekly, *Jet*, mirrored *Quick*. But for a brief period, Johnson considered using *Quick* to break into publishing magazines for white readers. The pocket-sized weekly had a circulation of more than a million readers, and he surmised that one of its primary difficulties was overstaffing. He reasoned that if he could cut costs sufficiently, he had a chance to make the magazine profitable again. But the specter of race once again reared its head. Johnson did not have the freedom of white business owners, who saw an investment opportunity and weighed the various strengths and weaknesses of the acquisition. In addition to those necessities, Johnson also had to weigh the possibilities of racism. Specifically, he worried that if his white advertisers saw him publishing a magazine for white readers, they might have been so incensed that he had become "uppity" and was attempting to move out of his rightful "place" and publish material for whites that they would pull their advertisements from *Ebony*. Rather than take that unacceptable risk, Johnson passed on acquiring *Quick* and published *Jet* instead.[46]

As Johnson himself later admitted, his business needs often outweighed his sense of personal or racial pride. He had often had to bend and accept little indignities in pursuit of larger goals. He said, "I stooped all the time to get what I wanted. If I had to do it over again, I would."[47] To get the advertising account from the Elgin Watch company, he had to sit and say nothing when the head of the company told his advertising manager to give "this boy" some of the company's advertising budget. Or he had to carefully explain to Quaker Oats executives that even though blacks were then protesting the image of Aunt Jemima pancake mix, with its recognized trade character of the heavy-set, handkerchief-headed dark black woman, they still bought the product, and as such it should be advertised in *Ebony*.[48] Thus despite his personal feelings, his needs as a business owner won out. Plus, simply put, Johnson had been poor, and *Negro Digest* had introduced him to what it was like to have money. His personal experience had taught him that, at least in terms of the kinds of comforts and power that could be purchased, having money was better than not.[49]

Defending His Position

Throughout his publishing career, Johnson fiercely defended his position as the leading black publisher in the country. He promoted his magazines in every avenue possible and advertised in the trade press for potential advertising clients. Yet as his publishing enterprises grew, Johnson realized many potential advertisers considered all of the black press to be the same. Therefore, in order to increase his own chances of success, he routinely had to differentiate his periodicals from others in the existing Negro press. In contrast to white periodicals, Johnson recognized that there were limited dollars available for advertising to black consumers and that his profits rested on building a wall around his publications and then fighting off any interlopers. In 1952 Johnson took a more proactive and offensive stance in publishing not just market statistics of black consumers in a particular category, but *Ebony*'s penetration in the Negro market with a direct comparison to black periodicals.

The relationship between Johnson and other editors could be described as a kind of cautious cooperation. Neither he nor any other black publisher had the kind of confidence in their relationships with advertisers as did white-owned publications like those in the Henry Luce (e.g., *Time*) or Curtis Publishing (e.g., *Ladies Home Journal*) companies. Absent the specter of race, those publishers could expect to receive continued entreaties from advertisers to use their magazines to reach their millions of white readers. Black publishers, on the other hand, were fighting over the same limited pool of advertisers and agencies. Further, especially in the case of those periodicals with a national reach (e.g., *Chicago Defender*, *Pittsburgh Courier*, and *Ebony*), they could not necessarily expect that the ads placed in one would be replicated in the others. In other words, if an advertiser already felt they were reaching the national African American consumer market via the *Chicago Defender*, the publisher of the *Pittsburgh Courier* had reason to be concerned that they would not choose another black-oriented national periodical, as well. As a result, using the cudgel of a quantitative research report designed to proactively limit encroachment on his advertising revenue, Johnson launched what can only be construed as an open attack on the advertising potential of black newspapers. The report did not go as far as to say that they should never be used as a source to reach the black consumer, but that the magazines that were part of his publishing company were the most effective and efficient way to do so. His implication to potential advertisers was clear: black newspapers were a waste of advertising spending.[50]

Viewed through the lens of racial solidarity, Johnson's actions seem self-centered, cruel, and unnecessarily aggressive and oppositional to an important voice of the African American community. When viewed through the lens of the competitive marketplace, however, his actions were both reasonable and necessary. Competition was a fact of business life. Further, Johnson was both a realist and a pragmatist. While the number of black readers in the country could ably support multiple magazines that catered to their interests, the number of advertisers interested in targeting those readers would not. Advertisers accepted the need for ads in a magazine like *Life* to reach white readers and one in *Ebony* to reach black ones. They would not, he reasoned, pay for ads in black-oriented magazines whose content was even marginally similar. He was well aware of the limited pool of advertising available to black publishers and wanted to ensure that he received the lion's share of it. There was nothing anywhere in his history that suggests Johnson sought the demise of black newspapers, but rather that he wanted his periodicals to receive the primary consideration from any company spending money to advertise to black consumers.

Beyond black newspapers, the stiffest competition for the slice of the magazine world *Ebony* occupied came in the first few years of the magazine. *Our World*, a publication based in New York City, competed with *Ebony* for rack space and advertising schedules. Johnson said, "There were other competitors, but *Our World* kept me up more nights than any other publication."[51] Both *Our World* and *Ebony* were after the same everything: same employees, same content, same readers, and same advertisers. Billed as "The picture magazine for the whole family," *Our World* included the same kinds of general-interest content (sports, celebrities, entertainment, images of attractive men and women) used by *Ebony*. Johnson himself admitted that "*Ebony* was not that much better than *Our World*," but he believed that his need to focus only on his publication provided him the necessary edge.[52] In contrast, John P. Davis, publisher of *Our World*, often had other interests and commitments that detracted from his personal involvement. Over the long run, it was Johnson's personal involvement that allowed *Ebony* to succeed. It was his personal appeals to advertisers, he reasoned, rather than the existence of or the excellence of the magazine that resulted in advertising contracts and revenue. "While he [Davis] was off making speeches and dealing with the law and other things, I was in the trenches, digging, fighting, worrying, and even crying. In the end, persistence and doggedness won out. *Ebony* was not that much better than *Our World*—I simply tried harder."[53] Had Davis been able to pursue a similar focus, the outcome could have been considerably different in this "life-and-death struggle" between *Ebony* and *Our World*.[54]

In the case between *Ebony* and *Our World*, Johnson's singular focus on the magazine business was clearly an asset. Virtually all of his public appearances were directly related to *Ebony* or African American consumers. In contrast, Davis spent time dealing with various political and racial issues. Davis had been a founding member of the National Negro Congress (NNC), a civil-rights organization that supported interracial understanding and cooperation. Later, during the anticommunist furor symbolized by the McCarthy hearings of the 1950s, Davis had to defend himself against those who viewed his NNC membership as evidence of communism. As a result, in contrast to Davis, Johnson focused all of his energies on succeeding as a publisher rather than as a lawyer, public speaker (unless it dealt somehow with his publications), or in some other role.

Johnson recognized that at that time there was room for only one successful black picture-based magazine. As in the case of black newspapers, there simply was not enough national advertising directed to black consumers to support more than one (especially if the two were so similar that once you were past their covers you had difficulty discerning between them, as with *Ebony* and *Our World*). Consequently, the battle between the two men and their publications was bitter. Davis tried to recruit editor Ben Burns away from *Ebony* but demurred when Burns asked for a pay raise over his *Ebony* salary. Davis later used Burns's race as a cudgel with which to critique the contents of *Ebony*, saying, "*Ebony* reads like a white man's idea of what Negroes want in a publication."[55] Further, he verbally attacked Johnson for having a "white man [Burns] high on his staff,"[56] a curious observation considering Davis's history with the National Negro Congress (NNC), an organization interested in promoting interracial understanding and cooperation.

In 1955, listing over $200,000 in unpaid debts, Davis declared the *Our World* Publishing Company to be bankrupt.[57] When *Our World* was declared bankrupt and its assets put up for sale, Johnson submitted the highest bid at $14,000 and then scuttled the magazine. In so doing, he ensured that the magazine would never be published again. It would not be until the arrival of *Essence* and *Black Enterprise* magazines in the 1970s that Johnson again faced competition for advertising spending devoted to black consumers.

Expanding an Empire

Although *Ebony* and *Jet* were his primary focus, Johnson cannot be accused of resting on their success or of not seeking other business opportunities. As in the case of *Ebony*, it was another who catalyzed his first major venture outside of publishing. In the late 1960s, Johnson's wife, Eunice, approached him about the creation of a cosmetics line for black women. The development of the line proved the catalyst for one of his most successful ventures.

Eunice Johnson was the key architect of one of the other Johnson Publishing ventures, the *Ebony* Fashion Fair show. She established and maintained relationships with the international designers who provided the fashions, organized the traveling exhibition, and worked closely with the black models who wore the designer fashions presented in the show. Therefore, she was well aware of the difficulties that they had in finding cosmetics appropriate for their skin tones, tones that were darker than the Caucasian ones that then drew the attention from manufacturers. In the late 1960s, she approached her husband and he in turn went to some of the country's largest manufacturers of cosmetics to encourage them to create a line specifically for the varied hues of African American women. To a person, they showed no interest. Sensing an opportunity, Johnson and his wife went to a variety of chemists until they found one who could create the appropriate products for black women. Then, rather than using the mail-order route with which he had been so successful in the early days of *Ebony*, he decided that the products would be sold in "high-line" department stores. With the support of the *Ebony* Fashion Fair show and now a cosmetics line of the same name, "Fashion Fair," Johnson had potent name recognition if he could secure proper distribution.[58]

As was the case when he started his publications, Johnson initiated his efforts to market Fashion Fair cosmetics in Chicago. His primary initial target was Marshall Field's, the most popular major department store in the city. In 1974 his efforts toward Marshall Field's executives began in earnest. Of all the initial "high-line" stores, Marshall Field's was the most important. Johnson reasoned that if he could get the store, based in the city of Chicago, to carry his line, others would follow. If he could not, they would not. Through sales techniques similar to those he used in the early years of distributing *Ebony*, he succeeded in getting Field's to carry the Fashion Fair line. But in a request couched in caution and likely some racism, Field's executives asked him not to advertise the line's availability in Marshall Field's. The reason? Fear of offending white female customers with the presence of a black-oriented line in the store. As he had done with *Ebony*, Johnson found a way around the request. He had black women go into the store and purchase hundreds of dollars' worth of Fashion Fair cosmetics every week. As the popularity of the line became evident, Field's executives relented on their advertising prohibition. Beyond Marshall Field's, he also personally sold the line to major department stores like Dillard's and Nieman Marcus in the United States, as well as Harrods and Printemps in London and Paris, respectively. Over the next several years, Fashion Fair became the largest black-owned cosmetics firm in the country and was sold in over 1,500 stores.[59]

Beyond cosmetics and fashion, Johnson's final major efforts at empire building came in the area he knew best, publishing. Like other entrepreneurs and akin to billionaire investor Warren Buffet, Johnson primarily invested in businesses and enterprises within his sphere of understanding, black-oriented magazines. By his own admission, Johnson was not always supportive of other black publishers. He was friendly, but he always viewed them as competitors for advertising dollars and was wary of cooperating in any way. For example, the publishers of *Essence*, a magazine for black women, approached him with a cooperative plan to lower each magazine's printing costs, but Johnson refused. Later, when those same publishers proposed a potential joint advertising effort between *Ebony* and *Essence* magazine, Johnson said, "Madison Avenue will not allow *Ebony* and *Essence* to come together."[60] Edward Lewis, publisher of *Essence* magazine recalled, "John had been the first and only black magazine game on Madison Avenue for so long that he never really got used to the idea of four young upstarts launching a magazine for black women two and a half decades after he'd pretty much single-handedly laid the groundwork."[61]

Echoing Lewis's recollection, Earl Graves, publisher of *Black Enterprise*, a magazine geared toward black business executives, related a similar anecdote: In a meeting between Johnson and Graves, Johnson revealed that "from the moment BE [*Black Enterprise*] was published, he saw it as an encroachment on *Ebony*'s circulation and ad dollars. In meetings with potential advertisers, they'd ask him about BE and he'd tell them it wasn't serious or that Graves character was running numbers on the side—whatever he could to discourage their interest."[62] Nonetheless, perhaps because the content of *Ebony* and *Black Enterprise* was dissimilar, eventually the two competitors became friends.

Even if personally friendly, though, as a professional and aggressive businessman, Johnson's hostility to competition was sometimes war waged openly. In 1985 Johnson was part of a hostile takeover attempt of *Essence* magazine. During a period of internal managerial turmoil at *Essence*, he was part of a group that attempted to oust publishing head Lewis. Johnson bought up the shares of investors seeking to sell their interests in the magazine. With his already sizable shares bolstered, he positioned himself for control. Although the takeover effort eventually failed, it is intriguing to consider how the current landscape of black magazine publishing might be different had he succeeded. Would he have scuttled the magazine and combined its content with *Ebony*, or would he have allowed it to continue to run as a separate entity? Given his business acumen and the success of *Essence*, it is likely that his modifications, if any, would have been minor. What is certain, though, is the financial windfall his shares in Essence Communications eventually earned. In 2005, when the company was purchased by Time Warner, Johnson's shares were worth nearly $40 million.[63] A strategist and financially astute pragmatist, Johnson recognized that even if he could not control *Essence* as he did *Ebony*, there was still a great deal of money to be made, and he wanted, and got, his share.

The Legacy of John H. Johnson

"In a world of despair, we wanted to give hope. In a world of negative black images, we wanted to provide positive Black images. In a world that said Blacks could do few things, we wanted to say they could do everything. We believed in 1945 that Black Americans needed positive images to fulfill their potential. We believed then—and we believe now—that you have to change images before you can change acts and institutions," said Johnson.[64] It is easy to dismiss this idea when we live in a country that has elected an African American president. But in the mid-1940s the racist and derogatory images of Black Americans were centuries old and had not left blacks unaffected. In Johnson's understanding, too many African Americans unwittingly accepted the idea that whites were superior, if for no other reason than that this was what they had always been told. If you were *really* sick, you went to a white doctor. If you *really* needed legal help, you found a white lawyer. This was the time period of the *Brown v. Board of Education* experiment in which when asked which doll was better, the black or the white one, the little black girl said with no hesitation the white one was better. So we cannot dismiss the broader impact and benefits of *Ebony* just because it enriched Johnson. In the process of making him a considerable amount of money, the positive images in the magazine undoubtedly also were a part of the process of changing institutions, America, and blacks' pictures of themselves and their possibilities.

Johnson started from a basic premise: Black people wanted respect (in all of the myriad ways in which that respect can be displayed or gained). In going into media and, later, cosmetics, Johnson's work was a continuation and extension of the most successful traditions of African American entrepreneurship in Chicago. Heir to the groundbreaking work of people like Claude Barnett, Anthony Overton (who also owned a cosmetics company and a magazine), Annie Malone, and Robert Abbott, Johnson became the most financially successful of them all.

Johnson had a simple business mantra: "Ask not what you want but what the customer or the potential customer wants."[65] This was the foundation of his message to potential clients: Do not run a marketing program among African Americans because I want you to, or for social reasons, do it because it will enable you to make more money. Johnson was not naive enough to believe that he could win converts to the Negro market (and by relation using *Ebony* as the vehicle to reach it) with social arguments. Instead he positioned his company as having a bottom-line benefit to their corporate revenues. If Johnson could demonstrate that his company was a valuable partner rather than just a source through which to ease the pressure of a boycott or negative publicity, then he could occupy a much more stable position. Additionally, he lacked the power, and possibly interest, to try and threaten corporate leaders with boycotts or other forms of negative publicity. Instead, he sought to convince and to persuade them with statistics and consistent appeals as his weapons of choice. In so doing, he appealed to the financial interests of corporate executives across America. He later recalled, "The only way I got to where I am today was by persuading thousands of Blacks and Whites, some of whom were very prejudiced, that the only way they could get what they wanted was by helping me get what I wanted."[66]

Johnson built both a business conglomerate and a marketplace. As an individual he was directly responsible for much of the corporate recognition of black consumers as a viable target market and for changing the overall way in which blacks were depicted in advertisements and other forms of media. Fairfax Cone, head of the agency Foote, Cone, and Belding, said that advertising agencies once "genially accepted that the white people shown in advertisements were the models most black people accepted for themselves."[67] He went on to credit the work of John Johnson and the success of *Ebony* for being the catalyst through which change eventually came. Certainly others were engaged in the effort to change the depiction of blacks in media—some, like fellow Chicagoan Claude Barnett, years before Johnson even entered the fray. Yet the voice that carried the most weight during the important years between 1950 and 1970 belonged to Johnson or one of his representatives.[68]

Additionally, Johnson was perhaps one of the best salesmen of the twentieth century. He had to sell his ideas to blacks and whites, both parties coming with preconceived notations about the potential success of an African American–themed magazine. And then he had to sell corporate executives on black consumers as a legitimate and profitable target for their advertising and marketing dollars.

Johnson adroitly recognized that as consumers (and as people), blacks wanted respect, and that corporate executives wanted profits and ever-increasing revenue. Blacks could shop only on specific days in some stores, were prevented from trying on hats, clothing, and shoes in others, and knew far better than to even to walk in the doors of others. They could not stay in just any hotel, were sometimes forced to eat their dinner from the back window of restaurants, and when traveling never knew when their very presence or display of affluence might arouse the ire of a racist police officer or incite a mob. So the world that Johnson addressed was the one so expertly cataloged via Ralph Ellison's nameless protagonist, in his masterwork *The Invisible Man*, in which they were simply invisible.

Johnson's impact was social, but also economic, and went well beyond his own companies. Working at Johnson Publications also gave several blacks the experience they needed to start advertising firms (Vince Cullers and Emmett McBain, to name two). He supported the efforts of other black entrepreneurs, especially when their businesses could assist his own rather than become a source of competition. Black entrepreneurs in a variety of industries owe their business livelihoods to Johnson and the staff of Johnson-owned companies.[69]

Today *Ebony* retains its position as the most widely circulated African American magazine, but the edges of the Johnson empire are slowly crumbling. Events once deemed unthinkable—the ending of the Ebony Fashion Fair, the sale of the company headquarters building to Columbia College, the ending of printed versions of *Jet* in favor of a digital-only presence, and the sale of a percentage of the company to an outside entity—have all taken place. The proud history of the company stands in stark contrast to its present reality. The reasons for these events are beyond the scope of this essay to analyze. Suffice it to say that it is questionable whether a magazine-based company that has lasted for over seventy years will exist for another decade or more.

Notes

1. John H. Johnson with Lerone Bennett Jr., *Succeeding against the Odds: The Autobiography of a Great American Businessman* (New York: Amistad Press, 1992), 58.

2. Ibid.

3. Allan H. Spear, *Black Chicago: The Making of a Negro Ghetto, 1890–1920* (Chicago: University of Chicago Press, 1967), 226.

4. "John Johnson: My Mentor, Harry Pace/Inspiration for the Negro Digest," YouTube video, 9:00, posted March 19, 2010, by "visionaryproject," National Visionary Leadership Project, http://www.youtube.com/watch?v=iDAlRt5E4oI.

5. Mary Fuller Casey, *S. B. Fuller: Pioneer in Black Economic Development* (Jamestown, NC: BridgeMaster Press, 2003), 57.

6. Leonard Pearson, "Negro Chambers of Commerce" (September 30, 1937), Illinois Writers Project: Negro in Illinois Papers, Box 25, Folder 15, Vivian G. Harsh Research Collection of Afro-American History and Literature Chicago Public Library. Hereinafter referred to as the Illinois Writers Project Papers.

7. Ibid.

8. Casey, *S. B. Fuller*, 57.

9. On the fight with the War Production Board see Johnson, *Succeeding against the Odds*, 145–51.

10. Ben Burns, *Nitty Gritty: A White Editor in Black Journalism* (Jackson: University Press of Mississippi, 1996), 95.

11. Johnson, *Succeeding against the Odds*, 154.

12. Ibid., 118–19.

13. Burns, *Nitty Gritty*, 186.

14. Ibid., 90.

15. Johnson, *Succeeding against the Odds*, 236.

16. Ibid., 156.

17. On the factors supporting the emergence of a black consumer market, see Dwight Earnest Brooks, "In Their Own Words: Advertisers' Construction of an African American Consumer Market, the World War II Era," *Howard Journal of Communications* 6 (October 1995): 32–52; Jason Chambers, *Madison Avenue and the Color Line: African Americans in the Advertising Industry* (Philadelphia: University of Pennsylvania Press, 2008); and Robert E. Weems Jr., *Desegregating the Dollar: African American Consumerism in the Twentieth Century* (New York: New York University Press, 1998).

18. Johnson, *Succeeding against the Odds*, 205, 246.

19. For this description of the content of early *Ebony* magazine, see Roland E. Wolseley, *The Black Press, USA* (Ames: Iowa State University Press, 1971), 118–19.

20. On the recession and the changed advertising and subscription program, see Johnson, *Succeeding against the Odds*, 235.

21. Burns, *Nitty Gritty*, 122.

22. Ibid., 121.

23. Quoted in Burns, *Nitty Gritty*, 119.

24. Quoted in Tom Pendergast, *Creating the Modern Man: American Magazines and Consumer Culture, 1900–1950* (Columbia: University of Missouri Press, 2000), 251–252.

25. "Nation within a Nation," *Premium Practice* (May 1957): 29.

26. Johnson, *Succeeding against the Odds*, 179.

27. "Johnson, John Harold," in *African-American Business Leaders: A Biographical Dictionary*, ed. John N. Ingham and Lynne B. Feldman (Westport, CT: Greenwood Press, 1994), 373.

28. Johnson, *Succeeding against the Odds*, 187.

29. Ibid., 188.

30. Burns, *Nitty Gritty*, 126.

31. Ibid., 113.

32. Stuart Rankin, interview by author, November 18, 2011.

33. Ron Sampson, interview by author, November 8, 2011.

34. Ibid.

35. Burns, *Nitty Gritty*, 140.

36. Johnson, *Succeeding against the Odds*, 235.

37. Quoted in Burns, *Nitty Gritty*, 94.

38. On rumors of *Ebony* ownership, see Johnson, *Succeeding against the Odds*, 200–201, and Burns, *Nitty Gritty*, 129–30.

39. Chambers, *Madison Avenue and the Color Line*, 42–43; Pendergast, *Creating the Modern Man*, 253; and Weems, *Desegregating the Dollar*, 74–75.

40. Chambers, *Madison Avenue and the Color Line*, 146–47; and Weems, *Desegregating the Dollar*, 75–77.

41. Burns, *Nitty Gritty*, 121.

42. Johnson, *Succeeding against the Odds*, 157.

43. M. L. Stein, *Blacks in Communications: Journalism, Public Relations, and Advertising* (New York: Julian Messner, 1972), 34–35.

44. Pendergast, *Creating the Modern Man*, 255.

45. Burns, *Nitty Gritty*, 103–5.

46. Ibid., 166–67.

47. Ibid., 112.

48. Ibid., 124.

49. Ibid., 123.

50. Chambers, *Madison Avenue and the Color Line*, 47–49.

51. Johnson, *Succeeding against the Odds*, 190.

52. Ibid., 190.

53. Ibid., 190.

54. Ibid., 190.

55. Burns, *Nitty Gritty*, 130.

56. Ibid., 130.

57. "'Our World' Folds; Sale Set Nov. 3," *Baltimore Afro-American*, November 5, 1955, 1.

58. Johnson, *Succeeding against the Odds*, 342–45.

59. Ibid.

60. Edward Lewis with Audrey Edwards, *The Man from Essence: Creating a Magazine for Black Women* (New York: Atria Books, 2014), 218.

61. Ibid., 217–18.

62. Earl Graves, "John H. Johnson: Leader, Legend, and Friend," *Black Enterprise* (October 2005): 13.

63. Lewis, *The Man from Essence*, 218.

64. Johnson, *Succeeding against the Odds*, 159.

65. Ibid., 117.

66. Ibid., 118.

67. Fairfax Cone, *With All Its Faults: A Candid Account of Forty Years in Advertising* (Boston: Little, Brown, 1969), 308.

68. On John H. Johnson's role as a "broker," see Dwight E. Brooks, "In Their Own Words: Advertisers' Construction of an African American Consumer Market, the World War II Era," *Howard Journal of Communications* 6 (1995): 49.

69. Johnson, *Succeeding against the Odds*, 231–32; Chambers, *Madison Avenue and the Color Line*, 57.

CHAPTER 7

Jim Crow Organized Crime

Black Chicago's Underground Economy in the Twentieth Century

WILL COOLEY

J. Levert "St. Louis" Kelly was an entrepreneurial gangster of the first rate. During his career in Chicago from the 1910s through the 1940s, he dabbled in gambling, pimping, and political fixing. Lean and dapper, with piercing eyes and a hard-earned knife-wound scar on the back of his neck, he carried a Luger in the front of his trousers, which he brandished frequently. According to journalist Frank Marshall Davis, he wanted to be "the toughest man on the South Side."[1] In addition to his vice activities, Kelly presided over two unions. The legitimate retail clerks local engaged in civil-rights struggles, bolstering Kelly's "race man" credentials. In the restaurant union, however, Kelly enforced solidarity with his gun. When a new tavern opened, Kelly walked in, put his Luger on the counter, and told the owner, "Send the boys over to the union meeting and with a $20 initiation fee."[2]

Regardless of the tactics, Kelly delivered raises and rights for workers, making him a popular figure with his constituents.[3] Kelly had an extended history of trouble with the law and was undoubtedly a "bad" man, yet he was also finalist for the ceremonial post of "Mayor of Bronzeville" in 1934, revealing the blurred lines in Chicago's black community between the shady and the upright.[4] Before being cut down by a rival in 1944, Kelly established himself as a powerful racketeer. So why isn't Kelly listed alongside other fabled Chicago gangsters in histories of the

Outfit, Chicago's crime syndicate? Why has this charismatic figure been lost to history?

Kelly's career reflects the limits imposed by racism and discrimination in Chicago's informal economy. Though he wielded impressive clout, Jim Crow unionism and the Outfit's color line curbed his authority and compelled him to pay tribute to white gangsters.[5] Success in organized crime, historian Mark Haller shows, involved securing collaborative partners and achieving political cover.[6] Unfortunately for Kelly and many other talented and resourceful African American gangsters, whites rarely extended the fruits of full and equal partnerships to them. This exclusion was no small thing. Organized crime was a lucrative industry, a path for generational mobility, and an agent of social capital. In Chicago and its suburbs, white mobsters assimilated into communities that barred blacks.[7] The structural racism embedded in the underground economy amplified the difficulties blacks encountered in twentieth-century Chicago.

To make matters worse, white officials steered vice into segregated black neighborhoods, and then denied African Americans chances to take full advantage of these markets. The resulting dysfunctions in black communities owed much to this discrimination, but critics blamed blacks' supposed unsophistication in criminal rackets.[8] According to one historian, African Americans could not maintain successful organized crime syndicates because their "family patterns were matrilineal and less orderly. Most of the young black hoodlums had no fathers on hand to emulate."[9] When whites seized black rackets, observers claimed African American mobsters were not murderous enough. When black gangsters drew intensified law-enforcement scrutiny, it was because they were too murderous to properly organize crime.[10] In these cases and others like them, scholars and journalists understated the role of racism in consigning blacks to second-class underworld status.[11] This chapter focuses on African Americans' mixed responses to vice, the hostile white takeover of black organized crime, and the rise of gangs and the drug trade. It demonstrates that racism and discrimination were so thoroughly entrenched in the city that they extended into its illicit sectors, creating lasting problems for Black Chicagoans.

The Rise of the Black Underworld

Before the Great Migration brought thousands of African Americans to the Windy City, black entrepreneurs achieved success in politically protected outlaw capitalist enterprises. Men such as Henry "Teenan" Jones and Robert Motts ran gambling emporiums and expanded into other entertainments.[12] Dan Jackson used gambling proceeds for contributions that bolstered not only the black submachine, but his own electoral ambitions.[13] He and Robert Cole also served as the first two presidents of the Metropolitan Funeral System Association, showing how illicit money often funded conventional ventures.[14] As the historian Humbert Nelli notes, most Chicagoans abhorred poverty more than crime, and for racial and ethnic minorities the underground economy offered lower barriers to entry than mainstream pursuits.[15]

Even the most fastidious African Americans usually realized that black participation in vice occupations was more about necessity than moral failings. The preacher and sociologist Richard R. Wright Jr. came to this conclusion soon after arriving in Chicago. Gambling boss John "Mushmouth" Johnson boosted Wright's struggling church by purchasing all the raffle tickets for fundraisers. Taken aback, Wright denounced Johnson as a "menace to the community," but parishioners objected to this description, regarding Johnson as a generous individual and a good man to know if you were in a tight spot. Wright agreed to meet Johnson and was surprised to encounter a civil, churchgoing man who lived by a code. Johnson was not proud of his line of work and did not want his daughter to know how he made his money. Wright urged him to quit, but Johnson responded that if he did, odds were someone with fewer scruples could easily take his place. Besides, Johnson reasoned, "I need money to support my family and educate my children; this seems to be the only way in this town a colored man of my limited learning can get the money he needs." Wright, who later became the first African American to earn a PhD from the University of Pennsylvania, realized that many participants in the shadow economy were not there by choice, but because "they were the victims of economic circumstances."[16]

Many African Americans squeezed by the discriminatory labor market gravitated to policy gambling, a vice that mostly avoided controversy while attracting significant numbers of African Americans as bettors, workers, and operators. By the late 1930s, the wildly popular daily numbers lottery included an estimated 4,200 gambling stations employing 10,000 Black Chicagoans that handled 100,000 players per day.[17] Commentators regularly overstate the "organization" of organized crime, as rackets such as prostitution and drugs proved difficult to manage and control.[18] Policy gambling, however, was a hierarchical, structured venture because it required not only customer faith and trust, but sophisticated operations. The "policy kings" at the top of the pyramid needed order and efficiency to attract repeat customers, and paid protection fees to law enforcement to turn a blind eye or actively shield the game. In 1916 a reporter noted that if an operator made the "proper" arrangements he could "run without molestation," but if he overlooked that important detail, "he may safely bet that he will be raided the first night."[19] Unlike other forms of gambling in the Black Belt, such as noisy casinos and rowdy craps games, policy kings generally ran well-ordered, peaceful ventures. Police officers placed bets, safeguarded the receipts, and sometimes served as "tellers" during drawings.[20] While the game engendered some criticism and soul-searching in the black community, most tended to see it as a benign pastime. One prominent citizen who resided in the Lilydale neighborhood, an area of "people of higher ideas and people of self-respect," bragged that his neighbors had facilitated the closing of a local nightclub casino, yet tolerated the two policy stations that operated nearby. "Almost everybody plays policy," he reasoned, "but our organizations don't bother the policy station because that is the only form of gambling that most people think is all right."[21]

Policy was an integral part of black cultural, political, and community formation in the Windy City. It created social capital, bringing people together through a common amusement.[22] Depots were easily recognizable, as barbershops and newsstands hung signs in their windows such as "We Write All Books." One researcher claimed that children in Chicago were "unaware of the fact that the operation of policy is illegal."[23] There were occasional crackdowns on numbers businesses, but they were usually motivated by partisan concerns rather than law and order. Policy syndicates, with small armies of runners in daily contact with customers, could influence and turn out voters, and politicians used the contributions and syndicate manpower to win elections.[24] Anton Cermak definitely understood this. In 1931 the newly elected mayor closed down policy wheels until they agreed to shift their allegiances to the Democratic Party.[25]

In Chicago, where money mattered most, policy kings vaulted to the top of the city's social scene. The "sports" of Black Chicago were a varied bunch. Some members of the "overdressed underworld" clad themselves in flashy suits and brandished diamond rings with matching stick pins, and drove vividly colored open-topped vehicles. Their female consorts wore silk stockings and low-slung dresses, draped themselves in jewels, and carried parasols.[26] Others fit in to black middle-class society, eschewing glamour for the decorum of respectable professionals. One informant noted that the Jones brothers, policy kings through the Depression into the 1940s, "appear to be businessmen first. It is not their fault that the law considers policy to be a racquet [sic]. They are not racketeers. Only colored boys who cannot enter legitimate business because of the color barrier, & must turn to illegitimate policy." The Jones brothers were college-educated and from a middle-class family, a background that was not unusual inside gambling organizations.[27]

Policy barons also helped drive the local economy. A 1937 survey estimated that nineteen policy kings owned at least twenty-nine different businesses, and the game spurred ancillary firms such as the White Paper Supply Company, owned by Mississippi-born migrant Edward White, which supplied gambling slips in Chicago and Detroit.[28] Many blacks viewed policy kings as role models, shining examples of making it in the big city. "There was nothing I wanted more than to run policy," journalist Warner Saunders recalled, "like any other boy in that community." The future newsman knew that gambling was technically illegal, but policy kings were his "greatest heroes" and discrimination made it hard for blacks to concretely define "illegitimate" activity.[29]

Black Chicagoans realized that the game was rigged in the house's favor, but at least the beneficiaries were local men made good, a source of pride when nearly everything appeared to be white-owned and -operated. The upper crust of black society regularly interacted with policy kings, though some preferred not to admit it. Reverend Harold Kingsley of the prestigious Good Shepherd Church was an outspoken opponent of the game, but eased his opposition after gambling entrepreneur Julian Black donated $50,000 to Kingsley's community house.[30] The South Side Community Committee, a distinguished civic organization, sought to impress upon black youths that the "swaggering racketeer" was not the local "big shot" in comparison to the hard-working, legitimate businessmen "who had the confidence and respect of his neighbors." Yet the chair of the women's committee was Mrs. James Knight, whose husband rose up from being a Pullman porter to a policy king, owner of the celebrated Palm Tavern jazz club, and first Mayor of Bronzeville. "Some of the women on my committee obtain their money from businesses which cannot be called exactly uplifting," a member admitted. "But that's all right. We don't mind. As long as they are willing to contribute money we are glad to receive it." An observer of the group remarked that they made little distinction between the criminal and the conventional, but because the black middle class was a little embarrassed by the intermixing, they made a big show of attacking the criminal element. "This, however, is strictly a type of play acting which has little reality so far as the residents themselves are concerned." The gambling bosses were "well integrated in the total pattern of dominance in the community." The observer recommended that the South Side Community Committee should "refrain from mentioning the fact" in public, though, because the "outside world" would not understand.[31]

More significantly for blacks seeking adequate wages, policy required thousands of workers to function. Black men and women worked as door-to-door solicitors (writers), fielders, doormen, checkers, pickups, stampers, bookkeepers, and overlookers. The slots higher up in organizations were more and more lucrative, with managers drawing weekly salaries of up to $320 and making millionaires of the policy kings. Weekly pay during the Depression for checkers, pickup men, and guards ranged from $25 to $45 dollars a week, and unlike many white-owned firms, gambling operations had a merit system where employees with skill and ability secured choice positions.[32] By comparison, stockyard workers earned from $20 to $30 dollars a week during times of regular employment in the 1920s, while those who kept their jobs during the Depression took home around $11 weekly. Though policy work included many perils and occasional harassment from the police, it was less dangerous and more invigorating than the jobs left to African Americans on the killing floor, in the mill, and in domestic service.[33]

During the Great Depression, black banks and insurance firms went under, and many college-trained African Americans entered gambling operations, applying rationalized principles of organization to the industry. Policy kings added lawyers, bookkeepers, and experienced accountants to the payrolls. "Many men have given up the legitimate pursuits of insurance collecting, Pullman portering and waiting to engage in number writing," policy critic J. Saunders Redding remarked. "They are not all stupid men. They feel that the income from the racket is permanent."[34] The presence of black white-collar employees in policy operations further muddled lines of respectability.

Segregated Vice and Community Standards

Though many African Americans supplemented their wages, made their living, or enjoyed the entertainment diversions of the underground market, the vice econ-omy also had drawbacks for Black Chicagoans. City officials had tolerated vice in the Levee District until 1912, when reformers successfully closed it down. How-ever, gambling, prostitution, and drug dealing simply moved into other areas of the city, especially the Black Belt, with the approval of law enforcement.[35] In 1917 the *Chicago Tribune* observed that a dozen "disreputable" houses operated openly within a few hundred yards of the Twenty-Second Street police station.[36] One flabbergasted judge stated that "crime conditions among the colored people are being deliberately fostered by the present city administration. Disorderly cabarets, thieves, and depraved women are allowed into the section of the city where colored people live."[37] Many blacks decried this situation, as prostitution, narcotics, and all-night casinos created chaos in places where people were raising families.[38] By 1928 the *Chicago Defender* reported that there were 2,750 "buffet flats" (offering a full assortment of illegal services) and brothels in the majority-black Second, Third, and Fourth Wards that did business without interference, with some of them vis-ited regularly by policemen.[39] The situation was not exclusive to Chicago. Across the country many black neighborhoods abutted vice zones, serving as a glaring reminder of municipal racism.[40] The *Chicago Whip* accepted that prostitution and gambling were unlikely to disappear anytime soon, but "we can only hope that that it will be segregated and removed from residential sections where people make the pretense of decency."[41] While some African Americans profited from the underground economy, others wanted it out of their communities, initiating disputes between vice entrepreneurs and their neighbors.[42]

African Americans not only turned their fury toward city officials permitting unruly vice in black neighborhoods, they were also incensed that most of the proceeds left the black community. In 1928 the *Chicago Defender* estimated that whites living elsewhere owned 60 percent of brothels in black areas. This added insult to injury, because "when money leaves the district in this fashion it never returns."[43] As white gangsters moved to take over the policy racket in the late 1930s, racist expropriation became more acute. By this point, policy and numbers rackets in cities across the North were probably the largest black-owned businesses in America. Though some historians argue that white gangsters thought the opera- tions were nickel-and-dime amusements not worth their time, white hoodlums surely must have been aware of policy's massive profits and payoffs, and could not miss the nattily dressed policy kings about town.[44] Indeed, in the 1920s Jew- ish gangsters failed in attempted hostile conquests of black operations in Harlem and Detroit, respectively. African Americans rallied to push back against these incursions, with the black press decrying the attacks and black bettors resisting from the bottom up, preferring runners and numbers kings of their own race.[45] In addition, the game made a lot of people rich and powerful, including many politicians and law enforcement officials, and they wanted no interference with the gravy train.[46] White competitors salivated at the thought of getting a piece of this lucrative racket, but black policy kings were too well connected for this to happen.

The Takeover

Something changed, however, beginning in the late 1930s. White gangsters mur- dered Walter J. Kelly, the numbers racket chief in Gary, Indiana, in 1939. The Jones brothers gave up their gambling enterprises after Outfit associates kidnapped Ed Jones and held him for ransom in 1946. Nine bullets ended the life of Buddy Hutchen in 1948, and the *Defender* noted that the mob's color line had claimed another civic- minded entrepreneur. "Had he been white," the newspaper noted, "he'd probably have been Lake County's gambling boss." On the West Side, a botched assassina- tion in 1950 convinced "Big Jim" Martin to change occupations, leaving Ted Roe as the last independent black policy king remaining in Chicago.[47]

His time on this lonely throne was fleeting. On August 4, 1952, a hired gun pumped two bullets into Roe. The funeral drew one of the largest crowds in the South Side's history, and the *Chicago Defender* reported that the Outfit had "dethroned the last king of a rapidly vanishing policy empire—silenced the 'Last of the Mohicans' of a fabulous gambling world." African Americans smoldered with resentment. "Mexico or Timbuktu, you can't hide from the mob," a resident fumed. "They'll follow you to the ends of the earth. They'll find you and cut you down."[48] The *Chicago Tribune* suggested that black policy operators had lost their patrons, noting that the Democratic Party could have stopped the lethal purge, but "their hearts aren't in it."[49] This transfer of power was not unique to the Chicago area. The black magazine *Color* lamented that the "war on numbers racket kings" had also led to white command over formerly black operations in New York, Pittsburgh, and Cleveland.[50]

In the 1950s and 1960s, the Outfit colonized organized crime in black areas of Chicago. White gangsters skimmed an estimated 85 percent of the before-expenses revenue from policy wheels, and they strong-armed bookmakers into paying street taxes. According the Kefauver Committee report in 1951, Outfit boss Tony Accardo earned the lion's share of his sizable income from policy proceeds.[51] They also presided over the drug importation. As one police detective remarked, the Outfit protected this commerce with extreme prejudice. "The family isn't going to allow any brothers to bring stuff into the country because this will cut right into their pockets."[52] When enterprising African Americans attempted to challenge the syndicate, they were rubbed out. After the Outfit executed an independent policy operator in 1958, Ed Jones, in exile in Mexico City, stated that the mob intended to "whip Negro policy boys in line" and would not tolerate a "smart, hard-working independent operator bucking them."[53] While policy kings had been potent powerbrokers, a *Chicago Defender* reporter noted, the Outfit had reduced black criminals to mere "underlings and errand boys."[54]

Racism in the rackets even stalled civil-rights struggles. In 1967, at a meeting with Coca-Cola executives, Operation Breadbasket leaders stated that they would pressure chain stores to do more business with black-owned sanitation haulers. The Coca-Cola officials warned that this effort was sure to bring "syndicate and union problems." Operation Breadbasket pushed ahead anyway, securing garbage contracts with forty stores in African American neighborhoods. White gangsters responded by threatening black workers, destroying refuse containers, and firebombing two garbage trucks.[55] Clearly, Chicago's exclusionary crime syndicate was another obstacle to black empowerment.

Across the country, white hoodlums regularly barred blacks from the upper ranks of organized crime hierarchies. "The Mafia is *not* an Equal Opportunity Employer," the *Wall Street Journal* reported in 1967.[56] In Chicago, the Outfit excluded African Americans though it was otherwise unmistakably multiethnic. Law enforcement and reporters frequently asserted that Italians were in charge, but by the 1930s Chicago's syndicate network included an assortment of men from different European backgrounds.[57] Though ethnic considerations were important to establishing trust, the profit motive could overcome suspicions, and the Outfit's management included men such as Frank "The German" Schweihs; Gus Alex, a Greek; and Jewish labor boss Allen Dorfman.[58] "We got Jews, we got Polacks, we got Greeks, we got all kinds," Outfit enforcer Jackie Cerone boasted. However, similar to most other large business operations in Chicago, the Outfit did not include blacks in management positions.

Gangs, Drugs, and Power

In the late 1960s, as the Black Power movement blossomed, African Americans began to break this white stranglehold, often with black gangs leading the way. In Chicago, groups—such as the Blackstone Rangers and Disciples on the South Side, and the Vice Lords on the West Side—grew from local sets to sizeable "nations."[59] Prior to this period, black gangs were largely neighborhood self-defense cliques, and members usually graduated out when they attained adult employment. The emergence of large and ambitious gangs coincided with deindustrialization, capital flight, and a slide in the urban job market. The informal economy, especially with the rise of drug employment, became an enticing route to supplement income or make a living in the battered landscape of inner-city Chicago.[60] To do so, gang members realized they would have to confront white racketeers. Law enforcement officials noted the signs of upward mobility by black gangsters in numerous cities: dealers wholesaling narcotics, numbers entrepreneurs circumventing white syndicates and banking their own operations, and arrestees posting substantial bail bonds. In Chicago, black gang members required Outfit associates to pay tribute to stay in business.[61] By 1974 the *Chicago Tribune* found that African Americans patronized black racketeers who had pushed aside the Outfit bosses.[62]

Black gang members frequently merged their ambitions with the mantras of the Black Power movement, casting their aims as part of the expansive move for "community control." In the 1960s, influential African American activists, intellectuals, and politicians asserted that blacks should take command of vice rackets in their neighborhoods.[63] According to the *Chicago Defender*, many blacks viewed the rising gang muscle as a justified "rebellion" against "the white racketeers who exploit heartlessly Negro slums."[64] Astute black gang members fervently endorsed this cultural zeitgeist. David Barksdale, a leader of the Disciples, indicated their growing aspirations: "We're not just a bunch of black boys out fighting and fooling around like we used to," he stated. "We're getting together. One of these days we're going to run the whole Southside for the black people."[65]

At first, some African Americans welcomed the gangs as a sign of nascent black clout. Youth gangs, politicians, and organized crime figures had customarily enjoyed reciprocal relationships. Hoodlums delivered money and votes, and elected officials sheltered the underground economy.[66] Some Black Chicagoans expected black gangs to continue this pattern.[67] Other activists tried to steer gangs toward civil-rights protests and revolutionary movements. In his open-housing marches into unfriendly white neighborhoods, Martin Luther King Jr. used gang members as bodyguards and was impressed by their discipline and commitment to nonviolence in the face of hysterical white hostility. Likewise, the Black Panther Party urged gangs to join their socialist uprising.[68]

These hopes were short-lived. As their power grew and the economy worsened, black gang members turned to exploiting their own communities. This was standard practice for organized criminals, but the extortion schemes, robberies, and intrarace violence clashed with calls for black unity and many black gang members' militant pronouncements. Some gang members did articulate an expansive view of Black Power, lamented intraracial violence, and pushed for augmented activism. Yet gang members could be of two minds and did not divorce political activities from struggles to secure a foothold in the informal economy. The fight for access to construction jobs and control over rackets were not mutually exclusive efforts, as both involved vigorously asserting demands for more opportunities for gang members. Larry Hoover, who rose from poverty in the South Side Englewood neighborhood to head the Gangster Disciples, recalled wearing the militant's dark blue beret by day, and then trading it for the hustler's fur-felt fedora and cashmere coat at night.[69]

In the meantime, gang extortion expanded from pimps and drug dealers to conventional businesses. A 1971 study claimed that nearly every white merchant on the South Side was extorted by gangs, driving up prices and hastening business flight.[70] In one case, the Blackstone Rangers forced the Red Rooster grocery chain to add twenty-two members to its payroll, including leaders Jeff Fort and Mickey Cogwell as "store inspectors." The shakedown put the chain out of business, laying off three hundred black workers. Red Rooster was unpopular with black customers. Operation Breadbasket boycotted and picketed it for unethical practices, and the city named it a "flagrant violator" of laws on labeling and measuring food. The closures infuriated displaced workers, but many shoppers were happy to see the exploitative chain go.[71] Unfortunately, Black Chicagoans realized that few merchants took the place of exiting stores, creating commercial wastelands. Even middle-class blacks complained about the dearth of retail outlets in their neighborhoods.[72] Furthermore, black gangs did not stop at white targets, but expanded their scope to black-owned businesses. Pleas for racial solidarity did not spare "soul brothers" from extortion schemes.[73] Black businesspeople already faced significant impediments due to discrimination, and their exertions became even more difficult with the added expenses of gang extortion and intimidation.[74]

Another enterprise, the drug trade, also drove a wedge between black gangs and their neighbors. Narcotics markets became more prevalent during the first decades after World War II, but the supply was small and mainly confined to subcultures. In the late 1960s, however, a "tidal wave of heroin addiction" swept through urban America.[75] Additionally, the rise of cocaine, an "easy-entry business" compared to heroin, created a "revolution in the criminal underworld" as strivers made connections with South and Central American producers.[76] Gang members sensed opportunity. In Chicago, white organized-crime figures trafficked narcotics, but blacks mainly served as street dealers.[77] Illinois lawmakers inadvertently incentivized drug selling by youth gangs by passing the Controlled Substance Act in 1971, which mandated severe penalties for adult dealers. The unintended consequence was that retail drug sales became a young man's game just as gangs made their ascent.[78] In the 1970s racial minorities ended the Outfit's monopoly on narcotics wholesaling.[79] While the organization of gangs probably encouraged the drug business, no "black mafia" had a firm grip on it. In contrast, the dispersion of the trade and its youthful, ad hoc characteristics contributed to the violence in the city.

Many blacks had long disdained drug dealing in their neighborhoods. Open-air markets brought addicts to street corners, prompted unwanted police attention, and contributed to dissipation while the bulk of the profits left the community.[80] As early as the 1970s, blacks linked the flood of narcotics to a conspiracy to keep blacks subjugated, and militants called for vigilante patrols to keep pushers out.[81] Skeptical gang members had varied feelings toward drugs and drug dealing, viewing it as socially destructive and seeing users as unreliable and erratic. "Gangbangin' itself is dying off," a former West Side gang member claimed in 1972. "Now, too many brothers are too busy noddin' off on the junk."[82] The prediction was premature, but some gang factions shunned dealing and others forcibly drove peddlers away.[83] Some sellers also harbored deep ambivalence, regarding the business as improper but necessary for economic survival. On wiretaps, Larry Hoover, who built his empire on narcotics, called trafficking "wrong" but a "cold reality" and a matter of "self-preservation" in the ghetto.[84]

For Hoover and other gangsters, the profits were usually too bountiful to ignore, and a drug economy took hold in impoverished inner cities. The willingness of gang members to mete out violence was innate to running illicit, highly profitable enterprises, and eradicating rivals and amassing market share were fundamental to the business plan. Turf battles raged as rivalries flared, dealers sought to manage an unwieldy marketplace, and the upsurge in handguns made rumbles more deadly.[85] As the urban employment crisis intensified, the growing narcotics supply created income paths for many youths, as gang leaders hired lookouts, runners, handlers, and managers of shooting galleries. Drug trafficking, Eric Schneider notes, was "the free market's answer to deindustrialization."[86]

Though Chicagoans close to the problem often understood that drug dealing was one of the few ways to make a living in distressed areas, gang chaos made neighborhoods unsafe and sometimes almost unlivable. Gunfire punctuated nights in violence-plagued neighborhoods, and parents fretted over the futures of their children. A black police officer summarized the stress many parents felt: "It's really a heart-breaking thing because sometimes they're doing the best they can," he stated in 1972. "They're out there beating their brains out, trying to make it for their kids, and they live in dread every day that they come home that their kid is dead, he's shot, or he's got an eye put out."[87] Firearm homicides in the city jumped from 197 in 1965 to 608 in 1973, while the number of black male victims ages fifteen to twenty-four increased 302 percent in the same period.[88] Most of these killings were not gang-related, but enmity between gangs such as the Disciples and Blackstone Rangers added to the carnage. The number of gang-related homicides in the Windy City shot up from 11 in 1965 to 70 in 1970.[89] It was an ominous start for groups that claimed to be working on behalf of all black people, and the violence worsened as gangs became more involved in drug capitalism.

In response, many Black Chicagoans turned their ire on the gangs, and their calls for tougher law-enforcement measures revealed their anguish.[90] One mother expressed justifiable anger and distrust toward police after they brutalized her sons for minor curfew violations. Yet when her son was shotgunned by gang members involved in a tit-for-tat battle, she demanded vengeance for his killers, even if it meant using rough tactics.[91] Tensions between black citizens and the Chicago police had historically run high, and blacks often simultaneously criticized homicidal gangs and brutish cops. One Chicago Urban League official stated that while black residents wanted the "criminal elements" of gangs weeded out, their call for help was not "a license for law-enforcement agencies to unjustifiably take off on youth gangs in the black community." Likewise, Urban League president Edwin Berry charged that the "war on crime" was actually "an endorsement of a war on black ghetto youth."[92] Unsurprisingly, people caught in a bad situation without straightforward solutions harbored contradictory feelings over what to do about the gang problem. A comprehensive approach to dealing with the economic decline of the inner city may have alleviated the growth of gangs and street crime. Instead, policymakers endorsed a law-and-order regime that focused mainly on punitive approaches, strategies that only worsened conditions in urban areas and did nothing to stem the supply of narcotics.

Larry Hoover and the Gangster Disciples were a particularly telling example of entrepreneurial expansion fueled by narcotics, the futility of the war on drugs, and the negative consequences of the collapse of employment markets in Chicago. Hoover was born in Mississippi and, like many before him, made the trip to the land of hope in the 1950s. As with many young men growing up on the South Side, he was attracted to gang membership. "I didn't get recruited," he recalled. "I just signed up. You want to be part of a street gang because it's the social club of the ghetto."[93] Exceptionally clever and ambitious, Hoover formed his own narcotics-dealing faction called "The Family" in the early 1970s while maintaining his ties to the Disciples. In 1973 Hoover was found guilty of the kidnapping and murdering of an associate who stole from his drug stash and was sentenced to 150 to 200 years in prison.[94]

Ironically, Hoover and his organization prospered behind bars. Gangs recruited vigorously in prisons, using sophisticated overtures to solidarity and racial pride along with fear and terror.[95] On the streets, gang factions frequently quarreled and fought each other, but in the confines of lockup Hoover consolidated his power by creating an organizational hierarchy, setting rules, offering protection, and directing exacting punishments.[96] The Gangster Disciples paid off guards, and their reach was so extensive that lieutenants could order beatings in other detention centers over the phone.[97] Though membership was not lucrative for most of the rank and file, the Gangster Disciples did provide a street code and certain benefits. Arrested gangsters usually could expect access to an attorney, bail money, and protection in prison. The gang also paid funeral expenses for deceased soldiers and bestowed payments to the families of those killed or incarcerated.[98]

All the while, the Gangster Disciples expanded their business operations, as through the 1980s Chicago gangs exerted tighter management over drug markets than gangs in other cities.[99] When federal agents took down the El Rukns (formerly the Blackstone Rangers and Black P. Stone Nation) in the late 1980s after the gang engaged in a bizarre terrorist plot involving Libyan leader Muammar Gaddafi, the Gangster Disciples emerged as a dominant gang on the South Side.[100] On tape recordings made by government investigators, Hoover discussed the elaborate taxing schemes directed at street peddlers in gang territory and ordered members to dedicate one day a week to dealing for him, which may have earned Hoover from $200,000 to $300,000 weekly.[101]

The tapes revealed how Hoover and the Gangster Disciples managed drug sales, but also demonstrated that even under corporate gangs, dealing retained many freelancing aspects. Dealers paid for the rights to sell on Gangster Disciple turf, and members used the connections provided by the gang to buy large quantities for resale, occasionally kicking some proceeds up the hierarchy.[102] In many respects, though, dealers were on their own. Gang leaders and the government claimed that the Gangster Disciples had a footprint extending into several states and boasted a membership in the thousands. While many of these factions networked to facilitate drug and gun sales, their connection to the leadership was loose at best.[103]

This diffuse structure, the rising prevalence of firearms, the faltering postindustrial economy, and the incarcerating drive of the war on drugs encouraged cycles of violence. Vendettas and feuds spiraled, and dealers tried to avoid harsh legal sanctions by vehemently discouraging snitching. Law-enforcement actions did little to help the situation. When prosecutors dismantled corporate gangs, dealing dispersed to small crews with little sense of the chain of command or solidarity. Though the Gangster Disciples had undoubtedly utilized violence, Hoover, like other organized-crime figures, understood that attention-grabbing incidents were generally bad for business and tried to keep a lid on them.[104] Smaller crews often had no such checks, and homicides mounted as corporate gangs lost jurisdiction and influence.[105] In court, prosecutors admitted that gang busts produced more underworld turmoil, as a murderous spate resulted from a "leadership vacuum in the Gangster Disciples" after the federal indictment of thirty-nine members in 1995.[106] Crew associates, untethered from gang rules, unable to secure mainstream routes to manhood, and involved in unlawful rackets, turned to violence as insults and challenges took on outsized importance. Small disputes became defining moments, instigating rounds of bloodshed and retribution.[107] Yet this havoc should not be dismissed as random and senseless. For peddlers in an unregulated business, reputation mattered. As legal scholar William Stuntz states, "One reason why violence by drug-dealing gangs remains high is that, from the point of view of the perpetrators, it pays."[108]

This violence and the moral panic surrounding illicit substances contributed to gangs' failure to become integrated in the politics-organized crime nexus that safeguarded earlier syndicates. Organized criminals traditionally had a clear interest in fostering agreeable, under-the-table relations with politicians, police, judges, and the public. Payoffs were a business expense, and they funded political machines and police-officer retirement plans.[109] Policy kings, for example, donated to charities and supported civil-rights organizations, and heavily invested in legitimate businesses, creating economic benefits for the community. Drug gangs, though, could not shield themselves from prosecutions, because they usually failed to achieve these elevated government connections and win the public's acceptance. Kingpins raked in massive profits, but at an exploitative cost, as little of this money trickled down to the street dealers taking the greatest risks and only scant amounts circulated through the neighborhoods damaged by the turmoil.[110]

Forward-thinking gang leaders certainly tried to burnish their reputations and protect their interests. The Gangster Disciples laundered money through a host of enterprises, including clothing, grocery, and jewelry stores. Hoover expanded the scope of his organization by changing the gang name to Growth and Development and by initiating voter-registration drives in the 1980s.[111] These movements fell short, especially since most gang members were socially and politically marginalized and just struggling to make ends meet.[112] Neighbors also remained wary, disapproving of how substance abuse ruined lives and how the commerce attracted addicts to crime-ridden areas. Few politicians wanted anything to do with drug money tainted by the stigma of violence and addiction, and those that associated with gang members were excoriated by the media.[113]

Discriminatory policing also foreclosed paths to political protection, as black neighborhoods received the worst kind of criminal justice. While Chicago cops collaborated with the Outfit, they subjected African Americans to intrusive, scattershot stop-and-frisk tactics and excessive punishment for minor crimes. Meanwhile, the department devoted too little time to targeting violence and other harder-to-solve major offenses.[114] The police concentrated raids and prosecutions on minority communities, even as they virtually ignored addiction issues in white, middle-class areas. Governments increasingly funded police operations through asset seizures that encouraged mass arrests, soaring incarceration rates, and community degradation.[115] The war on drugs had no effect on the availability, price, or potency of illicit substances, but it did damage poor communities by making offenders less employable, weakening families, and fostering distrust in the justice system.[116]

A wave of successful prosecutions in the 1990s and 2000s destabilized the Gangster Disciples, including sending Hoover to a Colorado Supermax prison where he could no longer direct operations. Law enforcement gloated, but the breakup of the gang solved few problems while instigating a rash of killings and power plays, producing a new set of headaches for Chicagoans.[117] The Gangster Disciples were "irreparably damaged" by the prosecutions, sociologist Andrew Papachristos notes, but other gangs swiftly filled the void.[118] Meanwhile, the jobs crisis remained, the drug supply resumed unabated, and violent episodes continued. "Life around here is real complicated," a young Gangster Disciple remarked. "It's been like that long before Larry Hoover came around. It'll be that way long after he's gone."[119]

Conclusion

Organized crime is the outgrowth of capitalism, regulation, and moralistic laws. In its essence, historian Robert Lombardo finds, it was a payola system "collected by the ruling political party from crime and vice in exchange for money and immunity from the enforcement actions of the police."[120] Corruption and patronage, though they undermined good governance, served a critical function in tying together Chicago's varied ethnic groups. For blacks, though, the underground economy replicated patterns of marginalization. As "St. Louis" Kelly discovered, being a skilled racketeer could get him only so far before he bumped up against the color bar. Whites denied Black Americans equality of opportunity, drove vice into black neighborhoods, and then castigated blacks for making the most of their limited prospects in illicit industries. This cycle became ever more injurious as industry deserted the city while government simultaneously ramped up the war on drugs. Skyrocketing incarceration rates and worsening violence further destabilized communities. In the absence of decent jobs, sociologist John Hagedorn observes, the justice system punished people "for the 'crime' of not accepting poverty."[121] Despite these constrained situations, Chicago's black outlaw entrepreneurs demonstrated impressive ingenuity.

African Americans often exhibited nuanced responses to vice activities in Black Chicago. They could accept and even endorse policy gambling as an acceptable racket, while fervently denouncing brothels and casinos in their neighborhoods. As newspaper columnist Vernon Jarrett explained, "survival has demanded that black

Americans have a capacity to see the fine shades of differences in everything in their social, physical, economic, and spiritual environment." Most came from the South, where laws ordered them to drink from separate water fountains, prevented them from attending the same schools, and made them use back doors. In Chicago—supposedly the Promised Land—they realized that obstructions to advancement still existed. Thus they commonly differentiated "illegality" and "wrongdoing." A policy king like Ted Roe was not a criminal, rather "just another brother from down home who had come to the big city and made good in one of the few business operations that blacks had been permitted to operate on their own without excessive interference by the white man." In contrast, Jarrett wrote, most African Americans were intolerant of the dealer who resorted to violence and lowered the quality of life in black communities, even if they had a better understanding of the root causes of these actions.[122]

Experience did not make African Americans more cynical; rather it engendered honesty about how the system worked. Organized crime was the "crooked ladder" to upward mobility. For African Americans, though, even the crooked ladder had missing rungs. No matter how cunning, innovative, and ruthless black gangsters were, whites declined to offer them full partnerships. Similar to the rest of Chicago's industries, the syndicate was no meritocracy.

Notes

1. Frank Marshall Davis, *Livin' the Blues: Memoirs of a Black Journalist and Poet* (Madison: University of Wisconsin Press, 1992), 113; Sunnie Wilson and John Cohassey, *Toast of the Town: The Life and Times of Sunnie Wilson* (Detroit: Wayne State University Press, 1998), 70–71.

2. I. A. Lipschitz, "A Study of Two Trade Unions on the South Side of Chicago," December 19, 1935, Ernest Burgess Papers (EWB), box 188, folder 3, Special Collections, Regenstein Library, University of Chicago.

3. Perry Thompson, "Letter to the Editor," *The Crisis,* July 1935, 221.

4. "Chicago's Underworld Shaken by Vice Probe: Gambling on South Side Under Fire," *Chicago Defender*, August 25, 1928, 1; "Pick 'Miss Bronze America' and Bronzeville Mayor on Sept. 22," *Chicago Defender*, September 22, 1934, 21; "Seize Union Official in Racket Purge," *Chicago Defender*, August 17, 1940, 1.

5. "Cops Probe Slaying of 'St. Louis' Kelly," *Chicago Defender*, April 15, 1944, 1.

6. Mark H. Haller, "Urban Crime and Criminal Justice: The Chicago Case," *Journal of American History* 57, no. 3 (December 1970): 635.

7. Gordon A. Chissom, "Normal Park," March 19, 1930, EWB, box 154, folder 6; Marian Badgley, "Flossmoor," January 26, 1932, EWB, box 159, folder 2; Edward Kirk, "Park Manor," 1933, EWB, box 160, folder 2; "The Chicago Wall," *Chicago Defender*, October 4, 1962, 1.

8. Ivan Light, "The Ethnic Vice Industry, 1880–1944," *American Sociological Review* 42 (June 1977): 472, 475.

9. Stephen Fox, *Blood and Power: Organized Crime in Twentieth-Century America* (New York: William Morrow, 1989), 415. See also Francis A. J. Ianni, *Black Mafia: Ethnic Succession in Organized Crime* (New York: Simon and Schuster, 1974), 311; Rufus Schatzberg, "African American Organized Crime," *Handbook of Organized Crime in the United States*, ed. Robert J. Kelly, Ko-Lin Chin, and Rufus Schatzberg (Westport, CT: Greenwood Press, 1994), 199.

10. "The Policy War," *Chicago Tribune*, June 22, 1951, 20; Gus Russo, *The Outfit: The Role of Chicago's Underworld in the Shaping of Modern America* (New York: Bloomsbury, 2001), 186; Fox, *Blood and Power*, 419; William Kleinknecht, *The New Ethnic Mobs: The Changing Face of Organized Crime in America* (New York: The Free Press, 1996), 11–12, 209–11.

11. Malcolm Gladwell, "The Crooked Ladder," *New Yorker*, August 11, 2014.

12. Junius Wood, *The Negro in Chicago* (Chicago: Chicago Daily News, 1916), 25–27; Robert M. Lombardo, *Organized Crime in Chicago: Beyond the Mafia* (Urbana: University of Illinois Press, 2013), 62.

13. Harold F. Gosnell, *Negro Politicians: The Rise of Negro Politics in Chicago* (Chicago: University of Chicago Press, 1935), 57, 80.

14. Robert E. Weems Jr., *Black Business in the Black Metropolis: The Chicago Metropolitan Assurance Company, 1925–1985* (Bloomington: Indiana University Press, 1996), xii.

15. Humbert S. Nelli, *Italians in Chicago, 1880–1930* (New York: Oxford University Press, 1970), 138–39.

16. Richard R. Wright Jr., *87 Years Behind the Black Curtain: An Autobiography* (Philadelphia: Rare Book Company, 1965), 111–13.

17. J. Winston Harrington, "Let 'em, Policy," *Chicago Defender*, November 25, 1939, 13; "Effect of the Depression on Insurance Business," 1934–35, EWB, box 134, folder 1; Lewis A. H. Caldwell, "The Policy Game in Chicago," unpublished MA thesis, Northwestern University, 1940, 58–59.

18. Alan Block, *East Side–West Side: Organizing Crime in New York, 1930–1950* (New Brunswick, NJ: Transaction Books, 1983), 148.

19. Wood, *Negro in Chicago*, 27.

20. Caldwell, "The Policy Game in Chicago," 87–88; "Effect of the Depression on Insurance Business," 1934–35, EWB, box 134, folder 1.

21. Ruth Evans Pardee, "A Study of the Functions of Associations in a Small Negro Community in Chicago," unpublished MA thesis, University of Chicago, 1937, 24.

22. Mathilde Bunton, "Taverns, Essay on African-American Owned Taverns in Chicago," 1937, 3–4, Illinois Writers Project Papers, box 26, folder 6, Vivian Harsh Research Collection of Afro-American History and Literature, Carter Woodson Library, Chicago.

23. Caldwell, "The Policy Game in Chicago," 3, 48.

24. Mark Haller, "Policy, Gambling, Entertainment, and the Emergence of Black Politics: Chicago from 1900 to 1940," *Journal of Social History* 24, no. 4 (1991): 720.

25. "Arrest Minister's Sons as Policy Racketeers: Mayor Issues Order in Clean-up of All Policy Racket Dens," *Chicago Defender*, September 26, 1931, 1.

26. Bricktop with James Haskins, *Bricktop* (New York: Atheneum, 1983), 29; Katherine Dunham, *A Touch of Innocence* (New York: Harcourt, Brace, 1959), 178; Roi Ottley, *New World a-Coming* (Boston: Houghton Mifflin, 1943), 159.

27. "Policy," n.d. but c. 1932, EWB, box 37, folder 5; Julius J. Adams, "Policy, Once a Big Industry, Hits Skids: Defender Reporter Spills the 'Inside' Dope on Rise and Fall of Numbers," *Chicago Defender*, April 22, 1933, 11; Haller, "Policy, Gambling, Entertainment, and the Emergence of Black Politics," 733.

28. "Policy: Negro Business," 9–12, IWP, box 35, folder 11.

29. "Gangs: Their Evolution and Essence," Hyde Park-Kenwood Voices, n.d. but c. 1969, Leon Despres Papers (LMD), box 94, folder 7, Chicago History Museum.

30. Herbert Morrison Smith, "Three Negro Preachers in Chicago: A Study in Religious Leadership," unpublished MA thesis, University of Chicago, 1935, 42; Samuel Strong, "Social Types in the Negro Community of Chicago: An Example of the Social Type Method," unpublished PhD dissertation, University of Chicago, 1940, 118–19.

31. South Side Community Committee, "Are These Our Children?" n.d. but c. 1942, and untitled journal, South Side Community Committee, May 13, 1942, Chicago Area Project Papers, box 98, folder 1, Chicago History Museum; "James Knight Rites Saturday," *Chicago Defender*, January 6, 1962, 3.

32. "Policy: Negro Business," 15–17, IWP, box 35, folder 11; Caldwell, "The Policy Game in Chicago," 32.

33. Cornelia Tilford, "Report of Mrs. Cornelia Tilford, Work Relief Employee Assigned through the Urban League, 1934–1935," 15, EWB, box 134, folder 1; Myra Hill Colson, "Home Work among Negro Women in Chicago," unpublished MA thesis, University of Chicago, 1928, 93; Gareth Canaan, "'Part of the Loaf': Economic Conditions of Chicago's African-American Working Class during the 1920's," *Journal of Social History* 35, no. 1 (2001): 157–58.

34. Caldwell, "The Policy Game in Chicago," 32–33; J. Saunders Redding, "Playing the Numbers," *The North American Review* 238, no. 6 (December 1934): 535–36.

35. Walter Reckless, *Vice in Chicago* (Chicago: University of Chicago Press, 1933), 3–5; Chicago Commission on Race Relations, *The Negro in Chicago: A Study of Race Relations and a Race Riot* (Chicago: University of Chicago Press, 1922), 343.

36. "Black and Tan Vice Wide Open in Old Levee: South Side Police Captains Face Investigation Following Raids," *Chicago Tribune*, August 25, 1917, 13.

37. Wood, *The Negro in Chicago*, 6, 29–30.

38. "The 'Red Light' Rumor: Chicago Colored Citizens Alarmed over the Social Evil Coming into Their Residence District," *Indianapolis Freeman*, March 11, 1916, 1; Edward E. Wilson, "The Responsibility for Crime," *Opportunity* 7, no. 3 (March 1929): 96; Southside Community Committee, *Bright Shadows in Bronzetown: The Story of the Southside Community Committee* (Chicago: 1949), 31–32; Drake and Cayton, *Black Metropolis*, 658; W. Lloyd Warner, Buford H. Junker, and Walter A. Adams, *Color and Human Nature: Negro Personality Development in a Northern City* (Washington, DC: American Council on Education, 1941), 199–200.

39. "Chicago's Underworld Shaken by Vice Probe: Gambling on South Side Under Fire," *Chicago Defender*, August 25, 1928, 1.

40. Ottley, *New World a-Coming*, 158.

41. "Under the Lash of the Whip," *Chicago Whip*, August 5, 1922, 8.

42. For examples of African Americans using the cultural sphere of Chicago, including vice spots, for self-expression, see Davarian L. Baldwin, *Chicago's New Negroes: Modernity, the Great Migration, and Black Urban Life* (Chapel Hill: University of North Carolina Press, 2007), 115, 165. For vice spurring African Americans to move, see Will Cooley, "Moving On Out: Black Pioneering in Chicago, 1915–1950," *Journal of Urban History* 36, no. 4 (July 2010): 485–506.

43. "Chicago's Underworld Shaken by Vice Probe," 1.

44. Bill Davidson, "How the Mob Controls Chicago," *Saturday Evening Post*, November 9, 1963, 22; Russo, *The Outfit*, 184.

45. Shane White, Stephen Garton, Stephen Robertson, and Graham White, *Playing the Numbers: Gambling in Harlem Between the Wars* (Cambridge, MA: Harvard University Press, 2010), 26, 103–4, 106–12, 138; "Capone Gang Plans Snatch of Chicago Policy Game," *Chicago Defender*, June 6, 1942, 1.

46. Orville Dwyer, "Policy Racket Pays Million in Protection," *Chicago Defender*, May 14, 1946, 1; Roger Biles, *Big City Boss in Depression and War: Mayor Edward J. Kelly of Chicago* (DeKalb: Northern Illinois Press, 1984), 107.

47. Raymond Grow, "De King Is Daid!" *American Mercury*, October 1939, 212–15; "Threats of Death Sent to Jones Boys," *Chicago Defender*, May 4, 1940, 2; " 'Hired Killers' Murder Policy King: Buddy Hutchen Is Victim of Capone Hoodlums in Gary," *Chicago Defender*, June 26, 1948, 1; "Jim Martin Decides to Quit City," *Chicago Defender*, December 2, 1950, 1; "Roe Bosses Huge Policy Empire; Defies Syndicate," *Chicago Tribune*, June 20, 1951, 2; "Ted Roe Bares Inside Story of Jones Kidnapping," *Chicago Tribune*, June 23, 1951, 4; "Lucky Ted," *Time*, August, 18, 1952.

48. Albert N. Votaw, "Chicago: 'Corrupt and Contented'?" *New Republic*, August 25, 1952, 12–13; "Ted Roe, Policy Boss, Slain," *Chicago Tribune*, August 5, 1952, 1; Lee Blackwell, "Midnight Street Echoes Dread Tale Roe Is Dead—You Can't Beat Mob," *Chicago Defender*, August 16, 1952, 4.

49. "The Policy War," *Chicago Tribune*, June 22, 1951, 20.

50. "War on Numbers Racket Kings," *Color* (June 1951): 32–35.

51. George Bliss, "Mob Takes Over Policy Games," *Chicago Tribune*, August 18, 1958, 1; Sandy Smith, "The Charmed Life of Tony Accardo," *Saturday Evening Post*, November 24, 1962, 32.

52. Donald Mosby, " 'Negroes on Outside Say Police," *Chicago Defender*, November 15, 1967, 10.

53. "Rankins Victim of Gang Greed," *Chicago Defender*, May 12, 1958, A1.

54. Donald Mosby, "Negro Crime 'Barons' Days Gone," *Chicago Defender*, November 14, 1967, 8.

55. Operation Breadbasket meeting with Coca-Cola executives, August 24, 1967, Vernon Park Church of God, Addie Wyatt Papers, box 149, folder 2, Vivian Harsh Research Collection of Afro-American History and Literature, Carter Woodson Library, Chicago; "Operation Breadbasket News," October 1967, Abbot-Sengstacke Family Papers, box 191, folder 8, Vivian Harsh Research Collection of Afro-American History and Literature, Carter Woodson Library, Chicago; "Black Pocketbook Power," *Time*, March 1, 1968, 17;

Peter Prugh, "Tobacco Industry Is Target in Aim to Help Negro Employment," *Wall Street Journal*, February 19, 1968, 4.

56. Nicholas Gage, "Bias in the Mafia: Negroes Are Barred from 'Executive' Posts in Organized Rackets," *Wall Street Journal*, October 26, 1967, 1; Ralph Salerno and John S. Tompkins, *The Crime Confederation: Cosa Nostra and Allied Operations in Organized Crime* (Garden City, NY: Doubleday, 1969), 119.

57. U.S. Senate, "Organized Crime and Illicit Traffic in Narcotics, Report of the Permanent Subcommittee on Investigations," 89th Congress, 1st Session (Washington, DC: Government Printing Office, 1965), 13, 37–38, 119; William F. Roemer Jr., *Roemer: Man against the Mob* (New York: Donald I. Fine, 1989), 167–68; John H. Hagedorn, "Race Not Space: A Revisionist History of Gangs in Chicago," *The Journal of African American History* 91 (Spring 2006): 198; Mark H. Haller, "Illegal Enterprise: A Theoretical and Historical Interpretation," *Criminology* 28, no. 2 (1990): 218.

58. U.S. Senate, "Organized Crime in Chicago, Hearing before the Permanent Subcommittee on Investigations of the Committee on Governmental Affairs," 98th Congress, 1st Session, March 4, 1983 (Washington, DC: Government Printing Office, 1983), 23–24, 162; "Allen Dorfman Is Given Year in Prison, Fined in Teamster Fund Case," *Wall Street Journal*, April 27, 1972; John Gorman, "Court Told of Mob-Negotiated Gambling 'Tax,'" *Chicago Tribune*, April 12, 1991.

59. "Rising Black Mafia," *Chicago Defender*, August 6, 1969, 15; R. T. Sale, *The Blackstone Rangers: A Reporter's Account of Time Spent with the Street Gang on Chicago's South Side* (New York: Random House, 1971), 15–16; David Dawley, *A Nation of Lords: The Autobiography of the Vice Lords* (Garden City, NY: Anchor Books, 1973).

60. Useni Eugene Perkins, *Explosion of Chicago's Black Street Gangs: 1900 to the Present* (Chicago: Third World Press, 1987), 18; Harold M. Baron and Bennett Hymer, *The Negro Worker in the Chicago Labor Market: A Case Study of de Facto Segregation* (Chicago: Chicago Urban League's Studies of the Labor Market, 1965), 7; William Julius Wilson, *When Work Disappears: The World of the New Urban Poor* (New York: Knopf, 1996).

61. Fred J. Cook, "Black Mafia Moves into the Numbers Racket," *New York Times*, April 4, 1971, SM26; Salerno and Tompkins, *The Crime Confederation*, 119, 376; Bob Wiedrich, "Tower Ticker," *Chicago Tribune*, March 16, 1970, 31; Bob Wiedrich, "Tower Ticker," *Chicago Tribune*, June 30, 1971, 16; Art Petacque and Hugh Hough, "The Mob Mourns South Side Empire," *Chicago Sun-Times*, February 4, 1973, 1, 48; "With Youth-Gang Violence on the Rise—One City's Answer," *U.S. News and World Report*, September 17, 1973, 63; Roemer, *Roemer: Man against the Mob*, 246; Kleinknecht, *New Ethnic Mobs*, 61.

62. Bob Wiedrich, "The Old, Gray Mob," *Chicago Tribune*, April 21, 1974, G24.

63. Charles Grutzner, "Dimes Make Millions for Numbers Racket," *New York Times*, June 26, 1964, 1; Robert S. Browne, keynote speech delivered at National Black Economic Development Conference, April 25, 1969, 11, Inter-Religious Foundation for Community Organizations Papers, box 15, folder 5, Schomburg Center for Research in Black Culture, New York Public Library; Donald R. Cressey, *Theft of the Nation: The Structure and Operations of Organized Crime in America* (New York: Harper and Row, 1969), 196.

64. "Is There a Black Mafia?" *Chicago Defender*, December 11, 1969, 23.

65. Rufus Schatzberg and Robert J. Kelly, *African-American Organized Crime: A Social History* (New York: Garland, 1996), 40–41; Ianni, *Black Mafia*, 94–97; Jonathan R. Laing, "The 'Black Disciples,'" *Wall Street Journal*, September 12, 1969, 1.

66. Frederic Thrasher, *The Gang: A Study of 1,313 Gangs in Chicago* (Chicago: University of Chicago Press, 1927), chapter 21; Hagedorn, "Race not Space," 196–98; Andrew Diamond, *Mean Streets: Chicago Youths and the Everyday Struggle for Empowerment in the Multiracial City, 1908–1969* (Berkeley: University of California Press, 2009), 20–22.

67. Phyl Garland, "The Gang Phenomenon: Big City Headache," *Ebony* (August 1967): 103; "Blackstone Rangers: Gang or Emerging Social Order?" *Science News* (July 1968): 80–81.

68. Alan B. Anderson and George W. Pickering, *Confronting the Color Line: The Broken Promise of the Civil Rights Movement in Chicago* (Athens: University of Georgia Press, 1986), 219–20; Ralph David Abernathy, *And the Walls Came Tumbling Down* (New York: Harper and Row, 1989), 376–77; Jon F. Rice, "Black Radicalism on Chicago's West Side: A History of the Illinois Black Panther Party," unpublished PhD dissertation, Northern Illinois University, 1998, 89–90.

69. Alex Poinsett, "The Craft Unions," *Ebony* (December 1969): 33; Ann Scott Tyson, "Journey of Chicago's Ultimate Street Tough," *Christian Science Monitor*, December 31, 1996, 1.

70. IIT Research Institute and the Chicago Crime Commission, *A Study of Organized Crime in Illinois* (Chicago: IIT Research Institute, 1971), 180.

71. "Negroes Picket Rooster Chain; Owner Closes All Seven Stores," *Chicago Tribune*, March 2, 1969, 14; Joseph Boyce, "Red Rooster Probe Asked by Sen. Chew," *Chicago Tribune*, March 5, 1969, A6; William Jones, "How Blackstone Rangers Helped Scuttle Red Rooster Food Chain," *Chicago Tribune*, March 8, 1970, 2; Robert B. McKersie, *A Decisive Decade: An Insider's View of the Chicago Civil Rights Movement during the 1960s* (Carbondale: Southern Illinois University Press, 2013), 168–71.

72. Small Business Administration, *Crime against Small Business: A Report of the Small Business Administration transmitted to the Select Committee on Small Business United States Senate* (Washington, DC: US Government Printing Office, 1969), 44, 153; Don Debat, "Chatham, Pill Hill: Pride Builds Values, Black Families Prosper in Stable Neighborhoods," *Chicago Daily News*, February 22, 1974.

73. Robert Pearman, "Black Crime, Black Victims," *The Nation*, April 21, 1969, 501; "Gangs: Their Evolution and Essence," *Hyde Park-Kenwood Voices*, n.d. but c. 1969, LMD, box 94, folder 7; "Gang's Demand for 3 Pastors' 'Tribute' Told," *Chicago Tribune*, February 27, 1970, A2; "Report Fear of Gang by Sammy Davis Jr.," *Chicago Tribune*, March 6, 1970, 7; "What Source Gang Funds?" *Chicago Defender*, August 11, 1970, 1; Patricia Leeds, "Police Accuse 2 of Extortion," *Chicago Tribune*, September 1, 1970, 19.

74. "The Dilemma of a Black Businessman," *Chicago Defender*, August 20, 1970, 1; "Ambushes in Chicago," *Time*, August 24, 1970; William Griffin, "After Lifetime of Labor, He Refuses to Give in to Gangs," *Chicago Tribune*, September 24, 1974, A1.

75. Eric C. Schneider, *Smack: Heroin and the American City* (Philadelphia: University of Pennsylvania Press, 2008), x.

76. Thomas Plate, "Coke: The Big New Easy-Entry Business," *New York*, November 5, 1973, 66, 71.

77. Joseph Spillane, "The Making of an Underground Market: Drug Selling in Chicago, 1900–1940," *Journal of Social History* (Fall 1998): 39.

78. Felix M. Padilla, *The Gang as an American Enterprise* (New Brunswick, NJ: Rutgers University Press, 1992), 15, 95–98.

79. Donald Jansen, "Drug Inquiry Asks Police Be Aided," *New York Times*, December 21, 1973, 74.

80. Spillane, "The Making of an Underground Market: Drug Selling in Chicago, 1900–1940," 39; South Side Community Committee, "Dope Must Go Crusade, Progress Report," December 15, 1950, and March 12, 1951, CAP, box 98, folder 6.

81. "Blacks Declare War on Dope," *The Courier*, May 6, 1972, 29; David T. Courtwright, *Forces of Habit: Drugs and the Making of the Modern World* (Cambridge, MA: Harvard University Press, 2001), 173.

82. Donald Jansen, "Youth Gangs' Violence Found Rising in 3 Cities," *New York Times*, April 16, 1972, 1.

83. Jesse Hoffnung-Garskof, *A Tale of Two Cities: Santo Domingo and New York after 1950* (Princeton, NJ: Princeton University Press, 2008), 153–55; Natalie Y. Moore and Lance Williams, *The Almighty Black P Stone Nation: The Rise, Fall and Resurgence of an American Gang* (Chicago: Lawrence Hill Books, 2011), 86, 127, 249.

84. Ann Scott Tyson, "The Many Faces of a Reputed Gangster," *Christian Science Monitor*, May 6, 1997, 4; John M. Hagedorn, "Homeboys, Dope Fiends, Legits, and New Jacks," *Criminology* 32, no. 2 (1994): 210.

85. Tony Griggs, "Gun-battle Termed Bout for Profit," *Chicago Defender*, March 11, 1972, 5; John O' Brien, "Black P. Stone Nation Muscling into Drug Racket, Police Say," *Chicago Tribune*, June 11, 1972, A18; Joseph Longmeyer, "Gang War Stuns CHA," *Chicago Defender*, May 4, 1974, 1; Jonathan Laing, "Urban Arms Race," *Wall Street Journal*, March 12, 1975, 1.

86. Eric C. Schneider, *Smack: Heroin and the American City* (Philadelphia: University of Pennsylvania Press, 2008), 203.

87. Ridgely Hunt, "Requiem for Virgil White," *Chicago Tribune*, January 23, 1972, 32.

88. Richard Block, "Homicide in Chicago: A Nine-Year Study (1965–1973)," *Journal of Criminal Law and Criminology* 66, no. 4 (1975): 497, 504.

89. Irving A. Spergel, *The Youth Gang Problem: A Community Approach* (New York: Oxford University Press, 1995), 37–38; Carolyn Rebecca Block and Richard Block, "Street Gang Crime in Chicago," *National Institute of Justice: Research in Brief* (December 1993), 4.

90. John Hall Fish, *Black Power/White Control: The Struggle of the Woodlawn Organization in Chicago* (Princeton, NJ: Princeton University Press, 1973), 129–30; James Alan McPherson, "Chicago's Blackstone Rangers (II)," *Atlantic Monthly* (June 1969): 96; Harry Golden, "Black Communities Back War on Gangs, Daley Told," *Chicago Sun-Times*, June, 30, 1969; Irving Spergel et al., "Youth Manpower: What Happened in Woodlawn" (Chicago: University of Chicago School of Social Service Administration, 1969), 185.

91. Hunt, "Requiem for Virgil White," 32.

92. "Blacks Form Crime-Fighting Body," *Chicago Sun-Times*, August 7, 1970; Edwin C. Berry, keynote address, Freedom from Fear Conference, March 27–28, 1970, CUL, series II, box 242, folder 2440.

93. Neil Pollack, "The Gang That Could Go Straight," *Chicago Reader*, January 26, 1995; Josh Tyrangiel, "Ghost in the Machine," *Vibe* (September 1995): 123.

94. Andrew V. Papachristos, *A.D., After the Disciples: The Neighborhood Impact of Federal Gang Prosecution* (Peotone, IL: National Gang Crime Research Center, 2001), 28.

95. James B. Jacobs, "Street Gangs Behind Bars," *Social Problems* 21, no. 3 (1974): 399.

96. Papachristos, *A.D., After the Disciples*, 30–34.

97. Don Terry, "Chicago Trial Could End Long Reach of Man Said to Run Gang from Jail," *New York Times*, March 23, 1997; Mary Mitchell, "Gang Boss Had Free Rein in Prison, Prosecutor Says," *Chicago Sun-Times*, January 30, 1996.

98. Susan Chandler, "Gangs Built on Corporate Mentality," *Chicago Tribune*, June 13, 2004; Matt O'Connor, "Ex-Member Testifies on Gang Life," March 21, 1997.

99. Isabel Wilkerson, "Crack Hits Chicago, Along with a Wave of Killing," *New York Times*, September 24, 1991, A1; Scott Decker, Tim Bynum, and Deborah Weisel, "A Tale of Two Cities: Gangs as Organized Crime Groups," *Justice Quarterly* 15, no. 3 (September 1998): 395.

100. "Gaddafi's Goons," *Time*, December 7, 1987; George Papajohn and Tracy Dell'Angela, "Indictments Open Door for Next Gang," *Chicago Tribune*, September 3, 1995.

101. *United States of America v. Larry Hoover, et al.*, in the United States Court of Appeals for the Seventh Circuit—246 F.3d 1054, argued March 2, 2001–April 12, 2001, accessed July 16, 2014, at http://law.justia.com/cases/federal/appellate-courts/F3/246/1054/469083/.

102. Matt O'Connor, "Cash, Cocaine Part of 'Street Tax,'" *Chicago Tribune*, February 9, 1996.

103. In the Supreme Court of the United States, *Larry Hoover, et al., Petitioners v. United States of America*, On Petition for a Writ of Certiorari to the United States Court of Appeals for the Seventh Circuit, Brief for the United States in Opposition, Theodore B. Olson, Solicitor General, accessed July 16, 2014, http://www.justice.gov/osg/briefs/2001/0responses/2001–0529.resp.html; Decker et al., "A Tale of Two Cities: Gangs as Organized Crime Groups," 410, 413, 418.

104. Chandler, "Gangs Built on Corporate Mentality."

105. Papajohn and Dell'Angela, "Indictments Open Door for Next Gang."

106. *People of the State of Illinois v. Clifton*, Modified Opinion Pursuant to Supervisory Order of the Illinois Supreme Court, August 3, 2003, 1-98-2126 and 1-98-2384, accessed July 14, 2014, at http://www.state.il.us/court/opinions/appellatecourt/2003/1stdistrict/august/html/1982126.htm.

107. Randolph Roth, *American Homicide* (Cambridge, MA: Belknap Press, 2009), 24; Andrew Papachristos, "Murder by Structure: Dominance Relations and the Social Structure of Gang Homicide," *American Journal of Sociology* 115, no. 1 (July 2009): 76–77.

108. William J. Stuntz, *The Collapse of Criminal Justice* (Cambridge, MA: Belknap Press, 2011), 273.

109. Haller, "Policy, Gambling, Entertainment, and the Emergence of Black Politics," 720; Aaron Kohn, ed., *The Kohn Report: Crime and Politics in Chicago* (Chicago: Independent Voters of Illinois, 1953), 8, 12.

110. Steven D. Levitt and Sudhir Alladi Venkatesh, "An Economic Analysis of a Drug-Selling Gang's Finances," *The Quarterly Journal of Economics* (August 2000): 770–771; Sudhir Venkatesh, *Gang Leader for a Day: A Rogue Sociologist Takes to the Streets* (New York: Penguin, 2008), 247–48.

111. Papachristos, *A.D., After the Disciples*, 42–47; George Papajohn and John Kass, "21st Century Vote Giving Gangs Taste of Real Power," *Chicago Tribune*, September 28, 1994.

112. Don Terry, "Gangs: Machiavelli's Descendants," *New York Times*, September 18, 1994, 27.

113. Richard Roeper, "Calls Show No Ringing Endorsement of Hoover," *Chicago Sun-Times*, August 10, 1993; Mike Royko, "No Reason to Hail the Gangs All Here," *Chicago Tribune*, October 22, 1993; "A 21st Century Tragedy," *Chicago Tribune*, February 27, 1996.

114. WTTW, "Our People," Chicago, 1968, and WMAQ, "Whatever Force Is Necessary," Chicago, 1972, Peabody Awards Collection Archives, University of Georgia, Athens, Georgia.

115. A. Rafik Mohamed and Erick Fritsvold, "Damn, It Feels Good to Be a Gangsta: The Social Organization of the Illicit Drug Trade Servicing a Private College Campus," *Deviant Behavior* 27, no. 1 (2006): 101; Stuntz, *Collapse of Criminal Justice*, 55; Heather Ann Thompson, "Why Mass Incarceration Matters: Rethinking Crisis, Decline, and Transformation in Postwar American History," *Journal of American History* 97:3 (December 2010): 709, 716.

116. Dan Werb et al., "The Temporal Relationship between Drug Supply Indicators: An Audit of International Government Surveillance Systems," *BMJ Open* 3 no. 9 (2013), accessed July 30, 2014, at http://www.bmjopen.bmj.com/content/3/9/e003077.full.

117. John McCormick, "Winning a Gang War," *Newsweek*, November 1, 1999, 46.

118. Gary Marx and Matt O'Connor, "Prison Officials Hope to Crimp Hoover's Style," *Chicago Tribune*, May 11, 1997; Papachristos, *A.D., After the Disciples*, 50–51.

119. Terry, "Chicago Trial Could End Long Reach of Man Said to Run Gang from Jail."

120. Lombardo, *Organized Crime in Chicago*, 77.

121. Hagedorn, "Homeboys, Dope Fiends, Legits, and New Jacks," 216.

122. Vernon Jarrett, "Telling Illegality from Wrongdoing," *Chicago Tribune*, September 28, 1973, 18.

CHAPTER 8

The Politics of the Drive-Thru Window

Chicago's Black McDonald's Operators and the Demands of Community

MARCIA CHATELAIN

The McDonald's restaurant at 6550 Stony Island Avenue, in Chicago's Woodlawn neighborhood, resembles most of the fast-food chain's thousands of U.S. outlets, except for a simple square plaque embedded in the reddish-brown facade. The marker announces: "On December 21, 1968, this location was franchised to the first African American Owner and Operator." The plaque honors Herman Petty, a local barber and Chicago Transit Authority bus driver who suddenly entered the burger business months after one of the city's most troubling times.[1] Dr. Martin Luther King's assassination ignited rioting and violence on Chicago streets and in other major cities. Shortly after the chaos subsided, white business owners who had long done business in Woodlawn, and in other black sections of Chicago, wondered if their enterprises could survive in the urban core. McDonald's was no different. The corporation's recruitment of Petty was an attempt to put a new face on the brand, and his franchise agreement with the restaurant chain required him to navigate complicated economic and social terrains.

Throughout the 1970s, McDonald's corporate offices recruited franchisees of color to aid in an ambitious plan to open and reopen stores in urban areas. In the three years after Petty assumed control over the Woodlawn store, the roster of black McDonald's franchisees grew from four to nearly fifty, representing close to 10 percent of all the chain's franchise contracts.[2] Though scattered across the

Midwest, the first cohort of African American McDonald's franchisees found that they shared common problems. Black McDonald's operators often inherited stores with poor equipment, managed properties located in high-crime areas, and desperately needed advice on how to secure their stores. The operators also held mutual desires to uplift their communities and actively sponsored local programs and charities. In 1972 Petty joined other black franchisees to form a small affinity group, and he hosted the first convention of the National Black McDonald's Operators Association (BMOA); the founders hailed from Milwaukee, Kansas City and St. Louis.[3] The BMOA created a space for black operators to leverage their collective power within McDonald's and to serve as leaders in the predominately black and working-class communities that supported their restaurants.

This essay examines the economic and political factors that contributed to the building of black McDonald's franchise ownership in Chicago. Urban violence, Black Power movement ideologies about economic self-determination, and community demands for socially responsible businesses in the inner city undergirded McDonald's approach to winning over black customers.[4] The BMOA of the 1970s represented a synthesis of late nineteenth- and early twentieth-century notions of the special role of business elites in racial-uplift projects, and Black Power's emphasis on business ownership as a means of remedying economic and political injustice.[5] This merger of ideological approaches allowed for black McDonald's operators to mediate black resistance and skepticism toward the Golden Arches. Nationally, BMOA members' approach toward black consumers helped accelerate the proliferation of fast-food restaurants within communities of color, which today represents a crucial segment of the industry's most loyal consumers.

Where McDonald's Grew Up

McDonald's was founded and developed in a place far different than Herman Petty's Woodlawn and the South Side of Chicago of the 1960s. Richard and Maurice McDonald's first restaurant to offer hamburgers was born in 1940 in San Bernardino, California, a suburb sixty miles east of Los Angeles in the San Bernardino Valley.[6] Where once the town was tethered to the agricultural industry, World War II ushered in San Bernardino's growth with new military bases and government offices.[7] Many early San Bernardinos who enjoyed McDonald's barbecue sandwiches, hot dogs, and, later, burgers sought out the California suburb for its promises of well-paying industrial and military jobs, affordable tract housing, public schools, and access to local entertainment. San Bernardino was also the final destination for motorists heading west on Route 66, so hundreds of thousands of travelers on their way in and out of California visited the city and its distinctive McDonald's drive-in.[8]

McDonald's owed its early success to more than just its menu. Easier access to home and car purchasing, and higher education after the war, contributed greatly to the communities McDonald's served. McDonald's first customers were among the millions of white families who moved to suburbs and claimed the American dream of homeownership with assistance from generous Federal Housing Administration–backed loans. These new homeowners could also improve their career prospects and attend college under provisions in the G.I. Bill. By 1960, more Americans lived in suburbs than in cities, especially in the Sun Belt of the United States, where the mild weather and job opportunities lured families out of cities. These suburban, planned communities regulated the racial makeup of neighborhoods with "restrictive covenant" clauses, agreements prohibiting sales to African-Americans, Latinos, and Jews. Realtors supported this system of segregation even after the Supreme Court ruled it unconstitutional in the 1948 *Shelley v. Kramer* case, by steering families of color away from certain suburbs. Some banks simply refused to make mortgages available to black home seekers.[9] Within these suburban paradises, driving became a critical activity to allow for life outside of the city. Families relied on cars to take them to jobs in the city, shopping malls in the suburbs, and weekend getaways via a growing interstate system. Between 1945 and 1960, car ownership in the United States increased from 25.8 to 61.7 million.[10] McDonald's capitalized on all these elements: suburban families, now with more disposable income due to a surge in white-collar jobs, could drive their cars to McDonald's on Saturday nights, give their orders to carhops, and enjoy dinner in their American-made cars.[11]

Salesman Ray Kroc's visit to McDonald's in 1954 would set the restaurant on a trajectory that would make it one of the most profitable fast-food chains in the world. Kroc, then a blender salesman, was far more overwhelmed by the way the McDonald brothers made food than by the food itself. The men were already local favorites when, in 1948, they decided to streamline their business and introduce what they called the Speedee Service System. The McDonald brothers fired their "slow" carhops, whom they deemed too flirtatious and inefficient, switched to disposable flatware, and reorganized their kitchen.[12] In this new self-service system, each kitchen worker preformed one distinct task in the process of grilling a burger or frying French fries. The food was prepared assembly-line style, with no customization, and patrons did not seem to mind because they could get their food fast, and the innovations in the kitchen allowed the McDonalds to slash menu prices.[13] The changes transformed McDonald's from a teen hangout to a family-friendly restaurant, and the brothers focused on accommodating young children, who could convince their parents to treat them to McDonald's.

Soon after the visit, Kroc was in business with the brothers and would immediately get to work at bringing McDonald's to Illinois suburbs and areas similar to the bedroom communities of Southern California. By 1958, Kroc announced a 151 percent increase in sales over the previous year, with a portfolio of ninety stores in nineteen states.[14] He credited the drive-in chain's success with his commitment to the three nos—"no tipping, no jukebox, and no carhops."[15] Kroc purchased the McDonalds' financial interest in the company in 1961 and set his sights on expanding the burger chain into a greater national, then international, force. He moved operations to Illinois and continued to pursue growth based on a mixture of company-owned and franchised outlets. Although willing to open a sprinkling of stores in Chicago, Kroc focused mainly on the suburbs, which by 1960 evolved into a lucrative market of concentrated wealth and youth buying power. Kroc initially was not looking to cities to expand the burger empire; he reflected: "Urban real estate is a different ball game than the one we play in suburbia, where McDonald's grew up."[16]

Forces greater than Kroc's ambition for McDonald's prompted him to reconsider the direction of the chain. As white flight, the process of white homeowners leaving city neighborhoods due to fear of racial integration, changed the demographics of some American cities almost overnight, McDonald's found itself catering to a clientele very different than the all-American family it promoted in its advertising. The rapidly changing racial dynamics of cities across the country sometimes turned its restaurants from white to black in a matter of months. Petty's store was a prime example of this phenomenon. Kroc personally granted the franchise, McDonald's twenty-ninth location, to a white owner in 1956, as the Woodlawn area was losing more and more white residents to the North Side and suburbs.[17] The population of white residents fell from 50,716 in 1940 to 42,615 in 1950, when African Americans constituted 40 percent of the area.[18] Roland Jones, one of the first African American McDonald's executives, described McDonald's "corporate mindset" as "firmly suburban, although stores inside large cities were often among the most profitable in the system."[19] It would take a national tragedy to push Kroc to intentionally envision new spaces and communities for his business to expand.

Where Herman Petty Grew Up

Before 1968, Kroc did not think about Chicago's South Side very much. He was at the helm of an ever-expanding restaurant organization, and as long as the suburbs provided a steady flow of customers, urban life was not his concern. April 4, 1968, would change Kroc's thinking. The announcement of King's assassination in Memphis dramatically challenged McDonald's thinking about how it did business, and the reaction to King's death reconfigured the role of black businesspeople nationwide. As news of King's death spread across the country, the nation's most impoverished communities, in racially embattled cities, ignited in flames. Grief over the leader's death and fear that little would ever change for black people or the poor stoked rioting, looting, and arson. Chicagoans and police waged battles on the city's streets for more than forty-eight hours. Mayor Richard J. Daley issued a "shoot-to-kill" order, and state and federal authorities deployed National Guardsmen to support local law enforcement and firefighters.

The riots frightened McDonald's executives, and other business interests, whose Loop offices stood only a few miles from the epicenter of the riots on Chicago's West Side. McDonald's leaders closely monitored the fates of restaurants in the 129 other cities confronting similar uprisings. Anecdotes of white McDonald's owners afraid to return to their properties in rioting cities like Washington, D.C., forced the corporate offices to formulate a survival strategy in their new territory, the inner city.[20] Due to McDonald's insistence that its franchise owners spend time in their stores and manage employees, in the 1960s customers knew who personally owned their local McDonald's. Corporate officers dispatched black managers to temporarily run stores before they could decide what to do with inner-city properties. White business owners had long operated businesses in black communities in Chicago's South Side, Harlem, and Detroit, but it was a new day. McDonald's executives may have read the anger and frustration expressed in the riots as a warning sign that they would not be able to garner the support of community members after heads cooled. Even if their properties survived the destruction, would black customers care to order their new Big Mac sandwich or treat their families to dinner at the white-owned McDonald's in their neighborhood?

Though peace and quiet were eventually restored, the rioting in Chicago alone took eleven lives; the police wounded forty-eight citizens, and citizens returned fire, injuring ninety officers. More than two thousand people were arrested, and miles of city streets were left in ruins.[21] The West Side, where many black residents lived in previously white ethnic enclaves, suffered the most losses, alongside pockets of the South Side and a few North Side neighborhoods. The entire world was shaken by King's death, but it was mostly black communities that were left with destroyed homes, shuttered businesses, and shattered hopes that change would ever come.

Woodlawn, which borders the Gothic masterpieces of the University of Chicago campus and the tony brownstones of the Hyde Park neighborhood, was spared much of the destruction. But the 1968 riot propelled more white families in the neighboring communities and white business owners to flee the area. Historians and social scientists have long focused on the residential and educational impact of white flight, but the loss of white-owned businesses is also an important part of the narrative of urban decline in the 1960s and 1970s. Petty's ability to open a McDonald's in Woodlawn was the result of what I call *commercial white flight*. In an oral history of the South Side and white flight, one white business owner recounted that she resented the neighborhood's changing demographics and fled after the

1968 riot because she could no longer keep her business: "When I really came to the point of loathing them [blacks] was when we went through the final stages of having to give up the store." Her husband agreed. "For me," he reflected, "it was intimidating to go from being a respected member of the business community in South Shore to an outsider."[22] The couple was a member of a close-knit Jewish community—some who had lived in Woodlawn for nearly half a century—that left the South Side en masse throughout the late 1960s and early 1970s. The formerly unified group of South Side Jews eventually sold their neighborhood synagogue to the Chicago Public Schools, and most moved to the northern suburbs of Skokie and Evanston.[23]

McDonald's head-office team wondered if their restaurant would become an outsider, too. While white families fled to racially homogenized suburbs, African Americans usually remained in the cities where their families had settled during the Great Migration, the mass exodus of African Americans from the South to the North. By the late 1960s, more than 5 million African Americans had moved to the North in search of higher-paying jobs and more social freedoms.[24] Many were shocked and disappointed to experience segregation and racial inequality in what was said to be "the promised land." Relatively speaking, cities like Chicago provided a wider variety of social experiences, political participation, and educational opportunities than the South. Yet, on the whole, black life in major cities did not mirror that of the families captured in early McDonald's advertising. Father did not come home every evening wearing a gray flannel suit. Mother did not stay home and tend to the domestic duties. And the children did not learn from the very best teachers in their brand-new public schools. Children and youth, McDonald's major consumer market, were also changed by the riots, and mistrust of white people and businesses permeated the community. The political climate of the 1960s, coupled with the explosiveness of the riot, also changed Woodlawn's black youth, leading some to take a Black Power stance on the future of their community. One black South Sider remembered that the mood of his racially integrated high school shifted in the days after King's murder. "There was a definite attitude change in the black students at Bowen [High School] after King was killed. They were no longer Negro students—they were black students . . . wearing Afros and African clothes."[25]

Burgers and Black Capitalism

After the once-smoldering piles of rubble burned out and the curfews were lifted, Chicago's politicians and leaders sought answers as to the causes of the riot. Despite a long history of race riots in the city dating back to 1919 and having experienced riots the previous summer, Mayor Daley appointed an eleven-person

Riot Study Committee to illuminate the public about the specific causes of this particular riot. The Riot Committee included in its report the problems facing "ghetto business" as contributing to black rebellion. The committee recommended "businessmen come to grips with ghetto problems and that there be increased efforts by the business community to develop black ownership of retail outlets in the ghetto." The commission wanted community members involved in "policing ... fraudulent merchants" and the creation of "ghetto better business bureaus," consumer education, and more affordable insurance policies to secure businesses in high-crime areas.[26] This report highlighted the pervasive grievances of black consumers—overcharging, an inability to secure capital to build businesses and insure them adequately, and the scarcity of market competition that forced residents to spend too much money for too little service.

The Riot Committee's talk of business echoed national conversations and suggestions. Historian Robert Weems has argued that King's assassination prompted presidential candidate Richard Nixon to take seriously the plight of black businesspeople, because he wanted to suppress further rebellions and galvanize the white conservative vote for the Republican Party. By co-opting the Black Power movement's language around economic self-determination, Nixon believed he could subvert the radical political organizations monitored by FBI director J. Edgar Hoover and later by Nixon's White House.[27] Nixon immediately began reaching out to powerful black leaders to pledge his commitment to government programs to infuse capital into ignored sections of urban areas. A week before King's murder, Nixon declared that black militancy was not about separation, but a call for black economic freedom. Before a Milwaukee audience, the Republican nominee declared: "What most of the militants are asking is not for separation, but to be included in—not as supplicants, but as owners, as entrepreneurs—to have a share of the wealth and piece of the action." Nixon suggested the federal government play a part in orienting black people "toward more black ownership, for from this can flow the rest—black pride, black jobs, black opportunity, and yes, black power, in the best, the constructive sense of that often misapplied term."[28] By the following week, Nixon had the weight of King's assassination and legacy to contend with in his appeal to black voters. Weems aptly reminds, "If King had been alive when Nixon took office, he likely would have rejected black capitalism and may have even led demonstrations opposing this policy."[29] Ironically, King's message of economic justice for the poor and challenges to capitalism did not especially resonate with corporate leaders, but the aftermath of his death did, as the era of black capitalism took hold.

The message of black capitalism could be heard across Chicago's South Side, which housed disparate black empowerment movements, from black churches seeking to build businesses to the Black Panther Party for Self-Defense and the Woodlawn Organization, a local action group that used federal funds for community-improvement projects. In Horace Cayton and St. Clair Drake's revised edition of the epic *Black Metropolis*, the sociologists highlight that Chicago's call for black capitalism momentarily stirred interest in rebuilding the damaged parts of the West Side, despite fundamental differences among African Americans over the definition of and approaches toward building black capitalism. But soon the focus shifted when the Black Panthers questioned the means of true transformation. The Panthers insisted, "Only revolutionary reconstruction of the entire society could solve the problems of the black "internal colony."[30] Panther members did not come to a consensus on the issue of black capitalism, with some party members partnering with the Nixon administration for community-development programs, and others remaining skeptical of the federal government. Regardless of the particular position on the issue, Nixon's capture of the term *black capitalism* ushered in an era of federal assistance programs, minority business loan schemes, and incentives to cultivate business ownership within black communities; all of these initiatives helped open crucial doors for Petty and his BMOA colleagues.

Chicago's post-riot damages and Nixon's message about black business did not escape Kroc; his company was on a mission to find African American operators. In his autobiography, Kroc described his action in searching for black franchisees as a response to "the social changes of the late sixties" and called McDonald's "a leader in advancing black capitalism."[31] The social changes Kroc refers to included more than Nixon's call for black ownership. In 1969, less than a year after Petty opened the Woodlawn McDonald's, Black Power activists protested Cleveland's four East Side area franchises, citing their irritation with the white-owned chain in their community. The protests turned violent, and McDonald's dispatched black store managers to tend to the restaurant while black McDonald's corporate manager Bob Beavers defused the situation. The standoff ended with an agreement that allowed white operators to transfer their stores to black owners and move outside of black areas.[32] In its scheme to quell black resistance to the chain and negative publicity, McDonald's supported its own sort of white flight. These types of internal franchisee transfers provided the entry for future black franchisees, but sometimes the price they paid proved to be incredibly high.

Grand Openings

McDonald's application of black capitalism was not necessarily true to the definition set forth by Nixon or Black Power advocates. Early BMOA members often relied on white investors to obtain franchise agreements, which would later prove harmful to their business interests. Though McDonald's claimed they were actively searching for black operators, they allowed white financial backers to dictate black franchisee deals. Two white businessmen recruited Petty to take over the Wood-lawn store, and after meeting with the McDonald's franchising office in the morn-ing, Petty was sent to McDonald's internal-training program, dubbed Hamburger University, that same afternoon.[33] In McDonald's enthusiasm to install a black owner, they waived the requirement that Petty personally provide 100 percent of the franchising fee. In the 1970s, a McDonald's franchise fee could cost up to $150,000.[34] The white investors provided the financing, and Petty was to tend to the store and be its public face in the community. Crudely called "zebra" or "salt and pepper" partnerships, as long as black operators maintained a majority stake in the franchise, they could receive backing by white silent investors and partners. The investors could charge the black operators administrative and management fees, and some were rumored to remove cash from registers at closing time.[35] Even-tually the most exploitative of "salt and pepper" relationships were dissolved and McDonald's successfully forced out the problematic white investors. McDonald's action on the partnership was too late for some franchisees; some lost their busi-nesses and considerable sums of money.

Petty's partnership with the white investors was not the only difficult relation-ship he had to manage. The well-organized South Side Blackstone Rangers gang also made demands on the owner. The Rangers gang had overtaken the store under its previous ownership. Petty was able to leverage some of his goodwill from his barbershop to terminate employees and to "clean up" the scene around the restaurant, asking loiterers to stay away and negotiating with the members of the Blackstone Rangers gang.[36] A good working relationship between Petty and Rangers members allowed him to safely remove gang employees. Rangers gang leader Jeff Fort, who migrated to Woodlawn from Mississippi as a child, was also a proponent of black capitalism, so much so he famously received an invitation to Nixon's 1968 inauguration.[37] Fort organized his gang into a political group, the Grassroots Independent Voters of Illinois, and received a million dollars in grants and donations, including monies from the Office of Equal Opportunity, to open businesses and provide job training.[38] A month before Petty's McDonald's store opened, in November of 1968, the Rangers debuted their own nonprofit, twenty-four-hour restaurant at 4651 South Woodlawn Ave. Funded by a $3,000 loan from the Kenwood-Oaklawn Community Organization, a local body who drew the funds from another program named Toward Responsible Freedom, the restaurant was supposed to provide job training to local youth. But the restaurant's greatest challenge before it even opened was Fort's federal indictment over how he secured so much funding for his projects, which provided him with a salary.[39] The Rangers' restaurant would not prove to be very much competition for Petty, but he was ever vigilant about the consequences of gang violence and intimida-tion for his business.

Petty's cooperation or agreement with the Blackstone Rangers was critical, as area gangs intimated other South Side business owners. White business owners complained of shakedowns from gang members who asked for cash in return for protection. According to a *Chicago Tribune* report, gang members even formalized their extortion, getting themselves on the "payroll of a south side food store chain."[40] The payroll scheme started after a March 1969 boycott of Red Rooster grocery stores. Led by Jesse Jackson and Operation Breadbasket, the economic-justice wing of the Southern Christian Leadership Conference, the protestors accused the store of "selling poor quality meat, overcharging and short changing." The store agreed to hire more black residents, and the Rangers got the manager to add twenty-two gang members to their budget line. The positions and the subsequent intimidation caused the store to report the Rangers to the police, before closing seven of its stores and dismissing three hundred black workers.[41]

Petty's problems existed inside his restaurant, as well. Roland S. Jones, a regional consultant for McDonald's who worked with Petty and other pioneering franchisees, believed that Petty and other black owners were usually assigned to facilities that were "run down and the equipment mostly broken."[42] This was a common problem for black franchisees; they inherited some of McDonald's most damaged city properties and watched with envy as white franchise owners acquired suburban stores and newly built restaurants. By the first anniversary of King's death, Petty had gained a hold of his business. He broke with McDonald's convention and began employing women in his restaurants. He figured out how to upgrade the facilities. He was a regular fixture in the kitchen and dining room to oversee operations. At the end of his first year, his restaurant sales increased by 75 percent.[43] Petty's success allowed him to add a second South Side property to his portfolio; he became a multi-unit franchisee when he took over a store on Vincennes Avenue in 1969.[44] In April of 1969, Ralph Abernathy of King's SCLC visited Petty, and the proud McDonald's owner presented him with check for $1,300, a day's worth of sales.[45]

Petty's success proved that black operators worked well in black neighborhoods, and by 1969, eleven other black McDonald's franchisees trained at Hamburger U. At McDonald's regional meetings and trainings, the black franchisees would casually exchange war stories, give advice, and collaborate on community-improvement projects. The shared struggle and interests of the baker's dozen of entrepreneurs laid the foundation for the BMOA. McDonald's management did not endorse an all-black group but tolerated what seemed like a regional network of midwestern franchisees. Like the National Negro Business League of the Great Migration era, BMOA members were regular contributors to community programs and were elevated to the status of community hero for their philanthropic contributions and their presence in communities with so few businesses, and even fewer black-owned businesses. Petty, in particular, believed that he could use McDonald's ownership to serve a larger mission. In August 1969 he personally brought food, drinks, and cakes to children at the La Rabida Children's Hospital in Jackson Park, who were forced to celebrate their birthday in the hospital. A clown acting as Ronald McDonald gave gifts to the children.[46] In 1970 Petty joined a group of South Side operators in sending more than fifty children to YMCA camps in Michigan and Wisconsin.[47] BMOA members financed the expansion of the DuSable Museum of Afro-American History, the renovation of the historic Wabash YMCA, and scholarships for their teen workers to attend college.

Black McDonald's owners' presence in their communities undoubtedly helped to reinvigorate McDonald's chains; but they were not solely responsible for McDonald's success in the early 1970s with black consumers. McDonald's popularity among black diners and the success of black franchisees also rested on the economic climate of the 1970s, which included further commercial white flight, recessions, and capital divestment in black communities. Woodlawn reflected many of the economic trends facing Black Americans in the post-Nixon era: high unemployment, few retail options, and a growing reliance on fast-food outlets to meet their needs.

Within a few years of the riots, despite Petty's and McDonald's continued success, Woodlawn was in the midst of an urban tailspin. Social psychologist Loïc Wacquant has characterized this period after the riots as one in which "the wage labor market and the welfare state both retrenched from the area in the wake of the rageful riots of 1968," causing "economic involution and organizational desertification." Evidence of this decline was apparent a few blocks from Petty's restaurant in the formerly "bustling commercial artery of 63rd Street," which had "mutated into a lugubrious strip dotted with burnt-out carcasses of stores, boarded up buildings . . . and vacant lots strewn with weeds, broken glass and garbage."[48] The local press regularly reported on the loss of businesses in Woodlawn. In an article on the departure of Kahn's Department Store from the neighborhood, the *Chicago Tribune* cast doubt that federal programs and community-development grants were making a difference in Woodlawn. "Despite elaborate plans by the Department of Urban Renewal and the massive influx of federal money," the article claimed, "business [has] pulled out and those residents who could fled to other parts of the city."[49]

Supermarkets and grocery stores, like the Red Rooster, were among the businesses closed after the riots and not replaced by comparable stores. Eventually, McDonald's provided one of the few sources of affordable foods in blighted communities. As food prices soared during the recessions of the 1970s, McDonald's offered a cheap and fast alternative to expensive urban grocery stores, which were rapidly going out of business. Jones credits the lack of "regular access to suburban supermarkets and their lower prices" as integral to McDonald's popularity in cities and its remarkable period of urban expansion.[50] McDonald's had to reconsider its commitment to suburban markets when the oil embargo crisis of 1973 reduced the amount of gasoline available to drivers. Suburban residents now mindfully monitored their fuel tanks, and trips to McDonald's were now a greater financial investment. Urban residents were less likely to drive to McDonald's, and in many cities low-wage white-collar workers could walk to McDonald's counters in office building food courts.[51] A study of McDonald's growth in the 1970s reported that despite the 1973–74 recession, McDonald's successfully increased its number of new store openings, while smaller fast-food chains slowed their expansion or closed stores.[52] By 1974, McDonald's was opening an average of ten restaurants weekly.[53] McDonald's new strategy, called "nook and cranny expansion," concentrated their efforts in "opening in central-city neighborhood locations that had been previously ignored in favor of exclusive suburban orientation."[54]

BMOA members, many of them having grown up or lived near their stores, prioritized providing jobs and job training to locals, a move that engendered trust among populations in the throes of chronic unemployment. In the spring of 1968, Chicago's black unemployment rate was 8.5 percent, three times the rate of whites.[55] Yet community-action organizations suggested that the real unemployment rates in black neighborhoods was much higher, with some estimating that after the riots, unemployment was as high as 30 percent, despite overall job growth in Illinois. Large employers also left the city after the riots. They opened offices in suburban office parks and moved jobs into far-flung suburbs, where custom rather than law excluded black families and was virtually inaccessible by public transportation.[56] According to a case study of Chicago's Great Migration business center Bronzeville and its decline in the 1960s, between 1963 and 1977, factory jobs in areas surrounding the South Side fell nearly 50 percent. The researcher discovered that during this time, "the newly unemployed could not follow their jobs out of the city, nor were they prepared for the service jobs being created by glittering Loop revitalization."[57]

As McDonald's infiltrated urban markets, they in turn helped BMOA members increase their franchise holdings, and people like Petty managed multiple inner-city stores until the 1980s, when black franchisees advocated for store ownership outside of what had become their exclusive territory—black and Latino neighborhoods. This was partly possible because of McDonald's commitment to keeping labor costs low and resisting union protection for its employees. McDonald's regularly lobbied Washington to kill bills that called for a raise in the minimum wage. In 1972 Kroc donated $250,000 to Richard Nixon's reelection campaign; Kroc claimed to spontaneously provide the donation, but some observers wondered if he was supporting a second Nixon term to prevent minimum-wage increases.[58] Kroc and other business interests supported, instead, a proposed wage bill that would exempt companies from paying students at the current minimum wage.

The bill became known as the "McDonald's bill" after the press discovered Kroc's donation.[59] McDonald's also aggressively fought unionization to prevent wage increases in the 1970s. In one instance in Lansing, Michigan, when McDonald's employees sought union recognition and completed a successful card-signing campaign with the Teamsters, McDonald's shuttered the store to prevent a vote. They reopened another restaurant within walking distance of the original store and refused to hire the pro-union employees.[60] In the 1980s, ACORN (Association of Community Organization for Rights Now) tried to organize a union drive among black McDonald's workers in Detroit, coming face-to-face with a BMOA member. With assistance from the United Auto Workers, ACORN organizers tried to unionize the BMOA's Ralph Kelly's stores in 1980. Most of the workers were teens, and others were related to unionized autoworkers. McDonald's stepped up the pressure, planning parties for employees, firing troublemakers, and challenging the legality of the vote. The BMOA members suggested that union wages would drive up the cost of doing business in Detroit and limit opportunities for neighborhood youth. A few days before the union election, McDonald's brought Houston Oilers star Earl Campbell to dissuade a pro-union vote. Only one third of workers signed cards, and the plans were dead.[61]

BMOA members also built their success on the growing segmentation of black consumers in advertising, which sought to reflect the realistic conditions of black life in print and television advertisings. Unlike earlier generations of black advertisers, who used an aspirational tone in black marketing by largely depicting middle-class family and community life as a means of combating racism, a new generation of advertisers took a different approach to the black consumer market. McDonald's growth in the 1960s required the company to develop its brand identity and produce advertising to introduce the concept to new markets. Beginning with print ads and local commercials in the early 1960s, McDonald's advertising has been some of the most persuasive and influential strategies in fast-food marketing. From the introduction of Ronald McDonald and his McDonaldland friends to the use of celebrities in pitching value meals, McDonald's advertising has worked incredibly well. BMOA members played a critical role in challenging McDonald's to develop content that spoke to its growing base of black consumers. BMOA members expressed their concern that the 1971 "You Deserve a Break Today" campaign failed to speak to their customers. Jones recalled: "It had only a marginal effect in McDonald's growing urban markets. Black owners began to complain that they were getting little, if any return for the fees they paid out of their gross sales for national advertising."[62] After lobbying from the BMOA, McDonald's enlisted Burrell Communications, a Chicago-based advertising agency that specialized in black marketing, to create a more relevant campaign.[63] Burrell's limited "Get Down with McDonald's" campaign depicted black families in cities visiting the restaurants, and though the BMOA was happy with the concept, McDonald's corporate offices initially buried the ads in publications and radio stations that exclusively catered to blacks. Agency head Tom Burrell persisted and would become one of the leading authorities on black consumers for McDonald's and other companies. Burrell and McDonald's agreed on another campaign, "McDonald's, sure is good to have around." Jones credits Burrell's success in crafting successful black advertising with his understanding of the fundamental differences between "the hardcore urban black consumers and middle-class suburban white consumers." In his experiences at McDonald's, Jones determined that "for most inner-city blacks, McDonald's wasn't a fun break in the daily routine; it was just to eat, 'a feeding station' in Tom's words."[64] Burrell addressed the 1973 BMOA convention and discussed strategies on capturing black consumers. The "McDonald's, sure is good to have around" campaign featured everyday life in a black community, which included a postal worker making an ordinary lunch break stop at McDonald's. Postal work was an area opening fast for African Americans with limited education, and the phrase "good to have around" may have also referred to McDonald's permanence in an age of business white flight.[65]

McDonald's popularity in the inner city, coupled with the efforts of the BMOA, rendered black franchisees a critical part of their neighborhoods' social and economic life. An incident in the spring of 1974 illustrates just how ingrained McDonald's had become in Black Chicago. Residents of the Altgeld Gardens public housing development, which housed two thousand families, found a cloud of hydrochloric acid hovering over their apartments after a silicon tetrachloride leak at a nearby chemical company. City officials failed to warn many of the residents the afternoon the cloud of acid appeared over the area, and they didn't take steps to safely evacuate them until late in the evening, compromising the safety and health of the community. One resident said that she called the police, "but they didn't send anyone." She revealed, "If I'd known what this was I could have been ready to take my family out of here. They should have told us so we would have been ready."[66] Those who fled their homes without anything to eat were relieved when McDonald's stepped in with 1,050 hamburgers and drinks for the evacuated Chicagoans, who waited for further instructions at a local high school. In a statement to the press the BMOA remarked, "We at McDonald's are sincerely interested in community involvement and can always be counted upon in a crisis."[67]

Within Black Chicago, crisis was not hard to come by, with high unemployment, continued gang violence, and a growing drug epidemic, alongside near total managerial abandonment by the city. The BMOA provided vital resources. A December 1977 *Chicago Tribune* feature on the black operators remarked, "Social critics often point to the fast-food franchise as one of the prime ways the rich [almost always white] get richer and the poor [almost always black] keep profits on the rise with every hamburger, chicken leg, and fish fillet they consume." The article suggested black-owned McDonald's restaurants were a sound means of diverting black money away from wealthy whites and maintaining profits with their community. The president of the BMOA, William Pitchford, buttressed this point in the article. "Just about all of the McDonald's that are located in the black community are owned by blacks, and I've never heard anybody charge that the black community is being milked by whites who don't live in the city."[68] The article and Pitchford's rhetoric suggested that exploitation was inherent among white-owned businesses in black neighborhoods. Pitchford's comments assured patrons that eating at his McDonald's essentially kept money inside the black community, where it rightfully belonged. The average customer who visited Pitchford's restaurant regularly or his kitchen crew may not have fully understood the real-estate fees and revenues that all franchisees had to deliver to McDonald's headquarters in suburban Oak Brook. It did not matter. McDonald's had successfully fulfilled the mission inspired by those days after 1968—they had used black franchisees to ingratiate the brand to the community and obscured their corporate identity so well that if the streets of Chicago were to burn again, they probably thought, McDonald's would be immune.

Every Building but McDonald's

After the violence of 1968, Chicago has yet to experience a riot of such magnitude and devastation. Yet for those old enough to remember the violence of 1968, the 1992 Los Angeles riots may have triggered terrible nightmares of the days following the King assassination. When four white police officers were acquitted of police-brutality charges after they beat a black motorist, Rodney King, Los Angeles's streets were reminiscent of Chicago's West Madison Street and Roosevelt Road. Within hours of the verdict's announcement, looters and rioters took to the street antagonizing business owners, starting fires, and suggesting that little had changed in the nearly twenty-five years since King's assassination. Los Angeles's South Central area, the core of black life in L.A., was the hardest hit. Soon after the rioting ended, the McDonald's corporation dispatched stories proudly proclaiming that their L.A. restaurants were spared in the destruction of more than a thousand buildings totaling a billion dollars in damage.[69] Seeing it as an integral part of the community, rioters avoided the fast-food outlet and directed their ire elsewhere. The corporation claimed that none of the thirty-one McDonald's locations in Los Angeles were affected by the rioting.[70] Then-CEO Edward Rensi explained, "Our businesses there are owned by African-American entrepreneurs who hired African-American managers who hired African-American employees who served everybody in the community."[71] An article on McDonald's survival during the riots described the company's fate as "vindication of enlightened social policies begun more than three decades ago." The Los Angeles chapter of the BMOA had long supported area sports teams and, in the wake of the riot, provided lunches for schools that could not access cafeteria supplies and food shipments. So, McDonald's was spared, and the narrative of progress that infiltrates the corporation's public-relations materials could claim the Los Angeles riots as proof of its racial progressiveness and community commitments.

From Greensboro to the Golden Arches

The history of African American entrepreneurship is an important, yet woefully underexamined, topic in explorations of the legacy of the post-1968 movement toward racial and economic justice. African American fast-food franchisees represent the tensions and ambivalence about the direction and terms of progress in light of growing economic gulfs between poor and middle-to-upper-income black communities and constituencies. Fast-food restaurants, from the minority-ownership schemes to their employment practices to their menu offerings and their marketing, provide a rich arena for assessing the complicated ways that African American business interests leveraged their power in both community-affirming and harmful ways.

Restaurants are places in which both bodily and social needs are met. For African Americans who were barred from entry into dining establishments under Jim Crow and segregation, the 1964 Civil Rights Act was supposed to signal an ability for black citizens to expand their ability to participate as consumer citizens and validated their ability to access a form of pleasure they saw whites routinely enjoy. Yet discriminatory practices continued in individual businesses, and the trauma of participating in or merely witnessing the struggles to integrate lunch counters and diners rendered black diners cautious or altogether avoidant of certain restaurants. Fast food, in many ways, mediated black consumer anxiety and frustration in its expansion years. Fast-food restaurants' goals readily remedied traditional restaurant problems by the very nature in which they operated. For the most part, each outlet charged consumers the same amount of money for their items; service was limited to the taking of orders and food delivery; and with the rise of ethnic marketing, chains crafted messages that affirmed the desirability of black customers. These strategies, coupled with the personalizing of fast food with operators of color, ensured that fast food would connect to black consumers.

As important as it is to uncover this rich history and these relationships, it is also critical to understand the current state of black health and income inequality to grasp the impact of fast food. Today, food activists concerned about African American obesity rates and food deserts in poor communities, indict McDonald's and their counterparts for harming people of color. In 2011 the Robert Wood

Johnson and Rudd Foundations conducted a study tracking advertising marketed toward children of color and found that "African American children and teens see at least 50% more fast food ads than their white peers." McDonald's marketed to black children mostly with banner ads on websites and television advertising. The report also concluded that "African American children see nearly twice as many calories as white children see in fast food TV ads every day."[72] Currently, obesity rates are highest on Chicago's South and Southwest Sides. According to a Northwestern University Medical Center survey, 22.6 percent of black high school students are overweight, twice the rate of their white peers.[73] With a population of 33 percent of the city's residents, Black Chicagoans encounter a 21.4 percent unemployment rate; in 2010, black families earned an average annual income of $28,725 versus $63,625 for white families. More than 30 percent of black families live below the poverty line.[74] The Woodlawn community, and most of Chicago's South Side, continues to struggle. Woodlawn is now 98 percent African American, and its population declined by half between 1950 and 1990.[75] Despite some efforts at community revitalization, including University of Chicago initiatives, Woodlawn's population is still 50 percent lower than in 1950, and the 2008 mortgage crisis caused housing values to plummet.

The greatest sign of hope for some in the community is the Woodlawn McDonald's, which is now owned and operated by Keith Allen, a local man who first worked for Petty in 1976, earning $2.10 per hour. He regularly receives hundreds of job applications for positions at his reopened store.

Notes

1. Patricia Sowell Harris, *None of Us Is as Good as All of Us: How McDonald's Prospers by Embracing Inclusion and Diversity* (New York: Wiley, 2009), 31.

2. John A. Jakle and Keith A. Sculle, *Fast Food: Roadside Restaurants in the Automobile Age* (Baltimore: Johns Hopkins Press, 1999), 156.

3. Harris, *None of Us*, 45, and "Now That's 3 Burgers with Ketchup," *Chicago Daily Defender*, June 19, 1972, 24.

4. For more on Black Power capitalism, see Peniel Joseph, *Waiting 'til the Midnight Hour: A Narrative History of Black Power* (New York: Owl Books, 2006); and Devin Fergus, *Liberalism, Black Power, and the Making of American Politics, 1965–1980* (Athens: University of Georgia Press, 2007).

5. For more on racial uplift, see Kevin Kelly Gaines, *Uplifting the Race: Black Leadership, Politics, and Culture in the Twentieth Century* (Chapel Hill: University of North Carolina Press, 1996); and Willard B. Gatewood, *Aristocrats of Color: The Black Elite, 1880–1920* (Bloomington: Indiana University Press, 1990).

6. John F. Love, *McDonald's Behind the Arches* (New York: Bantam Books, 1986), 12.

7. U.S. Department of Commerce, U.S. Census of Population, 1950 (Washington, DC: Government Printing Office, 1950), 5–20.

8. Love, *McDonald's Behind the Arches*, 10–14.

9. For more on race and housing policy, see Arnold Hirsch, *Making the Second Ghetto: Race and Housing in Chicago, 1940–1960* (Chicago: University of Chicago Press, 1998); Thomas Sugrue, *The Origins of the Urban Crisis: Race and Inequality in Postwar Detroit* (Princeton, NJ: Princeton University Press, 2005); and Becky M. Nicolaides, *My Blue Heaven: Life and Politics in the Working-Class Suburbs of Los Angeles, 1920–1965* (Chicago: University of Chicago Press, 2002).

10. Tom McCarthy, *Auto Mania: Cars, Consumers, and the Environment* (New Haven, CT: Yale University Press, 2007), 152.

11. Love, *McDonald's Behind the Arches*, 11–12.

12. Ibid., 14–22.

13. Ibid., 13–16; Eric Schlosser, *Fast Food Nation: The Dark Side of the All-American Meal* (New York: HarperCollins, 2001), 19–21.

14. "McDonald's Drive-in Chain's Sales Up 151%," *Chicago Daily Tribune*, January 18, 1959.

15. Ibid.

16. Ray Kroc, *Grinding It Out: The Making of McDonald's* (New York: Bedford St. Martin's, 1992), 203.

17. Loïc Wacquant, "Urban Desolation and Symbolic Denigration in the Hyperghetto," *Social Psychology* 73, no. 7 (September 2010): 215–19.

18. Gladys Priddy, "From Marshland to Maturity—Fast Growing Woodlawn," *Chicago Daily Tribune*, February 7, 1954, S1.

19. Roland S. Jones, *Standing Up and Standing Out* (New York: World Solutions, 2000), 119.

20. Harris, *None of Us*, 30; Jones, *Standing Up and Standing Out*, 78.

21. *Encyclopedia of Chicago*, s.v. "West Madison." For more on the race riots after Dr. King's assassination, see Janet L. Abu-Lughod, *Race, Space, and Riots in Chicago, New York, and Los Angeles* (Oxford: Oxford University Press, 2007); and Louis Rosen, *The South Side: The Racial Transformation of an American Neighborhood* (Chicago: Ivan Dee, 1998).

22. Rosen, *The South Side*, 141.

23. Ibid., 141–49.

24. Lisa Krissof Boehm, *Making a Way Out of No Way: African American Women and the Second Great Migration* (Oxford: University of Mississippi Press, 2009), 3.

25. Rosen, *The South Side*, 130.

26. Sheryl Fitzgerald, "Chicago Riot Panel Rejects Conspiracy in April Violence," *Chicago Daily Defender*, August 6, 1968, 1.

27. For more on Nixon's FBI and the COINTELPRO, Counter Intelligence Program, of the 1960s and 1970s, see Kenneth O'Reilly, *Racial Matters: The FBI's Secret File on Black America, 1960–1972* (New York: Free Press, 1991); and Ward Churchill and Jim Vander Wall, *The COINTELPRO Papers: Documents from the FBI's Secret Wars against Dissent in the United States* (New York: South End Press, 2001).

28. Robert E. Weems Jr., *Business in Black and White: American Presidents and Black Entrepreneurs in the Twentieth Century* (New York: New York University Press), 115.

29. Ibid., 113, and Dean Kotlowski, "Black Power Nixon Style: The Nixon Administration and Minority Business Enterprise," *Business History Review* 72, no. 3 (Autumn 1998): 409–45.

30. Horace Cayton and St. Clair Drake, *Black Metropolis: A Study of Negro Life in a Northern City*, 2nd ed. (Chicago: University of Chicago Press, 1969), lxvii.

31. Kroc, *Grinding It Out*, 167.

32. Nishani Frazier, "A McDonald's That Reflects the Soul of a People: Hough Area Development Corporation and Community Development in Cleveland," in *The Business of Black Power: Community Development, Capitalism, and Corporate Responsibility in Postwar America*, ed. Julia Rabig and Lauren Warren Hill (Rochester, NY: University of Rochester Press, 2012), 68–93.

33. Harris, *None of Us*, 32.

34. Ibid., 31.

35. Jones, *Standing Up and Standing Out*, 169–75; Harris, *None of Us*, 33.

36. Harris, *None of Us*, 32.

37. Tom Brune and James Yliselany, "The Making of Jeff Fort," *Chicago Magazine* (November 1988).

38. Russell Freeburg, "Justice Dept. Probe of Rangers Is Asked: Fraud Is Hinted in Chicago Project," *Chicago Tribune*, September 14, 1968, 1.

39. "Rangers to Open Restaurant," *Chicago Tribune*, November 11, 1968, A18.

40. William Jones, "How Blackstone Rangers Helped Scuttle Red Rooster Food Chain," *Chicago Tribune*, March 8, 1970, 2.

41. Ibid.

42. Harris, *None of Us*, 33.

43. Ibid.

44. Ibid.

45. Untitled (photo standalone), *Chicago Daily Defender*, April 29, 1969, 4.

46. "A Treat for a Customer," *Chicago Daily Defender*, August 2, 1969, 27.

47. Untitled (photo standalone), *Chicago Daily Defender*, July 4, 1970, 9.

48. Wacquant, "Urban Desolation and Symbolic Denigration," 216.

49. James Jackson, "Store to Close in Woodlawn," *Chicago Tribune*, March 8, 1973, S4.

50. Jones, *Standing Up and Standing Out*, 120.

51. Andrea Freeman, "Fast Food: Oppression through Poor Nutrition," *California Law Review* 95 no. 6 (2007): 2,221–59.

52. Robert L. Emerson, *The New Economics of Fast Food* (New York: Van Nostrand Reinhold, 1990), 10.

53. James W. McLamore, *The Burger King: Jim McLamore and the Building of an Empire* (New York: McGraw-Hill, 1998), 153.

54. Jakle and Sculle, *Fast Food: Roadside Restaurants*, 156.

55. "Black Unemployment Still Nags Cities," *Chicago Daily Defender*, March 16, 1968, 26.

56. Robert McClory, "Discouraged Workers Struggle and Starve," *Chicago Daily Defender* November 23, 1974, 5.

57. Michelle R. Boyd, *Jim Crow Nostalgia Reconstructing Race in Bronzeville* (Minneapolis: University of Minnesota Press, 2008), 48.

58. Love, *McDonald's Behind the Arches*, 87.

59. Ibid., 360.

60. Schlosser, *Fast Food Nation*, 77–78.

61. John Atlas, *Seeds of Change: The Story of ACORN, America's Most Controversial Antipoverty Community Organizing Group* (Nashville, TN: Vanderbilt University Press, 2010), 53–56.

62. Jones, *Standing Up and Standing Out*, 208.

63. For more on black advertising agencies and their impact on marketing, see Jason Chambers, *Madison Avenue and the Color Line: African Americans in the Advertising Industry* (Philadelphia: University of Pennsylvania Press, 2009).

64. Jones, *Standing Up and Standing Out*, 210.

65. Ibid., 212; Blacks and the postal service is the topic of Philip F. Rubio's *There's Always Work at the Post Office: African American Postal Workers and the Fight for Jobs, Justice, and Equality* (Chapel Hill: University of North Carolina Press, 2010).

66. Jon Van, "Gas Victims Help Each Other; Kept in Dark, They Assert," *Chicago Daily Tribune*, April 28, 1974, 2; Frank Zahour, "Fume Victims Still Feeling Symptoms," *Chicago Daily Tribune*, May 5, 1974, 22.

67. "Big Mac Helped Big Leak Victims," *Chicago Daily Defender*, June 1, 1974, 15.

68. Michele Gaspar, "McDonald's Does It All to Help Minorities," *Chicago Daily Tribune*, December 28, 1977, E8.

69. Ian Warden, "How Marketing Saved McDonald's from Arson," *Canberra Times*, December 19, 2001, A7.

70. "Odds and Ends," *Wall Street Journal*, November 16, 1992.

71. Edwin M. Reingold, "America's Hamburger Helper," *Time*, June 29, 2001.

72. Kelly D. Brownell, Jennifer L. Harris, and Marlene B. Schwartz, *Evaluating Fast Food Nutrition and Marketing to Youth* (New Haven, CT: Yale Rudd Center for Food Policy and Obesity, 2010).

73. Romana Hasnain-Wynia and Juliet Yonek, *A Profile of Health and Health Resources within Chicago's 77 Communities* (Chicago: Northwestern University Feinberg School of Medicine, Center for Healthcare Equity / Institute for Healthcare Studies, 2011).

74. U.S. Census Bureau, *American Community Survey 5-Year Estimates* (Washington, DC: Government Printing Office, 2009).

75. Wacquant, "Urban Desolation and Symbolic Denigration," 216.

CHAPTER 9

Positive Realism

Tom Burrell and the Development of Chicago as a Center for Black-Owned Advertising Agencies

JASON P. CHAMBERS

"Good entrepreneurs make money. Great ones make a difference."
—Earl Graves, *Black Enterprise*, June 2011, 12

For many people, New York City's Madison Avenue is the idealized "home" of the advertising industry. Beginning in the late nineteenth and early twentieth century, agencies began establishing offices on the street to service their clients in the expanding metropolis. So, despite the work of agencies in cities like Chicago and Philadelphia, by the middle of twentieth century, "Madison Avenue" became the geographical shorthand used to reference the advertising industry.

In contrast, the center of the African American–owned agency sector has been in Chicago. Like their counterparts in the black newspaper and magazine fields, Chicago proved a fertile location for African American–owned agency development. Black-owned companies such as the Associated Negro Press, *Chicago Defender*, and John H. Johnson's *Negro Digest* and *Ebony* magazines made Chicago a powerful seat of African American media creation and delivery. Supporting and supported by those media enterprises were black advertising agencies. These agency owners built upon the work of men like Claude Barnett, Robert Abbott, and John H. Johnson, who early in the twentieth century repeatedly told American corporations to recognize the value of the black consumer market and to invite its members to use their products. Therefore, in the early 1970s when Tom Burrell and Emmett McBain based their agency's unique selling proposition on their expertise in creating advertising campaigns to reach black consumers, they were planting seeds in soil actively tilled by others for decades.[1]

The tradition of successful black ownership of advertising concerns has a longer and more consistent history in Chicago than in any other city in the country. From Claude Barnett's pioneering work in the industry in the 1910s and 1920s, to Vince Cullers's advertising firm in the 1950s, African Americans in Chicago had greater opportunity to create advertising firms of significant size, scope, and longevity than in any other city in the country. A significant part of that black-owned agency success has been Tom Burrell. Burrell played a key role in the development of the Chicago advertising community. He was also one of the major actors in transforming the advertising industry from its insular white, Ivy League, WASP orientation that dominated the profession for much of the twentieth century.[2]

This chapter analyzes Burrell's experience within the mainstream advertising agency segment and moves through the foundational years of his experience as an agency owner. The first four years of the agency's life were key, as they established a base of clients that enabled it to survive. Also, in those inaugural years the Burrell philosophy of advertising was clearly enunciated and displayed in the firm's work. This philosophy, "positive realism," meant the firm's work depicted blacks in ads as they realistically existed in life rather than as caricatures from a racist imagination. The central argument here is that being in Chicago allowed Burrell unique opportunities that, if based elsewhere, he would have been unable to leverage. Specifically, these opportunities were Burrell's mainstream agency experience, an unparalleled client roster, and the ability to develop and then leverage his connections within the Chicago network of African American professionals and entrepreneurs. This last factor was particularly key in enabling him to draw experienced African American personnel from other Chicago-based agencies, men and women whose talents catalyzed his success.

Burrell founded his advertising agency in 1971. He did so alongside several other black entrepreneurs who opened agencies, as well. Therefore, examining the factors that allowed his agency to survive the tumult that claimed several other black agencies and to then thrive in the post–civil-rights era is key. Burrell created an agency that withstood the competitive landscape that between 1971 and 1981 decimated the ranks of the original black agency cadre. Understanding how he withstood the difficulties that battered his agency in its early years provides clarity in locating Chicago as a unique center for black business development generally and for the black advertising agency presence in the city specifically.

An Entrepreneurial Family

Thomas Burrell Jr. was born into an entrepreneurial family in 1939. The family lived in an apartment near the corner of Fifty-Ninth Street and Calumet Avenue in the Washington Park area of Chicago's South Side. His father, Thomas Burrell

Sr., operated a string of businesses, including a bail bonds office and a tavern on Chicago's West Side where blues legends like Muddy Waters played. He also dabbled in residential real estate and owned a series of buildings on the West Side. Regardless of the enterprise, the elder Burrell, like other black entrepreneurs of the period, sought to work for himself in order to both reap the lion's share of the profits and to avoid the sting and limitations of race that came when working for whites. Although his father had varied experiences in business ownership, he passed none of those lessons on to his son. Instead he was physically present yet emotionally distant from him. His cruelty reached the point that he even refused to speak directly to his young son and instead relayed messages to him via his mother.[3]

In many ways Tom Burrell's life turned on the results from a single test. After his sophomore year, on his own initiative he had transferred from Englewood High School to Parker High School. Even as a young man he recognized that the academic preparation at Englewood was unlikely to lead him to even minimal opportunities. As a result, he sought out the opportunities that he envisioned could be possible through coursework at the academically stronger Parker High. At Parker he enrolled in a course on careers taught by Ethel Buland. Part of that course required him to take an aptitude test on which he scored highly in the areas of persuasiveness and creativity. When he asked Ms. Buland what type of career these areas were suited for, she answered without hesitation, advertising copywriting. Whether she did so with or without forethought, the white Ms. Buland did not restrict her answer only to jobs deemed suitable for blacks. Her response was unique because it ran counter to the traditional restrictions white teachers often put on the aspirations of their black students.[4]

When examining the role of teachers in the career aspirations of black youth in Chicago, Arvarh Strickland noted that "Negroes needed special motivation to help them break the pattern of accepting the status quo. Since many jobs had been closed to them, Negro youth developed a 'psychological attitude' which discouraged high level job preparation."[5] Or as one young black girl observed, "[My] teacher said not to take a commercial course because there were no jobs opening up for colored. So there's nothing but housework and cleaning left for you to do."[6] Hence both Ms. Buland and the young Burrell stepped outside of the constrictive racial mores of their time. She did not restrict her advice only to opportunities that were clearly open to blacks, and he did not restrict his professional aspirations to occupations already open to blacks. Instead he began to pursue a career path that, based upon race alone, was largely closed to him. Further, by introducing Burrell to a career that neither he nor his friends knew anything about, she fueled him toward a goal. And rather than keeping his goals to himself, he began telling his friends and family that he was going to be an advertising copywriter. Her encouragement gave him a goal to pursue through high school and a major to select when he entered college.

Still, it was a final interaction with his father that strengthened his resolve and determination.[7]

Burrell's parents divorced when he was thirteen, and the young man became estranged from his father, seeing him sporadically over the next several years. Finally, at the age of eighteen and upon learning of his father's ill health, Burrell went to visit him in the hospital. Dying of cancer, the elder Burrell still kept his son at an emotional arm's length. The young man made a final effort to reach out to his father and let him know that he was enrolling in Roosevelt University in a few weeks. The elder man refused to offer even a modicum of support. In a raspy voice he spoke some of his final words to his son. "College? What the hell makes you think you can get through college? You'd be lucky if you could pass the post office test."[8] A few days later, the elder Burrell died.

Burrell's treatment by his mother and father were worlds apart. For where his father repeatedly and openly doubted his son's abilities, Burrell's mother was a fountain of strength, encouragement, and expectation. She also encouraged him to think for himself and to be something of a leader in the family, a role he took to eagerly. Beyond his expected matriculation through school, he also developed a strong work ethic. "I always worked," he said. "I always had this work ethic that I needed to get a job and earn some money."[9] Over the course of his childhood and teenage years he worked in a bowling alley and at the freight yards, sold soap door-to-door, delivered newspapers, and shined shoes. In having that one person believe in him and continually expect success, Burrell had the support and drive he needed to pursue his goals. While those goals evolved over the years, the foundational base of his pursuit of success remained the same. "What I was determined to do was to prove her right and prove him wrong."[10]

Being motivated, having a strong work ethic and drive to succeed sound trite without knowing how Burrell translated these traits into action. In his case they directly influenced his actions in college, at first negatively. His eagerness led him to take on more work than he could actually handle. In his first semester at Roosevelt University, he enrolled for eighteen credit hours (with twelve being considered a normal class load), plus additional courses at the nearby Art Institute, as well as a position as an editor at the school newspaper.

Also, in contrast to Ms. Buland, some of his instructors discouraged him from pursuing a major in advertising. "What do you think you're doing," one asked. "There's nobody hiring black people in the advertising business. What are you going to do with it?"[11] Consequently, he found himself with low grades, little motivation, and eventually placed on academic suspension.

When Burrell returned to school the next semester, he trimmed his workload and adopted better study habits. Therefore, when the opportunity came to apply for a position at Wade Advertising, he was intellectually ready and prepared to incorporate a job into his academic work. Although one would not have expected much from the lowly beginning in the agency mailroom (where he was working in an advertising agency, though not necessarily *in* advertising), the time at Wade Advertising was a key experience in Burrell's advertising career.

Mainstream Advertising Experience

When Burrell began working at Wade Advertising in 1960, there were few white-collar blacks in Chicago and no blacks working in a professional capacity in any of the city's major advertising agencies. At Wade, the third-largest agency in the city, the decision to hire an African American was made with caution. Led by Lou Nelson, a senior vice president and director of marketing services, the agency moved to integrate voluntarily rather than in response to public pressure or fair employment laws. Instead, they planned to hire an African American college freshman into the mailroom and advance him slowly up the agency ranks as he matriculated through college. After he graduated, they intended to integrate him into the professional areas of the agency. Based on those plans, Tom Burrell was not what they had in mind.[12]

Executives at Wade wanted to integrate their firm, though they did not want any negative publicity for doing so. As a result, instead of running an ad or a public job search, they sought help from the only black professional they knew, Don Brown, their representative from *Ebony* magazine. They told him that they wanted black applicants for a position in their mailroom. This gave them the advantage of having applicants already vetted by their *Ebony* representative and spared them from any negative publicity arising from their decision to integrate the agency. In fact, Burrell heard of the opening only through a fraternity brother who had a connection with another *Ebony* representative, Ron Sampson. From that connection, Burrell gained the interview with the executive leadership team at Wade Advertising.[13]

Although he was the one eventually hired, Burrell was not the ideal candidate in the minds of Wade's leadership. They wanted a college freshman majoring in marketing; he was a junior majoring in English and advertising. They wanted an eighteen- or nineteen-year-old who could be advanced through the professional ranks over a period of years; he was twenty-two years old with visions of joining the agency's professional ranks within a period of months. The challenge for Wade executives was that he was the only individual who had applied for the job.[14]

Through his own initiative, Burrell's timetable proved more accurate than that of Wade executives. He hustled. He arrived early and stayed late. He did not limit himself only to his mailroom duties, but also sought ways to expand his network in the agency. Since his mailroom duties required him to deliver parcels around the agency, Burrell got to know the other employees in the firm, particularly the creative director. As a result, he landed a position as a copywriter within a few months of joining the company. From that position he developed the experience that allowed him to move to other major advertising agencies, including Leo Burnett, the London office of Foote, Cone & Belding (FCB), and finally Needham, Harper & Steers (NH&S).

Burrell moved to the Leo Burnett agency in 1964. The time at Leo Burnett taught him that employees should not feel as though they were competing with their boss for the development of a client's advertising. During Burrell's time with Leo Burnett, the organizational structure had several layers of approval for advertising development. Before the final decision was made on the execution of an advertising campaign, everyone on the respective creative team, including managers, submitted creative work. In other words, management was a part of the process of creation rather than of analysis and evaluation of the work done by the professionals hired to do just that. To Burrell, that process created a sense of internal competition in which the employee was unlikely to win, and it stifled the professional growth of the employees. Thus when he had his own agency, he decided that he would actively encourage employees to develop their own ideas; he would critique and be the final authority on what the agency would submit to the client, but he would not directly compete with his employees.[15]

When he moved to the Needham, Harper & Steers agency in 1968, Burrell found himself in a position that drew on his creative acumen and gave him responsibility and authority. His time at Wade, Leo Burnett, and FCB helped Burrell hone his creative acumen, but he credits his experience at NH&S with providing him with the knowledge and confidence to start his own advertising agency. At NH&S, as a copy supervisor, he was in a management-level position. He learned how to guide other employees in their creative executions and overall development. His position also allowed him to study the process of client acquisition. Additionally, at NH&S he evolved from being a copywriter into being a marketing strategist. Specifically, he learned to remain focused upon the key selling points or features of the product and to utilize those ideas when developing the advertising campaign. Hence his time at NH&S was a thorough education in advertising and marketing. "I got a chance to produce," Burrell said. "I got a chance to interface with clients. I basically learned the agency business there, and it really helped prepare me to go out on my own."[16]

In terms of experience, Burrell took something different from each of the agencies that he worked for. For example, from Wade Advertising he learned not to place too much of the agency's billings in the hands of one client. Wade was the longtime agency for Miles Laboratories, makers of Alka-Seltzer, with Miles eventually providing over 80 percent of the total billings for the agency. When Miles executives decided to move the account to another firm, they ended a client-agency relationship over three decades old and effectively forced Wade's closure.[17]

At each of the four mainstream agencies where Burrell worked, he viewed himself as more than an employee marking time and collecting a paycheck. Instead he consciously observed how each agency was structured and run. With the benefit of hindsight, he recognized that he had "spent those years with some kind of thought or feeling about watching how advertising agencies work and with the thought of someday applying that to my own business."[18] By approaching his time at each agency as a training experience, Burrell developed a wealth of knowledge unparalleled among the cadre of blacks who started advertising firms in the late 1960s and early 1970s. He had honed his creative and management abilities and gained important experience in finding clients and, due to his experience as a supervisor, in attracting and retaining employees. While other black agency founders may have had some experience in mainstream firms, none could match the length of time and breadth of experience Burrell obtained. So rather than opening the doors of Burrell-McBain and having to spend time learning on the job about advertising, he could draw on the key lessons he learned over the prior eleven years. Of how his experience differed from that of other black agency owners he noted, "One of the things that I felt I had going for me, which Vince [Cullers] or nobody else had is, I had experience. I had managed to get through the door of major advertising agencies and then do major stuff once I got in there."[19] Hence Burrell had key experiences and insights he was able to draw upon when he joined Emmett McBain in launching the Burrell-McBain advertising agency in 1971.[20]

Burrell-McBain Advertising

During his last few years at NH&S, Burrell began investigating the possibilities of opening his own advertising firm. He had tried a number of combinations of partnership groups, none of which worked out to his satisfaction. His initial plan was to quit his job at NH&S only after he had secured some clients with which to open his agency. Unfortunately, he and his partners were caught in the classic entrepreneurs' dilemma. They were able to find clients who might give them some business once their agency was open, but none willing to give them business before they had actually opened it. As a husband and father with a steady paying job, Burrell hesitated to start an agency without any clients. Emmett McBain, on the other hand, familiar with operating in a far smaller agency with much smaller margins for error, looked at the problem simply and said, "There is always going to be a reason not to do something."[21] So, instead of waiting until they had clients, the two men set January 3, 1971, as their date to open and, even with no clients, did so. As a testament to their resolve, they did so even after the third original member of the partnership group, Frank Mingo, an account executive at the J. Walter Thompson agency, backed out at the last minute and decided to remain in his current position.[22]

When Burrell-McBain opened, both men had considerable experience in the advertising industry. Like Burrell, McBain, an award-winning graphic artist, had worked at a mainstream advertising agency, J. Walter Thompson. In addition, he had also worked at the Chicago-based Vince Cullers agency, one of the oldest black-owned agencies in the country. Therefore, the two men brought together an important combination of skills and experiences, Burrell in the application of time-tested advertising and marketing techniques, and McBain in having worked at a small shop that specialized in advertising campaigns to reach the black consumer market.[23]

Opening a business with no clients was a challenge and ongoing financial hardship. Therefore, Burrell kept his focus upon client acquisition and keeping expenses down. In its early months, the agency consisted of Burrell, McBain, a secretary, and three desks from which to operate. Despite the logic of the fiscal restraint, the lack of operating capital and clients was difficult. "It was painful. Not only was it painful from a financial perspective, but also my health suffered tremendously. I went from, in that first six months of the business, 215 pounds down to about 175. People thought I was dying because I was totally, totally stressed out."[24] Neither man collected a paycheck in those initial months, and at one point Burrell collected unemployment compensation. In fact, it was only a small loan from Burrell's uncle that helped to keep the agency afloat.

Despite their difficulty, the two men held fast to the unique positioning of their agency. It was, they told prospective clients, an agency with the marketing and advertising skill and experience to sell products to African American consumers. Rather than trying to create "just another advertising agency," Burrell and McBain actively courted clients interested in reaching the black consumer market. They reasoned that black people were culturally distinct enough and profitable enough as a consumer group to be worthy of a separate advertising initiative. Or, as Burrell put it more succinctly, "Black people are not dark skinned white people."[25] Thus Burrell emphasized how the agency could help clients sell more products through the creation of unique campaigns, rather than ask them to simply recast mainstream advertisements by replacing white faces with black ones. Neither did Burrell accept corporate handouts then used by some companies as a kind community-relations effort—programs in which they gave money to black-owned companies but required little in the way of professional execution or actual deliverables. As a selling proposition for the agency, it was a unique, measured, and professional approach. Unfortunately, it was not one that led to business.[26]

Burrell and McBain were not the only black agency owners with experience in advertising and marketing. For example, both Junius Edwards and John Small, two black agency owners in New York, also had some mainstream agency experience. The key difference was that neither man positioned their agencies as experts at reaching black consumers. Instead they focused on accounts to reach the general rather than a racially segmented market. As such, they failed to stand out in the crowded agency landscape. Still, though the Burrell-McBain approach was unique within the industry, it made business difficult to come by, and the two men struggled to keep the agency afloat. Fortunately, after a few months, the agency landed an account with the Edison Theater Company that paid a monthly fee of $1,000. Over that same period, Burrell developed important contacts that lead him to the agency's first major client, Philip Morris.[27]

During the mid- to late 1960s a broad push took place within the advertising industry to find and employ more black professionals. Pressure from civil-rights groups and both state and federal equal employment committees led to (relative to their past employment numbers) large numbers of blacks joining mainstream advertising firms. While the employment experiences of those blacks is not the focus of this chapter, one key difference is clear in the experiences of blacks in Chicago versus in New York. Whether or not Chicago agencies were more liberal or open-minded in terms of their treatment of black employees, blacks were able to work their way into key decision-making positions in Chicago-based agencies well in advance of those in New York. Combined with the decades-long spirit of group self-help among blacks in Chicago, Burrell's visibility among black corporate professionals meant that his agency was positioned for growth.[28]

In Burrell's case, being in Chicago had allowed him to advance at each of the agencies in which he was employed, particularly at Wade Advertising and Needham, Harper & Steers. Further, it brought him into contact with other blacks who were later integral to the early successes of Burrell-McBain. One of the most important of these was Stuart Rankin, a black agency executive at Leo Burnett. Rankin went to work at Burnett in the late 1960s and eventually became one of the account executives on the Philip Morris account. Around the same time, Philip Morris board chairman Joseph Cullman III made the decision to move more aggressively in hiring blacks to work within the company. As an extension of this effort, he also asked Leo Burnett to find a black advertising agency to work with Philip Morris. Cullman's motivations were both social and economic. Several of Philip Morris's competitors already employed African American agencies, so Cullman's request was in part based on a desire to maintain competitiveness. As the lone African American on the Philip Morris accounts, Rankin fell into the task of finding the black agency. As a result, Rankin became the conduit between Philip Morris and Burrell-McBain, and Philip Morris became the agency's first major client.[29]

Rankin and Burrell had known of each other even before either man joined the advertising industry. They had mutual friends in the city and crossed paths socially. The two men met in a professional capacity when both became members of an ad hoc collection of African American advertising professionals in Chicago known as the Black Advertising Group (BAG). The members of BAG met on a regular basis to share their insights and agency experiences. The network provided the foundation of the relationship between Rankin and Burrell and also later provided Burrell with the first black professionals for his agency. So when Cullman asked Rankin to craft a report and provide a recommendation of a black-owned agency to work with Philip Morris, Rankin steered them toward Burrell-McBain.[30]

Rankin's choice of Burrell-McBain went beyond his personal relationship with the agency's founders. After all, Rankin was relatively new to the Philip Morris account, and if Burrell-McBain failed, he would have damaged his credibility with both Philip Morris and Leo Burnett. Therefore, he examined the agency closely to ensure that they had the capability and insight necessary to service the account. Rankin recalled: "I called them and told them, 'Look, Philip Morris is looking for a black agency. Where are you in your development?' They invited me down and I saw their offices and everything, not that I needed to see that, but I really came down to talk to him so we could set it up and make sure that if I did recommend them that there weren't any loose ends. Because the last thing I wanted them to think was that I was doing it because of a friend."[31]

He also met with the two men before their initial meeting with Philip Morris to familiarize them with the company's product lines as well as with the executives they would meet. Hence, rather than on friendship, he based his recommendation on personal knowledge, the proficiency of the agency, and his knowledge of the training and experience the two men received before they opened their agency. Of his final recommendation he observed, "It was all again based on my experience at Burnett and knowing that Tom had not just experience at Burnett but good rudimentary experience from Wade. I knew that he knew the process, the whole process of product to advertising. I just had confidence in him and I knew I couldn't go wrong."[32]

The acquisition of the Philip Morris account was a major stepping-stone for Burrell-McBain. First, it provided them a $3,500 a month retainer that they desperately needed. Additionally, it gave them a relationship with one of the nation's major advertisers. The company was one of the twenty-five largest advertisers in the country, with advertising expenditures of nearly $60 million annually. Philip Morris was the type of blue-chip account that gave the agency visibility and credibility. Further, rather than working on one of the less important brands that were part of the Philip Morris brand family, the agency was asked to craft an advertising campaign to black consumers for Marlboro, their flagship cigarette product.[33]

With the goal of relating client products to black consumers, Burrell and McBain quickly surmised that the trade character of Marlboro cigarettes, the independent cowboy alone with his horse, was a problem. For whites the cowboy was an independent hero, a symbol of America; to blacks he was a "loser." Burrell's research indicated that blacks felt that the cowboy was alone because he did not have friends and was not known in his community. Rather than being a figure of independence and a source of emulation, the cowboy image hampered Marlboro's sales among black smokers.[34]

In addition to the image, the Marlboro slogan, "Come to where the flavor is," was also a problem. So they dropped the first two words and changed the tagline for black smokers to "Where the flavor is." This immediately made the line more relevant to black smokers. Although the emphasis remained on the word "flavor," Burrell-McBain's seemingly simple change evolved the slogan into the Soul-oriented meaning of the word, one that encompassed the cultural richness of the black experience. The black flavor in jazz or soul music, the black flavor of personal style, all became encapsulated within the word "flavor." Additionally, by using images of black men who through their clothing, the objects they carried, or the settings in which they were placed supported the tagline and urged readers to conclude that black Marlboro men were men with style and who were known to and emulated by members of their urban community.[35]

The Black Marlboro Man campaign attracted black smokers but ultimately lasted only a few months. Executives at Leo Burnett, the agency responsible for the original Marlboro Man campaign, actively argued to Philip Morris executives against any alteration of the image of the trade character. Even more problematic were consumer complaints and legal threats connected to the campaign. In using scenes framed on busy city streets, McBain's photographs had caught passersby in some of the shots. He failed to secure the written release from those individuals, one of whom threatened to sue Philip Morris for using his image without consent. Consequently, the combined pressure from Leo Burnett executives and possible legal action against Philip Morris led the company to terminate their contract with Burrell-McBain.[36]

Although the Black Marlboro Man campaign ended quickly, the account showcased the advertising prowess of the young agency. It also provided them with a connection to a blue-chip advertiser that helped them acquire large national clients. Being able to show clients work that the agency did for Philip Morris was far more persuasive to other national clients than work done for the locally based Edison Theater Company. Working with Philip Morris allowed Burrell-McBain to demonstrate the types of accounts they could service. That experience was vital in proving the agency's capabilities, particularly as Burrell targeted his next blue-chip client, the McDonald's fast-food chain.

McDonald's

In the twenty-first century, McDonald's is a recognized multinational corporation with a well-known logo and a history of slogans that made their way into the nation's lexicon. In the early 1970s, however, the Chicago-based company had only recently begun to run advertisements on a national level. Instead, most McDonald's advertising came from local McDonald's store owners. Therefore, executives at the company had only just begun to explore developing a national identity for McDonald's.[37]

At that time, the national advertising agency for McDonald's was NH&S. While Burrell worked at NH&S for several years, he never worked on the McDonald's account. Therefore, in order to cultivate a contract with McDonald's, he needed relationships with people beyond those at his old agency. In this case, his networking efforts were aided by the physical location of the Burrell-McBain offices. The original offices of the agency were at 360 North Michigan Avenue. Located on the tenth floor, the agency was next to Cooper and Golin, McDonald's public-relations agency. Burrell eventually met one of the owners of the firm, Al Golin, who in turn introduced him to executives at McDonald's. Therefore, when the opportunity came to work for McDonald's, there were already people at the company who knew the young advertising man. Even more important than Golin, however, was Roland Jones, one of the first black field-service operators at the fast-food giant.[38]

Out of all the relationships Burrell cultivated in securing work with McDonald's, the one with Jones proved to be key. Jones came to Chicago in 1969 at the behest of McDonald's executives. His initial charge was to help them understand and adapt to ongoing consumer changes at the local store level. The evolving racial demographics of urban neighborhoods meant that stores once located in white neighborhoods were now located in African American ones. Thus McDonald's, which at the time of Jones's arrival had no black store owners in Chicago, had to adjust to a customer base with which they lacked familiarity. Also, as the neighborhoods changed, the owners of several of the affected stores began reducing the time and energy they put into running them. Walter Pitchford, a black McDonald's manager, recalled, "A lot of the [white] operators didn't even come into the city. They operated their stores through the telephone. They'd come in at 12:00 p.m. maybe to collect their deposits and stuff and get the heck out of there by 1:00 p.m. or 2:00 p.m. And in most black areas where there were McDonald's you didn't see any white people after 2:00 p.m. in the evening."[39] Further, several of those owners began looking for African American buyers and managers to either take over or at least run their stores. To guide those new black owners and managers through their difficulties, McDonald's executives brought Jones in for help.[40]

As part of his job responsibilities, Jones came into contact with all of the members of the growing cadre of black store owners and managers in Chicago. Therefore, he was uniquely positioned to be aware of their challenges and to suggest solutions for common problems. One of his suggestions was that, rather than meet individually with store owners to provide them training or to address issues common to other owners, they should meet together regularly so his work could be more efficient. Out of those early meetings emerged the Black McDonald's Operators Association (BMOA), a group that along with Jones proved essential to cementing Burrell's relationship with McDonald's.[41]

McDonald's today is renowned for its operational systems. Store owners are provided with specific machinery, products, and instructions that allow the customer experience to be the same whether eating at a McDonald's in Chicago or in Philadelphia. In the early 1970s, however, one result of that standardization was the corporately held belief that all store owners faced the same problems and that all customers viewed their McDonald's experience the same way. They did not. Instead the research conducted by Burrell into the African American perception of and experience with McDonald's, combined with the in-store knowledge generated by members of the BMOA, illustrated that urban blacks and suburban whites had widely differing views of the restaurant. One area in which this contrast was most clearly illustrated was in the rationale that each group used for visiting the restaurants.[42]

Of the original research that supported the development of McDonald's first national advertising efforts, NH&S executive Keith Reinhard said, "All of our consumer research was showing us that a trip to McDonald's was an event for each member of the family that could be likened to an escape to an island of enjoyment. Kids could see the mountains of french fries, moms could escape from meal planning, and dads could escape the hassles of business."[43] This insight formed the basis for one of McDonald's most recognized slogans in its history, "You deserve a break today." To whites, McDonald's was a respite from the demands of life, and it was a special treat to visit and enjoy the hamburgers, shakes, and fries. As a break, McDonald's was a place that they did not visit regularly but instead reserved for a weekend meal or used to reward kids for an accomplishment. Burrell's research into the black experience at McDonald's showed something quite different. In contrast to being a "treat" or a "break," to urban black consumers, the main patrons of the stores of BMOA members, McDonald's was "a feeding station." McDonald's was a place close to home where parents could get inexpensive, filling food for their families. Additionally, rather than being a place only visited on special occasions, McDonald's was someplace that black youths might visit several times a day, with the restaurant acting almost as a babysitter while parents were at work.[44]

After analyzing these broadly variant consumer motivations between blacks and whites, Burrell cogently argued that McDonald's needed to launch a targeted advertising program to blacks. Fortunately, he found a receptive audience in Jones and the members of the BMOA. "We knew that there was something wrong, and the problem was that the black franchise owners were paying the same thing that the general market consumer owners were paying for advertising," Jones recalled.

"But we were not getting our money's worth out of it. As a matter of fact, we got very little out of it, because those dollars were directed toward the general consumer market. Black consumers were not related to the general consumer market."[45] Led by Carl Osborne, a black franchisee from Columbus, Ohio, black store owners began agitating for an advertising program to target the African American consumers who visited their stores. Osborne and others met with McDonald's leadership, including Paul Schrage, the company's chief marketing officer, as well as representatives for NH&S. From that meeting Burrell received approval to create the new advertisements specifically targeting black consumers.[46]

Supported by an understanding of black consumers' use of McDonald's, Burrell and McBain created a series of print advertisements featuring the tagline "Get down with McDonald's." Placed in *Ebony* magazine, the advertisements featured a limited use of black slang and were illustrated with black families eating at McDonald's or black men interacting closely with their children at the restaurant. As they had done with their reworking of the Marlboro Man, Burrell and McBain continued their emphasis on prominently featuring images of strong and capable black men. Surprisingly, even though black store owners credited the work with increasing their sales, Burrell was informed that he would receive no more assignments from McDonald's. Instead, a unique combination of racial fear within McDonald's and corporate competition from NH&S worked against him.[47]

Initially, Burrell-McBain worked as a subcontractor through NH&S to create a series of print and radio advertisements. Consequently, all of the agency's McDonald's work first went through NH&S for their approval rather than to the head of the McDonald's marketing department. The creative executions were vetted by NH&S, who then decided what advertisements would be forwarded to McDonald's and even what media sources would be used. In fact, of the initial work Burrell completed, NH&S executives rejected the use of the radio ads his agency completed because they were "too black." Hence NH&S acted as a roadblock between Burrell-McBain and McDonald's. Beyond their lack of appreciation for the work completed by Burrell-McBain, NH&S may have also resented having another agency with influence on what they viewed as their account. Their competitive instincts likely made them loath to lose any part of the McDonald's account to an outside agency. Instead, NH&S leaders were concerned over any efforts by McDonald's, a major agency client, to allot even part of their advertising work to another agency. Therefore, behind the scenes they encouraged McDonald's executives not to work directly with Burrell-McBain.[48]

Beyond the machinations of NH&S executives, McDonald's executives were hesitant to support any further development of an advertising program they did not fully understand. This was especially true of an advertising plan based on developing a program around racial differences. Rather, they worried that a visible advertising effort to reach black consumers might offend white consumers and result in the loss of sales. This fear was based on their assumptions of white consumer reaction rather than any actual experience. In fact, major manufacturers of various products had featured blacks in their advertisements since the early twentieth century and had experienced few negative reactions from white consumers. Regardless of that history, Burrell knew that if he could not establish a direct relationship with McDonald's rather than work through NH&S, his association with the company would never appreciably increase. Instead, as in the case with Philip Morris, the agency would be able to complete work for a blue-chip client, but that work would not result in steady revenue.[49]

Rather than accept rejection, Burrell reached out to Roland Jones for help. In doing so, he utilized a relationship with a vocal advocate for their work within the client company. As one of the leading members of the BMOA and one concerned with the development of black-owned McDonald's franchisees, Jones offered Burrell invaluable support. Well aware of BMOA members' feelings that their advertising needs were not being met by the current national advertising program, Jones avidly believed Burrell offered the solution. Therefore, at the 1973 BMOA convention, Jones organized a meeting where Burrell presented his research to the entire BMOA membership and showed some prospective advertising work. When finished, he left the room while Jones and the BMOA members discussed his presentation. Jones's summation of the issue was simple: if the BMOA did not stand behind Burrell and press the need for a national-level advertising effort targeting black consumers, black storeowners would never receive an equitable return on their advertising expenditures.[50]

Like their white counterparts, black McDonald's franchisees contributed 1 percent of their gross sales to the Operators National Advertising Fund (OPNAD). This fund was the advertising cooperative that supported the national advertising of the McDonald's corporation.[51] Therefore, Jones and others in the BMOA argued that they had a right to expect their wishes on the direction of the company's advertising to be heard. Jones put the matter succinctly: "If McDonald's national advertising was going to increase sales for black owners in black communities, we needed a black ad team in control."[52] Thus the BMOA voted to support a formal contract for Burrell-McBain as an agency of record with McDonald's rather than one assigned project-based assignments on an as-needed basis.

Although they did not immediately acquiesce, eventually McDonald's executives listened to the BMOA's recommendation. They did so in part out of fears of negative publicity and in part out of respect for the needs of their franchisees. As an organization, McDonald's had a history of listening to the wishes of their franchisees rather than insisting that all decisions on products and strategy come from corporate headquarters. For example, franchisees created some of the company's most recognized products, like the Big Mac and the Egg McMuffin. In the case of black franchisees, they recognized that the store owners knew their client base in a far more specific and intimate way than could executives based at corporate headquarters. They were in their stores on a daily basis and witnessed their consumers' particular interaction with the company and its products. Therefore, when members of the BMOA supported Burrell's analysis of McDonald's black consumers, they did so with the benefit of their own experience. As a result, McDonald's established a direct working relationship with Burrell-McBain that has lasted into the twenty-first century.[53]

With McDonald's as a contracted client, by 1974 the Burrell-McBain agency was on surer economic footing. Despite this new blue-chip client, however, Emmett McBain decided to leave the agency to pursue an art career. Therefore, by mid-1974 the agency that once was to have been Mingo-McBain-Burrell, and then Burrell-McBain, became simply Burrell Advertising. The agency was now completely at Burrell's discretion to move in whatever direction he envisioned.

After McBain's departure, Burrell began gathering a staff of professionals that could support his vision of the agency and assist in developing advertising for McDonald's. Led by Burrell, the new staff crafted a more inclusive vision of McDonald's customers. They created print advertisements featuring black men, women, and children enjoying the restaurant. More important, because McDonald's spent a significant amount of its advertising budget on television work, Burrell also received the opportunity to develop television commercials.[54]

Television work placed the Burrell agency on a significantly different level than other black-owned agencies at the time. "Well, it [television] helped establish us," he said. "It helped separate us. It helped give us tremendous visibility. We were doing television commercials that were running outside the country, that were running in places like Norway."[55] While other black agencies were also gaining accounts with blue-chip companies (particularly cigarette and alcoholic-beverage manufacturers), their work was largely restricted to print and radio advertisements placed in black-oriented media. In contrast, through television commercials featuring black construction workers undergoing a "Big Mac Attack" or black children running to the store to get a Happy Meal, Burrell's work for McDonald's gained the agency a level of visibility unmatched by other black agencies. The television work not only attracted new major clients like the Coca-Cola company to the agency, but also helped attract other black professionals. African American professionals with a mainstream advertising-agency pedigree similar to Burrell's own left their positions at Chicago agencies like Foote, Cone & Belding or Leo Burnett to join a black-owned company. Thus by the late 1970s, with a growing stable of clients and with a growing staff of new employees, the agency was well on its way to the success that propelled it for the next three and a half decades into the Burrell brand recognized across the industry.[56]

Positive Realism

From the beginning, Burrell sought to build a top-flight agency that helped its clients meet their advertising goals. Therefore, he encouraged his employees to constantly tweak and refine their work in order to meet his exacting standards. "My philosophy," Burrell said, "was that we will do it over and we'll do it over again, as long as there is time and money left. If that meant doing it over again, recasting, reshooting, whatever the hell it was, rewriting, that's what I did."[57] The results from such high standards came quickly after the acquisition of the McDonald's account. Not only did the agency acquire more blue-chip clients like Coca-Cola, but it also began to win industry awards like the Clio, one of the highest honors in advertising, or Communications Excellence to Black Audiences (CEBA) awards. Thus, Burrell Advertising received recognition from their clients, from their peers in the industry, and from African American consumers.

Burrell understood that one of the central tenets of reaching black consumers was for the advertising to demonstrate a respect for their patronage and for their self-vision. As John H. Johnson observed of the state of black consumers when he began publishing *Ebony* in 1945, "Respect. For more than one hundred years, that had been the cry of the Black soul. One hundred years of 'boy' and 'girl' and 'George' and 'Mary' and 'nigger' had created an almost inexhaustible thirst for recognition and respect."[58] Building on the work of fellow Chicagoans like John H. Johnson and Claude Barnett, Burrell's agency practiced a philosophy of advertising that he labeled "positive realism."

Although black images were slowly becoming more visible across the media, they were still largely absent in advertisements. Aware of blacks' thirst for recognition and for realistic images of themselves and their lives, Burrell focused on developing advertisements that showed black people using products in the unique ways in which they did so. His theory was simple: "If we could just show black life, portray it in a positive, realistic way," he reasoned, "people will come to the product."[59] Further, his advertisements depicted blacks in urban settings or other locales with which black consumers would be familiar. Although he did not shy away from using black celebrities and sports stars when necessary, he actively sought to use everyday, non-celebrity black men and women, as well. For example, the model in several of the ads the agency did for Philip Morris was Adolph Barmore, a man with whom Burrell had gone to high school and who represented the kind of strong black male image he wanted to portray. This approach of depicting regular black people as they realistically existed garnered an immediately affirmative response from consumers. Black consumers purchased the products and services of Burrell clients, and the agency gained broad recognition for its advertising and marketing prowess. In the process, the work Burrell developed helped shift the advertising depiction of blacks away from that of stereotyped caricature to that of valued consumer.[60]

Over the course of his forty-plus-year career, Tom Burrell easily proved his father's perception of his abilities and potential societal contributions wrong. For companies like McDonald's, he demonstrated the positive impact that respectful and appreciative depictions of Black America via advertising could have on their product sales. Over the years, the agency attracted a veritable who's who of black advertising professionals. A number of former Burrell employees later went on to high-level positions in other agencies or with client-side companies. In addition, some, like Eugene Morris and Don Coleman, created significant advertising agencies of their own. Additionally, Tom Burrell built a company that became a brand unto itself. Whether through the constant pursuit of perfection for his clients or in the development and application of his philosophy of positive realism, Burrell created a firm that has lasted for over four decades. Further, he built an institutional structure that allowed the agency to continue to thrive after his retirement in 2004. Along the way his firm has won nearly every major award given in the industry. As an individual, Burrell has been acknowledged with numerous honors, including induction into the American Advertising Federation Hall of Fame, the industry's highest recognition. Known today as the Burrell Communications Group, the small firm that started with a few desks and three employees has grown to be the leading advertising agency for reaching the black consumer market. In the process, it also helped cement Chicago as the center of the black advertising agency community.[61]

Notes

1. On the work of Claude Barnett and John Johnson in the development of the black consumer market, see Jason Chambers, *Madison Avenue and the Color Line: African Americans in the Advertising Industry* (Philadelphia: University of Pennsylvania Press, 2008), 22–30 and 41–49. On the work of Robert Abbott in developing the *Chicago Defender*, see Allan H. Spear, *Black Chicago: The Making of a Negro Ghetto, 1890–1920* (Chicago: University of Chicago Press, 1967), 185.

2. On the African American experience in the advertising industry, see Chambers, *Madison Avenue and the Color Line*.

3. Tom Burrell, interview by author, May 27, 2011.

4. Ibid.

5. Arvarh Strickland, *History of the Chicago Urban League* (Urbana: University of Illinois Press, 1966), 213.

6. St. Clair Drake and Horace R. Cayton, *Black Metropolis: A Study of Negro Life in a Northern City* (Chicago: University of Chicago Press, 1993), 259.

7. Tom Burrell, interview by author, May 20, 2011. Chambers, *Madison Avenue and the Color Line*, 242–43.

8. Tom Burrell, interview by author, May 27, 2011.

9. Tom Burrell, interview by author, March 22, 2011.

10. Ibid.

11. Laurence Minsky Calvo and Emily Thornton, *How to Succeed in Advertising When All You Have Is Talent* (Lincolnwood, IL: NTC Business Books, 1995), 120.

12. On the lack of professional and managerial opportunities for blacks in Chicago, see Harold M. Baron and Bennett Hymer, *The Negro Worker in the Chicago Labor Market: A Case Study of Defacto Segregation* (Chicago: Chicago Urban League, 1968), 21. "Historical Profiles of the Nation's Largest Agencies," *Advertising Age* (December 7, 1963): 22; Tom Burrell, interview by author, March 22, 2011; Tom Burrell, interview by author, January 26, 2001.

13. Tom Burrell, interview by author, March 22, 2011; Ron Sampson, interview by author, November 8, 2011.

14. Tom Burrell, interview by author, March 22, 2011.

15. Tom Burrell, interview by author, June 3, 2011.

16. Thomas J. Burrell (The HistoryMakers A2001.007), interview by Julieanna Richardson, June 5, 2001, The HistoryMakers Digital Archive, session 1, tape 5, story 3, in which Tom Burrell recalls his experience at Needham, Harper & Steers advertising agency. Accessed at http://www.idvl.org/thehistorymakers/iCoreClient.html#/&n=1624.

17. James Smith, "Wade Will Close Doors April 1, Toni Account Going Elsewhere," *Chicago Tribune*, January 26, 1966, B6.

18. Tom Burrell, interview by author, June 3, 2011.

19. Tom Burrell, interview by author, May 27, 2011.

20. Tom Burrell, interview by author, May 20, 2011; Thomas J. Burrell (The History-Makers A2001.007), interview by Julieanna Richardson, May 6, 2001, The HistoryMakers Digital Archive, session 1, tape 5, story 6, in which Tom Burrell talks more about going into business for himself. Accessed at http://www.idvl.org/thehistorymakers/iCoreClient.html#/&n=1627.

21. Tom Burrell, interview by author, May 27, 2011.

22. Tom Burrell, interview by author, May 27, 2011; Lynn Taylor, "Black Ad Agencies Look to Future," *Chicago Tribune*, February 23, 1972, C12.

23. Roi Ottley, "Reds Get Good Look at Negro's Artwork," *Chicago Daily Tribune*, February 7, 1960, N11.

24. Tom Burrell, interview by author, May 27, 2011.

25. Tom Burrell, interview by author, June 3, 2011.

26. Ibid.

27. Ibid. On Junius Edwards and John Small, see Chambers, *Madison Avenue and the Color Line*, 209–12 and 214–18.

28. Stuart Rankin, interview by author, November 18, 2011; Ted Plair, interview by author, December 21, 2011.

29. Tom Burrell, interview by author, May 27, 2011; Doris E. Saunders, "Have You Met the Bold Soul in the Dashiki," *Chicago Daily Defender*, May 13, 1969, 17; "Black Agency to Handle Reynolds Adv. Campaign," *New Journal and Guide*, June 14, 1969, B2.

30. Stuart Rankin, interview by author, November 18, 2011; Eugene Morris, interview by author, November 7, 2011; Sarah Burroughs, interview by author, November 7, 2011.

31. Stuart Rankin, interview by author, November 18, 2011.

32. Ibid.; "Black Firm Awarded Big Account," *Chicago Daily Defender*, May 5, 1971, 27.

33. In advertising parlance, "blue chip" is a term denoting an account with a major national advertiser. "Black Firm Awarded Big Account," *Chicago Daily Defender*, 27.

34. Behavioral Systems, Inc., "The Marlboro Image Revisited: An Exploration of the Masculinity Concept among Black Urban Male Cigarette Smokers," June 1971, downloaded June 3, 2010, from http://legacy.library.ucsf.edu/tid/jey25e00/pdf; Tom Burrell, interview by author, June 3, 2011.

35. Behavioral Systems, Inc., "The Marlboro Image Revisited."

36. Tom Burrell, interview by author, June 3, 2011; Behavioral Systems, Inc., "The Marlboro Image Revisited"; Chambers, *Madison Avenue and the Color Line*, 247–49.

37. Roland Jones, interview by author, December 6, 2011; Roland L. Jones, *Standing Up and Standing Out: How I Teamed with a Few Black Men, Changed the Face of McDonald's and Shook Up Corporate America* (Nashville: World Solutions, 2006), 207, 212; John F. Love, *McDonald's: Behind the Arches* (New York: Bantam Books, 1995), 304–9.

38. Jones, *Standing Up and Standing Out*, 206–7. During an interview with the author, Roland Jones said that the correct year of his initial meeting with Tom Burrell was 1972 rather than 1973 as he stated in his book *Standing Up and Standing Out*.

39. Walter Pitchford, interview by author, December 14, 2011.

40. Jones, *Standing Up and Standing Out*, 110–17; Love, *McDonald's: Behind the Arches*, 369–71.

41. Tom Burrell, interview by author, June 3, 2011; Roland Jones, interview by author, December 6, 2011; Walter Pitchford, interview by author, December 14, 2011. Also see Marcia Chatelain's chapter in the present work.

42. Tom Burrell, interview by author, June 3, 2011; Roland Jones, interview by author, December 6, 2011; Lisa D. Chapman, "Black Franchises under the McDonald's Arches," *Black Enterprise* (May 1974): 19–25.

43. Love, *McDonald's: Behind the Arches*, 305.

44. Jones, *Standing Up and Standing Out*, 207–10; Roland Jones, interview by author, December 6, 2011.

45. Ibid.

46. Jones, *Standing Up and Standing Out*, 207–10; Tom Burrell, interview by author, June 3, 2011.

47. Ibid.; Jones, *Standing Up and Standing Out*, 209–10.

48. Tom Burrell, interview by author, June 3, 2011; Roland Jones, interview by author, December 6, 2011.

49. Chambers, *Madison Avenue and the Color Line*, 133–48; Roland Jones, interview by author, December 6, 2011; Tom Burrell, interview by author, May 27, 2011; Jones, *Standing Up and Standing Out*, 207–10.

50. Roland Jones, interview by author, December 6, 2011; Jones, *Standing Up and Standing Out*, 209–11.

51. Love, *McDonald's: Behind the Arches*, 302; Ray Kroc with Robert Anderson, *Grinding It Out: The Making of McDonald's* (Chicago: Henry Regnery, 1977), 152.

52. Roland Jones, interview by author, December 6, 2011; Jones, *Standing Up and Standing Out*, 210.

53. Roland Jones, interview by author, December 6, 2011; Jones, *Standing Up and Standing Out*, 208–9. On the role of McDonald's franchisees in product creation, see Love, *McDonald's: Behind the Arches*, 293–98.

54. Tom Burrell, interview by author, June 3, 2011; Tom Burrell, interview by author, January 26, 2001.

55. Tom Burrell, interview by author, January 26, 2001.

56. Eugene Morris, interview by author, November 7, 2011; Sarah Burroughs, interview by author, November 7, 2011; John Stannek, interview by author, November 28, 2011; Ronald Sampson, interview by author, November 8, 2011.

57. Tom Burrell, interview by author, March 22, 2011.

58. John H. Johnson with Lerone Bennett Jr., *Succeeding against the Odds: The Autobiography of a Great American Businessman* (New York: Amistad Press, 1992), 118.

59. Tom Burrell, interview by author, June 3, 2011.

60. Joseph Winski, "Burrell Success Rooted in Ads Basic to Black Culture," *Chicago Tribune*, April 8, 1981, C1.

61. Stuart Elliott, "Four to Be Inducted into Hall of Fame," *New York Times*, January 21, 2005, C4; Sonia Alleyne, "Growth by Reinvention," *Black Enterprise* (June 2011): 158–63.

CHAPTER 10

Oprah Winfrey

The Tycoon

JULIET E. K. WALKER

In 1998 Oprah Winfrey, who has won fame, prominence, and celebrity as the world's leading television talk-show host, was selected by *Time* magazine as one of the "100 Most Influential People of the 20th Century." Beginning in 1985 with *The Oprah Winfrey Show*, she built a financial empire. As she tactically expanded her unparalleled abilities in hosting an award-winning television talk show, Oprah emerged as a leading entrepreneur in the television entertainment and communications industries. Indeed, in 1998 Oprah was also awarded an Emmy for Lifetime Achievement. Doubtless, at the dawn of the new millennium, this phenomenal African American woman will also have the distinction of becoming the nation's first black woman billionaire.[1] At the close of the century, Oprah Winfrey was included in the list of "Forbes 400 Richest People In America," with a net worth in 1999 of $725 million. In 2000 *Forbes* listed Oprah's wealth at $800 million.[2] She is the only African American woman with joint-venture ownership in a cable television station, and in addition to owning her own show, Oprah is one of only three American women in the television and movie industry to establish and own a production studio, HARPO, based in Chicago, Illinois. Moreover, by the end of the twentieth century, Oprah Winfrey, the television tycoon, who had emerged as one of the nation's leading captains of industry and entrepreneurs in the entertainment business, also had achieved the distinction of being an American cultural icon.

What accounts for "the Oprah Effect," a cultural commodification phenomenon that has generated almost a billion dollars for America's superwoman? In the post-industrial, postmodern mass-media age in America, celebrity status accords one a voice as influential as leaders in other ideological institutions who traditionally have monopolized power that has influenced not only the market in a global economy, but also societal practices and political agendas.[3] In the instance of Oprah Winfrey, as she achieved commodification of herself as a cultural icon, she also achieved significance beyond entertainment. Through her media activities to empower women, Oprah took American feminism to a new level. In 1993, when she hinted that she might leave television, the stock of King World, the syndicator of *The Oprah Winfrey Show*, dropped 3 points. In 1996, when Winfrey did a show on England's mad cow disease, the next day the price of beef dropped 11 percent on the Chicago Mercantile Exchange.[4] Also, since 1996, when Oprah launched her Book Club, she has revolutionized the publishing industry, emerging as the nation's most influential bookseller. All of the books selected by Oprah for review have become million-dollar best sellers.[5] She is also an advocate for children, and reflecting the magnitude and political power of Oprah's celebrity status, it was her support that led to the passage of the National Child Protection Act, also called the "Oprah Bill," signed by President William Clinton in 1993.[6]

Assessing the factors that contributed to the rise of Oprah Winfrey as both an African American entrepreneur and as an American cultural icon, then, provides the focus of this study. Here was a black person, a woman, who stood in the vanguard in capitalizing on the revolution in telecommunications technology. While Winfrey was not the first African American who achieved success as a result of this revolution, she emerged as the most successful. *The Oprah Winfrey Show*, the highest-rated talk show in TV history, which is distributed to 206—over 99 percent of—U.S. markets, and about 142 international markets in some 119 countries, gives Oprah a weekly global viewing audience of some 33 million.[7] In the American market, Oprah's success has rested particularly on the support of the middle-class white woman. Within the intersection of race, class, and gender, does the support of Oprah Winfrey by a collective cadre of middle-class white women reflect a heightened racial consciousness distinctive of professed white liberals in post–Civil Rights America?

Black Entrepreneurship in the New Economy

So, who is this American woman? Oprah Winfrey was born January 29, 1954, in Kosciusko, Mississippi. Her mother, Vernita Lee, and father, Vernon Winfrey, never married or even had a long-standing relationship. Oprah was the result of a "one-night stand" that her eighteen-year-old mother had with her father, a young soldier stationed in a military base in Mississippi. Until she was six years old, Oprah was raised by her maternal grandmother, who early recognized her precociousness and taught Oprah to read when she was three years old. Also, Oprah's ability to memorize speeches, which she delivered with great confidence and oratorical skill in local churches, won her recognition in the rural community. As Oprah said, "When I was 3 years old, people would tell my grandmother, 'Hattie Mae, this girl sho' can talk.'"[8] Until her early teens, Oprah lived primarily with her mother, a maid, in Milwaukee's black ghetto. Again, her intellectual ability was recognized and she was bussed to a white suburban school.

When she was sent to live permanently with her father, a respected barber and black community leader in Nashville, Tennessee, Oprah also attended an integrated high school, achieving status as a student leader as well as for her scholarship. Very early, then, Oprah found a level of friendly comfortableness and mutual respect with whites. On graduation Oprah attended historically black Tennessee State University, where she majored in speech and drama, initially, and then media studies. Oprah's career in the communication industry began in radio in 1972, when she was nineteen years old. By the age of forty-five, Winfrey had emerged as one of the nation's wealthiest people, as she was ranked 348th in the listing of "Forbes 400 Richest People in America."[9] Who in African American business history can compare with this success?[10] But in the New Economy of the post-civil-rights era "Rise of Black Corporate America," leveraged buyouts, joint ventures, mergers and acquisitions, and conglomerate building represented expansion trends and new forms of business ownership and entrepreneurial activities for African Americans.[11]

In the New Economy, the most distinctive phenomenon in black business history was that blacks for the first time had access to Wall Street venture and investment capital, which provided a base for black entrepreneurs to buy into white American's multinational corporations. James Bruce Llewellyn, who headed the second-ranked black business at the close of century, Philadelphia Coca-Cola Bottling Company, with sales of $395 million, was the black pioneer in leveraged buyouts with his 1969 Fedco purchase.[12] Yet it was Reginald Lewis (1942–1993) who became the first Black American to acquire majority interest in a multibillion-dollar business. In 1987, through a leveraged buyout and with white investment capital from Drexel Burnham Lambert, Lewis purchased a multinational corporation, Beatrice International. He has the distinction of becoming the first African American to hold majority ownership in a billion-dollar company, TLC Beatrice International, which he headed as CEO.[13]

In the New Economy, African Americans also expanded their participation in the entertainment industry, where the pioneering road to joint ventures was taken by black performers in television, such as Bill Cosby, and in the recording industry by music impresario Quincy Jones.[14] In the cable television industry, Robert L. Johnson established BET (Black Entertainment Television) in 1979. Some $500,000 in investment capital from cable giant Tele-Communications, Inc. (TCI) gave it a 35 percent interest in BET.[15] The wealth accumulation of post-civil-rights-era black entrepreneurs positioned them either to buy into or buy out controlling interests in various mass-media enterprises, as well as to secure holding in businesses in other industries.[16] Johnson's attempt to purchase US Airways' takeoff and landing slots perhaps points to a new beginning for black businesses to hold again majority ownership in billion-dollar enterprises, as Johnson's plans were to expand his newly formed DC Air from a "virtual airline," leasing craft and operations management, to acquisition of carriers. In the year following the proposed purchase, the Justice Department announced that it would file suit to block United's acquisition of US Airways, which ended Robert Johnson's plan to establish DC Air, which would have become the first major airline owned by an African American. BET Holdings at that time were said by a company spokesmen to have a "$2 billion market capitalization." In 1998, when Johnson took BET private, he said that "his personal stake in the company was worth $780 million." BET's market capitalization, however, increased beyond $2 billion. In late 2000, it was sold for $3 billion to Viacom.[17]

But along with new investment opportunities, the expansion of black participation in the entertainment industry can be attributed to changes in American popular culture, which saw black entertainment reaching a crossover market for the first time. In American business history, this phenomenon began with Berry Gordy's Motown Records. Capitalizing on a crossover market demand for the Motown sound in the American music industry, Berry emerged as the first among this new group of African American superstar entrepreneurs whose business success was not limited to a black consumer market.[18] In the Old Economy of Industrial America, race-based societal constraints in the marketplace and in financial institutions in the mainstream American business community limited black entrepreneurship. The revolution in civil rights in the 1960s did make a difference in the expansion of black capitalism. Yet, at the same time, black entrepreneurs who produced for black consumers faced competition from white multinational corporations that reached out to capitalize on the black consumer market, which by the end of the century had surpassed $500 billion.[19]

Particularly, the revolution in telecommunications marked a revolution in the visibility of Black Americans. The civil-rights and Black Power movements in the 1960s placed African Americans on the front pages of mainstream newspapers and featured news items on television. Also, in a nation propelled by innovations and creativity in its cultural life, African Americans took the music industry by storm, as blacks also invaded the sports industry. Blacks also became a presence in the entertainment industry in movies and television as actors and newscasters, while blacks appeared on local television shows as talk-show co-hosts and hosts, partly in response to the television industry's government-mandated affirmative-action programs. But increasingly, changing racial demographics in urban markets propelled by advertising contributed to a slow but steady perceptible increase of blacks on live TV and even in commercials, as white corporate America reached out to tap the black consumer market.[20]

Still, it would be two decades from the Civil Rights Act of 1964 before television audiences were ready to accept blacks as national talk-show hosts. Enter Oprah, a reflection of the black superstar phenomenon in post-civil-rights America. With the participation of black entrepreneurs in various aspects of the mainstream American entertainment industry, can we attribute Oprah's entrepreneurial success in postmodern America as specific to the economic opportunities capitalized on by blacks in business in post-civil-rights America? Or is Oprah's entrepreneurial success in postmodern America specific to the economic opportunities capitalized on by blacks in business in the New Economy of the post-civil-rights era?[21]

Television, Technology, and *The Oprah Winfrey Show*

The revolution in telecommunications provided the technological infrastructure for Oprah to emerge as a media tycoon. By 1999, after fourteen years on air, *The Oprah Winfrey Show* had won thirty-two Emmy awards, and it averaged some 33 million daily viewers in the United States, where she appeared on 206 channels, in addition to a global audience in the 132 countries where her show was syndicated. While television technology was available in the 1930s, it was only in the post–World War II era that there was an expansion of commercial television. In 1948 the three major networks, National Broadcasting Company (NBC), Columbia Broadcasting System (CBS), and American Broadcasting Company (ABC), launched regularly scheduled prime-time programming. In 1949, however, "there were less than 100,000 TV sets in America; two years later there were 20 *million*."[22]

The 1950s marked the expansion of national network television. Then, from the late 1970s to the early 1980s, as a result of direct broadcast satellite (DBS), launched in May 1974 by the United States National Aeronautics and Space Administration (NASA), commercial television expanded national boundaries. While the first venture was for public consumption, private companies saw the commercial advantages and launched their own satellites, with profits earned from advertising.[23] Cable and satellites consequently created international television in the 1980s. This innovative technology was capitalized on by people such as Ted Turner, who created the twenty-four-hour Cable News Network (CNN), and Australian Rupert

Murdoch, who created the satellite-cable networks, which led to an expansion in the number of television stations.[24]

In the case of Oprah, whose show was carried on ABC-TV, the network was purchased by Capital Cities, which used satellites to televise ABC shows internationally, including, eventually, *The Oprah Winfrey Show*, thus opening international markets that over time generated billions of dollars in advertising revenues.[25] Consequently, with the technological revolution in television cable and satellite, syndication—the system of selling television shows to individual stations, which had begun in the 1950s—expanded. Those shows that generated substantial viewership were in demand not only by advertisers, but also by television stations because of the spillover effect. Television analysts found that there was a tendency of viewers to continue watching the same network after a leading show ended, which increased advertising rates for shows that followed.

Oprah Winfrey's career in television began in 1972, when she was nineteen years old, as a news anchor for Nashville's local CBS television station, where she was the first black reporter and anchor for WTVF-TV. Then for eight years, from 1976 to 1984, Oprah worked in television at the ABC news affiliate in Baltimore, Maryland, where for one year she was a co-anchor for WJZ-TV news. Oprah, however, admits she was not successful as a newscaster. Her display of emotion in both obtaining and reading the news did not conform to the television image of a serious newscaster. That failure, however, was the first step to Oprah's subsequent success as a talk-show host, when WJZ-TV moved her to co-host its 5:30 A.M. *People Are Talking* show in 1977. This new position marked the turning point in how Winfrey viewed her future career in television, thinking, she said at the time: "Thank God! This is it. I've found out what I was meant to do. This is what I was born for. This is like breathing!"[26] Oprah stayed with the show until 1984, when she moved to Chicago to host a thirty-minute television talk show on WLS-TV, called *A.M. Chicago*. In the Chicago market, Oprah was an immediate success, and in 1985 *A.M. Chicago* was renamed *The Oprah Winfrey Show*.

Despite competition from the nation's leading daytime talk-show host Phil Donahue, also based in Chicago, Oprah was a spectacular success, which was the first step toward a one-hour nationally syndicated television show launched in 1986.[27] Donahue, an engaging, articulate, and entertaining talk-show host, provided his viewers with serious, often controversial and provocative topics in which he engaged the participation of his studio audience. Within twelve weeks, however, local ratings showed Oprah with a Chicago viewership of 265,000, surpassing Donahue's 147,230 viewers. Yet who could compete with a talk show in which irreverent topics, many of them taboo, especially on a prime-time daytime show, were discussed? Particularly, a show on female sexuality brought Oprah to the attention of the nation television industry, especially when the discussion eventually turned to penis size and female satisfaction. The topic was outrageous enough as it was, but what was even more scandalous was Oprah's comment, based on what she knew was in the minds of her female audience. For Oprah turned to her audience and said, girlfriend to girlfriend: "Now, if you had your choice, you'd like to have a big one if you could? Right? Bring a big one home to Mama!"[28]

Besides the spontaneity in response to her guests as well as to the studio audience, the key to Oprah's escalating success was not only that she had the courage to discuss controversial subjects of concern to women, but that also she shared her own heartbreaking experiences. It was an unprecedented talk-show format "where the audience identifies not merely with the program's guests . . . but with the host. In turn, the distinction between guest and host disappears as the audience absorbs frequent personal confession from the talk-show host."[29] "Confessional TV" was the format that distinguished Oprah as a talk-show host. It seemed to be a format that could not be replicated because, as *The Oprah Winfrey Show* continued, it appeared that virtually everything tragic that could possibly happen to a woman had happened to Oprah. And, indeed, Oprah's various confessions were startling. It was in 1985 that Oprah revealed that she had been a victim, from the age of nine to when she was fourteen, of sexual abuse, incest, and sexual assault from relatives and family friends, which led to sexual promiscuity, juvenile delinquency, and eventually teenage pregnancy. Invariably, her shows included guests who were victims of sexual abuse.

Increasingly, topics on *The Oprah Winfrey Show* examined virtually every issue that women considered important. Oprah presented shows on the problems of women finding a real man and of finding love and marriage. Other shows covered topics such as overcoming rejection and, especially, controlling weight.[30] Drugs and battered women were also discussed on *The Oprah Winfrey Show*. On one television show Oprah confessed that she used cocaine in an attempt to hold together a relationship with a man who did not want her. Also, Oprah confessed that she, too, had been in a relationship that degraded her, and that in her early twenties was involved with a man in which the two of them got into a "knock-down drag out fight." Other topics included pathological family relations, especially mother-daughter conflicts and sibling rivalry; family feuds; greedy, jealous relatives; interracial dating; divorce; and AIDS. In 1989 Oprah's half brother, who was gay and a drug addict, died of AIDS.[31]

Indeed, Oprah had faced virtually all of these problems and survived. Moreover, in her public persona Oprah did not exhibit any bitterness, any rage, any anger. Also, along the way, Oprah has shed a few tears, along with her studio audience and, most likely, with her television viewing audience, as well.[32] Most important, these wrenching topics of female distress and abuse were subjects a female audience could identify with or had concerns about, such as topics on women who had been sexually molested by their male doctors, dentists, teachers, coaches, and bosses. And always, Oprah raised questions that most people refrained from ask-ing in polite company. Indeed, Oprah continued to titillate her viewing audience with topics on everything you would want to know about sex, but were afraid to ask. Oprah was not!

Media analysts have indicated that the "Oprahfication" of the television talk show encouraged the development of confessional TV, therapy TV, and trash TV, as subsequent talk-show hosts emerged, all hoping to match *The Oprah Winfrey Show* in content, forum, and, most of all, earnings.[33] Still, perhaps, most important for her success, as one unauthorized biographer stated, was that Oprah, as a talk-show host, capitalized on her ability to schmooze, "a Yiddish word that means indulging in small talk, chitchat, the exchange of inconsequential intimacies."[34] More simply, I would say that in addition to schmoozing, Oprah provided her viewers with the kinds of topics that engage the great American pastime, gossip about other people's lives. Also, by 1985 Winfrey recognized that to "win friends and influence people" one has to engage them in a dialogue on topics that interest them not only person-ally, but also vicariously. Moreover, despite advances in higher education, many American women, challenged by the all-consuming demands of family life, really did not care about the long-range economic effects of a drop in stock market prices or spiraling inflation, when they had to contend daily with problems such as job advancement, cheating husbands, delinquent kids, interfering mothers-in-law, and, most of all, even if you were a size six, being fat.

Since its inception, *The Oprah Winfrey Show* has gone through various changes—starting with sensationalism and controversial topics, the basis of American talk shows, including one show on "mad-cow disease" that resulted in a lawsuit from the Texas beef industry and won by Oprah. By the mid-1990s, Oprah moved away from sensationalism and trash TV, however, to take on serious issues and to empha-size more redeeming topics. In a new format, "Change Your Life TV," she closed out the decade with an emphasis on self-empowerment by emphasizing a segment called "Remembering Your Spirit." As Oprah said in 1994, "I am not going to be able to spend time from now until the year 2000 talking about dysfunction." Indeed, in the 1990s Oprah had a show on angels, even confessing her belief in them, which prompted the formation of her Angel Network.

Empowerment, particularly of women, became her focus, as she changed the emphasis in *The Oprah Winfrey Show* from scandal to self-improvement in all aspects of women's lives, including their intellectual lives. In 1996 Winfrey introduced "Oprah's Book Club," a regular reading group to discuss works of merit she had chosen and encouraged her audience to read. The reaction was enthusiastic, to say the least. Moreover, each book selected for Oprah's on-air reading club became an instant bestseller, averaging over a million copies in sales. In 1997 Oprah was named *Newsweek*'s "Most Important Person" in books and media.

Oprah's "Change Your Life" focus has not driven away viewers, who continued to embrace Oprah for her warmth, generosity, sincerity, and the media acknowledgment she gives to people who have given of themselves to help others. The new format is both engaging and entertaining, even inspiring. As Oprah said in 1998, as she testified in her defense at the mad-cow disease trial: "I answer to the spirit of God that exists in all of us. . . . To go on the air every day is a responsibility. Before every show I say a prayer . . . because I see myself as an instrument of a higher power."[35] But back in 1985, at that stage in her journey, it is not quite clear if she understood just exactly what her purpose was in being "an instrument of a higher power," or how she was to achieve that purpose. In one of her "trash-TV" shows that featured porn stars, Oprah, responding to a guest's description of her intensive thirteen-hour workday, asked the question that she knew would be in minds of her predominantly female audience when she said: "Don't you ever get sore?"[36]

At that time Oprah recognized that these were topics that engaged her women viewers as much as their search for quick-fix remedies in attempts to solve the problems of their day-to-day existence. Winfrey also realized that, if she were to have continued success pursuing these often inane but audience-appealing topics, she would need to acquire complete control of *The Oprah Winfrey Show*. Such was the format—confessional TV, therapy TV, and trash TV—that catapulted Oprah to worldwide fame as a talk-show host and marked the beginning of her successful entrepreneurial ventures in the entertainment and telecommunications industries.

Business Deals, Oprah's Conglomerate

In 1985 *The Oprah Winfrey Show* was owned by Chicago's WLS-TV, an ABC network station. But was America ready for "trash TV"? ABC did not think so and did not want to take the risk to find out. Oprah's irreverence just might have to be censured, unless she had decision-making power to determine her show's content. To have control, however, meant that Oprah had to own *The Oprah Winfrey Show*. But Oprah was a risk-taker as well as an innovator, which are two of the most important characteristics of entrepreneurs in their ability to sense the wants of consumers and to create a market for their goods or services. How many television stars have had the courage and confidence after only one year of being on the air, locally at that, to buy out their television show, so they could have control of the content? But Oprah did. She sought legal advice, selecting attorney Jeffrey Jacobs, a sports and entertainment lawyer who represented many of Chicago's professional athletes and television and radio personalities, and who was described to Oprah as a "piranha." According to reports her alleged response was, "I like that. Piranha is good."[37] Jacobs, acting as an agent, represented Oprah in her 1985 negotiations to buy her show. Not only did he provide legal advice for Oprah when she moved to purchase her show, he also advised her on the profit that could be earned by taking her show national through syndication.[38]

The juxtaposition of events at this time, when Oprah decided to gain control of her show by buying it, was indeed remarkable, if not miraculous, in two ways. In 1985 Oprah appeared in Stephen Spielberg's production of *The Color Purple* from the Pulitzer Prize–winning book by Alice Walker. The movie won Oprah an Oscar nomination for best supporting actress in 1986, which gave her nationwide prominence. It was also at this time that King World Incorporated, syndicators of *Wheel of Fortune* and *Jeopardy*, was looking for another show to syndicate. What a syndicator does is to rent/lease/franchise television shows to both network and local television stations, numbering more than 700 throughout the United States.[39] As it was, Oprah's national prominence in 1986 provided her the basis for successful syndication negotiations with King World that would subsequently enable her to purchase her show from Capital Cities/ABC for $10 million in 1988.

The road to wealth for Oprah Winfrey, consequently, began in 1986. With the syndication negotiations made with King World, *The Oprah Winfrey Show* debuted nationally in 1986 in 138 cities. Advertising revenues from commercials were the key that opened the door to Oprah emerging as a television millionaire. Advertising also provides the revenue for the earnings of television networks and their respective affiliate stations. By the 1980s, daytime television revenues were showing increases of 30 percent annually. Indeed, the year before Oprah went national, the gross income of daytime television in 1985, both network and nonnetwork, was $2.56 billion, compared to $820 million ten years earlier.[40] Commercial advertising rates charged by television stations are determined by what advertisers will pay, based on ratings determined by a specific "cost per thousand" viewers. Generally, advertisers will pay $7 for each 1,000 viewers. With a million viewers, companies searching for TV advertising slots would pay $70,000.[41] The higher the number of viewers, the more advertisers pay; the figure is also determined by the amount of time the advertisement runs during a commercial.

Advertising revenues from commercials are divided between the television station that carries the program and the syndicator that sold the program to the television station. With *The Oprah Winfrey Show*, King World had to divide its revenue four ways to pay for "the production costs of the show, ABC's cut, the King's percentage, and, finally, Oprah's percentage." Viewership projection rates are made at the end of each year for the following year. And, based on the ratings of *The Oprah Winfrey Show* at the end of 1985, it was calculated that for the 1986–87 season, *The Oprah Winfrey Show* would earn $125 million. From that amount, "Oprah's cut would come to $30 million." Consequently, in just two years, Oprah's income had increased from $200,000, which she was paid when she first signed to ABC in Chicago, to $30 million. By 1990, however, Oprah was worth $250 million.[42]

From the first time that *The Oprah Winfrey Show* entered syndication in 1986, airing nationally, it became a television gold mine not only for Oprah, but also the stations, advertisers, and especially King World. Indeed, over half of the revenues generated by King World were derived from *The Oprah Winfrey Show*, which gave Oprah the leverage to negotiate for a greater cut from King World's revenues. In 1988, just two years after going national, Winfrey negotiated a deal with King World that gave her rights to 60 percent of all syndication revenues. In 1993 Oprah grossed $180 million, an increase of $150 million in six years. Moreover, in 1993 Oprah's negotiations also included the right to buy stock in King World. As a result, Oprah secured 500,000 shares of stock in King World Productions. By 1998, King World's revenues had increased to $750 million, with *The Oprah Winfrey Show* generating 42 percent of the company's earnings that year, some $300 million. *Wheel of Fortune* and *Jeopardy* generated, respectively, 21 percent and 18 percent. (See Table 10.1.)

Yet in 1998 Oprah was hinting that she might not continue *The Oprah Winfrey Show*. Some five years earlier, in 1993, when Winfrey had hinted that she might give up her show, King World stock had dropped 3 points on the market. In 1993 the stock had sold for $47 a share. Also, because of the volatility of the market, King World stock continued to drop. While it had shown a 27 percent increase from $19.98 in 1997 to $24.31 per share, by 1998 it was averaging around $39 a share.[43] Realizing how financially dependent they were on *The Oprah Winfrey Show*, King World bailed out to cut future losses by selling out to CBS. Oprah's 1998 contract with King World Productions, however, stipulated that Oprah would continue to host and produce *The Oprah Winfrey Show* through 2002.[44] Yet for Oprah, the sale of King

Table 10.1 King World Company Revenues, 1998 and 1999

	Nine Months Ended May 31,		Three Months Ended May 31,	
	1999	1998	1999	1998
The Oprah Winfrey Show	38%	42%	38%	42%
Wheel of Fortune	19%	21%	9%	21%
Jeopardy	16%	18%	16%	18%
*Hollywood Squares**	9%	—	10%	—
*The Roseanne Show**	7%	—	7%	—
Inside Edition	6%	7%	6%	7%
*American Journal***	4%	—	4%	—

Source: King World Productions Inc. (KWP) Quarterly Report (SEC form 10-Q), July 8, 1999, biz.yahoo .com/e/990708/kwp.html.
* *Hollywood Squares* and *The Roseanne Show* premiered in September 1998.
** The production of *American Journal* was discontinued after the 1997–98 broadcast season.

to CBS was a bonanza in profits. Having accumulated 3.6 million shares of King World, Winfrey realized $150 million when CBS bought King World.[45] Moreover, when CBS bought King in 1999, according to Hoover's Online Business Network, "the deal gives King World stockholder Winfrey a $100 million stake in CBS (which is now a stake in Viacom following its buy of CBS)."[46]

Yet for Oprah, her stock ownership interest in both CBS and Viacom was not the first time she had acquired investment interests in network TV as well as other media ventures. Indeed, in expanding her media holdings, as early as 1990 Oprah had purchased ownership interest in "WIVB-TV Buffalo, New York; WEEK-TV in Peoria, Illinois; and KBJR-TV in Duluth, Minnesota."[47] Also, by 1993 Winfrey held 45 percent interest in fellow African American W. Don Cornwell's Granite Broadcasting, a network TV affiliate, which in 1994 was rated the country's top-performing media stock. In 1994 Granite's Sales amounted to $119 million. In 1998, Granite ranked eighth on the *Black Enterprise* "B.E. Industrial/Service 100" list with sales of $193.934 million.[48] Moreover, beginning with *The Oprah Winfrey Show* in 1986, the talk-show host began building an entertainment media conglomerate.

In 1986 Oprah established the Chicago-based Harpo, Inc. (*Harpo* is *Oprah* spelled backward.) Then, in 1988, the year Oprah purchased *The Oprah Winfrey Show* from Capital Cities/ABC, she established the Harpo Entertainment Group, the corporate umbrella for Winfrey's entertainment conglomerate. The Harpo Entertainment Group owns all Harpo-related ventures, including *The Oprah Winfrey Show*. Harpo Productions Inc., which produces *The Oprah Winfrey Show*, was also established in 1988, the year Oprah purchased what is now known as the Harpo Studio. *The Oprah Winfrey Show* is filmed and televised from Harpo Studio, which with renovations was worth $20 million in 1990. Harpo Films, the features and television film division of the Harpo Entertainment Group, was established in 1990. Products have included *Oprah Winfrey Presents*, with the ABC Television Network. The Harpo Productions component also produces prime-time specials, movies for television, and after-school specials including *There Are No Children Here* (1993) and *The Women of Brewster Place* (1989), in which Oprah starred.

Then in 1995 Oprah entered into a multipicture four-year contract with the Walt Disney Co. and ABC television (subsequently purchased by Disney) to produce six made-for-TV movies, as well as to star in some of the films that she would produce.[49] *Beloved* (1998), based on the Pulitzer Prize–winning novel by black author Toni Morrison, in which Oprah starred with Danny Glover, was one of the productions from that agreement. Oprah Winfrey is chairman of the Harpo Entertainment Group, which is privately owned. Jeffrey Jacobs is president and chief operating officer. The success of Oprah's business ventures is reflected in her increasing wealth. Indeed, from the syndication of her *The Oprah Winfrey Show* alone, which grossed $280 million in 1998, Oprah's cut was an estimated $65 million after taxes. In 1995 *Forbes* placed Winfrey's earnings at $75 million and her wealth holding at an estimated $340 million.[50] In 1996 Forbes showed her wealth at $415 million, ranking her 400th among the nation's leading wealth holders. In 1998 *Forbes* estimated her wealth at $675 million, including her income that year of $125 million.[51] And by 1999, Winfrey had a net worth of $725 million.[52]

Doubtless Oprah's income will increase with the expansion of her business activities from television and movies to Internet, cable TV, and magazine publishing. In 1998 Oprah expanded her conglomerate by moving into a cable-TV joint venture, Oxygen Media, which advertises its purpose as being "Designed to super serve modern women by combining the best qualities of the Internet and television." Harpo Entertainment received an undisclosed stake in the Oxygen Cable Network, for which Winfrey's Harpo Entertainment Group will produce original programming. Also, in 2002 Oxygen will acquire the rights to reruns of *The Oprah Winfrey Show*. In addition to Winfrey's Harpo Entertainment Group, the partners include Geraldine Laybourne, chairman and CEO of Oxygen Media, who helped launch Nickelodeon, a successful cable network for children. The other partner is CWM LLC, an entity formed by Carsey-Werner-Mandabach TV Productions. In return for their undisclosed stake in Oxygen, CWM LLC will produce original shows. Marcy Carsey, Tom Werner, and Caryn Mandabach have had a string of TV successes with *The Cosby Show*, *Roseanne*, *Grace Under Fire*, *Cybill*, and *Third Rock from the Sun*.

Oxygen media investors include AOL (America Online); Disney's ABC Inc.; and Vulcan Ventures, Inc., the investment arm of Microsoft co-founder Paul Allen, who put up $100 million, and French billionaire Bernard Arnault, who put up $122 million. Arnault heads LVMH (Louis Vuitton, Moët, Hennessey, Givenchy, and Christian Lacroix) and *Europ@Web*, the Internet investment company recently established by Groupe Arnault, which has investments in thirty-three global Internet companies. With Arnault, the tradeoff for LVMH is sales expansion, based on the demographics of Oxygen's market, middle-class women. At the same time, "The investment also gives Oxygen a foothold into expanding beyond the U.S." As Oxygen's chief operating officer Lisa Gersh Hall said, "We're clearly thinking about the European space."[53] With AOL, Oxygen cable network is integrated with Oxygen's Internet and AOL properties. All of the investors have seats on Oxygen's board of directors.

Oxygen was launched in 1999, but that year, only 29 percent of U.S. women were on the web, according to Forrester Research, Inc., but close to 50 percent are expected to be online by 2003. Since women make the majority of household spending decisions, from health care to buying computers, they constitute an important market. Oxygen has twelve websites, but after a year in operation, it was still not one of the top online destinations for women. Ironically, too, while Oxygen's website ka-Ching provides free e-commerce development tools, Oxygen dropped its e-commerce site, Picky.com, in June 2000. Still, many believe Oxygen has staying power, especially if it can capture a strong following on the Internet. Oprah Online has two sites, the Oxygen site at www.oprah.com and the AOL site, Oprah online at AOL (Keyword), "which average 3,000 hits a month."

In addition to Oprah's Oxygen Media holdings, in 1999 Winfrey's Harpo Entertainment Group reached a licensing agreement with Hearst Corporation to create a new magazine, a publication version of *The Oprah Winfrey Show*, which would also reflect Oprah's business and personal principles. In April 2000, *O, The Oprah Magazine* was launched, and it was reported that "the debut issue of *O* sold out on newsstands with a distribution of 1.5 million copies, including an additional 500,000 copies printed for a second press run after the first distribution virtually sold out." In addition, "More than 135,000 orders for magazine subscriptions have also been received via the internet, the industry record." Circulation sales for the June-July issue were reported as "already ahead of the scales for the first issue." Monthly frequency of the magazine will begin with the September 2000 issue, and, as reported, *O, The Oprah Winfrey Magazine* "will increase its circulation rate base to 900,000, an increase of 80 percent, from the initial 500,000 rate base."[54]

But will Oxygen Media's success parallel that of *O, The Oprah Magazine*? Oxygen premiered in February 2000. Close to $450 million had been raised and 560 people hired, with nearly 10 million TV viewers, to launch the cable TV station. A complete weekly programming schedule is available online at www.oxygen.com. Oxygen's cable TV, however, is not carried in the big media markets of New York and Los Angeles. Currently, the cable network is available only through some local providers. Even in the Chicago metropolitan area, only 500,000 households, in the city's northwest suburbs, carry Oxygen. As stated in one assessment: "The cable network has been struggling to make an impact and has had distribution difficulties. At its launch, only 10 million of the nation's 100 million households with cable TV offered this channel."[55]

Oxygen Media's business strategy in partnering with AOL was that at the time, with the planned merger of America Online and Time Warner, the hope was that AOL's investment would result in Time Warner carrying Oxygen on its cable systems. This did not happen, "though Oxygen announced in March that it had struck deals that would put it in 27 million homes by the end of 2002."[56] Generally, it takes several years for new channels to be added on cable TV. Certainly, cable TV has not become a payola situation (which once existed with radio for commercial advantage, where bribes were paid to disc jockeys to play a particular record to introduce it to the public). But with cable TV, new cable channels invariable pay cable operators to get into their systems. Oxygen, however, has taken a different business tactic in "charging cable operators about 18 cents per subscriber per month." Still, to break even by 2004, Laybourne needs 50 million cable subscribers. But in 2000, Oprah's joint venture ownership in Oxygen represented the expansion of Winfrey's media entertainment conglomerate, which doubtless will expand into other ventures in the new century.

In African American business history, Oprah's closet competition, not just in the cable industry at the dawn of the new century, but also as the nation's leading black entrepreneur, is Robert Johnson. Before the sale to Viacom in 2000, his BET Holdings operated five major cable channels that reached 58.5 million U.S. homes, notwithstanding that Black Entertainment Television, a twenty-four-hour programming service, specifically targets African Americans. Indeed, more than 90 percent of black cable households carry BET. Also, Johnson's joint ventures in the entertainment industry were as extensive as Oprah's. At one time early investor Time Warner had a 15 percent stake in the company, but as part of its plan to reduce debt, in 1995 it sold its interest back to BET Holdings. In 1996 BET partnered with Microsoft to launch the MSBET website. Johnson also has joint ventures with Encore and Live Entertainment in BET Film Productions, a film producer and distributor. In 1998 Johnson and Liberty Media took BET private again, with Johnson's stake standing at 65 percent and Liberty Media's at 35 percent, with the company renamed as BET Holdings II.

In 2000 BET Holdings II partnered with Liberty Media, Microsoft, News Corp., and USA Networks to create the BET.com portal. It also struck a deal with publisher Vanguarde Media to jointly own the two companies' magazines. BET Holdings II also took a 50 percent stake in Vanguarde Media. The company continued to broaden its horizons in 1997 with the creation of BET Financial Services, BET SoundStage Restaurant (Largo, Maryland), BET on Jazz Restaurant in Washington, D.C., and the BET SoundStage Club in Disney World; in 1998 the company opened its Tres Jazz restaurant in Las Vegas. There are also BET Financial's and Johnson's plans for an airline. Indeed, *Black Enterprise* reported that in 1998 BET's sales amounted to $178 million, and increased to $225 million in 1999.[57] But the sale of BET to Viacom raised Johnson to billionaire status.

Ironically, at the dawn of the twentieth century, the leading black entrepreneurs were women, Annie Minerva Turnbo-Malone and Madame C. J. Walker. While they did not achieve millionaire status, they did have sales in the millions of dollars. Yet while these women pioneered in hair-care products and health and beauty aids for people of African descent, in the post-civil-rights era, the leading black entrepreneurs in this industry were black men. In the twenty-first century, will black women as entrepreneurs transcend race and gender to achieve the economic success of men, or will American hegemonic masculinities in finance and business remain the determining factor for American women, regardless of race or ethnicity? Will there ever be a female Bill Gates? More important, to what extent can or does gender influence as well as determine business success?

Conclusion

Ultimately, what accounts for Winfrey's financial success? After all, Oprah surely will have the historic distinction of becoming the nation's first African American female billionaire. But are her shrewd business decisions and activities a reflection of the elusive human-capital qualities that have distinguished the business activities and decisions associated with the nation's leading entrepreneurs? Or is Oprah's financial success a reflection of the carefully crafted business practices and decisions that historically have distinguished the wealth holding of the nation's few most successful African American entrepreneurs from slavery to the present, as these men and women manipulate a system of racial capitalism to their financial advantage? With Oprah, who is not only an entrepreneur, but also an American cultural icon, any analysis of her financial success must proceed with an understanding of the complementary and also contradictory relationship between societal and cultural values and business practices in the New Economy. This television tycoon is a woman and she is black, and we must not forget that business practices, as they have developed in America, continue to reflect a system of interacting institutions, conditioned by race, gender, and class.

What does the future hold for Winfrey in her new business deals in cable TV, the Internet, and magazine publishing? Particularly, in an organic sense, business behavior is influenced by the values of the social system in which the enterprise operates, which explains why "the Oprah Effect" has significance beyond entertainment and race relations. As indicated, the phenomenal success of Oprah Winfrey as an African American and as a woman reflects the juxtaposition of societal and political factors and the forces of race and gender in post-civil-rights America, which the impact of a multiplicity of economic factors in the postmodern Information Age propelled by a new technology. In approaching this topic, then, an assessment not only of a black businesswoman, but also one of America's most successful entrepreneurs, requires merging several distinct but interrelated historiographical traditions: African American history, American business history, women's history, race and culture in America, and the history of technology. At the same time, insight is also provided by considering critical feminist theories that focus on both public and private spaces in the lives of women in their various multifaceted roles.

Still, the questions must be asked and answered: are there specific human-capital skills requisite for blacks in business that enable the more successful ones to transcend the racist economic practices in the nation's mainstream business community? Can one say that Oprah's financial success, as some would argue, proves that capitalism is fundamentally hostile to prejudice and economic iniquities? I think not! In 2019 Black Americans will have had a history in this nation of almost four hundred years, from the first permanent settlement of Africans in English Colonial America in 1619. But why is it, after almost four centuries, in a nation of almost three hundred billionaires in 1999, that not one African American had achieved this status? While Winfrey's wealth is increasing, so, too, is the wealth of white America. In 1998, while Oprah ranked 298th on the Forbes list, despite her wealth increase, in 1999 she ranked 348th out of "Forbes 400 Richest Americans."[58] Consider, too, that African Americans, who constitute almost 14 percent of the population, have business receipts that make up only 1 percent, $59.3 billion, of the nation's total business receipts.

Despite Oprah's success as an entrepreneur, the persistence of racial capitalism cannot be ignored in any analysis of African American business activities. While we can celebrate Winfrey's and other economic achievements in African American business history, still, with the persistence of systemic racism in American life, how long will it be before any Black American will acquire even 10 percent of the personal wealth, $89 billion, of Microsoft's William "Bill" Gates? Simply put, the comparatively few successful black entrepreneur superstars cannot sustain the hype that black business is alive and well or, on the other hand, that race has nothing do with the limited comparative economic success of Black American businesspeople as a group.

Doubtless, Oprah is more than just a shrewd businesswoman. She is an entrepreneur, an innovator, and a risk-taker. Indeed, she stands in the Schumpeterian tradition of creative capitalist, where entrepreneurial motivation extends beyond the desire for the accumulation of profits—it is also motivated by noneconomic forces: "the will to conquer, the impulse to fight, to prove oneself superior to others, to succeed for the sake, not of the fruits of success but of success itself."[59] But what Oprah, in explaining her success, said in a commencement address at Wellesley College in 1997 appears to have expanded the Schumpeterian concept of a creative capitalist:

> [If] you were to ask me what is the secret to my success, it is because I understand that there is a power greater than myself, that rules my life, and in life if you can be still long enough in all of your endeavors, the good times, the hard times, to connect yourself to the source—I call it God, you can call it whatever you want to, the force, nature, Allah, the power. If you can connect yourself to the source and allow the energy that is your personality, your life force, to be connected to the greater force, anything is possible for you. I am proof of that. I think that my life, the fact that I was born where I was born, and the time that I was, and have been able to do what I have done speaks to the possibility. Not that I am special, but that it could be done. Hold the highest, grandest vision for yourself. [60]

Oprah ended the 1999–2000 television season with a four-city tour in June to promote *O, The Oprah Magazine*, a tour billed as "Oprah's Personal Growth Seminar."

These seminars were held in Detroit, Atlanta, Chicago, and Los Angeles. Each one was packed, with women of all races making up virtually 95 percent of the audience. They were there not just to see in person one of the most famous women in the world. Oprah had something to say that these women wanted to hear, as did her television audience worldwide. America's girlfriend will keep on keeping on. You go, girl!

Notes

This work originally appeared in 2002 as a chapter in the edited book *Black Business and Economic Power*, published by the University of Rochester Press.

1. The author wishes to thank University of Illinois at Urbana-Champaign students Randy Gillion and Olabisi Olivia Martin for their research assistance. A special debt of gratitude especially to Alusine Jalloh, who suggested Oprah Winfrey as a topic for his 1999 conference at the University of Texas–Arlington. This paper has expanded into a book manuscript that I am presently writing, which will be the first scholarly full-length study of the business activities and life of Oprah as an entrepreneur; it is tentatively entitled *Oprah The Tycoon*. There are no authorized biographies of Oprah Winfrey, but information on her life is provided in several books. See Robert Waldron, *Oprah* (New York: St. Martin's Press, 1987); Norman King, *Everybody Loves Oprah: Her Remarkable Story* (New York: William Morrow, 1987); Nellie Bly, *Oprah! Up Close and Down Home* (New York: Kensington, 1993); and George Mair, *Oprah Winfrey: The Real Story* (Secaucus, NJ: Carol Publishing, 1994; revised and updated, 1998). Voluminous newspaper and magazine articles are available on Oprah.

2. "Forbes 400 Richest People in America," 1999, http://www.forbes.com; *Forbes: Special 2000 Issue: The Richest 400 People in America* (October 2000): 161. With Robert Johnson's November 2000 $3.1 billion sale of BET (Black Entertainment Television) to Viacom, his virtual two-thirds ownership in BET resulted in him acquiring over $2 billion, which would give him the distinction of becoming the first black billionaire. See "Viacom to Acquire BET Holdings," at http://www.viacom./com.press. See also Joyce Jones, "Betting on Black: Robert L. Johnson Sells the Largest African American Television Network to Sumner Redstone and Viacom," *Black Enterprise* (January 2001): 68.

3. William Greider, *One World, Ready or Not: The Manic Logic of Global Capitalism* (New York: Simon and Schuster, 1997). Also Fredric Jameson, *Postmodernism: Or, the Cultural Logic of Late Capitalism* (Durham, NC: Duke University Press, 1991).

4. Mair, *Oprah*, 368; *Wichita Falls Times Record News* (TX), April 27, 1996. In June 1996, a group of cattlemen filed suit against Oprah, her production company, and a guest who appeared on her April 16, 1996, show in a case popularly known as "The Mad Cow Disease" that was heard in the federal district court in 1998 in Amarillo, Texas. See *Amarillo Globe-News* (TX), April 11, 1998.

5. Merrell Noden, *People Profiles: Oprah Winfrey* (New York: Time, 1999), 39–40; "Oprah Winfrey Named the Most Powerful Person in Entertainment," *Jet* 9 (November 1998): 11. As an on-air reading club, *The Oprah Winfrey Show* features a new title approximately once a month, in which a dinner discussion is held with Oprah, the author, and selected viewers.

6. "President Clinton Signs the National Child Protection Act," *New York Times*, December 21, 1993. Also see Mair, *Oprah Winfrey*, 224–25, 314.

7. Oprah Winfrey, "Harpo, Inc.," Company Profile, Hoover's Online: The Business Network, at http://bit.ly/2hizoJx; http://oprah.oxygen.com/about/press/about_press_globelist.html.

8. Oprah Winfrey, "Become More of Who You Are," *O, The Oprah Magazine* 1 (May–June 2000): 57.

9. "Forbes 400 Richest People in America," 1999, http://www.forbes.com.

10. Juliet E. K. Walker, *The History of Black Business in America* (New York: Macmillan, 1998).

11. Ibid., 333–37.

12. John N. Ingham and Lynne B. Feldman, eds., *African-American Business Leaders: A Biographical Dictionary* (Westport, CT: Greenwood Press, 1994), 443–45; Walker, *History of Black Business in America*, 333–35; "B. E. Industrial/Service 100," *Black Enterprise* (June 2000): 121.

13. Reginald F. Lewis and Blair S. Walker, *Why Should White Guys Have All the Fun? How Reginald Lewis Created a Billion-Dollar Empire* (New York: John Wiley, 1995); Ingham and Feldman, *African-American Business Leaders*, 434–40; Walker, *History of Black Business in America*, 334, 338–39, 358, 370–71. Within six years after Lewis's death in 1993, through divestiture and liquidation, TLC's Beatrice International Holdings no longer existed. See "TLC's Final Chapter," *Black Enterprise* (September 1999).

14. Walker, *History of Black Business in America*, 335–36. Black superstars in the sports industry have also used their wealth and celebrity in developing business ventures. See Walker, *History of Black Business in America*, 354–56, 363, and Jeffrey E. Walker, "Sports, Athlete Enterprises and Entrepreneurs," in *Encyclopedia of African American Business History* (Westport, CT: Greenwood Press, 1999), 530–40.

15. William E. Berry, "Robert L. Johnson," in *Encyclopedia of African American Business History*, 335–37, on Johnson's diverse enterprise. BET was the first black business to be listed on the New York Stock Exchange in 1991 but went private again six years later.

16. Walker, *History of Black Business in America*, 333–340. Also Pamela Johnson, "The Powers That Be," *Black Enterprise* (August 1990): 126. For example, with *The Cosby Show*, Bill Cosby opted for joint profits rather than a fixed salary. This arrangement resulted in his earning a reported $333 million in addition to later syndication receipts.

17. Don Phillips and Christopher Stern, "BET Chief Looks at New Market," *Washington Post*, May 24, 2000; Del Jones and Keith L. Alexander, "'Romance of the Air' Begins: BET Boss Embarks on Odyssey of Billionaires Past by Starting Airline," *USA Today*, May 25, 2000; Keith L. Alexander, "Airlines Kill Deal after U.S. Objects: USAirways, United Bow to Justice Dept," *Washington Post*, July 28, 2001. Also Stephanie Ernst, "Viacom Buys BET for $3 Billion, Rise in Black Spending Cited," at Diversityinc.com, November 3, 2000.

18. Walker, *History of Black Business in America*, 301–2, 321. See also Berry Gordy, *To Be Loved: The Music, the Magic, the Memories of Motown, An Autobiography* (New York: Warner Books, 1994).

19. Juliet E. K. Walker, "Black Business: Can It Get Out of the Box?" in *Urban League's State of Black America 2000 Report* (New York: National Urban League, 2000): 199–225.

20. Robert E. Weems Jr., *Desegregating the Dollar: African American Consumerism in the Twentieth Century* (New York: New York University Press, 1998). See also Robert E. Weems Jr., "The Revolution Will Be Marketed: American Corporations and Black Consumers during the 1960s," *Radical History Review* 59 (1994): 94–107.

21. Walker, *History of Black Business in America*, 264–371.

22. Mair, *Oprah Winfrey*, 62.

23. Hamid Mowlana, *Global Information and World Communication* (New York: Longman, 1986), 70.

24. Robert Goldberg and Gerald Jay Goldberg, *Citizen Turner: The Wild Rise of an American Tycoon* (New York: World Publications, 1995); William Shawcross, *Murdoch* (New York: Simon and Schuster, 1995). See Walker, *History of Black Business in America*, 323–24, on Harlem's Percy Sutton, first black to buy a cable TV system in 1983.

25. Greg MacDonald, *The Emergence of Global Multi-Media Conglomerates*, Enterprises Programme, Working Paper No. 70 (Geneva: International Labour Office, 1990); Wilson Dizard Jr., *Old Media/New Media: Mass Communications in the Information Age* (New York: Longman, 1994).

26. King, *Everybody Loves Oprah*, 96.

27. H. W. Brands, *Masters of Enterprise: Giants of American Business Form John Jacob Astor and J. P. Morgan to Bill Gates and Oprah Winfrey* (New York: The Free Press, 1999), 295–97.

28. King, *Everybody Loves Oprah*, 124; Mair, *Oprah Winfrey*, 78; Brands, *Masters of Enterprise*, 298.

29. Jeffrey Louis Decker, *Made in America: Self-Styled Success from Horatio Alger to Oprah Winfrey* (Minneapolis: University of Minnesota Press, 1997), 117.

30. Bob Greene and Oprah Winfrey, *Make the Connection: Ten Steps to a Better Body—and a Better Life* (New York: Hyperion, 1996), 1–32, on Oprah's weight struggle from 1976 to 1993. The image of a newly size-10 Oprah, pulling a wagon of 67 pounds of fat on an October 1988 *The Oprah Winfrey Show* to indicate how much she had lost, has become a classic moment in television history. Two weeks later she had gained 13 pounds, an increase in her weight from 142 to 155. In two years, Oprah was back up to 200 pounds.

31. Mair, *Oprah Winfrey*, 150–51.

32. Corinne Squire, "Empowering Women? *The Oprah Winfrey Show*," *Feminism and Psychology* 4 (1994): 63–79, reprinted in *Feminist Television Criticism*, ed. Charlotte Brunsdon, Julie D'Acci, and Lynn Spiegel (Oxford: Oxford University Press, 1997), 98–113.

33. Vicki Abt and Leonard Mustazza, *Coming after Oprah: Cultural Fallout in the Age of TV Talk Shows* (Bowling Green, OH: Bowling Green State University Popular Press, 1997).

34. King, *Everybody Loves Oprah*, 120.

35. Tim Jones, *Chicago Tribune*, July 18, 1999, Chicagoland Final Edition, Business Section.

36. Waldron, *Oprah*, 127.

37. Brands, *Masters of Enterprise*, 299. Federal Communications Commission (FCC) regulations prohibit major television networks from syndicating their shows to non-affiliates. In that *The Oprah Winfrey Show* was produced by WLS, which was owned by

ABC, as Brands said, "under the FCC regime, it was barred from distributing the show nationwide (if not mankind-wide)."

38. Matthew S. Scott and Tarik K. Muhammad, "Top 50 Black Powerbrokers," *Black Enterprise* (August 1990): 70, 126. With *The Cosby Show*, Bill Cosby opted for joint profits rather than salary, which "netted him a reported $333 million in addition to syndication receipts." In 1988 the show went into syndication "for $500 million."

39. Mair, *Oprah Winfrey*, 102.

40. King, *Everybody Loves Oprah*, 13; Mair, *Oprah Winfrey*, 99; Brands, *Masters of Enterprise*, 300.

41. Mair, *Oprah Winfrey*, 104. See also King, *Everybody Loves Oprah*, 199.

42. Mair, *Oprah Winfrey*, 100–101, 205.

43. *Business Wire*, October 14, 1998, and *Crain's New York Business*, September 15, 1997, 4. For 1993 see Mair, *Oprah Winfrey*, 287.

44. *Business Wire*, October 15, 1998.

45. Jim Kirk and Tim Jones, "Oprah Gets $150 Million to Keep Talking," *Chicago Tribune*, September 25, 1998.

46. http://www.hoovers.com/premium/profile.

47. Mair, *Oprah Winfrey*, 188. The Buffalo station investment was in partnership with the King brothers.

48. Mark Lowery, "Solid as a Rock," *Black Enterprise* (June 1995): 122–23; "B.E. Industrial/ Service 100," *Black Enterprise* (June 1999): 109.

49. "Oprah Winfrey's Harpo Studio Signs Deals with ABC Television to Produce Six Made-for-TV Movies," *Jet* (June 12, 1995).

50. Barbara Grizutti Henderson, "The Importance of Being Oprah," *New York Times Magazine* (June 11, 1989): 97; Oprah topped Cosby and Spielberg in earnings that year. Winfrey made her screen debut in Stephen Spielberg's production of black author Alice Walker's *The Color Purple*. See also "The Top 400," *Forbes* (September 1995).

51. "Forbes 400 Richest People in America," 1998, http://www.forbes.com.

52. "Forbes 400 Richest People in America," 1999, Http://www.forbes.com.

53. Kenneth Li, "Oxygen Media Flashes the Cash," *Industry Standard Magazine* (December 16, 1999), at http://www.thestandard.com/article.

54. Seth Sutel, "Editor of Oprah Winfrey's New Magazine Resigns," *Chicago Tribune,* June 2, 2000; "Amy Gross Named Editor-in-Chief of *O, The Oprah Winfrey Magazine,*" *Business Wire,* July 10, 2000.

55. Jennifer Greenstein, "Oxygen Takes a Breather," *Industry Standard Magazine* (June 7, 2000), at http://www.thestandard.com.

56. Ibid. Oxygen's launch numbers top most recent cable launches. *TV Land*, in 45 million homes today, premiered in 1996 with 5.4 million subscribers. E! Entertainment Television's *Style*, at 6 million today, began in late 1998 in 3 million homes. Industry insiders say Oxygen's chances of success are good. "Oxygen is . . . a wonderful amalgam of old and new media," says Leo Hindery, the former AT&T cable executive whose guarantee of 7 million subscribers (3 million at launch) helped put Oxygen in business. "The cable industry has been offering programming for 30 years, 50% of the audience is

women, and there's only one service (Lifetime) aimed at women, and that one is mostly an entertainment service."

57. "B.E. Industrial/Service 100," *Black Enterprise* (June 2000): 121. The history of black business in the last quarter of the twentieth century has been documented especially by Earl Graves, the founder and publisher of *Black Enterprise*. See Earl G. Graves, *How to Succeed in Business without Being White* (New York: HarperBusiness, 1997). See also Walker, *History of Black Business in America*, 335, on Graves's business holdings and joint ventures, and Derek Dingle, *Black Enterprise Titans of the B.E. 100's: Black CEOs Who Redefined and Conquered American Business* (New York: John Wiley, 1999).

58. "Forbes 400 Richest People in America," 1999, http://www.forbes.com.

59. Joseph A. Schumpeter, *The Theory of Economic Development: An Inquiry into Profits, Capital, Credit, Interest, and the Business Cycle* (Cambridge, MA: Harvard University Press, 1936), 93.

60. "Oprah Winfrey's Commencement Address," Wellesley College, May 30, 1997, http://Wellesley.edu.

CHAPTER 11

Racial Desegregation and Black Chicago Business

The Case Studies of the Supreme Liberty Life Insurance Company and the Chicago Metropolitan Assurance Company

ROBERT E. WEEMS JR.

In 1947 *Scott's Blue Book*, a Chicago African American business directory, featured 338 pages of advertisements and stories related to local African American enterprise. This publication not only praised the impressive diversity of black-owned businesses in the Windy City, but suggested that Black Chicago's business community could grow even bigger with the active support of the city's black consumers. Despite the decidedly upbeat tone of the 1947 edition of *Scott's Blue Book*, another 1947 publication suggested that the future of black business in Chicago and elsewhere was bleak. Edward Franklin Frazier's 1947 essay "Human, All Too Human: How Some Negroes Have Developed Vested Interests in the System of Racial Segregation" bluntly predicted: "if segregation were eliminated, the social justification for the existence of Negro business would vanish and the Negro would have to compete with other businessmen. Undoubtedly, many Negro enterprises would disappear, along with the sentimental justification which helps support them."[1] This chapter will use Frazier's prognostication as a reference point to examine how racial desegregation impacted Chicago's black businesses community. As the evidence indicates, Professor Frazier proved to be a fairly accurate prophet in this regard. Some of the city's long-standing African American enterprises, including the Supreme Liberty Life Insurance Company and the Chicago Metropolitan Assurance Company, have indeed disappeared from the landscape of American business.

The 1947 edition of *Scott's Blue Book* represented both a high point of Bronzeville business visibility and a classic example of how Black Chicagoans were imbued with a sense of business-oriented racial solidarity. Black newcomers to Bronzeville, especially, must have been truly impressed with the wide variety of black-owned businesses in the Windy City. By 1947, this widely distributed free publication noted that Chicago blacks not only owned and operated such traditional enterprises as beauty shops and barbershops, restaurants, and grocery stores, but also furriers, golf instruction schools, ice cream manufacturing plants, massage parlors, and a riding stable.[2]

Besides exposing Black Chicagoans to a wide variety of commercial enterprises operated by local African Americans, *Scott's* strongly urged Bronzeville residents to support these businesses. For instance, the 1947 *Blue Book* noted: "the most cordial reception awaits you at these shops. They are YOUR shops. Opened for YOUR convenience and catering largely to YOUR individual needs and comfort. When planning a purchase, won't YOU visit them FIRST? YOU ARE ALWAYS WELCOME."[3]

Ironically, within a few years, *Scott's Blue Book* assumed an entirely different public posture. Apparently motivated by the historic May 17, 1954, *Brown v. Board of Education* Supreme Court decision, which outlawed school desegregation and set the stage for the total dissolution of U.S. apartheid, the 1956 edition of *Scott's Blue Book* sought to situate African American business activity within a racially desegregated society. The publication's transformation provides a clear window to view black business supporters' muddled response to a changing social reality.

Whereas the 1947 edition of *Scott's Blue Book* presented an unabashed appeal for racial solidarity, the 1956 edition abandoned its earlier racial exhortations. In fact, this later publication featured the racially neutral title *Scott's Blue Book: A Classified Business and Service Directory of Chicago's Citizens With Interracial Features.*[4] Significantly, readers of the 1956 *Scott's Blue Book* would have been hard-pressed to find *any* "Interracial Features." All of the businesses and professionals listed in this publication were black. Consequently, this edition's interracial content appeared to be merely rhetorical rather than factual.

Scott's Blue Book's disjointed response to the *Brown* decision represented a concrete manifestation of the title of Robert H. Kinzer's and Edward Sagarin's important 1950 book *The Negro in American Business: The Conflict Between Separatism and Integration.* This work, similar to Edward Franklin Frazier's 1947 essay "Human, All Too Human," discussed the present condition and possible future of black business in America. According to Kinzer and Sagarin, the primary dilemma facing the mid-twentieth-century African American was how to "facilitate the breakdown of segregation, [and] enhance the possibilities of integration and infiltration, without endangering what little economic advantages [linked with racial segregation] he now enjoys."[5]

Kinzer and Sagarin, citing various distinct European ethnic neighborhoods that existed at the time, perceptively argued that separatism and integration were not necessarily mutually exclusive propositions. For instance, all of these enclaves featured merchants who spoke the language of their particular group, catered to the tastes of their ethnic brethren, and extolled the notion of homeland-linked solidarity.[6] Yet, at the same time, "side by side with their small restricted economy, the immigrants and their American-born children have taken their place as part of the general economic picture."[7]

Kinzer and Sagarin's analysis did include the important disclaimer that "the heritage of slavery on the one hand, and the comparative ease of biological distinctiveness of the Negro, on the other, have made integration [for African Americans] extremely difficult."[8] Considering this reality, Kinzer and Sagarin insinuated that it truly made sense for African Americans to maintain their business infrastructure, since custom and law inhibited their quest for more opportunities in the larger economy. In the end, Kinzer and Sagarin argued that, because separatism and integration were not mutually exclusive options for blacks, "it would be impossible at this time to suggest that either pathway be abandoned, because there would be an obvious sacrifice that the Negro people can ill afford to make" (emphasis added).[9]

The above assertion provides additional perspective to the editorial decision made by the 1956 Scott's Blue Book regarding the mission and scope of Bronzeville businesses. Before the mid-1950s, black businesspersons were perhaps the most respected segment of Chicago's black community. Yet in the wake of the Brown decision, supporters of black-owned businesses, apparently believing they could not simultaneously promote black economic nationalism and racial integration, abdicated a considerable portion of their community leadership role. Bronzeville businesses, which at one time proudly declared their "racial mission," appeared by the late 1950s to be uncertain and timid about their role in black Chicago. Moreover, because mid-to-late-1950s black businesses in Chicago had become unwilling to promote economic racial loyalty to Bronzeville consumers, they perhaps unwittingly assisted the marketing campaigns of the growing number of white companies that were seeking more black customers. In retrospect, had black businesses known that America's subsequent economic desegregation would be a one-way phenomenon (that primarily benefited white entrepreneurs), they might have taken Kinzer and Sagarin's advice regarding the continued need for actively promoting racial enterprises.

Of the many white business concerns that sought a larger share of Chicago's "Negro Market" during this period, insurance companies were especially aggressive. The fact that there are currently no black insurers in the city attests to the power and effectiveness of these campaigns to woo black policyholders. The last years of the now defunct Supreme Liberty Life Insurance Company and the Chicago Metropolitan Assurance Company provide a sobering case study of desegregation's impact upon iconic local black enterprises.

Supreme Liberty Life and Chicago Metropolitan, similar to other black insurers, were by-products of American apartheid. While historians have tended to focus upon the social and educational dynamics of Jim Crow racial segregation, overt racial discrimination existed in the commercial sphere of American life as well. In fact, the evolution of the U.S. insurance industry provides a classic example of how the reality of "separate and unequal" operated in the realm of business.

As early as 1875, prominent white insurance companies insured African Americans. Moreover, during their initial contact with blacks, companies such as the Prudential Insurance Company of Newark and Metropolitan Life of New York offered blacks and whites identical coverage at identical cost. Nevertheless, in March 1881, Prudential, citing an excessive black mortality rate, began charging blacks higher premiums than their white counterparts (for the same amount of coverage). Other white insurers soon followed Prudential's lead and established their own separate and unequal black insurance programs.[10]

Although Prudential subsequently denied that racism influenced its revised policy toward blacks, the company's later employment of Frederick L. Hoffman demonstrated the racial overtones of that corporate decision. Hoffman, a former insurance agent who joined Prudential in 1894, apparently attracted the company's attention through his 1892 article "Vital Statistics of the Negro." In this essay, Hoffman declared that freed blacks, without the tutelage of their former owners, could not survive in American society. Prudential subsequently placed Hoffman in its actuarial department and provided him the support necessary to transform his 1892 article into a book-length manuscript.[11]

In 1896 the American Economic Association published Hoffman's revised, expanded project as *Race Traits and the Tendencies of the American Negro*. While this work was replete with statistics, some of Hoffman's conclusions relied less upon quantitative data and more on personal notions of white supremacy. For instance, Hoffman predicted that whites "will not hesitate to make war upon those races who prove themselves useless factors in the progress of mankind." Consequently, "useless" races, such as African Americans, would suffer a dramatic decrease in their population.[12]

Hoffman's background provides additional evidence that *Race Traits and the Tendencies of the American Negro* was not the work of an objective, disinterested commentator. A German immigrant, Hoffman "had adopted the South as his own; as a young adult new to America he had travelled the Mississippi and had settled for a time in New Orleans and Georgia; later he married into an old Confederate family; and he continued to visit the South for the rest of his life."[13]

It appears that Hoffman's premonition concerning the future extermination of blacks contributed to Prudential's and several other companies' subsequent decision to sever all ties with African American consumers.[14] However, not all white insurers took this radical step. The most prominent mainstream company to continue insuring blacks was Metropolitan Life. Metropolitan Life's medical director, Thomas H. Willard, drew a different conclusion from Frederick L. Hoffman in assessing statistics demonstrating higher mortality rates for blacks than whites. While Willard believed that blacks were an "alien race, alien in color, alien in thought, alien in education," that did not necessarily mean they were doomed to extinction. This mindset coincided nicely with Metropolitan's plan to continue serving blacks, albeit under discriminatory terms.[15] In this setting of exclusion and discrimination, black-owned insurance companies, such as Supreme Liberty Life and Chicago Metropolitan, emerged to provide African Americans dignified insurance coverage.[16]

It is widely acknowledged that black insurance companies, during the early twentieth century, operated under a variety of racially based constraints. However, even in the midst of conducting business in an overtly racist society, they exhibited the African American cultural trait of "making a way out of no way." In his 1962 study of African American insurance companies during the period of 1930–60, David Abner's findings included "the percentage increase in insurance in force, total income, total admitted assets, and policy reserves was substantially greater for the Negro companies than for the industry."[17]

Abner identified the decade of 1940–50 as being especially profitable for black insurers. Between 1940 and 1950, "insurance in force grew in the Negro companies at an annual rate three times that of the industry: 13.9 vs. 4.4 per cent." Similarly, "total income received by the Negro companies during the 1940–1950 decade increased at an average rate three times that of the industry: 13.4 vs. 4.4 per cent." Moreover, "the average annual rate of growth in total admitted assets was more than twice as high in the Negro companies than in the industry during the 1940–1950 decade: 15.9 vs. 6.7 per cent." Finally, "during the 1940–1950 decade, policy reserves grew in Negro companies at an average annual rate more than twice that of the industry: 14.5 vs. 6.1 per cent."[18] In sum, during the 1940s, African American insurance companies outperformed their white counterparts in several key areas. Moreover, the evidence indicates that this did not go unnoticed.

White insurance companies, perhaps surprised by their black counterparts' strong performance during the 1940s, began to reevaluate the African American consumer market during the 1950s. Contrary to Frederick L. Hoffman's predictions, the black population was steadily growing and increasingly proliferating in

America's major markets such as Chicago. Table 11.1 demonstrates the significant growth of Chicago's African American population during the first decades of the twentieth century. Moreover, other large U.S. cities experienced a similar simultaneous increase of their black residents.[19]

Not only were mid-twentieth-century African Americans increasing their numbers in America's largest cities, but they were experiencing a significant increase in their collective spending power. At the dawn of the twentieth century, the vast majority of blacks were ensnared as virtually penniless peons and sharecroppers in the southern agricultural economy. Nevertheless, a significant migration of southern blacks to northern cities (such as Chicago) during World War I, World War II, and afterward would result not only in a change of address for African American migrants, but also a dramatic improvement in their economic status.

Black movement during World War II, to take war-related jobs, appeared especially significant. As an assessment of African American participation in the U.S. economy from 1860 to 1960 noted, between 1941 and 1945 "the number of Negro skilled and semiskilled men doubled." Similarly, African American women benefited financially because "large numbers shifted from farms and domestic service to other types of personal services, to factories, and to clerical jobs." Moreover, "the postwar years showed continued advances in most regards."[20]

Significantly, there appeared to be a circumstantial linkage between the increased income of African American consumers during the 1940s and the increased profitability of African American insurance companies during the same period. Table 11.2 provides a graphic depiction of African American economic gains during the mid-twentieth century.

These important demographic and economic developments, coupled with a series of U.S. Supreme Court decisions that supported blacks' quest for equal treatment, prompted Prudential, Metropolitan Life, and other large insurers to end their

Table 11.1 Chicago's African American Population, 1910–70

1910	44,103
1920	109,458
1930	233,903
1940	277,831
1950	492,265
1960	812,637
1970	1,102,620

Source: Jeffrey Helgeson, "Striving in Black Chicago: Migration, Work, and the Politics of Neighborhood Change, 1935–1965," PhD dissertation, University of Illinois at Chicago, December 1989, 6.

Table 11.2 Median Annual Wage and Salary Income of Nonwhite and White Persons
by Sex, 1939, 1947, 1957, 1960

Sex and Color	1939	1947	1957	1960	Percent Rise, 1939–1960
Male:					
Nonwhite:	$460	$1,279	$2,436	$3,075	568.5
White:	$1,112	$2,357	$4,396	$5,137	362.0
Nonwhite as a percent of white	41.4	54.3	55.4	59.9	
Female:					
Nonwhite:	$246	$432	$1,019	$1,276	418.7
White:	$676	$1,289	$2,240	$2,537	275.8
Nonwhite as a percent of white	36.4	34.0	45.5	50.3	

Source: Marion Hayes, "A Century of Change: Negroes in the U.S. Economy, 1860–1960," *Monthly Labor Review* 85 (December 1962): 1,364.

discriminatory policies toward African American consumers. This would have an increasingly negative impact on black insurers such as Supreme Liberty Life and Chicago Metropolitan.

In a situation dripping with irony, the historic discrimination practiced by Prudential, Metropolitan Life, and other white insurers against blacks actually helped them to generate new business in the African American community. Because African Americans had previously been denied equitable insurance coverage with industry giants, it quickly became a status symbol to possess a nondiscriminatory policy from a mainstream insurance company.[21]

Besides profiting from previous discrimination, companies such as Prudential and Metropolitan Life increased their market share in the African American community by recruiting the top agents from black companies like Supreme Liberty Life and Chicago Metropolitan. Similar to how Major League baseball teams secured the best talent from the old Negro Leagues, insurance industry giants, with promises of financial rewards, were able to secure a cadre of trained black insurance agents.[22]

David Abner's research provides additional verification of the successful quest of white insurers to reach the increasingly important Negro market. For instance, between 1943 and 1957 the number of white companies that insured African Americans nearly doubled, from 55 to 104.[23] Moreover, this expansion contributed to a significant profitability shift during the 1950s. Unlike the 1940s, the average annual growth of mainstream insurance companies' insurance in force, during the decade of 1950–60, "was almost twice that of the Negro companies: 9.6 vs. 5.3 per cent." Likewise, during the 1950s, the broad-based industry's figures for total income "averaged an annual rate more than one and one-half times as great as that of the Negro companies: 7.3 vs. 4.9 percent."[24]

To their distinct credit, Supreme Liberty Life and Chicago Metropolitan fought back against the new competition they faced. However, Supreme Life, during the early 1950s, faced a special challenge to its corporate viability. Supreme Liberty Life, which began business in 1919 as the Liberty Life Insurance Company, was the first African American insurance company organized in the North. From the beginning, Liberty Life portrayed itself as a racial enterprise worthy of being supported by fellow blacks. Moreover, from its inception, the insurer also sought to impress upon African American consumers the negative consequences of blacks not supporting each other. For instance, in a January 3, 1920, article in the *Chicago Defender* about the company, readers were informed that Chicago blacks had previously "made Millionaires among every nationality known to civilization that offered them the least bit of encouragement for their patronage." Yet, at the same time, Chicago blacks had "made a PAUPER of every Negro who dared enter into competition with these people for our trade." In the end, "the results of our loyalty to the other fellow find us without any State Banks, Legal Reserve Insurance Companies . . . necessary for the upbuilding of a Race."[25] By 1923, Liberty Life's insurance-in-force grew from zero to $3.5 million, and the insurer had gained favorable publicity in black Chicago by investing a significant portion of its premium income back into African American community real estate.[26]

In 1949, fifteen African American insurance companies were surveyed to determine the effectiveness of their agent training programs, as well as agent compensation. Supreme Liberty Life agents, according to the survey, received less training and lower incomes compared to most of the other black insurers examined. Other discouraging data generated about Supreme Liberty Life included the company's "high rate of agent turnover, low proportion of college-trained agents (an obvious disadvantage to Supreme Liberty in competition for new markets), and very low quality production."[27]

This situation changed for the better with the ascension of former company general counsel Earl B. Dickerson to Supreme Life's presidency in 1956. Company historian Robert C. Puth described Dickerson's first years at Supreme Life's helm as "a period of rapid change for the company, the Negro, and the entire nation. There could be no doubt that President Dickerson had been the force behind most of the [positive] changes which took place in Supreme Life."[28]

By the 1950s, the Chicago Metropolitan Assurance Company, similar to Supreme Life, was a long-standing pillar of Black Chicago. Chicago Metropolitan, founded in 1925 as the Metropolitan Funeral System Association, focused on serving the Windy City's African American working class. During the next couple of decades, it evolved from a company that solely provided economical burial insurance to local blacks into a legal reserve insurer that marketed a variety of insurance policies. Another highlight of Chicago Metropolitan's early history was its construction of the Parkway Ballroom at 4455 South Parkway (later renamed Martin Luther King Jr. Drive) during the winter of 1939–40. At a time when downtown hotels and ballrooms openly discriminated against blacks, the Parkway Ballroom quickly became the showplace of Chicago's black community.[29]

At the same time that Earl B. Dickerson assumed the presidency of Supreme Life, Chicago Metropolitan dealt with its own transition in leadership. After long-time president and chairman of the board Robert A. Cole Sr. died on July 27, 1956, Thomas P. Harris, the company's general counsel and board member, became Chicago Metropolitan's new president and board chairman.[30] Unfortunately, a strike by Chicago-based agents in 1957, protesting higher compensation given to Chicago Metropolitan agents working in Indiana and Missouri, hurt both company morale and profitability at a time when white companies were increasing their sales pitches to black consumers.[31]

In 1961 Chicago Metropolitan made a historic attempt to help erase the negative financial reverberations of the 1957 agent strike. On November 22, 1961, the insurer's board of directors passed a resolution that stated "it would be a future policy of the company to employ competent persons both in Agency and Office Administration without regard to race, creed, or color." The Chicago Metropolitan Assurance Company subsequently interviewed several whites for positions in the company's agency department.[32]

Three years later, at its January 20, 1964, annual meeting, company president George S. Harris squarely addressed the issue of black personnel "defections" to white insurance companies. He urged Chicago Met employees not to "look upon this company as some sort of stepping stone, a kind of training ground for some other job somewhere else," although he acknowledged that "this is the attitude of certain white companies, who are willing to let us go to the expense of training and preparing personnel, and then take them when we have completed this training."[33]

Harris, who assumed the Chicago Met presidency in 1961, concluded his remarks with a direct appeal to both company and racial pride. He declared, "look not at your company as a minor league outfit, where ambitious people prepare for the major leagues." Moreover, for good measure, he told the audience, "remember, we are Negroes and any insurance company that employs more than 500 people should not be considered minor league in our eyesight."[34]

Chicago Metropolitan's attempt to simultaneously promote racial desegregation and racial solidarity generated mixed results. By the late 1960s, Chicago Metropolitan had to face the fact that while some black insurance agents responded positively to recruitment efforts from white companies, white agents responded far less enthusiastically to recruitment efforts from black companies.[35] Yet, during the same period, the ascendancy of the Black Power movement, with its focus on racial pride and solidarity, helped both Chicago Metropolitan and Supreme Life experience growth in their operations. In fact, at the end of 1970, the combined total insurance in force of the two companies stood at $389,136,000. Among black insurance companies, this was second only to the industry's top firm, North Carolina Mutual, which reported total insurance in force of $748,855,000.[36]

Although Supreme Life and Chicago Metropolitan were unable to directly market their insurance products in the homes of white consumers, they were able to indirectly reach this market through group insurance. For instance, beginning in 1972, Chicago Metropolitan's new president Anderson M. Schweich announced group insurance agreements with General Foods Corporation, Jewel Companies, Inc., and Commonwealth Edison.[37] In fact, as time went along, group insurance, which consists of a coverage agreement between an insurance company and a corporate employer, represented the primary source of Supreme Life's and Chicago Metropolitan's premium income. For instance, by 1988, $2,146,957,000, or *91 percent* of Supreme Life's total insurance in force of $2,336,645,000, came from group insurance. Similarly, $2,332,930,000, or *91 percent* of Chicago Metropolitan's total insurance in force of $2,551,740,000, came from group insurance.[38]

On the surface, total insurance in force data from the 1989 edition of *Best's Insurance Reports* suggested that Supreme Life and Chicago Metropolitan were holding their own as business entities. Once again, the combined total insurance in force of the two companies, $4,888,385,000, was second only to North Carolina Mutual's industry-leading figure of $8,982,418,000.[39] Yet a closer look at Supreme Life's and Chicago Metropolitan's operations indicates that, notwithstanding their acquisition of group insurance contracts, they still suffered the negative effects of being trapped in the "economic detour" (of being forced to primarily serve black consumers) that Merah S. Stuart eloquently described in his classic 1940 book *An Economic Detour: A History of Insurance in the Lives of American Negroes*. Moreover, whereas Stuart in 1940 asserted that black insurers and other entrepreneurs, unable to find a "place on the economic broadway of America," had to "turn to a detour that leads he knows not where," by the late 1980s it became crystal clear that for Supreme Life and Chicago Metropolitan, the economic detour was the path to extinction.[40]

One of the major consequences of black insurers being historically able to serve only the most impoverished segment of American society was that it put a de facto limit on how large these firms could grow. Thus, in the context of the U.S. insurance industry, Supreme Life, Chicago Metropolitan, and other black companies (including North Carolina Mutual) were small entities with limited capital for corporate research. Conversely, Prudential, Metropolitan Life, and other industry giants, unfettered with such restrictions, had considerably more resources to develop new products and marketing strategies. One manifestation of this growth potential occurred during the mid-1970s when mainstream companies, sensing the market was right, expanded their services to offer consumers qualified advice on retirement strategies and other investments.

Although black insurers like Supreme Life and Chicago Metropolitan had been able to enter the group insurance market, data from the authoritative insurance industry publication *Best's Review*, for the years 1978–85, indicates that mainstream insurers' new direction helped to widen the profitability gulf between themselves and black companies. Between 1978 and 1985, the number of black firms listed in *Best's* compilation of the 500 leading life insurance companies in total premium income dropped from six to two. Chicago Metropolitan left the list in 1980; Supreme Life disappeared in 1982.[41] Moreover, the average premium income growth of the two remaining African American companies, North Carolina Mutual and Golden State Mutual, compared unfavorably to the industry average. Between 1978 and 1985, all U.S. and Canadian insurance companies experienced a 10.5 percent increase in premium income. During the same period, North Carolina Mutual and Golden State Mutual had premium income growth of only 4.2 percent and 3.6 percent, respectively.[42]

To make matters worse for Supreme Life, Chicago Metropolitan, and their cohorts, the 1970s and 1980s featured increasing calls to outlaw industrial insurance, the historic bedrock of the black insurance industry. During this period, industrial insurance, a form of coverage characterized by the weekly collection of premiums in policyholders' homes and by low policy face values, had been all but abandoned by mainstream insurance companies. For instance, in 1970, only 2.9 percent of all U.S. companies provided industrial insurance. However, industrial insurance represented 43.9 percent of black companies' total insurance in force.[43]

Despite the disadvantages of industrial insurance, which included high administrative costs that were passed on to consumers, black insurance company executives reminded their critics that this form of coverage represented the cornerstone of the historic personal relationship between black insurers and their policyholders. To this day, there are African American senior citizens who fondly remember the "insurance man's" weekly visit to their homes. However, in the context of E. Franklin Frazier's 1947 observations, by the 1970s it seemed increasingly clear that a growing number of African American consumers were becoming less interested in nostalgia and more concerned about contemporary money saving.[44]

Both Supreme Life and Chicago Metropolitan sought to proactively respond to the growing chorus of criticism directed toward industrial insurance. As Tables 11.3 and 11.4 indicate, these firms, from the 1960s to the 1980s, significantly reduced this type of coverage from their total insurance in force. In retrospect, it appears that black insurers' continued promotion of industrial insurance, after it had become an

Table 11.3 Categories of Insurance in Force, Supreme Liberty Life Insurance Company, 1965, 1975, 1985, 1989

Year	Whole Life	Term	Group	Industrial	Percentage Industrial
1965	$71,273,000	$9,921,000	N.A.	$125,160,000	60%
1975	$80,397,000	$14,625,000	$1,683,853,000	$123,509,000	6%
1985	$86,644,000	$18,437,000	$1,644,123,000	$99,155,000	5%
1989	$66,357,000	$34,549,000	$1,962,845,000	$81,044,000	3%

Source: *Best's Insurance Reports, Life-Health*, 66 (1971): 1,405; 75 (1980): 1,805; 85 (1990): 2,137.

Table 11.4 Categories of Insurance in Force, Chicago Metropolitan Assurance Company, 1965, 1975, 1985, 1989

Year	Whole Life	Term	Group	Industrial	Percentage Industrial
1965	$23,563,000	$5,357,000	N.A.	$118,253,000	80%
1975	$57,457,000	$28,922,000	$303,356,000	$134,568,000	25%
1985	$83,662,000	$34,391,000	$2,079,463,000	$107,469,000	4%
1989	$98,541,000	$33,428,000	$2,389,205,000	$82,129,000	3%

Source: *Best's Insurance Reports, Life-Health*, 66 (1971): 268; 75 (1980): 379; 85 (1990): 497.

anachronistic coverage option for consumers, was another manifestation of how their relative lack of resources (linked to the ongoing economic detour) retarded innovative corporate research and development.

As Supreme Life moved into the 1980s, besides dealing with the issue of phasing out industrial insurance, it also had to deal with public disclosure of other company problems. As early as 1981, Supreme Life began receiving a rating of "NA-7," or "below minimum standards," from the authoritative *Best's Insurance Reports*. Chief among Supreme's problems were above average lapse rates and above average real estate losses.[45]

Significantly, Supreme Life's economic problems were directly linked to economic problems faced by the broader African American community during the Reagan presidency. Chicago census data during this period literally verified the presence of two separate and unequal racial enclaves within the city limits. By 1989, twenty-five years after the passage of the Civil Rights Act of 1964, African American per capita income of $8,569 represented only 47 percent of European Americans' per capita income of $18,258. At the same time, 33.2 percent of Black Chicagoans, as compared to 11.0 percent of white Chicagoans, had incomes below the poverty line.[46] These disturbing economic figures, caused by the widening gap between black and white unemployment rates, prompted one commentator to conclude that "the economy has little interest in enlisting black contributions."[47] Black Chicago's tenuous economic situation during the 1980s had a deleterious effect on Supreme Life's operations. As cash-strapped policyholders let their policies lapse and cash-strapped mortgagors let their homes go into foreclosure, the insurer found itself in a helpless situation. For instance, between 1985 and 1990, Supreme Life wrote off nearly $4 million in bad real estate loans.[48] To make matters worse, the company also experienced a steep decline in new business generated. For instance, in 1988 Supreme Life added $27,305,000 to its insurance in force. The following year, the company generated only $17,520,000 of additional insurance coverage.[49]

By 1991, Supreme Life, facing mounting lapse rates, growing real estate losses, and declining new business, had to seriously reevaluate its situation. Seeing no other viable alternative, the company sold its admitted assets to the white-owned United Insurance Company of America. Supreme Life's chairman of the board, publishing magnate John H. Johnson, had wanted to sell his company's assets to a fellow black insurer. Yet, because Supreme Life's mortgage loan portfolio was extremely problematic, other African American insurance companies, facing their own problems in this regard, backed away.[50]

Chicago Metropolitan, for most of the 1980s, was in much better financial shape than Supreme Life. One concrete manifestation of this relative strength was the company's receipt of a consistent rating of "C+" (which denoted a "fairly good" insurance company) from *Best's Insurance Reports*.[51] Yet *Best's* examination of Chicago Metropolitan's operations during 1989 indicated that the Black Chicago insurer had also become an "economic detour" casualty. Similar to Supreme Life, Chicago Metropolitan received a rating of "NA-7," or below minimum standards, in the 1990 edition of *Best's Insurance Reports*. The authoritative industry publication apparently based its judgment on the fact that Chicago Metropolitan (in 1989) experienced a 61 percent decline in capital and surplus funds "due mainly to substantial unrealized capital losses reported from the mortgage and real estate portfolios."[52] Because Chicago Metropolitan's balance sheet was not as distressed as Supreme Life's, the company's assets remained in black hands when they were acquired by the black-owned Atlanta Life Insurance Company in 1990.[53]

The disappearance of Supreme Life and Chicago Metropolitan from the landscape of Chicago business represented a sobering milestone in local African American history. These iconic companies, literally located down the street from each other—Supreme Life's headquarters was at the corner of Thirty-Fifth and King Drive, and Chicago Metropolitan's headquarters was at the corner of Forty-Fifth and King Drive—were two of the few remaining bridges to the halcyon days of the 1920s. During that decade, the young Supreme Life and Chicago Metropolitan's previous manifestation, the old Metropolitan Funeral System Association, shared the stage with such legendary enterprises as the Douglass National Bank, the Binga State Bank, and the Victory Life Insurance Company. Moreover, while those three businesses were casualties of the Great Depression, Supreme Life and Chicago Metropolitan continued for another sixty years. Fortunately, the histories of Supreme Life and Chicago Metropolitan have been preserved in book-length studies. Thus future generations, at the very least, will be aware of their existence and contributions.

In the end, despite the seeming accuracy of E. Franklin Frazier's 1947 prediction regarding how black enterprises would fare in a desegregated society, support for African American–owned businesses has not been totally extinguished. Notwithstanding the desegregation of schools, workplaces, and public facilities, a significant number of African Americans continue to live in predominantly black residential areas. Thus the relevance of community-based enterprises, which can help keep black dollars circulating in black communities (rather than make a quick one-way exit to downtown and suburban shopping areas) is as meaningful today as it was in the past.

Notes

1. Edward Franklin Frazier, "Human, All Too Human: How Some Negroes Have Developed Vested Interests in the System of Racial Segregation," *Survey Graphic* 36 (January 1947): 75.

2. *Scott's Blue Book: A Classified Business and Service Directory of Greater Chicago's Colored Citizens' Commercial, Industrial, Professional, Religious, and Other Activities* (Chicago: Scott's Business and Service Directory, 1947), 180–82, 184, 207, 227, 278. Local African Americans could get free copies of this directory from Black Chicago churches and from many of the businesses listed.

3. Ibid., 28.

4. *Scott's Blue Book: A Classified Business and Service Directory of Chicago's Citizens with Interracial Features* (Chicago: Scott's Business and Service Directory, 1956), title page.

5. Robert H. Kinzer and Edward Sagarin, *The Negro in American Business: The Conflict between Separatism and Integration* (New York: Greenberg, 1950), 23.

6. Ibid., 151–52.

7. Ibid., 152.

8. Ibid., 153.

9. Ibid., 169.

10. Robert E. Weems Jr., *Black Business in the Black Metropolis: The Chicago Metropolitan Assurance Company, 1925–1985* (Bloomington: Indiana University Press, 1996), 39–40.

11. Daniel B. Bouk, "The Science of Difference: Developing Tools for Discrimination in the American Life Insurance Industry, 1830–1930, unpublished PhD dissertation, Princeton University, 2009, 180.

12. Ibid., 180–82; Weems, *Black Business in the Black Metropolis*, 40.

13. Bouk, "The Science of Difference," 181.

14. Weems, *Black Business in the Black Metropolis*, 40.

15. Bouk, "The Science of Difference," 184.

16. Ibid.

17. David Abner III, "Some Aspects of the Growth of Negro Legal Reserve Life Insurance Companies, 1930–1960," unpublished doctor of business administration dissertation, Indiana University, 1962, 226.

18. Ibid., 227–28.

19. Robert E. Weems Jr., *Desegregating the Dollar: African American Consumerism in the Twentieth Century* (New York: New York University Press, 1998), 11, 12, 13, 79.

20. Marion Hayes, "A Century of Change: Negroes in the U.S. Economy, 1860–1960," *Monthly Labor Review* 85 (December 1962): 1,364.

21. Weems, *Black Business in the Black Metropolis*, 102–3.

22. Ibid., 103.

23. Abner, "Some Aspects of the Growth of Negro Legal Reserve Insurance Companies," 229–30.

24. Ibid., 227.

25. "Liberty Life Insurance Company of Illinois," *Chicago Defender*, January 3, 1920, 8.

26. Reed, *Building the Black Metropolis*, 94.

27. Robert C. Puth, *Supreme Life: The History of a Negro Life Insurance Company* (New York: Arno Press, 1976), 175.

28. Ibid., 213.

29. Robert E. Weems Jr., "The Chicago Metropolitan Mutual Assurance Company: A Profile of a Black-Owned Enterprise," *Illinois Historical Journal* 86 (Spring 1993): 15–23.

30. Weems, *Black Business in the Black Metropolis*, 50–51.

31. Ibid., 52.

32. Ibid., 103.

33. Ibid., 104–5.

34. Ibid., 105.

35. Ibid., 103–4.

36. *Best's Insurance Reports, Life-Health 1971, 66th Annual Edition* (Morristown, NJ: A. M. Best Company, 1971), 268, 1,078, 1,405.

37. Weems, *Black Business in the Black Metropolis*, 110.

38. *Best's Insurance Reports, Life-Health 1989, 84th Annual Edition* (Oldwick, NJ: A.M. Best Company, 1989), 507, 2,181.

39. Ibid., 507, 1,710, 2,181.

40. Merah S. Stuart, *An Economic Detour: A History of Insurance in the Lives of American Negroes* (College Park, MD: McGrath, 1969; orig. pub. in 1940), xxiii.

41. *Best's Review: Life/Health Insurance Edition* 80 (August 1979): 35–38; 81 (August 1980): 39–42; 82 (September 1982): 71–74; 83 (September 1982): 44–47; 84 (August 1983): 46–49; 85 (July 1984): 76–79; 86 (August 1985): 66–69; 87 (July 1986): 25–28.

42. Ibid.

43. Jacob M. Duker and Charles E. Hughes, "The Black-Owned Life Insurance Company: Issues and Recommendations," *Journal of Risk and Insurance* 40 (June 1973): 225.

44. Ibid., 226.

45. Weems, *Black Business in the Black Metropolis*, 122.

46. "1990 Census of Population and Housing Summary, Tape File 3A, Chicago, Illinois," Southern Illinois University at Edwardsville, Regional Research and Development Services.

47. Andrew Hacker, *Two Nations: Black and White, Separate, Hostile, Unequal* (New York: Ballentine, 1992), 102.

48. "Holding On for Future Growth" (overview of African American financial institutions), *Black Enterprise* 22 (June 1992): 174.

49. *Best's Insurance Reports, Life-Health 1989, 85th Annual Edition* (Oldwick, NJ: A. M. Best Company, 1990), 2,137.

50. "Holding On for Future Growth," 174.

51. *Best's Insurance Reports, Life-Health 1989, 81st Annual Edition* (Oldwick, NJ: A. M. Best Company, 1986), 535; *84th Annual Edition*, 1989, 507.

52. *Best's Insurance Reports, Life-Health 1989, 85th Annual Edition*, 497.

53. Weems, *Black Business in the Black Metropolis*, 119, 121.

Contributors

JASON P. CHAMBERS is an associate professor in the Charles H. Sandage Department of Advertising at the University of Illinois at Urbana-Champaign. A graduate of The Ohio State University, Dr. Chambers has presented his research both nationally and internationally. His work has been published in books and both academic and advertising-industry trade journals in the United States, Asia, and Europe. His first book, *Madison Avenue and the Color Line: African Americans in the Advertising Industry*, examined the employment and entrepreneurial experiences of blacks in the advertising industry and their fight to diversify both the advertising industry and its advertisements.

MARCIA CHATELAIN is an associate professor of history and African American studies at Georgetown University. Chatelain is the author of *South Side Girls: Growing Up in the Great Migration*, which examines the experiences of young women during the historic urbanization of African Americans in the early twentieth century. She is currently researching African American communities and McDonald's. Chatelain has received research support from the Ford Foundation Diversity Postdoctoral Fellowship, as well as grants from the Duke University Libraries and the Summersell Center for the Study of the South at the University of Alabama.

WILL COOLEY is a historian of the twentieth-century United States at Walsh University. His scholarly work examines race, labor relations, and social mobility. He has published in *The Journal of Urban History*, *The Journal of Sport and Social Issues*,

Labor History, and *The Oxford Handbook on Immigration and Ethnicity*. Cooley is also active in criminal-justice-reform efforts. In 2012 the Stark County Bar Association awarded him the Liberty Bell Award, which is presented annually to a citizen who has rendered outstanding service to the community.

ROBERT (BOB) HOWARD has a wide-ranging professional background that includes serving as an adjunct professor in the College of Business at Roosevelt University; as a senior executive in retail for over thirty years; and as president/CEO of the Boys and Girls Clubs of Chicago. His memberships include the Black Chicago History Forum (BCHF) and the Society of African American Professionals (SOAAP). Howard's educational background includes an MBA from the Harvard Business School and an MA from Roosevelt University in Chicago. He has lectured and written on the history of black banks.

CHRISTOPHER ROBERT REED holds the rank of professor emeritus of history at Roosevelt University, Chicago. He has also taught at Northern Illinois University, the University of Illinois-Chicago, and the City Colleges of Chicago. He is the author of six books, including *The Chicago NAACP and the Rise of Black Professional Leadership, 1910–1966; All the World Is Here: The Black Presence at White City; Black Chicago's First Century, 1833–1900; The Rise of Chicago's Black Metropolis, 1920–1929; The Depression Comes to Chicago's South Side: Protest and Politics, 1930–1933;* and, *Knock at the Door of Opportunity: Black Migration to Chicago, 1900–1919.*

CLOVIS E. SEMMES is professor of black studies and sociology, University of Missouri–Kansas City, and professor emeritus of African American Studies, Eastern Michigan University. His PhD is in sociology from Northwestern University. Semmes is a recipient of a National Endowment for the Humanities Fellowship and other awards. Among his publications are *Cultural Hegemony and African American Development*, which received a *Choice* award as an outstanding academic book; *Racism, Health, and Post-Industrialism; Roots of Afrocentric Thought: A Reference Guide to Negro Digest/Black World, 1961–1976; The Regal Theater and Black Culture;* and *The End of Black Studies: Conceptual, Theoretical, and Empirical Concerns.*

MYITI SENGSTACKE RICE seeks to maintain the legacy of an impressive family tree. Her father, Bobby Sengstacke, is a renowned photographer. Her grandfather, John H. Sengstacke, was the longtime publisher of the *Chicago Defender* and a prominent civil-rights advocate. Her great grand-uncle was the legendary Robert Abbott, the *Chicago Defender*'s founder. Sengstacke Rice's professional accomplishments include being the founding editor-in-chief of the award-winning magazine *Uptown* and author of the book *Chicago Defender*, published by Arcadia Publishing. She is currently a college professor teaching African American studies and literature and working on a doctorate in educational leadership from Governors State University.

JULIET E. K. WALKER is a University of Chicago PhD and founder/director of the University of Texas at Austin Center for Black Business History, Entrepreneurship, and Technology. She has received numerous fellowships and awards in black business history, including the Carter G. Woodson Scholars Medallion and the Business History Conference's Lifetime Achievement Award. Her publications include award-winning books *The History of Black Business in America: Capitalism, Race, Entrepreneurship* (1998; vol. 1, 2009) and *Free Frank: A Black Pioneer on the Antebellum Frontier* (1983). Walker is editor of the *Encyclopedia of African American Business History* (1999), is author of 100 scholarly articles, essays, and encyclopedia entries, and presently is completing her book *Oprah Winfrey: An American Entrepreneur*.

ROBERT E. WEEMS JR. is the Willard W. Garvey Distinguished Professor of Business History at Wichita State University. A University of Wisconsin–Madison PhD, he previously taught at the University of Missouri–Columbia and the University of Iowa. Besides numerous scholarly articles, book chapters, and encyclopedia entries, his publications in the realm of black business history include three books: *Black Business in the Black Metropolis: The Chicago Metropolitan Assurance Company, 1925–1985*; *Desegregating the Dollar: African American Consumerism in the Twentieth Century*; and *Business in Black and White: American Presidents and Black Entrepreneurs in the Twentieth Century*.

Index

THE NEW BLACK STUDIES SERIES

The University of Illinois Press
is a founding member of the
Association of American University Presses.

Composed in 10.25/13 Marat Pro
with Trade Gothic display
by Kirsten Dennison
at the University of Illinois Press

University of Illinois Press
1325 South Oak Street
Champaign, IL 61820-6903
www.press.uillinois.edu